# Built to Meet Needs

# Built to Meet Needs

## Cultural Issues in Vernacular Architecture

**Paul Oliver**

ELSEVIER

Amsterdam • Boston • Heidelberg • London • New York • Oxford
Paris • San Diego • San Francisco • Singapore • Sydney • Tokyo

Architectural Press is an imprint of Elsevier

Architectural Press

Architectural Press is an imprint of Elsevier
Linacre House, Jordan Hill, Oxford OX2 8DP
30 Corporate Drive, Burlington, MA 01803

First edition 2006



**British Library Cataloguing in Publication Data**
A catalogue record for this book is available from the British Library

**Library of Congress Cataloging-in-Publication Data**
A catalog record for this book is available from the Library of Congress

ISBN-13: 978-0-7506-6657-2
ISBN-10: 0-7506-6657-9

For more information on all Architectural Press publications visit our web site at www.architecturalpress.com

Printed and bound in Italy

06 07 08 09 10 10 9 8 7 6 5 4 3 2 1

# Contents

# Acknowledgements

In view of the many people on whom I have depended, or who have worked with me on field trips and projects, and the kind friends and acquaintances that I have made over many years and in numerous countries, to my regret I cannot acknowledge them all here. When it is compared with other books that I have written it will be evident that the themes of the conference papers included in this book, have been selected. Here I wish to acknowledge collectively, but sincerely, the work of students who have accompanied me on a number of field studies and the welcome and help of our hosts while on location. The following were mainly colleagues and companion fieldworkers, guides and, in view of my linguistic limitations, translators, on the main projects included here. All are interested in vernacular architecture and many have published extensively on the subject, including entries in the *Encyclopedia of Vernacular Architecture of the World*, for which I am of course, very appreciative. Generally, they are associated with academic institutions but I have omitted their academic titles and affiliations as these change over time.

In Ghana, West Africa, my thanks for the life-changing experiences are to Michael Lloyd, and also to Miles Danby. As for East Africa, where I worked a dozen years later, I owe as much to Hubert Murray and his associated faculty members for our fieldwork. Likewise, to Ali Bakhtiar and the late John Donat for our intensive studies in Iran. My thanks too, to Francisco Javier-Lopez and Jorge Gonzalez-Claveran in Mexico, and again to Michael Lloyd who subsequently invited me to Costa Rica. To my co-author on another book, Richard Hayward I am indebted for my trip to Peru.

In the United States, I gave papers at the Built Form and Culture Research meetings, organized by David Saile in Arizona, Kansas and Cincinnati, to whom I send my warm thanks. I am also grateful to

Wayne Attoe, for invitations to speak at his conferences, and similarly to Simon Bronner in Pennsylvania. My participation in other conferences in the United States included some at the invitation of Jean-Paul Bourdier and Nezar Al-Sayyad, and the International Association for the Study of Traditional Environments. Like all members I am particularly thankful to Nezar and Jean-Paul, for other meetings in Italy, Egypt, Tunisia and Hong Kong. In the latter city, I am greatly appreciative of David Lung's guidance and companionship and, while on mainland China, for the invitations of Ronald Knapp and Davis Uzzell at conferences, profound thanks too, to the late Wang Wenqing, with whom I shared the comparative project in Huizhou, China, and West Mercia in England, with the support of the British Academy. My researches in Japan were initiated by the invitation of Toru Mitsui of Kanazawa, which I much appreciated.

It was Chotu Padamsee, who invited me to India, where I was also hosted by Jai Sen in Calcutta. Yasemin Cheema and her colleagues, among them Bil-Al and Fauzia Qureshi, were responsible for my going to Pakistan with the support of the British Council; my thanks to them all. In Indonesia I was guided and accompanied by Mauro Rahardjo, to whom I owed so much. My time in South-East Asia was enriched in Malaysia by the kindly help of Wan Salleh Wan Ibrahim, and in the Philippines by Rosario Encarnacion-Tan and Regina Lim.

I am indebted to Suha Ozkan and the late Hasan Fathy for the memorable trip to Cappadocia, Turkey, Among the longest of projects in which I was engaged was also in Turkey, in Gediz, Kütahya Province, and I wish to thank Dr Yasemin Aysan for all her work in planning the project, the field work and co-writing the final Report to the Overseas Development Administration. A particularly interesting project was in Kaluderica, in which she also participated. In this we were indebted to Milan Prodanovic, and to participants Georgia Grzan-Butina, Stuart Parker and Deirdre McDermott, among several others. In both these projects the work of Stuart Lewis and Ian Davis was invaluable, and I owe my interest in post-disaster aspects of the vernacular to Ian, with whom I attended a number of international conferences. Some of these were held in Turkey, where we were hosted by Mete Turan, while later conferences there were at the invitation of Hulya Turgut and Peter Kellet, to all of whom I send my sincere thanks.

For their guidance in shared trips, often with students of the ISVA course, I owe much to Borut Juvanec in Slovenia, Antonia Noussia in the Cyclades, Josef Vařeka in the Czech Republic, and Fernando

Vegas in Spain, and to the devoted planning of my colleague, Rosemary Latter. I am very sorry that I cannot list here all the many friends and students who participated in research, or otherwise assisted me in my trips in nearly every European country; my sincere thanks to you all. Back in England, I worked on the study of the suburbs with my co-authors Ian Davis and Ian Bentley, and then commenced the ten-year project of the Encyclopedia – 'EVAW' as we called it. The devoted work of the never-tiring Lindsay Asquith, who put the whole project on computer, and of my wife Valerie, who looked after the contracting of contributors and the illustrations, while I did the editing, made the whole undertaking possible. I am also most thankful for the research undertaken by Deirdre McDermott, and for the multilingual lexicon compiled by Rosemary Latter.

These acknowledgements do not account for the field studies and research in many other countries and locations when many of the contributors were found or contacted and who helped immensely. Most of these trips were of my initiation or that of my dear, late wife, Valerie, who participated in the research trips, conferences and projects in every continent, and whose help in all respects was incalculable, and for me, unforgettable.

Paul Oliver

# List of illustrations

# Illustration credits

All photographs were taken by the author and are copyright Paul Oliver, except in the instances listed below, copyright in their names:

Photographs by the late Valerie Oliver: 6.6, 6.10, 6.11, 6.13, 7.6, 8.11, 10.4, 10.5, 10.7, 11.2, 11.3, 11.12, 16.3, 17.10, 17.11, courtesy Paul Oliver

Photograph by Yasmin Cheema: 15.4

Photographs by Ian Davis: 14.5, 14.3

Photographs by Joseph Fortin: 3.5, 3.6

Photograph by Graham Paul Smith: 20.8

Drawings of Eski Muhipler and Yeni Muhipler by Shelter and Settlements Unit members, Oxford Polytechnic School of Architecture: 14.4, 14.7, 14.9, 14.13

Drawings of Asante shrine: the late Michael Swithenbank, courtesy Mrs Swithenbank

Drawing of Matakam Compound, courtesy Piere Pelloux of the Beaux-Arts team

Map of global culture areas, researched, compiled and drawn by Paul Oliver for the *Encyclopedia of Vernacular Architecture of the World*, courtesy of Cambridge University Press

Maps: Sketch drawings by Paul Oliver

Shaker map and sections derived from WPA Historic Buildings Research, by A.H. Mosley, 1939

Advertisements and early drawings from the collections of Paul Oliver and Ian Davis

# Introduction

Although dwellings constitute the majority of the world's buildings, diverse environments, economies, technologies, inherited skills, social and family structures, belief systems and symbolism, together with many other factors, contribute to the wide variety of built forms of different cultures. They are reflected in the barns and byres, granaries and mills, stores and shops, chapels, mosques and temples among innumerable other types of buildings, which are constructed by communities to meet the specific needs of their respective ways of life. In varying degrees these all constitute parts of the vernacular architecture traditions, the diversity of the buildings being expressions of the differing demands and values of the cultures concerned.

Studies of certain vernacular traditions commenced in the 1880s and were slowly pursued in the early twentieth century, although in dispersed and often unrelated ways, which depended on the training or pursuits of the investigators. Many of these worked for the colonizing western powers; rarely were any studies made by nationals of non-western countries, the methods of recording and documentation employed being those of European and North American architectural conventions. Architects and amateurs alike were involved, as occasionally were anthropologists, although most of the latter disregarded buildings. By the mid-twentieth century initial attempts were made to co-ordinate their description and documentation, particularly at a national level, leading to the formation of groups engaged in vernacular architectural studies in, for instance, England, France, the Netherlands and the United States. However, it was not until the late 1960s that serious syntheses were published of research which related the buildings to the cultures that produced them. Many of those who were involved in vernacular studies in other parts of the world felt the need for forums in which to share their research and to benefit from that of others.

In the mid 1980s the Built Form and Research Conferences, the International Association for the Study of Traditional Environments, and the International Association for the Study of People and the Physical Surroundings, among others, led to regular gatherings of students of these subjects across the world, although regrettably, rarely in the southern hemisphere. For those engaged in research the opportunity to present their work and its results to a knowledgeable audience was gratifying, as indeed was the ensuing debate on issues that arose.

Rewarding though the conferences have been, and continue to be, there are inevitable problems. Among these is the frustration of not being able to attend all sessions, however interesting they may be, which faces every participant in a conference that has 'parallel sessions' offered simultaneously on subthemes. Not least of the problems is the fact that other participants often have similar backgrounds, notably in architectural education and research; consequently, there is an awareness of 'preaching to the converted'. This also applies to the publication of the transactions of the meetings, which are generally distributed or sold to the participating members of the respective associations and may reach a very limited readership beyond this. Most of the papers selected for inclusion in this collection are on aspects of the subject that have been understated or unrepresented. Arising directly from fieldwork or from issues highlighted in projects, the majority have been undertaken with the involvement of colleagues and students, as well as with members of the communities concerned. The results of such projects have often had implications for future practice in relation to housing, planning and servicing and have motivated the writing of papers for conferences, in addition to the requisite reports. As much of the content is related to these projects I have sometimes referred to them in more than one instance, but with differing details or emphases.

The chapters that follow consider aspects of vernacular architecture which, in some instances, may be contentious. They do not attempt to classify or describe in detail the types and forms of building traditions across the globe; this was largely my intention in compiling and editing the *Encyclopedia of Vernacular Architecture of the World* and, for a broader readership, my discussion of *Dwellings: The Vernacular House World-Wide*. However, certain of the chapters are related to entries and themes that were introduced, and briefly summarized, in both these works. They are presented in more detail and provide the research basis for some of the statements made. Reference is made in certain chapters, to resources, technologies and construction, and to forms, plans and functions. However, the main purpose of the present collection is to consider the cultural factors that bear upon the subject. Specifically, these relate to the study and understanding of vernacular traditions, and to aspects which reflect the motivations, means and methods of those who undertake research in the field, who may be responsible for the care of some of its buildings, or who may design in vernacular contexts. These aspects include subject definition, cultural character, transmission of skills and values, vulnerability to hazards, building conservation, popular housing, architectural education and future applications of the vernacular. In no sense is this complete or comprehensive, and there is much to be researched as, in some instances, I have indicated.

Realistically, it has to be recognized that apart from the conference participants, there are comparatively few professional architects, planners or members of governing bodies, let alone Members of Parliament, who familiarized themselves with these subjects, or have responded to them. In view of the vast demands on housing, social buildings, and their servicing that will be made in the coming decades, they, and the students preparing to assume these roles, should be fully aware of the cultural factors that may affect their implementation. In particular, they need to comprehend the potential of appropriately supporting vernacular traditions to ensure sustainable solutions to these demands. To a large extent, the focus of the chapters reflects the broad themes of the conferences held by organizations and educational centres, such as those mentioned above. They have been given in a number of countries and in many instances are drawn, with permission, from the publications that have ensued. Minor deletions have been made where there are repetitions; for instance, of the definition of the term 'vernacular'. Occasionally, other adjustments have been made, in tense for example, where it does not adversely affect the content. For the convenience of the reader, I have grouped the chapters together in parts under related headings.

Not the least of the problems associated with the study of vernacular architecture is, nonetheless, the meaning of the term itself. As understanding of the term and how it is applied, is clearly necessary, **Part 1: Defining the Field**, discusses its meaning as it is used in the present context. Broadly speaking, the phrase 'vernacular architecture' is seen here as referring to the buildings of and by the people. Nevertheless, the question 'what is vernacular architecture' persists, as do many stereotypes based on perceptions of past traditions. In this section, some of the purposes of the study of the subject are explained. Many vernacular traditions have visual appeal, as is frequently exploited in tourism leaflets, and some have been a source of inspiration, or a partial confirmation of their objectives, for a number of leading architects. Yet, in view of the fact that few schools of architecture make more than a passing acknowledgement of the subject, I have made arguments for the furtherance of the study of vernacular architecture on a number of occasions. While its inclusion in education, both general and specifically architectural, is important, it is no less essential in the profession and in its recognition by major organizations that are concerned with conservation, housing and development. Definitions have to be comprehensive, even though they may lead to generalizations that embrace millions of examples. However, the specific is as important as the comprehensive, as was inherent in meeting the imperatives to classification and categorization made by the commissioning of entries for the compilation and editing of the *Encyclopedia of Vernacular Architecture of the World*. The objectives that drove that undertaking for an entire decade, are examined with hindsight.

A great diversity of vernacular traditions in buildings of all kinds can be perceived throughout the world. Such diversity reflects the immense variety of cultures within the broad spectrum of peoples and places, their specificity being dependent in part on their response to, and use of, their local environments. This is evident in comparative studies based on cultural similarities and differences in their relationships with particular environmental contexts, which I consider in **Part 2: Cultures and Contexts**. Attempting to adjust to the values and manners of specific societies emphasizes the relationship of behaviour to culture. Cultural traits and environmental contexts constituted the focus of vernacular traditions in building, which have often existed for centuries. Undoubtedly, physical, cultural and perceptual factors affect the degree of significance of certain features in form, structure, space use, or detail in buildings, bringing into question the validity of environmental determinism, or indeed, of any kind of deterministic explanation for the commonality or singularity of traditions.

Although changes over time are to be seen in most building traditions, the persistence of distinct and distinctive building types and forms, of material resources and methods of construction, and of space use and associated values, is undeniable. It is an oft-quoted cliché that traditions are 'handed down from father to son', or 'mother to daughter,' though by what means traditions are sustained within a culture is seldom explained. In **Part 3**, I examine some of the issues of **Tradition and Transmission** in the vernacular.

Traditions are sustained if they have meaning; they may be practical or they may be symbolic, but they are frequently of fundamental significance for the cultures concerned. In vernacular architecture they may be related to the appropriation, preparation and working of certain building materials and resources, which can require specific knowledge and skills. But the means of transmission can be far more varied; they confirm that vernacular technology is closely related to 'know-how', acquired as efficiency is tested over time. It appears that sustainability is achieved through independence rather than dependence, and that innovation and change result from diffusion and experiment rather than from inducement and intervention. Transmission, whether as technology transfer or interpersonal instruction, is nevertheless, still a seriously under-researched aspect of vernacular architecture.

What is of special value to a culture is not readily perceived by brief acquaintance; its modes and mores may be recorded but the essence of their meaning may remain elusive, finding expression in seemingly inscrutable customs or behaviour patterns. Devastation of buildings and settlements has called into question the provision of modern housing and planning controls, the reconstruction of traditional buildings or the continuity of vernacular traditions. The destruction of buildings and whole settlements, and the collapse of earthen buildings as the result of earthquakes in Gujarat and Iran and recently, of the unprecedented scale of devastation caused by the Asian tsunami in December 2004, raise serious doubts as to the policies of mass housing, relocation and planning controls, compared with those of reconstruction and the perpetuation of vernacular traditions. Under the suffering and stress of a major disaster, such as a volcanic eruption or inundation by flood, a people can react in ways that may reject or accept all help, including post-disaster housing. Subsequent reactions may appear perplexing, even irrational, but they can reveal the persistent values by which a culture reclaims its identity. Stress situations arising from the double trauma of a disaster and what are intended to be mitigating relief measures, are discussed in **Part 4, Hazards and Dwellings**. Cultural issues relating to the provision of housing, reflecting family size and structure, hierarchies, religious beliefs and values, customs and traditions that are essential to specific cultures are frequently overlooked in temporary, as well as permanent, post-disaster re-housing. My chapters in this section consider specific themes, including the effects on small populations of what may be overlooked as 'minor' disasters. The significance of cultural factors such as economy, language and religion, to zones of seismic activity is mapped in one chapter, while the long-term evaluation of post-disaster housing in Turkey and its failure to meet the cultural needs of the victim communities is presented in another. A case study considers the impact of a major flood in the Indus valley and the rebuilding and reoccupation of a destroyed settlement. Certain weaknesses in the structures remain, and the chapter argues for mutual participation in post-disaster housing.

Devastation of buildings and settlements in recent years, and the scale of destruction of earthen buildings as a result of the earthquakes in Gujarat and Iran, has called into question the reconstruction or the conservation of traditional vernacular structures. In **Part 5** some of the cultural issues related to **Conservation and Continuity** are addressed. Policies for the conservation of buildings in many countries have been applied to monumental structures, while the conservation of vernacular buildings is often regarded with much less concern. Some of the problems of conserving the vernacular are encountered in countries where the concept is unfamiliar, where resources are limited, and where aspirations are to the 'modern' in housing. Other cultural aspects related to the implementation of conservation are reflected in the so-called 'open-air' museums, or museums of regional architecture. Their achievements, as well as their anomalies and attempts at historic recreation, are compared while considering the problems inherent in the making of vernacular settlements into World Heritage Sites. This section also includes a consideration of the historic example of emigrant Shaker communities unified by their beliefs, whose settlements, buildings and design inventiveness have been sensitively conserved and are discussed in the context of the expressions of their philosophy, their stated values and in the manifestations of their design principles. Theirs was a community-built architecture, based largely on nineteenth century housing.

At what may be considered to be the frontiers of the vernacular are different kinds of building which might be regarded as being 'of and *for* the people'. Such housing for the people is discussed in **Part 6: Suburbs and Self-Build**. Prominent among the settlements of large communities are the suburbs of the great cities of the world. These might be distinguished as 'popular' architecture, erected for the people by speculative builders, though this term is used for the 'vernacular' in some languages. During the twentieth century, the dominant forms of settlement around the periphery of many cities in western countries were repetitive suburbs. Such suburban housing has been regarded by some as architecture 'for the people' and as a 'modern vernacular'. While suburban houses are not self- or community-built, the motivation to express their individual identities by their occupants is clearly evident in suburban housing estates. From the naming of homes to internal decoration and the maintenance of the gardens, families have left the stamp of their personalities on both the internal and external features of their new dwellings. When locally built council houses in Britain were made available for purchase, this personalization was immediately apparent. It is noted in a necessarily condensed review of the writings and opinions of architects and architectural historians on the suburban landscape and of 'the houses in between'. Suburban housing has occasionally influenced self-builders: in the former state of Yugoslavia, the countryside was dotted with irregular housing, among which a study was made of a 'wild settlement' which comprised new houses in a former peasant community, self-built by settlers and local craftsmen with aspirations.

Recognizing that there are already acute housing shortages in many parts of the world, some western countries and their agencies are attempting to cope with the problem. In **Part 7, Meeting the Challenge of the Twenty-first Century**, a number of the issues that may confront those who seek to house and rehouse are reviewed. The section considers whether standards of dwelling spaces, organization and construction should be predetermined, or whether they should be defined with the active participation of the affected cultures. These matters have important bearing on the education of architects, planners and all involved in design and implementation on an international scale. Measures for infrastructure and support of the so-called 'squatter settlements' are enlarged upon, as are issues concerning the ethics of architectural design and practice, related to world housing needs. Policies of intervention, housing provision, design criteria, environmental implications and cultural factors, including beliefs and values, are among them.

As this book and its chapters are based on papers delivered at conferences over a long period, I need to point out that where facts and figures are cited, they applied at the time of their presentation, which is indicated with each chapter title. Although the specific circumstances may be different now, broadly speaking the fundamental issues have altered little. However, the times they are a-changing and the impact of globalization may be as damaging on the world's cultures as, we are led to believe, it will be beneficial. Accommodation of the expanding global population will be a major issue, even if it is not acknowledged as such at present. Environmental, resource and technological implications will be immense, but I believe that they will only be met positively with informed support, based on recognition of those aspects of the vernacular traditions that have evolved to meet the needs of the cultures that they represent. Which raises the question, 'what are those needs?' I believe them to be implicit, as they are fundamental to the living of humankind. The need for shelter from certain natural elements, especially when in periods of climatic extremes, is fundamental, while protection from marauders, alien creatures and natural hazards is highly desirable in some regions. Further structures to accommodate aspects of the economy, whether agricultural, pastoral or craft-based, and in such forms as barns, byres, granaries or workshops, are needed in the lowland, steppe, montane, coastal, riverine, and desertic environments, among others. Over time, cultures have determined the buildings that will accommodate their needs, subsequent generations drawing upon their traditions and tempering them as changing circumstances warrant.

It is apparent that all cultures have distinct vernacular architecture traditions, even though some may share features with contiguous societies. In my experience, no two vernacular traditions are exactly similar, and to me it is evident that, whether self-built, household-erected or community-constructed, no buildings within such a tradition are identical either. Considerable or subtle, the distinctions emanate from the strength of the traditions, from the values associated with buildings, and from the personalisation and identification with the dwellings by the users, in the course of occupation over time.

More profound however, are the connotations of the spaces created. To the various cultures concerned they frequently have symbolic meaning, which may be spiritual, cosmic, anthropomorphic, animist or of other significance, reflecting their customs and beliefs. In some instances such connotations have further expression in carving, painting or other decoration. Elusive though their meanings may be, vernacular buildings are never unnecessary. They are not erected on a whim and are not intended to impress, but they help satisfy the pyscho-social, as well as the physical, needs of those that use them.

In compiling this collection of accounts drawn mainly from field projects that I have undertaken, I am not suggesting that the issues that arose and the needs that the structures were built to meet, are to any degree comprehensively covered; rather, they are indicative of the breadth and complexity of the cultural issues of vernacular architecture which, in my view, urgently need to be addressed.

# PART I

# DEFINING THE FIELD

# 1

# Why study vernacular architecture? (1978)

A score of years ago, there were very few schools of architecture in Europe or the United States where it was possible to study the buildings of tribal, folk or peasant cultures. Today a number of colleges include studies in vernacular architecture in the curriculum, and some schools in Africa, Latin America and the East are encouraging serious investigation into the built forms of the indigenous peoples of their countries. If the colleges and the architects who staff them, have introduced the subject into the spectrum of studies considered appropriate to the education of intending architects, we can be justified in assuming that they have firm grounds for doing so. Yet, as I visit different colleges in various parts of the world I am by no means certain that they have good reason for including this work; nor do I see much agreement in the way in which it should be approached.

When I joined the staff of the Architectural Association in the early 1960s, students in the first year were expected to make a model of some form of tribal or folk shelter – an Eskimo igloo in small sections of polystyrene perhaps, or a Colombian lake dwelling with its stilts standing on a mirror, and with chopped straw to imitate its thatch. No students at the school would make such a model today, but they might be deeply involved in the restoration of a crofter's cottage in the Scottish Highlands, or documenting the house types of the Southern Sudan through extensive travelling, drawing and photographing. Attitudes to the subject have changed, but it is still thought valuable to be involved in it, even though the reasons for considering such work important in architectural education are not expressed. It seems to me that it is necessary now to ask the question: 'Why study vernacular architecture?'

This question invites another: 'What do we mean by "Vernacular Architecture"?' Unfortunately it is not an easy question to answer; we can do much more by example than by definition. The etymological roots of the word 'architect', from the Greek *arkhi-* and *tekton*, mean 'chief builder', while 'architecture' is defined as the 'science of building'. The word 'vernacular' derives from the Latin *vernaculus*, meaning 'native', so the definition 'native science of building' is really quite appropriate. In usage however, 'vernacular' generally refers to language or dialect of a people, while architecture is given a qualitative status. To bring some measure of neutrality into the terms used I suggested 'shelter', which laid emphasis on the common motivation for the building of all the structures that man inhabits. I admit that it is not a satisfactory word, for it has associations of the rudimentary rather than the complex, the utilitarian rather than the aesthetically pleasing. In using the generally accepted phrase 'vernacular architecture', I am embracing all the types of building made by people in tribal, folk, peasant and popular societies where an architect, or specialist designer, is not employed. To me, so general a term is only of limited value and I am working on a more useful and accurate terminology, which I hope to introduce at a later date.

One reason why I think that a definition of the terms we use is important goes right to the heart of the subject. Students, teachers or professionals involved in architecture are concerned with the design process, whereby a specific set of solutions is posed to an

**Figure 1.1**
A dwelling of the Southern Sotho, with fine thatch and its earth wall decorated on the windward side with coloured stones. Lesotho, Southern Africa.

**Figure 1.2**
'Puddling' or treading clay and water, to achieve the appropriate consistency for building. Antipolo, Philippines.

architectural problem. The problem is usually the 'brief'; the solutions are co-ordinated into a 'design' or 'scheme', but it is evident to me that in the vernacular, this is hardly ever the case. An African man may describe a circle on the ground with a stick at arm's length which will constitute the plan of his dwelling, and he may mark out the boundary of his yard. However, when he builds he will use traditional forms, employ the technology of his ancestors and may have his hut plastered and decorated by his wife, with designs that are symbolic to his people and immediately identifiable with them. A limited degree of design is involved but the architectural solutions have been arrived at over generations. They may be subtly modified or developed in time, but as responses to experience of conditions and use rather than by the application of rigorous method, analysis of the problems involved, or even by the 'lateral thinking' that we call inspiration. On the other hand, the vernacular owner-builders will dig and puddle their own clay, mix it with straw and dung, mould the walls, cut the poles, harvest and trim the straw, construct and thatch the roof – build in fact, their own houses. We may seek to gain a little experience on site during training, but we do not expect to build every structure we design. Both at the design and the implementation stages the processes of formal architecture and vernacular architecture are very different; so I am obliged to repeat the question which forms the title of this chapter: 'Why study vernacular architecture?'

Up to now I have used the word 'we' several times to denote those involved in the studying, teaching or practice of architecture. Yet there are many who examine vernacular architecture who are none of these. It may help us to consider briefly why they study the subject – especially as we are so dependent on the results of their research. A substantial proportion of them have been amateurs rather than professionals, or they have been missionaries, district commissioners, even army surveyors. Their methods have not been those of architects and their motivations to study tribal, folk or peasant peoples have been quite different. Often, shelter plays a small part in their research, which has been intended to serve other purposes. In summarizing a few of them, I will consider the approaches taken, rather than the disciplines that such researchers represent. Of these, the first is an approach to pure research, with the sole purpose of extending the sum of human knowledge. The scrutiny of all aspects of an unfamiliar society, including its building, is pursued as an end in itself unjustified by any reasons related to its application or usefulness. The assumption is that with the knowledge gained, applications may follow, but this is unknowable until the knowledge has been acquired. This approach, although unusual in architecture, has its merits, for it means that in theory the data obtained are not prejudiced by underlying motives. Akin to this, but with the advantage of methodological techniques, is the approach of the anthropologist. Within this field objectivity is sought, although the 'observer paradox' is recognized: the very presence of the anthropologist makes it impossible to write an account of a society in its virgin state. Building techniques, the preparation of materials, the naming of parts, the functions of spaces and the symbolism of shelter may occasionally be recorded in the anthropological approach, even though some of the factors of special interest to architects, such as structural principles or the perception of spaces within a building, may not be revealed. If anthropology is 'the study of man', it should also be the subject of study of its own various disciplines: a social anthropologist is likely to come up with different information about a society and its architecture than one who is concerned with the documentation of material culture.

Among non-literate societies history often takes the form of myth, having a symbolic truth important to the people concerned, rather than being verifiable, factual evidence. The history of a building type has often to be inferred, or deduced from archaeological remains, when other data are not available. Shelter constructed of stone can leave more tangible evidence than that made from woven matting or wattle and mud. Archaeology is contributing to the study of early forms of vernacular building even though the evidence of long vacated sites is open to misinterpretation, or subject to wide approximations as to the numbers of occupants and the date or duration of occupancy. The archaeological approach is concerned with origins and the uncovering of primitive roots of a culture; historians apply themselves to the analysis of the material and documentary evidence of the past, reconstructing it in patterns that have their own logic. An inordinate emphasis has been placed in history studies on nations and states, on battles and conquerors, on kings, princes and prelates. As vassals and serfs, the bulk of the population has been acknowledged but, until recently, the culture of the majority has received little attention. Now, however, many historians are trying to understand the lives, economies, culture and social structures of the common people. If the written record in many cases is limited, much of the other evidence may remain with us, including weapons, artifacts of pottery and metal, items of clothing and adornment, and the essentials of shelter.

**Figure 1.3**
Archaeological evidence of Middle Bronze Age granite 'hut circles'. Grimspound on Dartmoor, Devon, England.

One reason for this recent trend has been political; Marxist historians have had good reason to investigate the culture of the working classes. Their researches have helped to restore some balance in historical studies and have undoubtedly influenced even those who do not share their political persuasion. Analogous to this has been the rise of young historians in developing countries, who have been examining their traditional institutions with an enthusiasm and pride which was not present in the years of humiliation and colonization. One outcome of these changes in historical method and motivation has been the conservation of old and traditional buildings. Museums of folk-life with artifacts assembled in conserved examples of vernacular architecture have developed since the 1930s in most European countries and in the United States; some countries in the developing world, anxious to reawaken pride in the indigenous cultures are following this lead. Like folkloric ballets and concerts, such museums are inclined to be idealized, but they are generally supported by thorough research into the vernacular architecture of the cultures concerned. Much is learned about the buildings from their dismantling and reassembly, and they continue to serve an important educational function.

Of course, there is a romantic interest in traditional buildings which is antiquarian, and sometimes, purely nostalgic. Vernacular architecture can offer shelter from the realities of the present, and encouragement to those who believe that life in past centuries was better than life today; or that traditional buildings, no matter how insanitary, damp, smoke-filled or insect-infested they may have

**Figure 1.4**
A house wall painted with animal motifs. National Museum of Handicrafts, Delhi, which includes a collection of Indian indigenous building traditions.

been, were superior to housing here and now. Less conspicuous, but perhaps as sentimental in its emotional source, is the 'low culture' attitude which idealizes popular and folk culture at the expense of 'high culture'. Resentment at the values placed on sophisticated and complex art and architecture, which appear to esteem the intellect at the expense of feeling, encourages a neoprimitivist view. Rousseau's image of the 'noble savage' survives in an uncritical admiration of all that is regarded as naive or unsophisticated. At the extremes of this position there are no criteria and no values.

In contrast to this subjectivity is the pragmatism of the geographer who considers settlement in relation to resources. The availability of building materials, the capacity of the land to support a population, the kind of economy that evolves and the trading relationships with other communities that can be identified – all these have direct bearing on the kind, form, location and density of buildings. Other factors also have bearing on vernacular form, especially the effects of climate which have to be controlled, modified or utilized. Further particularization of the approaches that have revealed to us much of what we know about vernacular architecture, is probably unnecessary: for the present purposes I have indicated sufficiently, I trust, the degree to which we are indebted to the amateur and professional researchers, anthropologists, historians, political theorists, antiquarians and geographers for much of the knowledge that we have of the subject. Perhaps we can recognize ourselves in some of them; if we respond favourably to the work of some and with less interest, or even uncomprehendingly, to the work of others we are probably acknowledging how much they have influenced our own attitudes. They all have reasons for studying vernacular architecture, and most of them are valid. So the question now is, 'Why should architects, and architectural students, study vernacular architecture?' Let us look first, at some of the ways in which architects use their study of the subject.

Few historians are architects, although a number of architects have become historians. One of the most important ways in which they apply their study of vernacular architecture is in the service of the historian. With the acquisition of knowledge of traditional building, architects can play an essential role in conservation. Their advice is sought not only in the selection of structures or complexes that should be saved, restored or removed for conservation elsewhere, but also for professional advice on the way in which these measures are undertaken. Whereas architectural conservation has a long history in relation to palaces, cathedrals, churches and the residences of the gentry, the conservation of modest peasant and

**Figure 1.5**
Destruction of a *machiya*, or traditional shop, to be replaced by a modern structure. Kyoto, Japan

yeoman buildings has been more by default than by policy. Losses sustained through wars, through rebuilding programmes, the siting of new towns, airports and industrial developments have been catastrophic in some countries like Holland or Denmark, or in Japan and in certain of the provinces of China. Conservation of the vernacular heritage, except in folk-life museums, has come almost too late for some of them, but fortunately, legislation and the listing of valued buildings has been undertaken in other countries. Conservation architects informed as to traditional building at domestic scale, are being slowly but increasingly employed by the more enlightened authorities.

More interpretative is the work of architects who seek to recreate the qualities of vernacular traditions without imitating them. This requires great sympathy for the work of unknown craftsmen and anonymous builders of generations past, but the 'neovernacular' architects do not slavishly copy their works. Recognizing in examples of their own choosing, qualities of space, form, use of materials, details, proportion and other expressions of native sensibility, they try to emulate them in their own design. They may appreciate that their approach to designing is fundamentally different but they endeavour to create buildings that stimulate similar responses in those who see or live in them. For them, the vernacular is a source of inspiration. At a more superficial level it is also a source for the designers of buildings for the tourist and 'second home' industries. They are less concerned with the lessons that they might learn, than with the copying of surface appearances. Tourism and the annual

**Figure 1.6**
Tourist accommodation in Corfu, with forms designed to accord with concepts of the vernacular architecture of the island (see also Figure 1.8).

holiday are ritualized escapes from urban life or from the familiar surroundings of home and office. Designing for these industries of escapism implies the provision of the comforts of home in romantic, even fictionalized settings. As in other forms of tourist art, the reduction in scale of some elements and the exaggeration of others, leads to a *kitsch* version of the authentic.

If the latter is the architecture of the unnecessary, exploiting the vernacular tradition of the necessary building, the architects and planners who are involved in designing for the developing countries

**Figure 1.7**
'Bustee housing', built from waste materials by migrants to the city. These examples in East Calcutta, India, have been destroyed, but the housing problem remains.

of the Third World are concerned with the essential. The critical problems of rapid urbanization in the cities of Latin America, Africa or the East have led to violent measures. Whole towns of 'illegal' settlements have been destroyed in the futile attempt to stem the flow of migrants to the cities; new squatter housing instantly takes their place. Although traditional village building has declined and the *barriadas* of Peru, the *bustees* of Calcutta or the *favelas* of Brazil are made from salvaged and scrap materials, some architects have seen in the peri-urban squatters' passionate desire to build their own homes, a first glimpse of a new vernacular. They try to provide the support systems that may make its emergence possible.

Poised between the eclecticism of vernacular-inspired architecture and the urgency of self-build in rapidly urbanizing centres, is a small, but not insignificant trend among those dissatisfied with the world of commerce, industrialization and conspicuous consumption of energy and resources. More prevalent among younger adults, and more possible in the United States where building regulations are less restrictive, the building of personally crafted dwellings is the proving ground for new ideas based on vernacular precedent. Log cabin construction has been studied and developed with ingenuity, respecting and learning from the tradition but introducing innovations appropriate to the present. Associated with the commune movement and the advocates of 'alternative' life-styles, it is more widespread than may be realized and is heavily supported by books and periodicals which promote rational technologies.

All these attitudes, and others shared by some architects, are reflected to some degree in architectural education and account, in part, for the increase in importance of vernacular studies in the curriculum. I am sure that we can recognize in such courses echoes of the methods, approaches and publications of researchers whose motivations have been discussed already: the searcher after new or lost knowledge, the anthropologist, the historian, the archaeologist, the political theorist, the antiquarian, the romantic idealist, the geographer and so on. Similarly, the work of the architectural historian, the conservationist, the neovernacular architect, the derivative designer, the advocacy planner in the development context, or the home-builder dedicated to alternative technology, influences our interpretation of the subject.

Underlying the inclusion of these studies in an architectural course is the belief that the knowledge gained is of fundamental value. Bearing in mind that, as I have explained already, the design process of the architect is very different from the means whereby a building in the vernacular gets built, what are the lessons that can

**Figure 1.8**
The diversity and clarity of built forms in a village street. Pelekas, Kerkira (Corfu), Greece.

be learned? It seems that most people who are attracted to vernacular architecture, have admired examples on aesthetic grounds, responding to the simplicity of line and purity of form that is to be found in, for instance, the dwellings in the small towns of the Greek islands, or the incorporation of sculptured relief on the compounds of the Hausa in northern Nigeria. Very little is known of the aesthetic of tribal and folk cultures, especially with regard to their shelter, so we rely on our own sensibilities and subjective responses to the buildings and their details.

Architects in the twentieth century developed a functionalist aesthetic which esteemed forms that expressed fitness for purpose. In vernacular buildings that have been constructed to meet a specific need we may see evolve over decades, or even centuries, structures that have been modified and adjusted in form and detail until they satisfied the demands placed upon them. In a great many countries, farm buildings – stores, stables, granaries and the like – demonstrate the 'close fit' of the structure made to suit the requirements of a specific function. In certain structures this functional role is achieved through the discovery or the exploitation of physical laws – I am thinking here of rope and fibre bridges, or of the membranes using tension principles that provide the dwellings of desert nomads over vast areas of Africa and the Middle East. Economy and life-support systems clearly play an important part in determining these tents, for they must be light, portable, easily dismantled and assembled. We can of course, learn a great deal about structural principles in vernacular buildings, which often demonstrate them in the use and placing of every constituent element. Often, remarkably sophisticated results are achieved with relatively simple technologies. This is sometimes evident in buildings that have been constructed in order to serve a technological purpose, such as windmills and watermills, which have been ingeniously developed to utilize natural, nonexpendable energies, in the service of a wide variety of functions. Such examples of vernacular technology can teach us much about creative extensions of use and, in the case of windmills, even of vernacular servomechanisms.

It is not only in the use of energy that we can learn about the employment of natural resources, for most forms of indigenous shelter have to be constructed from available materials. In different regions we can see the intelligent and sensitive use of stone, mud, timber and grasses, even of animal hides. Many different methods and techniques have been developed, sometimes extending the potential of the material to its optimum capacity to serve as a load-bearing or cladding element. Many societies have achieved an ecological balance which maintains, in a steady state, the relationship between the availability of a resource and their consumption of it; I need hardly emphasize that this is a lesson that we certainly need to learn. Humans are the most adaptable of mammals and through their intelligence they have been able to survive in regions of abundance and in others of limited resources: whether rain forests and swamps, arid deserts or icy wastes. In spite of extremes of heat or cold, these environments have been host to different peoples who have evolved cultures appropriate to such conditions. In their

**Figure 1.9**
Functional building, e.g. a windmill that drives a mechanism for draining land that is subject to flooding. A drainage channel with sluice-gate runs from the mill. East Anglia.

**Figure 1.10**
Many Tuareg nomads use tents made of dyed and sewn goatskins, stretched over light frames and held in tension with hide ropes. Sahara desert, north of Timbuktu, Mali.

shelter they have incorporated numerous ways of utilizing available resources and, according to the circumstances, of modifying climates by warming, insulating or cooling. We could be less wasteful in our employment of natural materials and in our methods of heating and refrigerating buildings, if we studied vernacular solutions and profited by them.

Although I could continue generalizing, I have probably cited here sufficient broad examples to indicate that we have much to gain as students and architects from the study of indigenous precedents and current practices. Particularization is certainly necessary and much could arise from original field research. Just as some fundamental architectural principles are to be ascertained in vernacular shelter, so too, the means whereby we study them can be educationally beneficial. For instance, there are methods of record, from measured drawings to statistical analyses, full-scale details to tests of structural performance or climate regulation, which we can apply to folk shelter as a preparation for their application to more complex architecture. The practical advantages in education are not difficult to enumerate. Why then, am I dissatisfied with all that I have summarized up to now? Why do I feel that these are not the most important reasons why we should study vernacular architecture? All the reasons I have discussed have their place and can be of great help to us; I do not discredit them. But it is in the embodiment of values that I feel the study is most rewarding. In tribal, folk and peasant societies, shelter symbolizes much more than can be visibly apparent. People who build their own dwellings invest them with something of their own personalities; societies that have developed traditional forms of vernacular architecture see their buildings as the focus of their social, ritual and spiritual life. Vestiges of these values still remain in the homes of the people in our own society, but professional architecture has done much to prevent ordinary members of the community from interpreting their value systems through their homes, and has inhibited their capacity to shape their domestic environment.

This is not the place to embark upon a critique of the problems and failures of contemporary housing. If however, we are to ensure and support humane and valued housing in the immediate, and in the more distant future, among peoples of the so-called Third World as well as in the 'developed' countries, we need to know much more about the meanings and symbolic roles of shelter in society. These are reflected in the siting, the orientation and the spatial relationships within buildings, as well as in the customs and rituals that frequently attend all stages of construction and use, and in much more. It is my firm belief that the study of vernacular architecture can help us gain the understanding that we so desperately need, in these as well as in many other cultural aspects of vernacular architecture.

# 2

# The importance of the study of vernacular architecture (1993)

Before we can begin to consider whether the study of vernacular architecture is important, or if so, in what ways its importance may be evident, we have to define what we mean by 'vernacular architecture'. The term 'vernacular' is a linguistic one, and when it is applied to architecture it becomes a part of the familiar linguistic analogy of 'architecture as a language of form', and vernacular architecture can be said to be 'the architectural language of the people' with its ethnic, regional and local 'dialects'. As a phrase it is still unknown and unused in many countries, but it is gaining greater currency across the world. Even so, vernacular architecture is often associated with 'popular' architecture. A distinction can be made between the vernacular – *of* and *by* the people, and 'popular' architecture designed *for* the people – whether in suburbs, main street services or the buildings of public institutions.

## Defining the vernacular

In the British Isles there is no doubt that the timber-framed houses and other buildings of East Anglia or the Weald of Kent are vernacular; nor is there any question that the characteristic stone-built villages of the Cotswolds are likewise. But houses of such solidity and construction are not perceived as vernacular in some countries, where the phrase is frequently applied to smaller, simpler buildings. Of short life and made of local, and often very light materials, they may be the constructions of ethnic or other minorities. But, if the substantially built houses of the Mindanao in the Philippines,

**Figure 2.1**
A characteristic Cotswold village with houses built of local stone, including stone roofs. A manor house and church are nearby. Gloucestershire, England.

with their sculptured 'horn bill' decorations and massive tree trunk columns are 'vernacular', are the pile dwellings of the Baja fishermen also vernacular? If the compounds of the people of Burkina Faso or Cameroon are considered vernacular, should the temporary structures of the nomadic Fulani who pass through their territory also be so regarded?

The mistake may be to take a structural, materials or formal view of the built forms of various societies and to classify them according to their degree of permanence, technology and form. It is better I believe, to consider these aspects of the architecture of cultures in the context of their environments and essentially, in relation to their capacity to meet the values and needs of the societies that have built them.

While this definition raises questions in specific instances in many parts of the world, it may be accepted as what it is – a defining 'tool' which we may use when discussing the buildings of cultures that come within the orbit of our concerns and studies. However, the question arises as to whether they are important, and if so, to whom?

The number of people present at an international seminar compared with the tens of thousands of architects and architectural students in Mexico alone, is evidence enough that it is not a subject that is important to the majority of Mexican architects and students. It is clear that the subject is important to those who do participate, but likewise, it is evident that there are thousands of architects, practising or studying, to whom it has no significance. The best we can

**Figure 2.2**
Stone and adobe houses line the steep cobblestone street that winds through Taxco village at a high altitude (8000 feet). Mexico.

say is that it is valued by *some* architects and by *some* anthropologists and indeed, by *some,* but by no means all professionals in a variety of disciplines. To the others it may indeed, be unrecognized by them as a subject that merits study.

## Approaches to the study of vernacular architecture

Ours is a subject without a discipline. It is not studied in the way that medicine, or law, or computer technology, or even formal architectural design are studied – with a curriculum, method and qualifications that may lead to specifically identified employment. This is both a weakness and a strength of vernacular architecture studies – permitting freedom from the constraints of discipline, but also promoting a high level of uncertainty as to its practicality and usefulness, with serious questions as to purpose and method. We should not forget the important contributions made to our subject by those whose discipline did not bear upon it, or whose interest is not related to any academic pursuits: the amateur historians, the enthusiasts and devotees of vernacular building who are directed only by their love of the vernacular. Their passion is not to be dismissed – on the contrary, it is our common ground. Most of those among us who have embarked upon serious study of the vernacular have been motivated by our delight in the buildings, our appreciation of their beauty, our admiration of their simplicity, their honesty or their appropriateness.

Yet, beyond the level of aesthetic appreciation, which discards as inferior all that we consider to be lacking in quality or merit, there is much to be learned and understood. This is where the specialists of particular fields – architects, anthropologists, historians, archaeologists, geographers and many others – can apply their perceptions, skills, knowledge and expertise to traditional buildings, revealing much that we in other fields may not see or comprehend. As yet we hardly have a forum, or even a publication for the sharing of this knowledge and the fruits of our research, while the specific nature of our respective disciplines often isolates us from a more rounded understanding. We are all aware of the anthropologist who cannot describe a structure or communicate through drawings; of the architect whose study is of form but who has given no thought to symbolism or meaning; or of the geographer whose concept of spatial relationships is quite different from the architects' notion of space.

Former commitments to singular approaches are now being questioned. The meticulous recording of structural information and building details has a place: through careful observation and documentation much has been revealed about the distribution of types, the prevalence of motifs, the diffusion of technologies, the history of techniques. But the endless accumulation of data without relevance is of dubious value. Ideas of resource determinism – classification of the vernacular by the prevalence of the use of 'local' materials has little significance in many parts of the world. Even climatic determinism has been shown to be a less reliable key to architectural form than it might seem. Anthropological studies in kinship, inheritance and activity systems reveal much concerning values – but often without reference to the buildings and environmental contexts that accommodate them. Art historians who have studied decoration and detail but neglected construction, museologists who have saved exceptional buildings but ignored the lesser structures, are now seen as having too narrow a focus in their research. Nevertheless, intensive research in specific cultures by anthropologists who are aware of the significance of buildings has demonstrated, for example, the complexity of binary classification within the Kabyle dwelling, or the concept of the community house as cosmos among the Tucanoans of Amazonia. Such research has brought new dimensions to the study of vernacular architecture.

In the past few decades there have been approaches that have not been tied to a single discipline: structuralist approaches that have related change in architecture to change in social development, phenomenological approaches which have stemmed from experimental analysis of the relationship of the individual to space; ethno-archaeological approaches that have sought to understand the patterns of living of former cultures through the study of presently surviving ones; behavioural studies which have related patterns of culture and custom to the built environment.

While there is evidence of an expanding awareness of the advantages of multidisciplinary work in vernacular architecture, the methods and tools of study are for the most part, still thoroughly entrenched in the specific professional disciplines. So for example, architects bring their capacity to express structure and form through plans, sections, elevations and orthographic projections, even though these are by no means always comprehensible to those without training in them. At another level, anthropologists place considerable importance on fieldwork and participant observation, very different from the objective recording and analysis of the architects. Some of the methods used by specialists in certain fields are applicable only to particular vernacular contexts. Thus the accounts, probates, civic records and other documents that may be of great value to historians in literate societies are inaccessible or nonexistent with reference to preliterate and nonliterate peoples. As a result of these problems we may often resort to the methods of record which are materially productive – typologies of buildings, plans or details; tables of occupancy and statistics of density; climatic analyses of diurnal range; tests of building materials and their performance; histories of buildings to establish their precise dates of construction or the dendrochronology of their timbers – and so on. All these methods have their uses, all are uncovering aspects of vernacular architecture in many countries and cultures. But they can also be limiting – displacement activities for energies which might be directed elsewhere if other purposes were known.

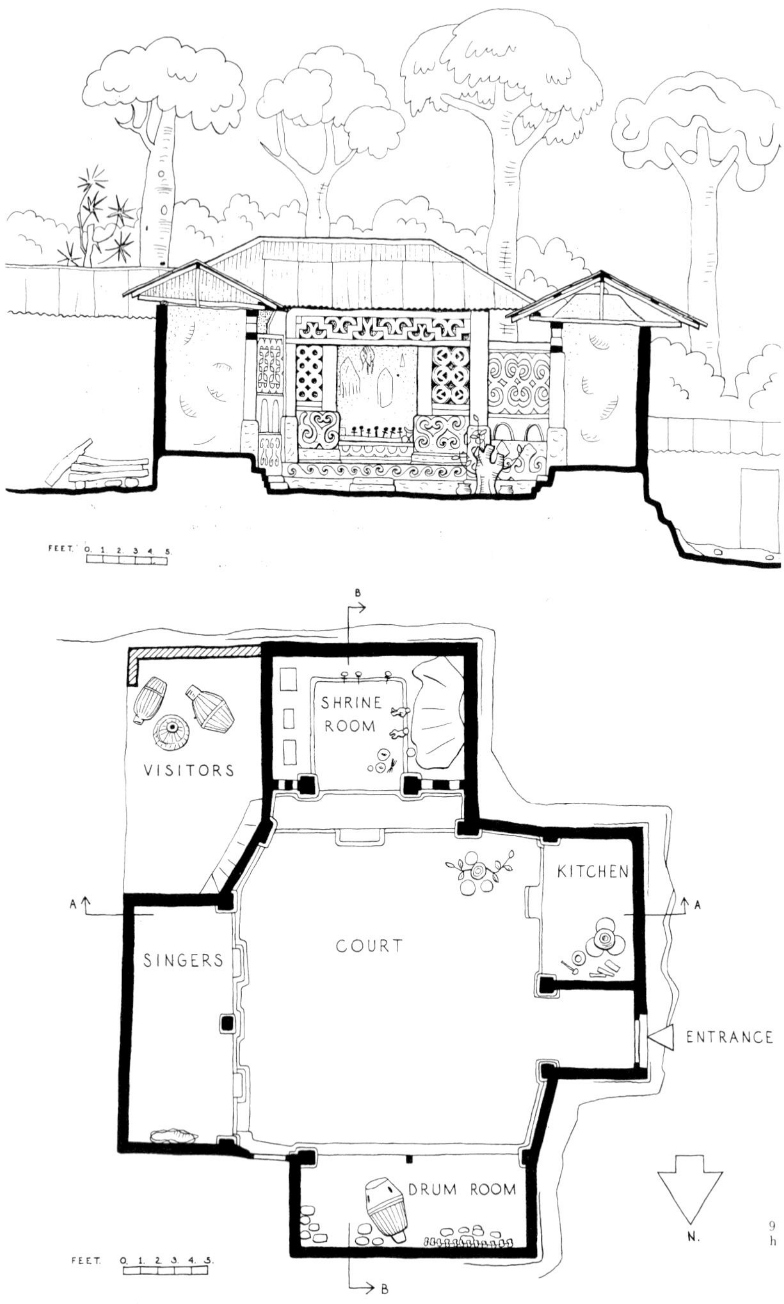


**Figure 2.3**
Plan and section of an Asante *abosomfie*, or village temple, drawn by the late Michael Swithenbank. Bawjwiasi, Ghana.

In the developing fields of vernacular research, methods employed in geography, archaeology or sociology, also demand methods in the acquisition and analysis of data involving specialized mathematical and computer skills. Other aspects, such as the analysis of spatial relationships within or between buildings, may inspire new kinds of diagrams and graphics to convey complex patterns. Occasionally, the methods of research and their presentation from more than one discipline may be brought together, as for example, when anthropological diagrams of kinship over generations are related to growth and change in domestic plan. We can expect to see more of such developments in the future as the scope of research, and the methods by which it is conducted, continue to widen.

How much importance is attached to the researches undertaken in vernacular architecture is frequently conditioned by the preferences and prejudices of professionals in specific fields. Our criteria are largely shaped by our understanding of what is of significance to our own discipline. Historians ignore geographical data; anthropologists may see little merit or value in architectural typologies or may question the evidence of diffusion in the light of current disregard of diffusionist theory; sociologists may have little patience for phenomenological accounts. As awareness of alternative methods of study and of the growth in knowledge of vernacular architecture increases, we may see these prejudices diminish. The day may come when certain anthropological and sociological studies may be included in the education of architects and environmental designers, who have already encompassed some geographical and historical studies within their courses. But the day when architectural studies are an integral part of the education of anthropologists may still be a long way off.

## Applications of vernacular research

If research in vernacular architecture is being developed and refined, it is reasonable to ask what the practical applications of such studies might be. Among the most visible is the selection of vernacular buildings for *in situ* conservation, or for dismantling and re-erection in open-air museums. There is a tendency to choose the most spectacular examples. When new buildings are constructed to old models, their decoration or forms are often exaggerated and even the open-air museums are often clinically clean. Then there is the response of architects who perceive the merits of vernacular architecture. Once it was the forms – and the white walls of Greek island houses – which inspired architects. But today, more are interested in regional qualities that are related to the use of local materials and they may seek inspiration in culturally specific building forms. Toraja roofs are erected in Sulawesi; the Sumatran Minangkabau house has obviously become a symbol, not of Indonesia, but due to the centuries-old presence of some Minangkabau in Negri Sembalan province, of Malaysia. But if some uses of the vernacular by architects are imitative and cosmetic, several have studied climatic modification by traditional techniques or made intelligent use of indigenous building methods.

Architects and planners engaged in development projects – such as settlement upgrading, sites and services schemes, or low-cost housing – have drawn upon a wide experience of vernacular skills and know-how. So for instance, the Nubian vault system 'discovered' by Hasan Fathy, the Egyptian architect, has been applied by teams of the Development Workshop in Angola and Niger. Such technology transfer, has the potential for overcoming the disastrous effects of the depletion of local resources. But there are problems. As structural anthropologists would argue, technological transfer will also mean corresponding changes in society, and there are serious cultural implications when new technologies are introduced. Often the values of a culture are difficult to ascertain.

## The importance of vernacular architecture studies

Vernacular architecture in countries throughout the world is threatened. Fortunately, the scale of deliberate destruction, such as the Ceaucescu regime perpetrated in numerous villages in Romania is not widespread, but the vernacular suffers from indifference and

**Figure 2.4**
Abandoned houses and entire villages in the Spanish Pirineos are numerous, their occupants having migrated to Barcelona, Zaragoza or other cities.

ignorance of its historic or social value, and from being assigned low status in housing. Mass migration from the rural areas to the cities of the developing world is driven by the push–pull factors of sophisticated urban living and fragile job opportunities. In the process, traditional homes and life-styles are abandoned, and in the villages, urban housing becomes a model. Confronting the widespread decline in respect for the vernacular, studies in the subject have become of major importance. They are necessary in the quest for knowledge of the diversity of mankind's solution to the problems of dwelling and accommodation of sacred and secular community functions. But they are also significant for the mutual benefit of cultures all over the world. With the reservations noted already, the transfer of skills may help solve resource depletion or improve climate modification. Practical applications of indigenous solutions to environmental problems may give a material incentive to the urgent recovery of vernacular know-how.

Yet, the need for vernacular studies is more complex than this. A culture without the presence of its history is a culture without roots and, very possibly, without meaning. The habitations of mankind are the scene of most of our activities from birth to death; the temples and shrines, meeting houses and communal social structures are the places where people meet their fellows, and commune with their deities. In scale and in detail, the vernacular offers antidotes to the architecture of power, to monumentalism and the profligate use of resources. It touches the well-springs of inheritance and points in many ways to technologically undamaging, culturally acceptable

**Figure 2.5**
A group of meeting houses, totem carving houses and other traditional structures, recently built by the Cowachin of Duncan, Vancouver Island, Canada.

and symbolically significant buildings in compatible landscape environments. This paper has a hidden agenda; to those who believe that the study of vernacular architecture is important, it is a plea for cross-cultural, interdisciplinary research. By sharing our perceptions and understanding, let alone our research methods, by endeavouring to resolve the dichotomy between those who study vernacular architecture and those who live in it, we may gain new, lasting and invaluable insights to the habitations of mankind. Such insights can lead to support and assistance for surviving vernacular traditions, and can inform policies and design in housing that will have to meet the exponential growth in populations in all continents.

# 3

# Problems of definition and praxis (1999)

## Cross-cultural and interdisciplinary perspectives

Having spent the greater part of my professional life studying the vernacular architecture of cultures in every continent, with extensive fieldwork and many projects, I became aware of the need for a resource which would bring together, at least in outline, what is known of the world's building traditions. In 1987, I was invited to draft a proposal for an encyclopedia which would perform this function, a task in itself which took me a considerable time to plan. In the previous few years, a couple of international organizations had been established whose meetings acted as forums for discussion of related issues. From these, from the contributors to my books published on the subject in the 1970s, from my colleagues on projects and from the authors represented in my ever-expanding library, I was able to draw up a list of potential contributors. A group of authors whose work I knew personally acted as an advisory board and the project was launched. The task was enormous, involving trips throughout much of the world and a vast correspondence. I encountered many problems, though perhaps none were as serious as the decision by the publisher to discontinue, as the work had grown beyond their capacity to publish it. Eventually, Cambridge University Press took on the task and *The Encyclopedia of Vernacular Architecture of the World* was finally published in three volumes at the end of 1997. It has 1.7 million words of text, a few thousand entries, illustrations on virtually every page, a glossary, a multilingual lexicon, a bibliography of some 9000 entries, indexes of cultures, of locations and of all subjects, the whole being extensively crossreferenced. All this could not have been achieved without the commitment of a small but dedicated team and the enthusiastic support of the contributors.

There is one further statistic which particularly relates to our overall theme – there were over 750 contributors to the work, drawn from some 80 countries and a wide range of disciplines. Why so many? Could I not have had a much smaller group – say a tenth or less – who could write the entries? Indeed, I would have been glad if this was the case, but in spite of my efforts I could find very few potential authors who had a sufficient spread of knowledge and interests. On the contrary, all but a small minority were specialists in their fields. In one respect this was an advantage, for it meant that they had detailed knowledge of the subjects on which they agreed to write. But there were also many problems that arose from this – problems both of definition and of praxis; problems which have bearing on both theoretical and practical issues relating to the study, and the preservation, of vernacular architecture. Not least of these was the term 'vernacular architecture' itself; unknown to many, objected to by some, but used by a growing number of writers and researchers in building traditions. Clearly, it had to be defined if it was to be used as the title of the encyclopedia.

The Latin root of 'vernacular' is *verna*, a slave, and the connotations still exist in Italy, even though *vernaculus* meant 'native'. Consequently, some of the Italian contributors to the encyclopedia, though they wrote with authority, tended to focus on the poorest and simplest shelters, and did not consider that Tuscan farmhouses

**Figure 3.1**
Main Street in Maryville, Tennessee, subject of an urban renewal programme.

**Figure 3.2**
Sea Ranch, a group of 'neovernacular' condominiums and service buildings on the north California coast, designed by Charles Moore and Partners (MLTW) 1965.

were vernacular. In fact, I had to get an Italian-speaking English architect to write the entries for Tuscany and Umbria. But this basic problem of definition also applied to English-speaking countries like the United States, Canada and Australia. In these, the term 'vernacular' is used in a wider sense, and includes commercial, contractor-designed and built tract housing. It is also applied to 'main street' architecture – stores, supermarket chains, fast food outlets, even filling stations, though these are clearly not indigenous. Such buildings constitute what is referred to by some British writers as 'popular architecture', designed and built for the people, but not native to them. In California and the west generally, however, the term is often applied to buildings designed by architects, who respond to the local tradition, or use local materials. It follows that a phrase like 'vernacular architecture heritage' will have different meanings, according to the culture to which you belong or the language that you speak.

For the purposes of the compilation of EVAW (the acronym that we used for the encyclopedia), a definition was necessary that would be applicable to building traditions in all continents, and to communities of differing sizes and in diverse environments. A definition that would encompass all forms of building, every structural system and innumerable functions the world over, seemed scarcely possible. Even if it was defined in these terms it might still not indicate the purposes that the world's cultures require their vernacular buildings to serve. Nevertheless, it seemed that the latter might constitute a firmer basis for a definition than one that was essentially descriptive in technical or physical terms. After due consideration I proposed the following definition which, I hoped, would be indicative to authors of the nature of the contributions that I sought, and which would be adequate and comprehensible for readers of all disciplines and persuasions. It was printed opposite the title page of each volume of the encyclopedia, and read:

> Vernacular architecture comprises the dwellings and all other buildings of the people. Related to their environmental contexts and available resources, they are customarily owner- or community-built, utilizing traditional technologies. All forms of vernacular architecture are built to meet specific needs, accommodating the values, economies and ways of living of the cultures that produce them.

This, I felt could summarize the *what* of vernacular architecture: what environmental conditions prevailed, what it was made of, what its

**Figure 3.3**
Rubble stone wall with relieving arch to distribute load. Lefkara village, Cyprus.

types were, and for what purposes it was built. These matters were covered in the first volume in sections devoted to environment, materials and resources, production, services, symbolism and decoration, typologies, uses and functions. Within each section there are approximately six categories, as is the case with the section on materials and building resources. These categories include (in alphabetical order) animal products, earths and clays, grasses and palms, rocks and stone, timbers, used and manufactured materials. Each category has an average of 15 separate entries, so for instance, in the category rocks and stone, the entries are on ashlar, cave shelter, cobbles and setts, cobblestone, coral, coursed stone, fieldstone, flint, granite, mortar, rock shelter, rubble, slab, slate and tufa.

A related problem of definition was that of the area under discussion in any entry. Nations are often implied in discussions about vernacular architecture; 'Finnish', 'Nepalese', 'Mexican' vernacular, for instance. But Finland includes Sami (or Lapp) people; Nepal, the Newar, Ghurka and several others, while Mexico includes the Maya, Purapecha, Totenac and many more contemporary Indian peoples, as well as the *mestizo* majority. Clearly, nationality does not define vernacular traditions. Nor do provinces or counties: so, to take an English example: 'Gloucestershire' is not a defined area as far as architecture is concerned; the Cotswold building tradition is as characteristic of north Oxfordshire. Many identifiable peoples are not limited by political or administrative boundaries, as I learned in Ghana in the 1960s. The Ewe people are in both Ghana and Togoland, while the Gurunsi complex of peoples is in northern Ghana and in Upper Volta (or Burkina Faso as it is now called; frontiers and national names are not constants). After much deliberation, I decided to focus the entries in the encyclopedia on the cultures that produce the identifiable building traditions of specific regions, which of course, meant that both 'cultures' and 'regions' had to be identified.

Little had been done in the way of cultural mapping since the 1950s, and the evidence suggests that these did not consider the architecture of cultures while identifying them. For the purposes of EVAW I had to redraw the cultural map of the world, relating individual cultures to culture groups which shared certain characteristics or which occupied territories of comparable environments and topography. In particular, in view of the subject of the work, they had to have sufficient architectural features in common to justify the grouping. Much research is needed in order to ascertain how relevant these cultural areas are, and how well the cultures and their building traditions relate to them. The areas were not defined

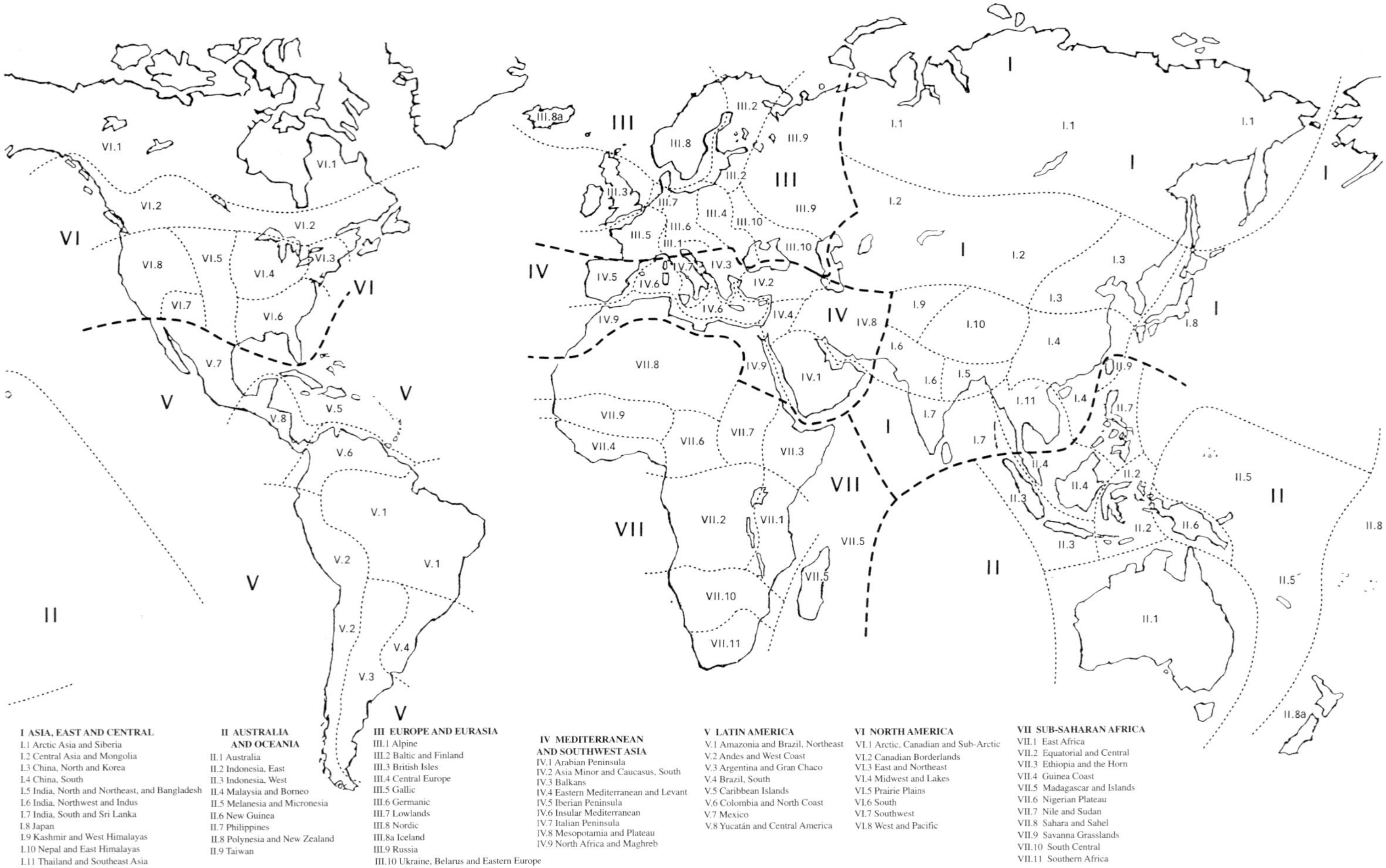


**Figure 3.4**
A map of the global culture regions and areas, as defined and drawn by the author, for use in the *Encyclopedia of Vernacular Architecture of the World*.

by political boundaries but reflected other factors, continental and regional; these I drafted in a simple linear map that served as end-papers.

For each cultural region so identified, reference numbers were assigned and expressed on regional maps. These accompanied the introductory text on each region, with many specifically identifiable but broadly related cultures indicated. They were grouped in the continental regions of Asia, East and Central; Australia and Oceania; Europe and Eurasia; Mediterranean and South-West Asia; Latin America; North America; and Sub-Saharan Africa. In excess of 65 culture areas were identified – between eight and eleven in each region. For Australasia and Oceania, these included Australia, Indonesia East, Indonesia West, Malaysia and Borneo; Melanesia and Micronesia; New Guinea, Philippines, Polynesia and New Zealand. In the course of study in the field it becomes apparent that we cannot usefully generalize about, for instance, 'South-East Asian', or 'Indonesian', vernacular. We learn that every island has a different architecture, and that this in turn may also be differentiated: there are similarities but also marked divergence between the building traditions of the Belunese, the Atoni or the Ema on the small island of Timor.

On a large island like Sumatra there is little correspondence between the buildings of the Minangkabau people in the south, the Riau of the centre, the Batak of the north or the Aceh people of the northern peninsula. The differences are not solely ones of materials,

**Figure 3.5**
A *torogan* or great house of a Maraneo lineage head. Raised on tree trunks and notable for the *panolongs*, carved foliated beam ends. Mindanao, Philippines.

or of structure, or of response to climate alone, but also of spatial organization, of status, of the age and gender of the owner-builders, and of the meanings that the buildings carry. They are in fact, essentially cultural differences, and the buildings cannot be understood outside their cultural, as well as their environmental, contexts, a fact which raises the issue of the *who* of vernacular architecture. So, for instance, in the culture area of the Philippines, listed above, the category is subdivided into approximately 20 cultures with distinctive architectural traditions. These included the Bajau, Bontoc, Ibaloi, Ifugao, Ifugao-Mayoyao, Ilocano, Isneg, Ivatan, Kalinga, Kankanay, Maranao, Sagada, Samal, Tagalog, Tausug, Tau't Batu, Visayan, and Yakan.

**Figure 3.6**
Badjao fisherfolk are traditionally the 'sea nomads' of the Sulu Sea. Some build one-roomed, unfurnished, stilt houses from which they trade. South-west Philippines.

In all, EVAW discusses the architecture of more than 1300 cultures. But it is not, and cannot be complete – we do not even know how many cultures there are. Every language indicates the existence of a distinct culture, and there are in excess of 6500 known languages in use today. But some languages embrace many cultures – think of the cultural groups that speak Spanish in Central and South America; does each one have a distinct vernacular tradition? We do not know how many vernacular building traditions there are in the world, or even what defines one as distinct from another. As I mentioned earlier, most contributors to EVAW were specialists and there were over 750 of them. The majority were specialists in particular cultures or cultural groups, who brought focused knowledge and research to bear upon building as an aspect of the way of life of their chosen societies. For some specialists, this research was based on 'fieldwork' undertaken to provide data for an academic study; for others, with a commitment to the survival of the vernacular, it was more the product of a quest in support of disregarded or threatened traditions. This raises a second issue of the *who* of vernacular studies: Who is engaged in them and to what end, for what purposes and by which means, is the study of the subject pursued? As the subject of EVAW is architecture, even if not designed by architects, it is probably to be expected that about 40 per cent of the contributors were architects. They brought the knowledge of their profession to the understanding of the technology of building, the properties of materials, the structural principles underlying certain solutions. They also brought the skills they had acquired in perceiving three-dimensionally, measuring and drawing to scale, expressing form, space and detail in plans, sections and elevations, and in many cases, in axonometric or isometric projections. They are valuable techniques, though they are frequently inadequate to express the forms of some vernacular traditions, and they do not communicate concepts of space use. On the social-cultural issues related to VA, some admitted to being rather less well informed.

Anthropologists, who were as numerous among the contributors as the architects, particularly emphasized the relationship of families to dwellings, kinship to settlement, social structure to status, beliefs to sanctuaries, and symbolism to decoration or associative meanings. But generally, they were less interested in the structural principles of architecture and ill-informed on the technological processes of constructing the largest and most essential elements of material culture: the buildings occupied by the peoples that they studied. The remainder of the contributors came from a variety of disciplines: ethno-archaeologists, who were interested in contemporary correspondences with occupational patterns of the past; historians, both professional and amateur, who studied documentary evidence and traced antecedents; cultural geographers, whose interests were in spatial relationships, economies, locations and communications; folklorists who probed traditional customs and practices in oral and material culture; conservationists who were concerned with the protection and preservation of the vernacular within the building heritage. There were several contributors whose explorations in the field of VA took them along the paths of art history, museology or development, but there were none whose primary disciplines were in engineering, planning, economics or politics; or at least, as they are understood in England. In Turkey, for instance, architecture is perceived as a branch of engineering, and hence as a science, while in Britain it is widely perceived as one of the arts. Similarly, there is no discipline of anthropology in Turkey, as it is considered to be part of archaeology in that country, while in some North American universities, archaeology is an aspect of anthropology.

Only in a very few instances were contributions drawn from interdisciplinary teams. This reflects the specialized nature of education and practice, over 80 per cent of the contracted authors being associated with an educational institution. The divisions went deeper, arising from the suspicion with which the humanities are regarded by the scientists, and by the failure of many to recognize the 'social sciences', whose methods they suspect are not 'scientific'. Even within the disciplines and among the practitioners there is disagreement on methodology. For instance, the 'participant observer' anthropologists disapprove of the active engagement of the folklorists. A principle such as 'diffusion' may be of interest to both the archaeologist and the geographer but be anathema to many a social anthropologist. Semiology/semiotics (the uncertainty of terminology itself indicates a philosophical division) may be valued by both linguist and architectural theorist, but their applications may be mutually exclusive. Who studies vernacular architecture is heavily conditioned by the nature, objectives and language of their respective disciplines, and the way in which both the subject of VA and the parallel disciplines are regarded. So diverse were the disciplines from which contributors came, that I felt it to be necessary to commence EVAW with a number of essays on approaches and concepts which discussed, from professional standpoints, the importance of VA within specific disciplines, and the contributions that such academic (and sometimes conflicting) directions have made to the study of VA – conservationist, developmental, ecological, ethnographical and museological, among them. These disciplinary summaries were augmented by philosophical positions which were shared by some researchers across a number of areas, such as the cognitive, behavioural, ecological, evolutionary, phenomenological or structuralist approaches.

This may be sufficient to indicate the *who* of the work; the kinds of cultures within related cultural groups who are included, and also the specialists and their representative disciplines or approaches who contributed entries for the text. But the examples of both the cultures about whom entries may be written, and the specialisms of contributors, emphasize the necessity for, but also the problems of, defining our terms so that we can mutually understand the content and the references. Making explicit, both individually and together, the locations of traditions situated in cultural areas, within larger regions, and related to the continental masses, should also have met the need to identify the *where* of vernacular architecture. Using the other ancient Anglo-Saxon interrogatives I will now introduce the issues of both definition and praxis of the *when*, the *how* and the *why* of the study of the subject.

In speaking of the 'vernacular architecture heritage' we immediately build in the assumption – very probably correct, but always open to question – of its presumed age. We have 'inherited' the vernacular; is it no longer constructed or is it still with us? I understand that within the boundaries of Romania there were, a decade ago, some 13 000 intact villages, within which there may have been a quarter of a million vernacular buildings. How recent were some of them? Are some still being built, adapted, modified, re-roofed? Is the tradition essentially past, has it been largely destroyed, or does it still survive in, for instance, parts of Russia and much of China? In Britain, where the study of the vernacular architecture is quite inflexible and defined by the national boundaries within the United Kingdom, it is contended that the tradition ended in the 1840s with the development of the railways, which moved materials and people. This contention is presumably based on the assumption that vernacular builders only used local materials, and that the structures were raised only by indigenous people.

One British scholar, whose interest is in houses built before the fifteenth century, remarked to me that a 300-year-old house was 'quite recent'. Not a view that would make much sense in North America. Age is not necessarily associated with a building; it can also relate to the persistence of a structural detail or form, of a plan type or the use of a particular technology. These can be traced over centuries, even, in the case of building in the Middle East, over thousands of years. Are these a part of the 'vernacular heritage'?

**Figure 3.7**
Medieval houses are still occupied for domestic and trade purposes. Cluny, France.

Yet in much of the world – in East Africa for example, we make assumptions about the age of a tradition even though we have no sound evidence for it, and the houses we study may only be a few years old. The *when* of vernacular architecture is therefore relative, and we need to indicate what we mean by age and heritage in the specific context that we study, and not depend upon sweeping assumptions. For the purposes of EVAW, I decided to include those traditions that had survived in use into the twentieth century, irrespective of when they were built; this ensured that it would cover medieval houses that were still lived in, as well as Maasai dwellings that had been raised since work on EVAW started.

Mention of Romania, Britain, China, Nepal, East Africa and elsewhere, emphasizes that just as vernacular architecture did not, and does not, exist solely in past times. On the contrary, if it has declined in much of the west, it is flourishing in Africa and Asia, and in much of Oceania and elsewhere. It is important that we do not bring the values and criteria that have been formed by the study of historical traditions to the study of living traditions, without seriously questioning their appropriateness. In the case of historical traditions we may feel forced to make unverified conclusions, about the craftsmen and their methods and about the people who occupied the buildings they constructed. Where the traditions survive we can learn much about these at first hand. Of course, their purposes, their technologies and their buildings may be very different in design, structure and function but our researches can be greatly enriched by studying them, if only because we can learn how buildings relate to society, to the community, to the family and kin. We can be reminded of their significance in access to resources, the conditions of differing environments, the cycle of the seasons and the progression of generations, aspects that have profound influences on the nature of vernacular traditions that can be overlooked, or be overgeneralized when they are not the specific focus of research.

A fundamental weakness of the study, understanding, and ultimately the survival, of VA is that it is not an identified, singular discipline, but within the province of many disciplines. It is a weakness that, in my view, could be its strength, necessitating cross-disciplinary discourse and interdisciplinary praxis. This is not where the subject stands at present, so it bears upon *how* the study of the vernacular is pursued. To a considerable extent the problems of, or barriers to, interdisciplinary research arise from ignorance of terminologies, an ignorance that can be basic – 'structure' has a very different meaning for the architect than its connotations for an anthropologist. Even terms like 'technology' or 'ethnology' have subtly variant meanings to academics coming from different disciplines or national backgrounds, with long-established approaches to the subject. Their objectives, research methods, modes of working, techniques of documentation, and conclusions, affect their perceptions and the definitions of the tasks before them. For example, in Britain vernacular architecture research is archaeological in nature with, among its objectives, the tracing of the earliest date of a

**Figure 3.8**
A *cabane* or *borie* of dry-stone construction, with rubble walls and dressed stone *quoins* or cornerstones. The bell-shaped roof is of corbelled stone. Quercy, France.

**Figure 3.9**
Notched log farm building, with turf roof. A stave church is beyond. Borgund, Norway.

building and the establishing of a chronology of structural methods and details. In the United States, researchers are motivated to establish typologies, though whether the concept of 'type' is one of form or of function is by no means consistent. In France, many researchers are interested in the primary forms and technologies used in building. Each have their obsessions; in England and Wales documenting the incidence of the 'cruck frame' is a prime objective, with the age of components ascertained by dendrochronology and radiocarbon dating. American researchers are as eagerly committed to the recording of notched log (*blockbau*) construction, with acres of print being devoted to the possible European provenance of the different corner-notching techniques. French publications and conferences give prominence to dry-stone construction methods and buildings.

**Figure 3.10**
Notched log cabin, with shakes (wooden tiles) cladding the roof. Nethers, Virginia, USA.



Only a few French, British, American, or other researchers into their own traditions, are customarily concerned with cultural issues.

I suspect that their approaches would be regarded by their exponents as 'scientific' or objective and free of value-loaded bias. Yet it seems clear to me, that these are as value-loaded in their emphasis on the tabulated and the factual as any ecological or sociosemiotic approach might be. It is true that, in compiling the list of approaches and concepts for EVAW, I decided against detailed discussion of ideological positions. Religious, political, feminist and other cross-disciplinary emphases do exist, although predetermining in a sense, the outcome of research. A measure of subjectivity is what drives most of us who study the subject, and the 'participant observer' learns to accept this when doing fieldwork. More important, but far more elusive, is the understanding of the values of the cultures that produce vernacular buildings. Of those from the past we can only surmise, but of those of the surviving traditions we need to know much more. Yet here the 'observer paradox' – that the observers influence by their presence that which they observe – makes knowing a culture 'from within' extremely difficult, if not impossible. Understanding the problem is, however, a step towards its resolution.

In the course of seeking, briefing, commissioning and editing contributions, I became increasingly aware of the problems of sharing knowledge and methods, essential to the *how* of interdisciplinary research. There was a risk of repetition of information (for example, of the method of building with rammed earth) or of examples (such as the *yurt* or *ger* tent) and of major gaps in contextual data in other subjects, like population distribution or the susceptibility of many vernacular buildings to natural disasters. More abstruse subjects to some writers, which were familiar enough to others with different academic backgrounds, also needed to be accommodated, like 'Central Place theory', or the theories of 'Spatial Syntax'. My solution was to divide EVAW into two parts, the first being a volume on theories and principles, and the second (in two volumes) on cultures and habitats, with sections, categories and entries of each, as briefly noted above. It took 18 months to devise the structure for EVAW and to draw up a provisional list of entries. This was made more difficult because I wished to see the subjects closely related to each other, so that they could be read in sequence, while the initial publisher required that it should be alphabetical. My solution was to use the three-tier structure of sections, categories and entries, each being alphabetical within its frame. Although there were those who considered the reconciling of related themes and alphabetical sequences impossible on this scale, I was helped by the appointed advisory board, and by the flexibility and rich variety of words in the English language.

This may seem to be more about the *how* of compiling EVAW than it is about the saving of the 'vernacular heritage'. But in my view it is closely associated with the last of those Anglo-Saxon questions: *Why?* The *why* of VA research differs for the members of various disciplines, as I have tried to show. The subject is too vast – it embraces, I calculate, in excess of 800 million buildings throughout the world – for there to be a single purpose, a sole objective. 'Saving the vernacular heritage' is indeed one aim, and the documentation of disappearing building traditions is another. But there are many more purposes related to the housing of peoples in the future, the continued involvement of cultures in shaping their own environments, and the study and understanding of existing traditions, failing or thriving, which are no less important. In a period when 'sustainability' is prominent in much architectural discourse, much can be learned from the most sustained of all forms of a architecture: the vernacular traditions.

Closely related to the *why* of research and praxis is education; the preparation of students of many disciplines to be able to work with others, to share and speak their languages, to comprehend what they bring to the subject, and to find their own place and role within it. And yet, I know of only a few modules or courses in vernacular architecture that are operating in schools of architecture, although these are to be found from Glasgow in Scotland to Makerere, Uganda and Jakarta in Indonesia. Some of them do attempt to bring into their projects a measure of anthropological study: I have noticed that architectural educators are more willing to involve anthropologists than vice versa. American folklore courses include the study of regional traditions, and there are extramural courses in the vernacular there and in the United Kingdom, but they are essentially local in their focus. Part of the problem has been the lack of technical and cross-cultural information that is readily available to students of the subject. This, it is my hope, the *Encyclopedia of Vernacular Architecture of the World* will provide in outline, bringing together under one roof, so to speak, much of the knowledge we have acquired on all aspects of the subject, and indicating the immense gaps in that knowledge. But the serious consideration of the world's vernacular traditions needs much more than this. We need to produce students who are fully educated in vernacular studies on a cross-cultural and, as far as possible, on an interdisciplinary basis. It is essential that we define what the subject is, when and where it applies and is applied, who is involved in its study, protection, conservation and support, how these are to be achieved and why, in a period of globalization, it is essential to the housing and well-being of humankind in the new century.

## References

Oliver, P. (ed.) *Encyclopedia of Vernacular Architecture of the World* (1997) Cambridge University Press. Three volumes: Vol. 1: *Theories and Principles*, including: Approaches and concepts, Culture traits and attributes, Environment, Materials and building resources, Production, Services, Symbolism and decoration, Typologies, Uses and functions. Vol. 2: *Cultures and Habitats. Asia and Europe*: Asia East and Central, Australasia and Oceania, Europe and Eurasia, Mediterranean and Southwest Asia. Vol. 3: *Cultures and Habitats: Americas and Africa*: Latin America, North America, Sub-Saharan Africa. *Appendices and Indexes:* Glossary of terms, Comparative lexicon (English, French, German, Spanish, Italian, Portuguese, Arabic), Bibliography (9000 entries), Index of cultures and habitats, nations and locations, General index. The three volumes are illustrated with over 2500 photographs, drawings and maps.

# PART II

# CULTURES AND CONTEXTS

# 4

# Learning from Asante (2000)

Many years ago, in the mid-1960s, I was invited to teach for a while in Ghana, West Africa, at the School of Architecture, Kumasi University of Science and Technology. Kumasi is in the heart of the Ghanaian rain forest, and we arrived in the middle of the rainy season. All the vegetation was green and glistening. I was fascinated by this jungle environment, and by the Asante villages that were buried deep in it, often linked only by unmade tracks of compacted red earth. Exploring the forest to some extent, I was impressed by the range of 'woody plants', as foresters termed them, from luxuriating palm trees, to giant cottonwoods with exposed root systems like immense buttresses. There was dense undergrowth throughout, which seemed impenetrable. Wanting to know more, I spoke to an agronomist at the university about it. 'It's not a jungle', he said, when I used the word; 'it's not even rain forest in the sense that you would find it in Nigeria or the Ivory Coast'.

I was disappointed and remarked that whatever they called it, it was primary forest. 'No', he said, 'it's not primary forest. It isn't even secondary forest; for the most part it's tertiary forest. And what you are looking at is Asante farms'. In other words, the original forest had been burned, felled, or utilized by distant generations to the extent that it had gone through successive transformations. But a farm? It was nothing like any farm that I knew. 'They grow bananas, mangoes, all kinds of tropical fruits and root crops', my agronomist friend explained. 'But what about these immense cottonwoods?' I argued. 'They've been here for hundreds of years'. 'Of course, they provide the canopy which protects the plants below', he replied. When I commented on the undergrowth he told me that 'it shades the soil and prevents the sun from turning it into concrete'.

**Figure 4.1**
Dense vegetation in the rain forest region of central south Ghana.

This was hard to understand, but my informant, and others including a geologist at the university, told me what generations of Asante had known and passed on to their successors: when the sun beats on the red soil it turns it into a hard crust, which cannot be cultivated, so it has to be shielded from the sun's heat. 'We argue whether laterites are soils which can behave like rock, or rock in which you can grow plants' said the geologist, with a laugh. For me it was no laughing matter, for I realized that what I understood to be the 'jungle environment' was far from being a simple and generalized phenomenon. Likewise, the Asante 'tribe' who lived there had a profoundly sophisticated understanding of its ecology and behaved accordingly, in order to nurture its growth and harvest its produce.

**Figure 4.2**
A forest farm by the coast, where trees and undergrowth protect crops. Exposed lateritic earth is infertile, but is used for the construction of houses. Ghana.

I have summarized this experience – which really changed the direction of my life – in some detail, because I had begun to learn that what I had taken to be 'the environment' was based on erroneous perceptions, and what I had understood to be Asante 'behaviour' was, in fact, a complex of collective know-how, passed on through a subtle process of cultural transmission. Since then, for decades I have regarded generalizations about the environment with discomfort, and descriptions of individual or group behaviour with scepticism. I will endeavour to enlarge on these misgivings, but first we should ascertain what is meant by these words. For guidance I turn to those standard works the *Oxford English Dictionary* and *Webster's Dictionary*. In these, we find that the verb 'to environ' means to 'encircle' or 'surround', and the 'environment' is that which surrounds an object or living thing: 'whatever encompasses'. Biologically, it is 'the aggregate of all external *and internal* (my emphasis) conditions, affecting the existence, growth, and welfare of organisms'. It can be argued that there is no entity that is 'the environment', but an infinite variety of environments for all physical phenomena. Similarly, we may discover that 'behaviour', while meaning for some 500 years, 'conduct or course of action *towards* or *to* others' has also meant for nearly as long a time, the 'handling, or disposition of *anything*', such as the 'manner or action of a machine, a chemical, substance, organ, organism, etc'.

If we consider what is meant by the terms used to identify persons who study these subjects we may find that a 'behaviourist' is one who advocates 'behaviourism' or the 'theory that human behaviour and activities are the result of individual reaction to definite objective stimuli or situations and not of subjective factors'. In other words, the theory of 'stimulus and response' virtually eliminates free will or motivation. As for the 'environmentalist' we find that this applies to one who attaches more importance to environment than heredity as a determinant in the development of a person or a group. Only the definition of 'one who advocates preservation of the environment, as from commercial exploitation' do we recognize the features of some who link together 'behaviour' and 'environment'. As far as I am aware, it was Amos Rapoport who first defined, by this name at any rate, the field of research termed 'environment–behaviour studies', or EBS. It was not always so: his first book, as many readers will know, was *House Form and Culture*. In this seminal work, he barely discussed either concept, mentioning 'behaviour' only four times, and 'environment' five (Rapoport, 1969). Nevertheless, these gave an indication of the direction to which he would turn, as he argued that an understanding of behaviour patterns is 'essential to the understanding of built form' and that 'forms, once built, affect behaviour and the way of life'. In his view the forms of vernacular buildings result from 'the aims and desires of the unified group for an ideal environment' and sociocultural forces 'become of prime importance in relating man's way of life to the environment'. Whether the 'ideal environment' is indeed, an objective or, in many cultures, is even a concept, remains to be demonstrated.

Several years later, in 1976, Professor Rapoport edited the proceedings of the IXth International Congress of Anthropological and Ethnological Sciences under the title *The Mutual Interaction of People and Their Built Environment*, to which he contributed an introduction outlining a programme for research in the newly defined area, and a paper on 'Socio-cultural aspects of man–environment studies' (Rapoport, 1976). The following year Rapoport's *Human Aspects of Urban Form* was published, subtitled 'Towards a man–environment approach to urban design' (Rapoport, 1977). Some time after this, perhaps under feminist persuasion, the 'man' was dropped and 'environment–behaviour studies' replaced it. This phrase was being used in the reverse form by Robert Altman (Altman *et al.*, 1980), Roger Downs, David Stea (Downs and Stea, 1973) and others, as 'behaviour–environment' research, but the other came into broader currency. Clearly, the meaning of the words has been made to fit a more unified usage, although a precise definition remains curiously elusive. The field of study was soon narrowed still further to the 'built environment'. Even so, this term, with its uncertainty as to the nature of the 'built' – whether this means constructed, enclosed, erected or simply made by mankind – has been loosely employed.

The behaviourist B.F. Skinner was the principal advocate of the theory of 'stimulus and response', applied to the actions of mankind (Skinner, 1953). As noted above, subjective factors are not included in this theory, though it seems to me that this position is indefensible. Intuitive, emotional and intellectual responses that inspire behaviour are all of significance. But they *are* signifiers, the behaviours that we may observe are the perceptible symptoms of cultural intentions and meanings that may be obscured, because they are based on shared understandings that are not necessarily articulated. In fact, all societies develop codified behaviour patterns that are formed to conceal behavioural impulses. We used to speak of 'manners', 'comportment', 'good conduct' – being sanctioned cultural, rather than individual, behaviours that symbolized, solemnized or simply screened more profound meanings. A curious aspect of this is our tendency to project our behaviours *on* the environment: we talk of 'the hostile desert', 'the cruel sea', the 'peaceful valley', the 'noble mountain', of being 'in the teeth of the gale' and innumerable other figures of speech which we employ as we try to humanize the world around us. But the environment has no motivations, no intentions, no impulses: the environment that surrounds any phenomenon is neutral; it is we who personalize it and often obscure its nature by our romantic projections.

In the commonly employed term, a society often seeks to 'tame' the environment, behaving to the environment as it does to its members. By mutual agreement or by authority, a society may control, suppress or 'civilize' impulsive behaviours for the good of the community, though the customs so employed may be inscrutable to those outside the culture. I soon discovered this when I decided

**Figure 4.3**
Asante elders including the chief (centre), the Queen Mother behind him, and the *okyeame*, or spokesman (with yellow staff), assembled to confer near their village.

that we should make a comparative study of a small number of Asante villages, ascertaining what generated their plans and the organization of their dwellings and their buildings of religious or hierarchical importance. To prepare for this we had to meet the chief and elders of a village and engage in prolonged explanation of our proposed study. All were men who were present, except for one elderly lady who spoke in whispers to the chief. Discussion was in subdued tones, but the dialogue with the village elders was only through a single elderly man with a golden cane – the *okyeame*. We were obliged to appoint our own *okyeame*, but he had to be one who could speak the formal language of such dialogue (Rattray, 1927). Fortunately, one of our students was the son of just such a spokesman, and had acquired the appropriate speech patterns and terminology. I learned that in this matrilineal society the woman who whispered to the chief was his Queen Mother, who advised him on decisions. The solemn chief himself, whose features I could faintly recognize, I later realized was the clerk at my Kumasi bank by day; their behaviours served both to obscure and to protect the cultural realities.

It was much the same with 'the environment', both natural and man-made, which I encountered in the bush or rain forest. There was no part of the forest that had not been felled, cultivated, coppiced, planted, cleared, quarried; no part of the village that was not constructed in *swish*, moulded and thatched for designated functions of dwelling, authority or ancestor and spirit worship. The drum orchestras that played under awnings and palm leaf shelters, or in the

**Figure 4.4**
At an Asante funeral, dancers in mourning cloths mime the occupation and other activities of the deceased. Relatives watch from temporary shelters.

*pato* of the shrine houses were not the freely improvising musicians that I had anticipated, but well-rehearsed and organized performers whose playing helped unify the complex rituals. I attended one occasion in which dancers performed exaggerated but stylized gestures and flowing movements; through interpreters I learned that these postures and sequences symbolized the activities and lifeways of deceased members of the community, whose spirits were recalled to the village within a specially constructed enclosure at 40-day intervals in the year. My perceptions of their behaviour and of their environment, both natural and shaped, had been superficial and it was only over an extended period of time, and with much difficulty that I began to gain a little understanding of Asante culture and its contexts.

I could continue, and would like to do so, extending my examples within and beyond the Asante, to cultures in their contexts in many parts of the world. But this is essentially the issue: for me, the definition of the field of study in behaviour and environment is unclear. As I have endeavoured to show, the terms are in effect, applied to external appearances, and as such are only symptomatic of the much more fundamental bases of culture and context. It can be argued of course, that these are simply alternative words for the same concepts, but I believe that culture in all its complexity lies beyond 'behaviour', which often even seeks to obscure it. Similarly, 'environment' summarizes the physical surroundings of a phenomenon which may have other, more profound implications in time, condition, cultural expression, and other varied contexts, than the word suggests. Culture and context, I believe, bear upon study and research in buildings, and in particular, on the vernacular architecture which constitutes the overwhelming majority of mankind's structures.

## References

Altman, I., Rapoport, A. and Wohlwill, J.F. (eds). (1980). *Environment and Culture*. New York: Plenum Publishing.
Downs, R.M. and Stea, D. (eds). (1976). *Image and Environment: Cognitive Mapping and Spatial Behavior*. Chicago: Aldine Publishing.
Rapoport, A. (1969). *House Form and Culture*. New Jersey: Prentice-Hall.
Rapoport, A. (ed.). (1976). *The Mutual Interaction of People and Their Built Environment*. The Hague: Mouton Editions.
Rapoport, A. (1977). *Human Aspects of Urban Form: Towards a Man–Environment Approach to Urban Form and Design*. Oxford: Pergamon Press.
Rattray, R.S. (1927). *Religion and Art in Ashanti*. Oxford University Press.
Skinner, B.F. (1953). *Science and Human Behaviour.* New York: MacMillan.

# 5

# Cultural traits and environmental contexts: Problems of cultural specificity and cross-cultural comparability (1999)

At a recent meeting of conservationists in that part of England in which I live, I made a case for the conservation of the 'built environment'. The phrase was challenged by one member of the committee who argued that it was a contradiction in terms. His reaction drew my attention once again to the semantic confusion that can arise from terms loosely used. We assume that we all know what we mean by a phrase such as the 'home environment' and that the theme of 'culture, space and the home environment' need not be questioned or defined. The term 'to environ', or the environs, refers to surrounding, forming a ring about or around, or to enclose. So the environment is the state of being environed, or that which does environ. Since the 1960s, by extension, the term is used by geographers and natural scientists to mean the totality of the surrounding, external conditions, within which an organism, a community or an object exists (Monkhouse and Small, 1978). When, however, the term is applied to an abstraction, such as 'home', we may question whether it has any real meaning.

Environmental scientists identify a number of branches of their discipline, including the study of the natural environment, the nonsocial, noncultural landscape before the intervention of mankind. This also embraces the geographical environment which is concerned with the spatial relationships of identifiable qualities, and the physical environment, or everything that is not within a social system. Monkhouse and Small warn that 'they are all slightly different, and unqualified use of the term can be misleading'. I would contend that one task that should be undertaken in a discussion on 'culture and space in the home environment' is to determine an agreed definition of what is meant by 'home environment'. But that of course, assumes that we agree on the meaning of 'home'. Home, it seems to me, is a very inexplicit word identifying a subjective involvement with a loosely defined sense of place. The astronaut declares that he is 'home again' when he sets foot on earth; the long-term prisoner in a foreign jail, greets 'home' as the soil of his country; 'my home country, my home town, my home' are degrees of scale and specificity that are familiar to English and American people. The landlady of an English guest-house advertises a 'home from home', the collector of bric-a-brac finds a 'home' for his latest acquisition; the point of a nail, even the point of a story is 'driven home'. Consideration of the use of 'home' as a prefix suggests its subjective nature – especially homely, homemaking, homesickness or homecoming. But other usages suggest a simpler, domestic but less romantic connotation – homemade, homespun, homebrew, home and away, home counties, homeless. Some of these usages may be unfamiliar, or unrecognizable to many people, which helps to underline that the word, like many others, is culture-bound.

I am no linguist, but I am interested to know whether the connotations of 'home', as distinct from 'house', translate, or whether they are differentiated in many languages. My impression is that the distinction is essentially Teutonic, its parallels to be found in German – *das haus*, the house, and *das heim*, the home; distinctions that are less evident in romance languages, and more distant still in nonEuropean cultures. This suggests to me that the concept of home is linked with sedentariness, and is often associated with the acquisition of property, furniture and domestic articles or ornaments. 'In Italian, *casa* is the nearest equivalent yet it is much closer in meaning to house than to home', wrote Csikszentmihalyi and Rochberg-Halton. 'The same is even truer of the French *maison*, and by the time one gets to the Hungarian *haz* the references are almost exclusively to their physical structure rather than to the emotional space'. They concluded that 'although we live in physical environments, we create cultural environments within them' – while neglecting to define what they meant by 'environment' (Csikszentmihalyi and Rochberg-Halton, 1981).

Many cultures have no evidence in their language or in their behaviour of a concept of 'home'. 'Patched and repaired from year to year, abandoned when not needed, or burned when death occurred in them, Paiute shelters were mainly protection from the elements. They were never "home"', Margaret M. Wheat observed (Wheat, 1967). A similar problem arises with the use of the term 'space'. It has been part of the architectural vocabulary for less time than may be imagined. Discussion that anticipates Bruno Zevi's *Architecture as Space* is comparatively rare (Zevi, 1957), although Siegfried Giedion's *Space, Time and Architecture* (Giedion, 1941) is among the small number of works that did. In anthropology, works such as Durkheim's *Primitive Classification* (Durkheim, 1903) considered space, but as a system of classification related to territory and to social structure. More recent studies, such as Christine Hugh-Jones' *From Beyond the Milk River* (Hugh-Jones, 1979), on spatial and temporal processes among the Piri-Pirana in north-west Amazonia, consolidate the link between concepts of space and of time, while cross-disciplinary approaches to archaeology and anthropology have enriched the study of archaeological evidence.

Here I wish to emphasize that the space is a concept, an abstraction, but not a universal one. Half a century ago, Benjamin Lee Whorf showed that 'space' as a concept did not exist in the language of the Hopi pueblo Indians (Whorf, 1956). It has been observed that their neighbours, the Navajo, with whom they share the northeast quadrant of Arizona, have six co-ordinates – north–south, east, west,

**Figure 5.1**
Hopi spatial organization is conditioned by topography, cultivation and the clan system, as in Moenkopi pueblo, by the Colorado River, Arizona.

zenith and nadir, and can therefore locate in space the position of say, a bird, with greater precision than could most 'Anglos'. Yet their lack of a concept of spatial relationships in other aspects led to a Dutch team endeavouring to devise a means of teaching geometry to Navajo Indian children through experimental means (Pinxten, 1987). In the Navajo world view, all is in motion and all is changing within an overriding concept of order and harmony. Space is related to movement, and as Witherspoon observed, 'the verb "to go" is for Navajo language and thought what the verb "to be" would represent for westerners' (Witherspoon, 1977).

Clearly, there is a problem: do the Navajo have an inbuilt perception of their world, of their 'environment', that does not require the concept of space, but does require certain terms that relate to movement through space? Is this simply the result of cultural conditioning? If a word does not exist in a language it may be argued that, broadly speaking, the concept does not exist either. But we are aware that a phrase may often serve as the equivalent to a specific term, to identify a concept. It must be evident that I am concerned that the terms we use and assume to be shared by others, are often interpreted differently by users from within a particular group, be it a profession or a tribe, or it may not be used at all. There are built-in assumptions in any discussion that arise from the interpretation given to the terms used, which are expressive of the language of a culture and are clues to the concepts of that culture.

For 10 years, I was totally involved in the compilation of the *Encyclopedia of Vernacular Architecture of the World*, to which a number

**Figure 5.2**
Navajo use of the landscape is not constrained, but its cosmic connotations are spatially and symbolically expressed in the form and plan of the *hogan* (dwelling). Canyon de Chelly, Arizona.

of conference participants contributed. In the course of this work, it was necessary to define the terms used, including 'environment', 'home', 'spatial organization' and 'culture', each of these having its own section or entry. It soon became clear that the diversity of approaches to the subject of vernacular architecture, whether disciplinary or interdisciplinary, required explanatory essays, while those aspects of culture which are broadly common to cultural groups also needed to be discussed. Which brings us to the fundamental question: What do *we* mean by 'culture'?

Culture as a concept, has a comparatively short history. It was first used and defined by the nineteenth century British anthropologist Edward Burnett Tylor, who gave the following definition: 'Culture is that complex whole which includes knowledge, art, morals, law, custom, and any other capabilities acquired by man as a member of society' (Tylor, 1871). The term was appropriated and widely applied to what were considered to be advanced, 'civilized' societies as distinct from 'primitive' societies. In the 1950s culture was still associated with the acquisition of skills, the production of, or the study of 'the arts' – painting, music, drama and the like. This position was summarized in the work of F.R. Cowell, who loftily asserted that culture was transmitted orally by traditional societies and 'objectively' by those that were literate, to enhance the quality of life with value and meaning by making possible 'the achievement of truth, beauty and moral worth' (Cowell, 1959). Such an interpretation persists in the name of UNESCO, and in numerous public functions and exhibitions. In 1952 the anthropologists Alfred L. Kroeber and Clyde Kluckhohn published their critique of more than 160 definitions of culture offered by their fellow anthropologists. The consensus, in their view, consisted of patterns of behaviour, both explicit and implicit which had been acquired and passed on by the essential core of cultural concepts and traditional ideas and their related values. They argued that culture systems could be considered as the products of action and also as 'the conditioning elements of further action' (Kroeber and Kluckhohn, 1952). This dynamic view of culture was somewhat at odds with Kluckhohn's later painstaking record of material culture – in his case, also of the Navajo (Kluckhohn *et al.*, 1971).

Apart from any implied aesthetic status, culture embraces both activities and artefacts, and the recognition of their worth. 'It is not true', wrote Durkheim, 'that society is composed of individuals only; it also includes material objects which play an essential role in the common life', giving as an example, 'houses, buildings of all kinds which, once constructed become autonomous realities, independent of individuals' (Durkheim, 1903). For the purposes of the encyclopedia, I defined 'culture' as 'the totality of values, activities and products, including buildings, of a society which give meaning and direction to the lives of its individual members. Culture is learned and is not transmitted genetically. A "culture" is a society whose members share such a totality'. 'Culture traits' I defined as 'aspects of social structure and group behaviour or values which may be defined and compared with those of other cultures. A "trait complex" refers to the interaction of a number of traits. Since the mid-eighteenth century, the term "trait" in English has meant "a distinguishing quality, or characteristic"'.

Cultural traits are seen by some anthropologists as the irreducible characteristics of cultural behaviour that can be recognized within a culture. In order to avoid unnecessary repetition in EVAW entries, it was important to discuss certain complexes of cultural traits in a separate section, which could then be compared or applied in the studies of specific cultures (I.II). These could not be discussed at length; only those culture traits, within broader trait complexes that related to the use or meaning of vernacular architecture, are considered. Certain of these are examined in greater depth in subsequent sections, where they had considerable bearing on the physical or functional aspects of vernacular architecture.

As the majority of cultures discussed in EVAW are sedentary and exist in specific physical–environmental contexts, some review of economy, whether subsistence or surplus, seemed necessary, while

**Figure 5.3**
When building her dwelling within an *enkang*, or Maasai settlement, a woman uses bark strips to tie the hut framework from within. Maasai Mara, Kenya.

nomadism, the major exception to sedentariness, also required discussion. An ecological approach to the study of vernacular architecture is included in the opening section of the encyclopedia. Encompassing the study of, response to and modification of the environment by human intervention or exploitation such an approach is largely focussed on the purposes of stock-raising, agriculture or horticulture for the obtaining of food as the basis of life support. Food is not a trait, but the traits involved in its acquisition and preparation are discussed. Whereas the cultivation and consumption of food are expressed in many culturally identifiable traits, those of cooking which require a separate structure, or may be related to heating systems, are discussed under Services (I.VI). The drive to obtain and consume food and water is essentially biological; the behaviours and means by which collectives of humans do so, are cultural. Moreover, these are culturally differentiated, developed by groups who communicate their discoveries, educating their children and sharing their activities in patterns which may eventually distinguish them as discrete cultures. The drive to bond, to engender children is innate, but the forms that the family may take are cultural and diverse. Family types may ultimately relate to the basic biological unit of parents and child, but the nuclear family is a particular cultural construct. So are the various forms of stem family or extended family whose unfolding over generations in the cycle of life from birth through childhood, maturity, old age and death establishes continuities through time and frequently generates lineages, descent groups and hierarchies. Family types and structural cycles take expression in kinship systems and these, in turn, in residential patterns. Raising the children is frequently, but by no means exclusively, the province of women. Women in some societies are the builders; in others they may prepare materials or finish surfaces, while the men do the structural work; this differentiation of gender roles in many aspects of human activity, may also have spatial expression in the dwelling or settlement and in the daily, weekly or periodic domestic routines of living.

Social structures, including the exercise of authority, whether by rulers, councils of elders or other administrations, make their impressions on the spatial organization of territory, land units and in some societies, of property. The complexity of these political issues and their economic implications, is significant in large, multilayered societies requiring skills in communication on the one hand, and signals of cultural identity on the other. Whether it was the family, or the need for cooperation in the obtaining of food, that was the underlying reason for the emergence of language as a human attribute is not our concern here, but language as a means of conveying and also at times, of circumscribing culture, undoubtedly is. The encyclopedia demonstrates that concepts of the dwelling, or of abstractions such as that of the 'home', are culturally and linguistically defined. Customary usages and technologies, or methods of construction or space use in the building, are frequently embodied in traditions which are transmitted over successive generations in the educative processes. But they are also observed, rehearsed and learned in children's play and socialization, still a seriously under-researched aspect of the sharing of values and behavioural norms related to the built environment. Such values are sometimes embodied in rule systems of use and behaviour about, and within, the building; in other cases they are implicit, perceivable to the visitor by avoidance cues, or sometimes supported by litigation and enforced by law.

Buildings may embody in expressive ways the qualities that we relate to our value systems. I say systems, because values and beliefs rarely lie outside a system – if they do, we may regard them as unformed or unrelated superstitions. But belief systems may be closely bound to religious convictions and practices, through which we endeavour to understand the cosmos or the spirit world. Temples, synagogues, churches, cathedrals, mosques, stupas, gadwaras, monasteries, madressehs – the range of religious edifices is great, and many of them being architect-designed, fall outside the vernacular. But others are vernacular shrines and furthermore, domestic dwellings may also be sited and planned on religious principles and contain within them places dedicated to deities, which may be spiritually sacrosanct. As extensions of the temporal and spatial patterns of movement, buildings can accommodate rituals and ceremonials which may correspond to the calendar of religious memorials and events, but which may also mark the rites of passage through the gateways of puberty, marriage and the life cycle. Ceremonials are never random but follow patterns sanctioned by traditional belief, often being symbolic enactments of the revered lives of priests and prophets. Symbols in speech, sound, movement, and gesture have their counterparts in the permanent symbols of religious edifices and their constituent elements, in orientation, form or embellishment. Whether they are codified as symbols, or expressed in formal and instructive language, the traditions by which a society maintains its links with the past and projects its future, constitute another field in which much research remains to be done. Even in the making of vernacular buildings, the means of tradition and their transmission are not well understood. But traditions are always under pressure

**Figure 5.4**
A local shrine with a figure of the many-armed goddess Durga, symbol of beauty and violence, good and evil. Bhaktapur, Nepal.

and influence, sometimes political, sometimes religious or ideological, seeking to denigrate or replace the vernacular with a 'superior' architecture, backed by power. Culture change may take place as a result of the diffusion of ideas or artefacts, or by the modification of tradition and intermittent bursts of innovation, acceptable within the norms of the group. Such processes have been accelerated with imperialist expansion, particularly of the European colonial powers in the nineteenth and twentieth centuries. Present trends to globalization arising from the electronic and communications revolution will inevitably impact upon traditional cultures. Yet, it is to be noted that tendencies to cultural independence and the retention of many aspects of their cultural inheritance, have been evident in a great many societies, including those of Central Europe and the Balkans in the last quarter of the twentieth century. These reactions may well continue, or retrench, for many decades in the face of westernization and cultural interaction (I.II.20).

Complexes of cultural traits that bear upon architecture and the built environment may be summarized as relating to economies and life support, family and social structure, communication and education, beliefs, values and symbols, and sociocultural continuity and change. There are others of course, and many subsets within those I have noted, but their identification helps to guide and balance research, and is used in the encyclopedia as a contextual setting against which entries on specific cultures can be placed and compared (I.II). Augmenting this, is a section on the environment, as it shapes, or is shaped by, human occupation – including the diversity of location and site conditions, climates and their extreme conditions, population distribution and demographic trends, settlement patterns and land utilization, and issues of territory and tenure (I.III). While other sections in the first volume are progressively concerned with resources (I.IV), production (I.VI) and servicing (I.VI) of the vernacular, a further section considers the nature of symbolism and ornamentation on and within buildings, including the use of inscriptions and motifs. Rule systems of spatial ordering, the rituals of the building process, and the symbolism of building structures and defined space are disclosed in a number of case studies (I.VII). The potential of some materials and the constraints of others, the ergonomics of height and space use, the volumes encompassed and the requirements of access, illumination and circulation, are among the factors which facilitate the comparability of structures. Eleva-

**Figure 5.5**
Terracing and cultivation of mountain slopes, and the siting of Newar farms are in response to the location, climate and to subsistence needs. Central Nepal.

**Figure 5.6**
Barns and byre are among the functions of this typical Padonian L-plan farm complex. Water is drawn from the well with a *shadouf* system. Eastern Slovenia.

tions, forms and plans are among the features examined in Typologies (I.VIII). In popular parlance – or 'the vernacular' – the uses for which buildings are intended to accommodate are also frequently regarded as their 'types'. With the discussion of uses and functions, a bridge is established between the contextual themes and the specifics of cultures where, apart from dwellings, the buildings that accommodate many of the cultural traits are reviewed. Among them are the edifices which reflect social structures, placing their emphasis on authority and status, on hierarchies, administrations and councils. Buildings that are designed for economic purposes and the production of commodities from sericulture to chicken farming, are reviewed, as are outbuildings, such as barns and byres, granaries and hunters' stores, where animals are raised and produce protected. The transformation of cereals and other processes requiring or benefitting from technological developments are examined, including wind, water and animal powered machinery (I.IX).

Structures related to belief systems including the sanctuaries and temples of the major religions and the shrines and funerary constructions of cultures large and small throughout the world are given, as are social buildings which offer shelter for comfort, leisure or communal activities. Not all buildings are permanent nonetheless, and temporary and transportable structures used for periodic events, occasional functions or by nomadic and travelling cultures are also considered. Many of the examples are specific to a single culture, even to a small subregion, but they are included because a sense of comparative scale is necessary. But the question arises: to what

**Figure 5.7**
A decorated funerary structure to support a coffin is built for transportation through a village to the cremation site, where it is burned. Bali, Indonesia.

extent can they be compared on a cross-cultural basis? By identifying certain major complexes of cultural traits I hope that comparative data can be more effectively assembled and correspondences and differences more clearly delineated. But further problems are generated from the determination of these issues. What, for instance, are the defining characteristics of a culture, and what indicates its boundaries? In fact, cultural traits can be as useful in demonstrating correspondences between cultures, as indicating their differences. By a process of comparison cultures may be grouped into culture areas, where a number of groups demonstrate a measure of similarity of traits within traits complexes.

Unfortunately, very little has been done on the mapping of cultures since the 1950s, but for the purposes of the encyclopedia it was clearly necessary (Russell and Kniffen, 1951; Price, 1990; Gaisford, 1983). Culture traits such as language, or economy, as well as building methods, types and meanings were key features in this. National boundaries proved to be a poor basis for the definition of cultures, or of culture areas, though in some cases (such as the Pyrenees between the Gallic and Iberian clusters) a physical and political boundary may be drawn. In all, approximately 80 cultural areas were defined, of various scales which principally reflected population densities and cultural complexity. Between them, the borders are necessarily uncertain, and the attempt to accommodate, where possible, distinct cultures, culture traits, nationalities, physical boundaries and climatic zones necessitated compromises. These, however, can be considerably reduced and the classification more finely tuned with further research. In all, the vernacular traditions of approximately 1300 cultures have been classified within some 66 culture areas, arranged in a triple alphabetical sequence (continental region, culture area, and specific cultures) moving from north to south and from east to west, approximating the generality of population and cultural movements. Until now, no worldwide resource giving discursive summaries of the housing of specific cultures has been available, and as comparative data have been difficult to obtain, the basis of cross-cultural debate has been severely constrained. Notwithstanding the disputes and disagreements on definition that are almost certain to arise, it is my hope that the identifying of cultural trait complexes relating to dwelling, and the mapping of cultures within the socio-environmental contexts of culture areas in the *Encyclopedia of Vernacular Architecture of the World*, will make a contribution to the debates that must follow, as we confront the issues of appropriate housing and cultural identity, let alone culture, space and home environment, in the future. Many of the characteristics that are shared in the buildings of differing cultures across the world may relate to the employment of materials, such as reed or bamboo, granite or adobe, or to the physical features of the landscape, whether montane or riverine, desert or steppe. They may reflect climatic conditions or the economies, subsistence or surplus, of the peoples concerned, although they may not be determined solely by any of these factors. Clearly, the mapping of these and many more such aspects of the vernacular on a worldwide basis, is necessary for the better understanding of common elements, of differing features and of future needs perceived on a comparative basis. This work is well advanced and *The Atlas of Vernacular Architecture of the World* should complement the documentation of the vernacular in the encyclopedia.

## References

Cowell, F.R. (1959). *Culture in Private and Public Life*. London: Thames and Hudson.

Csikszentmicalyi, M. and Rochberg-Halton, E. (1981). *The Meaning of Things; Domestic Symbols and the Self*. Cambridge University Press.

Durkheim, E. and Mauss, M. (1903, 1963). *Primitive Classification*. London: Cohen & West.

Gaisford, J. (1983) ed. *Atlas of Man*. London: Marshall Cavendish.

Giedion, S. (1942). *Space, Time and Architecture*. Harvard University Press.

Hugh-Jones, C. (1979). *From the Milk River. Spatial and Temporal Processes in Northwest Amazonia*. Cambridge University Press.

Kluckhohn, C., Hill, W.W. and Kluckhohn, L.W. (1971). *Navajo Material Culture*. Belknap Press of Harvard University Press.

Kroeber, A.L. and Kluckhohn, C., (1952). *Culture, A Critical Review of Concepts and Definitions*. Papers of the Peabody Museum of Ethnology, Vol. 47, No. 1., Cambridge University Press.

Monkhouse, F.J. and Small, J. (1978). *A Dictionary of the Natural Environment*. London: Edward Arnold.

Oliver, P. (ed.). (1997). *The Encyclopedia of Vernacular Architecture of the World* (3 vols) Cambridge University Press.

Oliver, P. and Vellinga M. (eds), with Bridge, A. cartographer. *The World Atlas of Vernacular Architecture* (in preparation).

Pinxten, R. *et al.* (1987). *Towards a Navajo Indian Geometry*. Ghent: Boeken Press.

Price, D. (1990). *Atlas of World Cultures*. Sage, with Human Relations Area Files, Yale.

Russell, R.J. and Kniffen, F.B. (1951). *Culture Worlds*. New York: MacMillan.

Tylor, E.B. (1871). *Primitive Culture*. London: John Murray.

Wheat, M. (1967). *Survival Arts of the Primitive Paiutes*. Reno: University of Nevada Press.

Whorf, B.L. (1956). Linguistic factors in the terminology of Hopi architecture. In: *Language, Thought and Reality*. Cambridge, MA: MIT Press, pp. 19–206.

Witherspoon, G.J. (1977). *Language and Art in the Navajo Universe*. Ann Arbor: Michigan University Press.

Zevi, B. (1957). *Architecture as Space*. New York: Horizon Press.

# 6

# Huizhou and Herefordshire: A comparative study (2001)

It is by no means unusual to discuss the issues of culture and space in the built environment with reference to a particular society in an identifiable environmental context. This framework helps us to understand the nature of the customs and mores of the people concerned and how these bear upon building form and living space, while relating them to such conditioning factors as climate, terrain or settlement pattern. Such an approach is appropriate in any study of a vernacular architecture tradition and makes more relevant the familiar description of types, materials, structure, technology, plan, section, elevations and detail by which many vernacular studies follow conventional architectural practice. There are problems in this of course, arising in part from the difficulties inherent in any cultural analysis and depiction, and partly from the complexity of what constitutes 'culture'.

The very concept of culture has been questioned by some anthropologists for it is a theoretical construct rather than a scientifically demonstrable entity. Nevertheless, we may be obliged to accept the premise that 'culture and space' can be paired and are related, recognizing that we are all members of a culture, which occupies territory and which largely shapes our values and behaviour, even though we may act as individuals within it. In order to comprehend those of another culture, whether the distinction is subtle or profound, we tend to make comparisons with our own. Sometimes, as tourists or travellers, we do this spontaneously, but as scholars we attempt to do so with considered analysis. Still, when we choose to describe a culture, or aspects of its behaviour and productions, including its buildings, we make comparisons implicitly. It is our perception of aspects of cultural difference, rather than of cultural similarity, which is the most common motivation for such research and which constitutes the main content of resultant publications.

We are at the threshold of a period of increasing globalization and of a century which may well witness attempts at highly repetitive and prefabricated mass housing, frequently designed by absentee or foreign, often western-based architectural firms and construction industries. This process has begun, with housing in Siberia being designed and fabricated in Canada, and housing for hundreds of thousands of Chinese, displaced by the Yang-tse Three Gorges Dam project, being initiated in Britain. Before too many disastrous decisions have been made and implemented it seems to be vitally necessary that structured cross-cultural studies, related particularly to housing, settlement and patterns of use, should be undertaken. It is remarkable, but nevertheless true, that cross-cultural and comparative studies which are explicitly made between specific traditions of vernacular building in their socio-environmental contexts, are exceptionally rare. Consequently, there are virtually no precedents and hence no methodologies advanced for this purpose. It was to remedy this that a leading authority on Chinese traditional building and contributor to *The Encyclopedia of Vernacular Architecture of the World* (Oliver, 1997), the late Professor Wang Wenqing of Southeast University, Nanjing, (Wang, 1997) and I proposed a joint bicultural project.

In a field of study made over such a distance and between such distinct cultures, it was necessary to make a number of decisions concerning the nature of the research. As others have been identifying buildings, measuring and drawing them up, we felt that it was desirable to choose accessible locations where this work had been, at least partially, done. More importantly, we considered it necessary to identify those aspects of context and environment that we perceived to be directly comparable (in the sense of being similar), so that a basic commonality might be established. The architectural traditions had to share some elements in common: for example, in the selection of the building materials used. There also had to be a measure of comparability in the scale of the cultural groups that we selected, the topographical and climatic conditions in which they lived, and the economies in which they were engaged. Finally, after careful consideration of a number of alternatives Professor Wang and I decided to make the focus of our research the Huizhou region in the counties of Tuxian and Shexian in the southern part of the province of Anhui in southeast China, and to compare this with the

West Midlands (West Mercia) of England, particularly the counties of Herefordshire and Worcestershire.

It should be noted that in English usage the process of comparison is one where two or more subjects are shown to have characteristics in common, or which are similar; the phrase often used in academic circles, 'to compare and contrast', was an injunction to find both similar and totally dissimilar characteristics in the subjects chosen. For the purposes of the present project and for this presentation, the use of the word 'comparison' and its derivatives is primarily one of similarity, but is also broadly understood to include 'contrast' where this applies. Most published studies of vernacular traditions, comparative or not, have been made by researchers from outside the cultures that produced them. An argument could be advanced that this made the research more objective. We recognized that there was a risk of cultural bias, but we decided to make a virtue of this by explicitly declaring our responses to newly encountered traditions, and drawing upon our respective cultural backgrounds and personal knowledge of their vernacular architecture. In doing so, we found that it was more valuable to share our first impressions when in a new location, rather than to suppress them. We became more aware of our cultural 'baggage', but also found that such first impressions highlighted aspects that could, through familiarity on the part of either one of us, be overlooked. Nevertheless, meeting our self-imposed conditions sometimes proved to be difficult.

While the selection of the locations and cultures for this initial research constituted what may be the first step for any such undertaking, the selective process is made more difficult when a comparative basis is sought. In this instance I can only summarize a few of the issues concerned, and am mainly giving attention to the comparative environmental and spatial features of the settlements and the structural and spatial characteristics of the dwellings. Their broad cultural implications are noted, but a more detailed comparative cultural study would reflect both the inheritance of the past and the social revolutions of more recent history in both regions.

## Anhui and West Mercia

What, one may ask, are the comparable features of the two regions, that justifies their choice? Topographically they have much in common. Both areas studied are in country where hills rise from lowland plains. For the most part the hills are not high – many being less

**Figure 6.1**
The small town of Xidi in its landscape context, with rice paddy fields and other crops adjacent to a river, and distant hills. Huizhou, China.

than 600 metres, although Huang Shan mountain is three times that. They rise quite steeply and serve to protect the agricultural plains from climatic extremes. The plains are well-watered – in Anhui, south-east of the Chang Jiang (Yang-tse) by the Liang river and its tributaries, and in West Mercia by the Severn and the Wye, and their tributaries. In the contexts of their respective larger regions both enjoy temperate climates, although each can be subject to flooding as a result of winter rains. Much of the landscape of the plains was

**Figure 6.2**
In the West Mercian landscape, fields are cultivated on gentle slopes between compact villages and dispersed farmsteads.

cleared for cultivation centuries ago, but with careful and traditional means of nurturing, they remain highly fertile.

Economically the regions are different, but comparable to quite an extent, Herefordshire being recognized as 'the most rural county' in England. Both are predominately agricultural, producing fields of cereal crops. Climatically, Huizhou lends itself to the cultivation of rice; the saturated ground of the rice fields under several centimetres of water being planted, weeded and gathered by manual labour, largely in family groups. Beans, sugar cane and cotton may be grown, there are bamboo groves and along the river banks, mulberry trees. The soil is tilled by hand-ploughs, sometimes drawn manually but more frequently by single oxen. In this, as in much else, the stage of technological development in the Huizhou villages compares with that of the West Mercian villages of the 1940s.

**Figure 6.3**
An ox drawing a plough in a paddy field, prior to re-planting. Tuxian province.

Attempts to use small tractors invariably fail as the machines capsize in the waterlogged fields. Apart from water buffalo, there are few cattle in evidence in Huizhou, but in West Mercia, where the 'white-faced' Hereford cattle are prized, large herds are pastured. On the hill slopes cattle and sheep are free to graze, while in the plains there are apple orchards for the cider industry and regimented fields for the growing of hops under pole frames, for the production of beer. In Anhui, their place is taken by tea plantations and tobacco fields, a number of small towns and villages employing local labour in the partially mechanized production. Among the most active of cottage industries, which engages virtually all families in many of the Huizhou villages, is sericulture, or the raising of silkworms and gathering of their silk.

**Figure 6.4**
In sericulture, silkworms are fed on mulberry leaves in trays. After 3 months, the cocoons are ready for collection and sale to the silk industry. Huizhou.

Agriculture implies farm buildings; in Herefordshire and its adjacent parts of Worcestershire, Shropshire and the Welsh Marches, isolated farmhouses with their auxiliary farm buildings, including cattle barns, hop-kilns, granaries and stables, are not uncommon. Some however, are integrated into the villages with their farmlands stretching beyond them. This integration is the customary pattern in Huizhou, where farms in isolation are rare (although a few exist), the farmer's house and functional buildings being essentially a part of the village. Typically, a village in either region may consist of some 200 buildings, with a total population of around a thousand. Settlement patterns include both nucleated and linear villages, depending in part upon the topography, physical communications and access to water. The latter proved to be especially important, though in Anhui linear villages like Yuliang, are frequently sited beside a river, or on both sides with the houses facing the water, as in Tangmo, the waterway constituting a major communication route (Dekun, 1996). In West Mercia, villages and small towns are often turned away from the water-front, as at Upton-on-Severn, or are placed on higher ground as is the case, in spite of its name, of Hay-on-Wye. This marked distinction in the settlement orientation of West Mercia appears to be due to the infrequent, but when they occur, highly damaging and disruptive floods, such as those experienced in England early in 2001. Houses in Huizhou are defensively built against floods, but their location and orientation is determined by the interpretation of the landscape, using the *Feng Shui* principles.

A West Mercian riverine village, like Eardisland, is usually reached by a single bridge which may still have its refuges for pack animals. Anhui riverside villages, on the other hand, may have several bridges serving groups of houses, while some may have a covered bridge, as at Tangmo, Huizhou which functions both as a pedestrian crossing and as a covered market. In both regions markets are significant, though recent European Union directives have exercised controls on the food sold in English markets, such as at Ledbury, whereas the market in a small town like Shendu remains a lively centre where pigmeat is chopped and quartered in the open street. Fresh vegetables are obtainable in the markets of both regions. Fish caught by tethered cormorants, and eels ensnared in the zeppelin-shaped willow traps are available in the Huizhou markets, while Wye salmon and trout, among a variety of river fish, are caught in Herefordshire. Until recently, fishermen in both areas used cane-and-pitch coracles of remarkably similar design. Beside the embanked river in many an

**Figure 6.5**
A covered bridge links both halves of the village and accommodates market stalls within. Anhui, China.

Anhui village, there is a broad walkway which permits social gathering, as well as the loading and unloading of boats. In some, a long covered section shades continuous wooden seating which faces the path, and which is cantilevered over the water so as to facilitate viewing without obstructing pedestrian movement. Mercian streams may also have a path, mainly used for fishing and casual strolling, the village streets being lined with sidewalks which may open on to larger social spaces before public buildings and village halls. Narrow lanes flanked by high walls are common in Anhui; they are

**Figure 6.6**
An open village market where meat and vegetables are sold. Shendu, Anhui.

frequent in Mercian villages too, but the scale is more intimate and side doors may open on to them.

The most conspicuous difference between the spatial organization of the Anhui village and that of West Mercia, is the symbolic focus of the settlement. As in other English counties, the village church provides the vital core even if there is a village green, market place or other prominent social space at its centre. In Anhui, the Ancestral Hall and the Buddhist temple both performed this function, though they were generally less dominantly located than the churches in England, which were erected on whatever hill or mound rose above the plain. Mercian villages seldom announce themselves but are recognizable as the accretion of buildings intensifies towards the centre where a few shops and one or two 'public houses', or inns, become evident. Whether church or non-conformist chapel, the religious buildings of Herefordshire are less used today, though most are well cared-for and attended by small but devout congregations. Half a century of atheistic Communist rule has annulled the significance of the Buddhist temples in Huizhou, and some ancestral halls have been stripped of much of their fine carving. Yet massive memorial gateways, symbolic of the ancestral families who founded and sustained the villages, still mark their entrances; in the case of Tangyue, with a succession of five great stone archways at 50-metre intervals (Gong, 1992).

As is to be expected, it is the domestic architecture which comprises the majority of the buildings in the villages and small towns

**Figure 6.7**
At Berriew, in the Welsh 'Marches', houses are close to the churchyard at right.

**Figure 6.8**
Buddhist temple, Tangmo, Anhui. Modern buildings are changing the character of the villages.

of both regions. In some respects they are comparable, being for the most part two storeys in height and fronting directly on to the roads. The use of hardwoods in construction is common to both – oak and elm in Mercia, cedar in Anhui. Fired brick is widely used and although it is now delivered from depots of the main brick industries in England, the domes of the former brick kilns and the more recent longer, covered kilns are still to be found in Anhui. Here, however, the similarities end. In Herefordshire and related counties the timber construction of village houses is of two main types. The first of these, almost unique to the west of the British Isles, is the use of 'crucks', or pairs of inclined curved wooden slabs, each pair being the split halves of a single curved tree-trunk. Several types of cruck frame, including half-crucks and raised crucks, have been identified and listed. Meeting at the crest and linked with collar beams, the pairs of crucks are ranged in line, forming bays, and are connected by purlins. While the main structure is customarily connected with the wall-plate, the walls are free-standing and take some of the roof load. Some cruck houses reveal their structure on their gable ends (Suggett, 1997).

Cruck frames may date from the thirteenth century and some were erected as late as five centuries after. More common in West Mercia are the box-frame houses which are constructed of posts and beams with pegged joints. Short, joined lengths are raised on a wooden cill above a brick or stone foundation. The roof is invariably of the truss type, with a transverse triangular assembly of rafters linked by tie and collar beams, supporting a ridge beam.

**Figure 6.9**
House with a raised cruck frame and box-framed wings. Willersley, Shropshire.

Principal and secondary rafters bear upon the ridge and the wall plate, carrying the purlins and battens which take the roof covering of thatch or tiles. Originally, the intervening panels between the box frames of the walls were filled with 'wattle and daub' (lath and clay); with the widespread introduction of brick in the sixteenth century, brick 'nogging', or infill panels, became common. Many cruck-framed houses may also have timber framing in the walls, and use a similar infill (Alcock, 1997). Both systems are to be seen in numerous Herefordshire villages, such as Pembridge, where the unpainted wood is grey and the red brick retains its colour, or in Weobley, where the timbers are painted black and the walls painted or rendered white. Weobley has a range of building types, including the most westerly example of a 'Wealden' hall-house, of a type normally associated with the south-east of England. Also present are some examples of the brick houses and cottages constructed in the eighteenth to twentieth centuries, although by being later they tend to be further from the centre of the village.

Superficially, the houses of Huizhou are apparently constructed entirely of brick under tiled roofs. Closer examination reveals that the walls often enclose courtyards and gardens screened from the street, while the buildings, of varying heights with their persistent rectangular plan, are often over-ridden by the height of the flanking brick walls. An impression of many roofs results from the tiling of the crests of these walls, as well as from the house ridges of buildings, while the varying wall-heights are created by stepping them, often with *matoufang*, or 'horse-head' terminal ornamentation, producing

**Figure 6.10**
Brick walls, with *matoufang* 'horse-head' capping and 'five peaks to the sky'. A modern school is at the rear. Hongcun, Anhui, China.

a 'five-peaks-to-the-sky' form (Feng and Ged, 1997). Rendered or painted white, the high walls with small openings beneath the black tiles, present a 'black-and-white' massing as striking as that of the Mercian houses, while being of very different form. These rising walls are an indication of the different structural system widely employed in the architecture of Huizhou. Within, the structure is remarkably consistent, bearing in mind that new houses were being constructed throughout the Ming and Qing dynasties, from the fifteenth to the late nineteenth centuries (Zhang, 1957). Fundamentally, the main structure consists of pairs of cedar columns spanned by massive beams, which support further struts and beams to carry the roof. Ranged in *jian*, or bays, the columns of the *tailiang* system, rather than the outside walls, carry the roof load (Steinhardt, 1984).

Houses in Huizhou often present a similar appearance, with symmetrical facades and doorways having carved and moulded lintels, approached by steps. Sometimes, the doorway reveals the evidence of the application of *Feng Shui*, the entrance being set slightly at an angle to benefit from auspicious orientation. It opens on a shallow court, often only a few metres deep; called a *tianjing* (skywell), it has a sunken stone trough that serves as a collecting vessel for rainwater from the roofs and, in some cases, also as a fish tank. Beyond this is the main living space defined by the cedar columns which also mark the *jian* bays and subdivisions of the internal space. Almost invariably this is symmetrical, with a large and open-fronted cubic volume, sometimes raised on a plinth, facing the central entrance. Here are placed the principal items of furniture, consisting of an

**Figure 6.11**
*Tianjing* skywell, with *yanlang* verandah supported by the *tailiang* system of columns and beams with additional struts. The living space is to the right. Huizhou.

honorific display table, a cabinet or two, and a few chairs. A wooden screen-wall between the side rows of columns and flanked by access passages, hides from general view a similar volume which may be used formally, or regarded as a covered extension of the enclosed rear garden. To one side, a kitchen may have been added, with a large brick furnace and woks set in the top. Above the main spaces, rooms with open screen walls constructed of light timber permitting air circulation, are also symmetrically arranged; here the daughters would sleep. A central upper hall is served by a timber staircase, usually placed at the side of the *yanlang*, or front-facing verandah. The *yanlang* overlooks the narrow front courtyard.

Shops and houses in the village centre are packed close together and many may share flanking walls. Often there is no enclosing facade wall such as is found in the larger, individual houses.

Instead, the house front may have a brick wall of ground floor height only, the upper level being fronted by a timber *yanlang* which overlooks the street. The doors are frequently open, many revealing the large circular wicker trays in which the silkworms feed in their thousands on mulberry leaves. Stacks of trays may be awaiting the maturation of the worms, which takes some 12 weeks, before the cocoons are gathered and taken by river to the spinning factory. The cycle of four crops a year is continuous and labour-intensive. In these nurseries and in many shops, the internal space generated by the *tailiang* system may be subdivided with brick or earth walls.

While the Huizhou house, as found in such small towns as Hongcun or Xidi, may be relatively large to accommodate the farmers and merchants who built them, dissolution of the wealthier houses and accommodation of the peasants during the Maoist era, resulted in the subdivision of the domestic spaces. Although the descendants of the original builders are still residing in many of the houses, three families who may be related, will occupy one house, dividing the communal kitchen and keeping their belongings in separate piles. The main room facing the entrance court still retains its simplicity, but is used by the residents for various functions – from making eel traps to playing *mah jhong*.

How then, does this domestic spatial arrangement compare with that of the houses of Herefordshire and its neighbouring counties? Whereas the plans and structures of the Huizhou houses remained remarkably consistent over five or more centuries, the plans of the Mercian houses were far more varied. Cruck-framing tends to produce a rectangular plan of two or three bays, but side extensions are common. The succession of living room, central hall and farmhouse kitchen is frequently found in both cruck and box-framed houses, with two or three bedrooms (and a bathroom, since the nineteenth century) above. Each might have a separate fireplace and chimney flue, the 'inglenook' being large enough to sit inside. Served by the kitchen and the hall, a separate dining room may be incorporated, sometimes by placing this behind a living room or by reducing the size of the hall. The box-frame system permits a freedom of arrangement which is sometimes expressed in an L-plan, with an asymmetrical gable over the extension. Gables and 'dormers' extending from the roof pitch to the wall plane have been built for centuries, as the steeper pitch of the English roof permits the conversion of the loft into habitable space. Internally a staircase, straight or 'dog-leg' if space allows, or winding (spiral) if not, may lead from the hall to a 'landing', off which access is gained to bedrooms.

**Figure 6.12**
Buildings of uneven stud-frame construction. Projecting upper floors are 'jettied', supported by extended floor beams. Ludlow, Shropshire.

To those unfamiliar with the culture, many Mercian houses present a somewhat confusing impression. The freedom of the framing system, the number of extensions, gables and dormers and the unaccustomed plans of houses of all sizes, are matched by the apparent lack of attention to geometry and precision in the construction. To many British and American eyes, this apparent randomness appeals, heightened as it is by the irregular forms and softened lines of traditional thatched roofs. During building construction, 'green' or unseasoned oak was used, as joints could be cut more readily. In time, oak hardens to become iron-like in its structural strength, so any twists or distortions which appeared in the hardening process were accommodated in the use of wattle-and-daub or brick infill. Externally there are few decorations, though in some of the wealthier houses window and door frames and lintels might be carved. Inside, the manor houses and those of more affluent families might have carved overmantels above the fireplaces, sometimes with armorial designs and supporting figures. Ceiling plasterwork might also be decorated though, in the vernacular houses, ceiling beams and even roof structures and cruck blades would be left exposed and undecorated.

By comparison with the houses of West Mercia, the houses of villages like Xidi or Hongcun appear more formal and more carefully crafted. The severe planes produce a geometric clarity which is contrasted with the decorated lintels or courtyard windows with their foliated or abstract ornamental details. Internally, the cedar screen walls may have open-work patterns which depict flora and fauna,

**Figure 6.13**
Finely carved internal decoration. Xidi, Huizhou.

while relief panels with intricate compositions of figures engaged in everyday pursuits, were carved in the round (Anon., n.d.). Regrettably, many of these have been sold to western antique dealers or found their way into tourist shops. Considerable though these spatial, structural and interior detail similarities and differences proved to be, among the most enduring of impressions were those of the hospitality of the residents in both cultures. Yet even here there were differences: it is virtually impossible in a Mercian village simply to request that one enters a dwelling, has access to all rooms, and makes drawings, photographs or measurements. But in Huizhou this presents no problems and such requests are met with little concern. The extent to which these differences of attitude relate to recent experience, political changes or the growth in tourism and visitor curiosity, is a question which remains with us.

However, many of the comparable and differing qualities of the vernacular traditions of Huizhou and Herefordshire relate to their respective histories, the buildings being largely constructed in Huizhou during the Ming and Qing dynasties, and those in Herefordshire and West Mercia in the Tudor, Stuart and Jacobean periods. Hierarchical and socially stratified in both regions, they reflected the wealth and social standing of their occupants.

Subsequent generations were subject to social revolutions, land reforms and Victorian industrialization in the case of England; the Bolshevik, Republican and Maoist revolutions leading to the introduction of the commune system in China. Clearly, such social changes and the many issues that arise from them have to be addressed in any thorough cross-cultural comparative study, while contemporary behaviours may be the subject of interviews and more personally focused research. This could extend to the intentions of recent house-builders in both Herefordshire and Huizhou; the lessons of this necessarily limited comparative cross-cultural project have convinced us of the need for more and immediate research of this kind, in order that housing provision by one culture for another in an era of globalization is not based on cultural stereotypes.

## References


Alcock, N.W. (1997). British Isles, Mercia. In Paul Oliver (ed.). *The Encyclopedia of Vernacular Architecture of the World*. Cambridge University Press, pp. 1272–74, 1293–94. All *EVAW* entries include bibliographical references. (See also Feng and Ged (1997) below).

Anon. (n.d.) *Old Houses: Family Houses in the Huizhou Style in Southern Anhui* (in Chinese). 2 vols. Jiangsu: Fine Arts Publishing House.

Dekun, Z. (1996). *Ancient Architecture in Huizhou: Yuliang Village*. Department of Architecture, Nanjing: Southeast University Press.

Feng, Y. and Ged, F. (1997). 'Anhui' (Huanan, NE). *EVAW*. Cambridge University Press, pp. 894–895.

Gong, K. (1992). *Ancient Architecture in Huizhou: Tanguye Village*. Department of Architecture, Nanjing: Southeast University Press.

Knapp, R.G. (1997). China, South. *EVAW*. Cambridge University Press, pp. 891–94.

Oliver, P. (ed.). (1997). *The Encyclopedia of Vernacular Architecture of the World Cambridge University Press* (3 vols).

Oliver, P. (2000). Cultural traits and environmental contexts: Problems of cultural specificity and cross-cultural comparability. In: Onugur, S., Hacihasanoglu, O., Turgut, H. (eds). *Culture and Space in the Home Environment*. 1997 Conference Proceedings. Istanbul: IAPS-CSBE Network, pp. 11–15.

Steinhardt, N.S. *et al.* (1984). *Chinese Traditional Architecture*. New York: The China Institute in America.

Suggett, R. (1997). Marches, Border Country. *EVAW*. Cambridge University Press, pp. 1291–1293.

Wang, W. (1997). Anhui. *EVAW*. Cambridge University Press, pp. 895–96.

Zhang, Z. *et al.* (1957). *The Dwellings of Ming Dynasty in Hui Zhou*. China: Architectural Engineering Press.


## Additional references


Kai, Y.-L. and Ho, P.-P. (eds). (1999). *Living Heritage. Vernacular Environment in China*. Hong Kong: Yungmingtang.

Knapp, R.G. and Lo, K.-Y. (eds). (2005). *House Home Family. Living and Being Chinese*. Honolulu: University of Hawaii Press.

# 7

# Tout confort: Culture and comfort (1986)

As I stepped out of the plane at Accra, Ghana, the atmosphere wrapped around my head like a hot, damp towel and seemed to remain there for several months. There was no escaping the heat and humidity as I moved up to Kumasi, deep in the Asante country, to teach at what was then known as the Kwame Nkrumah University of Science and Technology. On my arrival I was introduced to my new home – a large, lofty colonial bungalow, through which a light breeze blew. Its spacious interior was uncluttered by excess furniture; what furniture there was had been constructed of bent cane and there were no fabrics to cling to the skin. I changed into cotton shirt and shorts and sat back to watch the geckos (small lizards) chase each other over the wall and among the rafters.

After a day or two of introductions to colleagues in the Faculty of Architecture, I was taken to meet members of other faculties. We visited the home of a British engineer. He was out, and while we awaited his return his wife showed me and my wife into her living room. It was quite a shock to walk across the deep-piled figured carpet, and in the light filtered by draped net curtains, to see the cabbage rose patterns on the deep upholstery of a three-piece suite. It had been imported in its totality from their suburban house in England. Our hostess waved us to a settee: 'Well, it's home, isn't it?' she said, 'nice and *comfy*'.

In the ensuing years, I was reminded of her words innumerable times, as I encountered other Europeans far from their native countries. In Africa, Central America, the Indian subcontinent and elsewhere I frequently met expatriates who had settled in their adopted countries, but who had brought 'the comforts of home' with them. What were they, these comforts of home? Often they were cushions, tablecloths, light fittings, decorative objects, photographs of family, dogs and former homes, and personal, nondescript but valued keepsakes which had nostalgic associations of comfort in a different milieu. Generally this was comfort that had little to do with climate: it was comfort that was *comforting*. These comforts reassured the owners of the values of their countries of origin, reminded them of their heritage both national and familial, offered stability in the uncertainty of a new environment, and gave a measure of contentment in the disturbing circumstances of the unfamiliar and the alien. In the heat and humidity, in the tropical rainstorms and steaming aftermaths, these comforts provided nothing in the way of physical relief. On the contrary, as they curled or tarnished, damp-stained or grew moulds, and suffered the attacks of termites and beetles, they added to the problems of maintenance and therefore, of living. But their importance was not in their material value, but was far more elusive and abstract.

Comfort figures frequently in popular usage. Westerners are much concerned about their 'creature comforts', frequently if erroneously associating them with civilization. Visiting friends, or waiting for attention, they are customarily invited to 'make themselves comfortable'. They stay in guest houses and bed and breakfast accommodation that reassuringly inform them that the premises has 'all the comforts of home'; they take their continental holidays in France at hotels and *pensions* that offer '*tout confort*'. Generally speaking, these advertised amenities mean that they can sleep on soft beds with pocketed mattresses, they can relax in deeply upholstered and padded chairs, they can wallow in luxury: a luxury which in fact, may far exceed the actual comforts at home, but helps make up for separation from them.

Westerners seeking comfort surround themselves with objects, facilities and gadgets that simplify the process of daily living in an otherwise strange environment. Comfort, in these circumstances, is cushioning against physical reality. But it's more than that. Comfort is a modifier of the distasteful, a release from awareness of our human nature: it is no accident that a public lavatory in the United States is called a 'comfort station'. A euphemism of course, but then, comfort is so often an avoidance measure, a material euphemism. And not only material: in the hospital the victim of an accident or a violent assault spends 'a comfortable night'; his condition is reported as being 'comfortable'. As a United States Army spokesman said at a meeting with the press, following the incineration of hundreds of civilians in a Baghdad bunker during the 'first' Iraq war: 'I am comfortable with that'.

'Are you sitting comfortably? Then I'll begin' said the story-teller habitually, in Britain's most popular children's radio programme. To enjoy the stories, to be involved in them but not to be frightened, it was necessary to be comfortable. Comfort is an enduring atavistic memory of prenatal protection, and the pursuit of comfort is an impossible flight, an attempt to return to the womb. So the comfort of the stories of Beatrix Potter lies in the small, enclosing, maternal burrow: the Peter Rabbit syndrome comforting generations of children. But it is not children alone who seek its protection; 'It was a hobbit-hole and that means comfort', as Tolkein described the home of his mythical denizens. To the Puritan mind such padded insulation may be tantamount to sin, an indulgence in conflict with the severe, austere terms of the Christian ethic. Yet comfort becomes a virtue of Jesus Christ himself; the Saviour is also the Comforter. His birth is proclaimed in 'tidings of comfort and joy' and in hymns and spirituals his followers are entreated to 'tell them that the Comforter has come'. It is clear that the word 'comfort' in popular usage can assume many meanings and subtle shades of those meanings. To what extent does this popular use correspond with the lexicographer's definition of the word? Where, in fact, does the word originate? *The Concise Oxford Dictionary* notes that it comes from the Old French, *confort* which in turn derives from the Latin *con fortare* – with strength – from *fortis*, strong. It is, says the dictionary: 'Relief in affliction, consolation, satisfaction, well-being, things that make life easy'. That which is comfortable is 'such as to avoid hardship; saves trouble; promotes content'. Its synonyms in *Roget's Thesaurus* are: 'content; gracious living; ease, heart's ease, creature comforts, luxury, etc'. And that which is comfortable is 'comfy, homely, snug, cosy, comforting, restful, etc'.

So, it seems that in both popular and lexicographic understanding in the west, comfort is focussed on more than one aspect of the lives of individuals, and individuals within the family or society. In one cluster of definitions it relates to the physiological condition, ameliorating its negative, 'discomfort', and removing those physical obstructions which impinge upon the self. In a second cluster, just as important, it relates to a psychological condition, also ameliorating the miseries or unhappiness which discolour a perception of the personal world, offering the rose-tinted spectacles, seeking to remove the mental obstructions to tranquility. At the level of common usage, the two are believed to be bound together: relief of the physical condition and replacement with comfort is understood to promote well-being and the comfort of the state of mind.

'Comfort came in with the middle classes', observed the artist, critic and member of the Bloomsbury Group, Clive Bell. By this he presumably meant physical comfort: those 'things that make life easy'. It is demonstrable that the comfort that makes living easy is relative, and relative in particular to wealth: what is modest comfort for the aristocrat may be undreamed of luxury for the labourer or, conversely, what is comfort for the tradesman may be bare necessity for the banker. Discretely, but inevitably, the connotations of economics and class enter the discussion, as Clive Bell's aphorism observed. If the comfortable home as an aspiration of a significant sector of the populace developed with the advent of the middle classes – and there is much to support this view – its appearance was a concomitant of surpluses and profit.

When there was money to spare it could be expended on luxury. This was evident in any period in the west, although the luxury and comfort of the middle classes only became apparent with the expansion of international trade, of middlemen, merchants and merchant adventurers. How and when this occurred is a matter of history and beyond the purposes of this paper to delineate, but it found its first middle-class expression in the genre paintings of seventeenth century Netherlands. With money to spare and pride in their achievements, they sought to reflect, not the billowing clouds of the Assumption, nor the playful cavortings of Puck-like *putti*, but the image of their own class suspended between the labourers and the poor, and the rich and aristocratic. In the paintings of Gerard Terborch, Pieter de Hooch, Jan Vermeer or Gabriel Metsu can be seen the comfort provided by the profits of trade. Dutch genre paintings may still convey a somewhat austere image of the domestic interior. Tables may be spread with Turkish rugs and maps and paintings hang upon the walls, but the oak chests, swept tiled floors, leather-seated upright chairs and heavy drapes may have contributed only marginally to the creature comforts. These were provided as much as anything by tobacco and flagons of wine, if the paintings of Dutch interiors are reliable evidence. That they depicted a parallel to the aspirations for comfort of today's middle classes is reinforced by the popularity of the paintings in the twentieth century, as they held a mirror to contemporary desires. Nevertheless, it is clear that concepts of what made up the life of 'ease' and what was 'comfortable' among the western middle classes has differed greatly in different periods of time. Homes in eighteenth century France (or indeed, many French houses in the late twentieth century) were evidently finely crafted, delicately painted and detailed, the furniture decorated with ormolu mouldings and covered with exquisitely worked tapestry. They were elegant and refined within the taste of the times, but whether they offered 'comfort' is an open question. To contemporary values, such elegance of style in formal domestic interiors speaks more of discomfort.

That which sustained the home of the cultivated classes, whether aristocratic or middle class before the twentieth century in Europe, Russia, the United States, China or Japan, was the silent, acquiescent army of servants who maintained the standards of comfort of the affluent. It was they who groomed the horses, polished the furniture, prepared the food, starched the linen, and in a multitude of different ways from sunrise until their masters and mistresses turned to bed, maintained the expected standards of comfort. And in many countries, they still do. Their own comfort was not of serious concern to most of their employers, though many knew that the draughty garret and the back stairs to the servant's quarters, still represented a degree of comfort inaccessible to their families. Not until the end of the First World War did the picture change substantially, but with the rise between the wars of the 'servantless home' serviced by gas and electricity, life was 'made easy' for many, and the new technology 'saved trouble' for millions. Vacuum cleaner and refrigerator salesmen became stock characters in 1930s cartoons, just as the dealers in washing machines, air conditioners and double-glazing became stereotypical purveyors of comfort three decades later. If they did not 'obviate hardship' for those below the poverty line, credit systems and monthly repayments (termed in England, the 'never-never'), made service equipment and luxury items like radiograms accessible to the majority of the population in the countries of the west. Today their equivalents are accepted constituents of everyday life, no longer luxuries contributing to comfort but articles of common expectation. We might ask, as did Ronald Knox, whether creature comforts are 'more demoralizing when consciously enjoyed or when taken for granted?' Taken for granted they are, but do they contribute to our comfort? In the fully-serviced home, comfort may still be found in the simplest of adjustments – the patted pillow, the ad hoc footstool, that cliché of suburban contentment, slippers warmed by 'the fire', even the fire itself in a centrally heated home. There's pleasure to be gained from finding comfort in one's own modifications of the material world. Comfort is more than adjustment to temperature or humidity; it is intimately related to physical sensations and sensory perceptions of every kind. We experience discomfort when a flashlight is shone into our eyes, when we bite into a hot pepper, when we are stung by nettles, even when we may walk on an uneven city pavement. Yet we may enjoy virtually the

**Figure 7.1**
Advertisements for electric domestic appliances, manufactured in the 1920s to equip new suburban homes.

same sensations under different circumstances, seeking them out for our recreation. So we will bask in the flickering strobe lights at a discotheque, delight in fiery curries or Cajun gumbo, rub our skin vigorously in the bath with an abrasive luffa, scramble with excitement over rocks. We will spend blissful hours in deliberately selected uncomfortable conditions, backpacking over mountain trails and through undergrowth, standing thigh-deep in a stream on a rainy day with the hope of landing a fish or two.

Intention has a great deal to do with experiencing the sensations of comfort or discomfort. So has context. What may be comfortable in one situation can be uncomfortable in another. As I work before the VDU, I sit upon a typing chair which has been designed for my comfort. But it is not my choice of chair for relaxing in the back yard. I may choose a deckchair for that – though I don't choose a deckchair when I move inside the house. Nevertheless, these are seats of my own choice: travelling in an airplane I am comfortable even though I have another seat only a few inches in front of my knees, a proximity which I would find acutely uncomfortable in an office. Visitors to the United States find the winter central heating 'uncomfortably hot'; visitors to England complain of the low internal temperatures that are comfortable to Britons. West Indian and Pakistani immigrants far from their home environments take a long time to adjust to European or Canadian climates, and compare them unfavourably with those they've left behind. But the representative of a European firm who is posted to West Africa or Indonesia is just as likely to complain of the discomfort he experiences in the 'clammy' heat. In the 1960s, businessmen from the northern United States were still being awarded a bonus for suffering the climate in Houston, Texas. Comfort, in other words, is relative; relative to class, culture and context.

## Comfort and convenience

That the job of the architect is a multifaceted one is a truism, and the complex issues of design and realization, of form and space, site and services, structure and construction, progress and detail may all take precedence over comfort. But it is a part of the total process and, for the user or the consumer, often of prominent importance. In architectural discourse, comfort in the building is usually expressed in terms of 'comfort conditions'. These conditions are frequently considered as responses to climate, and the design response as 'climate control'. In fact, only rarely do buildings *control* climate, generating perhaps, a wind tunnel effect among the high-rise blocks,

**Figure 7.2**
Awnings lowered to shade and help cool the open-fronted metal-workers' shops. Isfahan, Iran.

or changing temperature by the shade they cast. Sitting and baking in a house whose walls are exposed to the midday sun, or whose plate glass 'picture' windows raise the temperature of the room, we are experiencing the intensification of a climatic phenomenon. Or, benefiting from the cooling of an awning or ventilators we may enjoy the modifying effects of building design or details. Buildings planned with, among other things, comfort conditions in mind are usually designed to act as climate intensifiers or as climate modifiers.

A shelf of books has been published on designing for climate, especially for hot and arid ones. Few discuss comfort, as such, in more than the most basic physiological terms: when the skin temperature rises above 93°F (34°C) or drops below 84°F (29°C); or when the air temperature rises above 104°F (40°C), we experience discomfort, we are told. It is part of the task of the architect to create a physical ambience that lies 'comfortably' within these extremes. All of which lays emphasis on temperature as the basis of comfort, though 10 minutes spent on a bed without mosquito netting, even in the most ambient of tropical temperatures, can give the lie to that assumption in many tropical parts of the world.

The pursuit of comfort does not stop at pleasurable sensations, or insulating the occupants of buildings against their awareness of climatic conditions. Comfort is not merely to be experienced as a neutralized physical environment; for the residents it is frequently important for it to be *seen* to have been achieved in particular buildings. Roman villas and Renaissance palaces bore the evidence of the wealth of their owners in every detail; the emperors and their successors from Hadrian to Hearst displayed their affluence in an excess of conspicuous comfort. Images of superfluous comfort are statements of power, the power that accrues with wealth. Pop artists and film stars, oil magnates and multinational conglomerates alike proclaim their accomplishments by symbols of comfort, far beyond the thresholds of necessity: gold fittings in the onyx jacuzzi.

Architects are willing enough to meet the fantasies of comfort of wealthy clients, as the work of such gifted designers as Julia Morgan or Sir Edwin Lutyens testifies. Many modernist architects were opposed to tasteless displays of luxuriating opulence and instead, sacrificed comfort to high style. At its most extreme, this comfortless, expensive aesthetic found its expression in the 'red-blue chair' of Gerrit Rietveld. Le Corbusier was a little more subtle, co-operating with Charlotte Perriand to produce chairs in chrome and canvas which at least gave the illusion of comfort. Illusion because, as anyone will know who has sat in a Corb 'grand confort' chair and had the canvas cut behind their knees, it is more beautiful than comfortable. As for Rietveld's chair, many an architect has it on display in his house, but who would do so if the designer was Jan Schmidt? Some of us who live in the west are the designers and occupiers of the buildings examined in Reyner Banham's book, *The Architecture of the Well-Tempered Environment*. Published in 1969, it is still one of the very few books to examine the climatic performance of modern buildings already built, rather than to give generous advice on how architects should design for comfort. None of the examples cited by Reyner Banham lies east of Berlin, and most are west of

**Figure 7.3**
Designed by Julia Morgan for newspaper magnate William Randolph Hearst, the indoor swimming pool of 'Hearst Castle' epitomized luxury and comfort. California, US.

**Figure 7.4**
*Gassho* ('praying hands') farm houses and cultivated land, are well adapted to a defined area, with no 'social inconvenience'. Gokayama, West Central Japan.

New York. To open his argument, however, Banham acknowledged that man could 'exist' in almost any environment, 'but only just; in order to flourish, rather than merely survive, mankind needs more ease and leisure than a barefisted, and barebacked, single-handed struggle to exist could permit' (Banham, 1969). His stereotype of mankind's 'struggle to exist' was not supported by evidence from even one culture. Nor was his assumption that 'ease and leisure' was unachievable by a 'real tribe'; the 'inheritors of ancestral cultural predispositions', whose response to resources was not rational. Reyner Banham left his theoretical tribes at this point, only returning to their vernacular architecture briefly at the end of his book. 'Most of the vernacular houses of the past . . . show these generalized adaptations to a fairly well-defined area – the Cotswolds, western Norway, central Japan, New Orleans'. But these were achieved 'only at the cost of human and social inconvenience'. That they may still be insufficient to deal with particularly adverse conditions 'is especially true where the local type is applied too rigidly, for reasons of ancestral custom, status seeking or commercial inertia' (Banham, 1969). There was both truth and misrepresentation in his summary dismissal of vernacular examples, convenience and inconvenience apparently being the basis of criteria that over-rode ancestral custom, societal structure or social intercourse.

When I left the air-conditioned building of the School of Architecture at the University in Kumasi it was to work with the Asante of the forest region of Ghana, and later, with the peoples of the northern savannah. I was confident that I would find the vernacular solution to housing in the heat and humidity of the rain forest: I began to study the Asante compounds with enthusiasm. They were unprepossessing, thick-walled, earthen buildings constructed of layers of compacted balls of laterite mud. The roofs were occasionally thatched, but most were now of reused galvanized, corrugated sheet metal. The rectangular plan, hipped roof units were grouped around a courtyard, the entrance to which was from a corner. There was no crossventilation or induced draught through the courtyard, no windows in the mud walls of the houses over whose open doorways cloths hung limply. To my dismay the interiors were close and airless during the day, but as the daily activities were conducted in the courtyard, where the cooking fire burned, or in open-sided shelters where weavers sat at their looms, it didn't appear to matter. As I became more acquainted with Asante life, I realized that virtually all activities, until late in the evening, took place in the compound courtyards or in the large, open space at the centre of the linear villages. The question, of course, was whether the Asante were forced to work and pass their leisure hours in the courtyards and open spaces because the dwellings were unlivable, or whether the way of life did not require their cover except in the rains, and during the night. Convenience – or comfortless compromise? Slowly, I realized that even my clothes exacerbated my own discomfort as I observed the animated, voluble Asante in their loosely draped togas, dancing gracefully and demonstratively in the public open spaces. Others watched from their low, curved stools, knees drawn up or legs stretched before them; they were at home with their environment because social life and its setting were intimately bound. Compared with social intercourse, comfort was of little significance.

A case for the climatic determinism of vernacular architecture has been made with reference to a number of cultures, most notably by the American historian James Marston Fitch. But whether the Bedouin tent is primarily a response to the desert climate, or a highly portable shelter used by a nomadic society whose economy exploits the limited resources of a desert environment, is a question that can only be asked outside the culture. Within it there is no distinction; the tent is indispensable on both counts. But any argument that all vernacular cultures demonstrate such equilibrium between the climatic and the economic cannot be supported; there are far too many factors that affect the forms and functions of vernacular traditions to be so simply summarized.

On the tropical east coast of Africa, the Swahili house is built with mud packed into the interstices of a mangrove pole frame. Though the construction is lighter than that of the Asante it is as resistant to through draughts. An Islamic people, the Swahili value their privacy and particularly that of their women. A large pitched *makuti* roof oversails the whole house, which may contain half a dozen rooms. Supported and braced by a forest of poles, its gable ends are open to catch the breeze and cool the interior spaces. But there is another Swahili house built of coral ragstone by Swahili labour, but under Arab direction. Many examples have been destroyed, but on the island of Lamu a large number still remain from the early nineteenth century (Donley-Reid, 1990). They take a form of successive narrow spaces which become progressively more close in atmosphere and with less movement of air, the deeper one penetrates. Though they were built in Africa their forms are those of the Arab Gulf states; to the Arab colonists their cultural values were more important to them than the devising of a new architecture that would sacrifice some of their requirements of a house in the interests of climatic adjustment. On the rooftops of the Lamu houses there is usually another shelter with woven palm leaf walls and a thatched roof. It is the accommodation for the house servant, of inferior status but undeniably more appropriate to the climate, the loose weave of the walls permitting the air to circulate and the layers of thatch allowing the warm air to escape. Too small to emulate the *makuti* houses, they have some of their climatic merits (Ghaidan, 1975).

**Figure 7.5**
Swahili *makuti* house of pole-and-clay construction and a light thatched roof. Open gable ends create through-ventilation. Lamu, Kenya.

**Figure 7.6**
Minangkabau 'saddleback' roof. The lower central section and open raised gable frames facilitate the exhalation of warm air. Negri Sembalan, Malaysia.



As a means of cooling the dwelling, in spite of exposure to the sun, the 'saddleback' roof types of many cultures in South East Asia are very appropriate. They are seen at their most graceful in the palaces and houses of the Minangkabau of Sumatra, but though the houses of the Batak or the Malays have marked differences, they share the saddlebacked roof. The rising gable ends are occasionally left open; more frequently they have a decorative pierced screen which defines the gable but permits the passage of air through the roof. The volume of air that passes through is determined by the dimensions of the roof at its narrowest point, or 'waist'. As the warm air issues from the rising gable it expands, and in doing so, brings down the temperature. Many theories have been advanced to account for the prevalence of the saddleback roof. It has been proposed by Vroklage and others that the boat-shaped roofs were derived from a maritime tradition (Lewcock and Brans, 1975). Domenig proposed a structural evolution from a conical, pole construction (Domenig, 1980); there is evidence to relate the forms to the Dong-Son culture of Vietnam. For their part, the members of these cultures refer to their symbolic association with the horns of the sacred water buffalo; none account for it in terms of comfort or climatic performance.

On the Malay peninsula the indigenous houses are complexes of units which are assembled in varying configurations, and in accordance with local traditions. The levels rise from a common family space, the *jemurung* or open verandah, to the main building known as the *rumah ibu*, the 'mother house'. The mother house is the

**Figure 7.7**
Malay houses on piles, with open eaves and a separate ventilator on the ridge. Social spaces are shaded by low-pitched pentice roofs. Malay peninsula.

ultimate private space, the parental sleeping room and a place for laying the deceased. Spaces are distinguished according to age and gender, and are further divided between clean and unclean zones. The interiors are kept cool by wooden shutters, decoratively pierced partitions and open eaves which maintain a continual air flow (Lim, 1987). The system of spatial regulation contributes to the comfort of the occupants, while the patterns of use ensure the respect with which the guardian spirits, and each member of the family, are entitled (Gibbs, 1987). Differentiation of spaces is often required for the preservation of privacy and, in Islamic communities, for the seclusion of the women. But in many circumstances, social constraints of this kind may find their architectural expression more by direct segregation than by internal partitioning. This is the case with the men's club houses that are to be found in Papua New Guinea, Polynesia and many other parts of Oceania (Morgan, 1988). Micronesia for instance, where, on the island of Yap the great *pebaey* or community meeting houses still stand. Built of mahogany pillars set deeply in stone footings, and with a ridge beam of palm trunks wrapped in bamboo that is lashed with coconut husk cords, the Yapese meeting house may be 80 feet long, over 30 feet wide and as high from the slatted floor to the ridge. Open-sided, the lofty *pebaey* is cool in the day, while firepits warm the air at night and discourage pests. Nearby will be the *faluw*, the 'bachelor's' clubhouse where the young men of the village sleep. Spanning a third of the area of the community meeting house, the *faluw* stands like the other Yapese buildings, on a coral plinth with a schist facing.

The high, reeded gables form an obtuse angle, so that the plan is an elongated hexagon. Walls of narrow, woven bamboo poles have top-hung ventilators allowing the flow of air while affording protection from high winds and heavy rains. Among the Yapese, every building has its house spirit, and every village is divided in matrilineal and patrilineal groupings, each with its separate cookhouse and stratification by age and gender. The relationship of Yapese villagers to caste and ancestry, and to their neighbours within a rigid hierarchical system of social ranking, was far more significant than comfort. Nevertheless, it is evident that Yapese buildings have been constructed with due consideration given to the regulation of the hot and humid Micronesian island climate. Interior furnishings are simple, the spaces uncluttered by partitions or structures that would interrupt crossventilation. Softly sprung floors of palm slats are covered with woven coconut matting for sleeping, with transverse half sections of palm trunks dividing the floor areas and serving as head rests (Hunter-Anderson, 1983).

Further particularization of the value placed on comfort and the means by which it has been achieved, relative to the norms of differing cultures, could be made at length. While the citing of specific instances investigated in depth is of undoubted interest, it is important to note that some solutions are widely distributed among many peoples. Sometimes this may be the result of diffusion: the passing on of methods of improving living conditions from one society to another, and thence to others. The top-hung ventilator noted in Yap above, which is also found in Indonesia (e.g. in Nias), is one instance. The sleeping hammock slung from the poles of house shelters found in Mexico, Central America and throughout Amazonia is clearly another.

If diffusion accounts for the distribution of some techniques of obtaining a measure of comfort in hot and humid climates, independent genesis might be assumed when cultures are far apart. The plinths on which the Yap buildings were raised enable them to benefit from sea breezes and protect the structures from damage by inundation. For the Yapese their importance lies in their permanence as ancestral sites. Plinths are found on many Pacific islands, but buildings are also frequently raised on piles. Pile-houses, sometimes supported on short, stout posts, sometimes lifted high on forests of poles, are to be found across Oceania. They are numerous in New Guinea, in Borneo and Sulawesi, and in island societies throughout Indonesia. But, like the Malay example already noted, pile structures are common in mainland South-East Asia (Frankowski, n.d.). Not only in the Pacific and South-East Asia however: pile structures are distributed across Equatorial Africa and in coastal West Africa; they are scattered through northern Amazonia and Venezuela and are far from rare in the Caribbean. While we may list the cultures who employ pile structures, it is significant that the raising of the floors above ground level, often (as in Macronesia or Colombia) at a considerable height relative to the size of the occupiable spaces, is ubiquitous in these regions of almost unrelenting heat and high humidity (Waterson, 1990).

It would seem reasonable to argue that such buildings on piles are constructed so as to take advantage of any air movement or cooling breezes, and to benefit from air circulating through slatted floors. But is it? Many of these pile structures are on coastal fringes, like Ganvié in Dahomey, where the economy is mainly based on fishing. Piles allow members of such societies to live directly over their fishing grounds and so ensure their control, while the height of the piles accommodates the rising of the tides. Inland cultures, many of them living in communal village longhouses as in regions as far apart as Assam and Kalimantan, gain protection from raiding parties and animal predators, by being raised above them. In some countries they raise the accommodation above the level of mosquito flight while, with the addition of capstones, they can repel rodents. The latter is an important factor in the distribution of pile structures such as granaries, in regions outside the hot and humid zones.

Economic and defensive imperatives can over-ride any that may relate to climate, but for many peoples living in pile dwellings it is

**Figure 7.8**
Pile house of the Dai, a Chinese ethnic minority related to the Thai of Thailand. Animals and stores are kept beneath the house and its single-pitch extensions. Yunnan, south-west China.

on their faithful adherence to rituals associated with the erecting of the piers, that their fortunes depend. Evidently, the concept of comfort has many ramifications, both physiological and psychological, some of which we can briefly recapitulate. Our comforts nurse and cosset the infant in us, protecting us from reality, insulating us against the natural environment in which we ultimately must learn to live. To command others to meet our need for comfort requires privilege; enjoyment of the artefacts designed to facilitate our comfort frequently implies status and wealth. What is comfortable to each of us is relative to the nature of the part of the world in which we reside, and the social niche we occupy within our culture. Not that these conditions are static: in time we become accustomed to modest comforts and demand still more to satisfy our sensory perceptions and physical dispositions. Yet we may gain pleasure from the minor comforts of our own devising, and seek enjoyment in the deliberate choice of uncomfortable environments that test our personalities and our potential. To be wholly comfortable is to deny our awareness of the Self. Still, people in the west expect buildings to provide comfortable environments; frequently ones in which 'comfort conditions' are interpreted in terms of climate 'control' or, more accurately, modification. Often the desire to demonstrate the achievement of such aims is expressed in the conspicuous comfort of unashamed luxury, which designers are willing enough to satisfy. Yet paradoxically, the acme of high style and status was also expressed in the austerity of Modernism. Professedly rationalist, the modernist architect might be the antithesis of the vernacular builder, but the comparison is not irrelevant, for the cultural values of the modernist aesthetic dominated any need to satisfy mere physical comfort.

Among the most common myths about vernacular architecture are those that argue that it is climatically determined. It is true that many kinds of traditional building are ideally suited to their climatic contexts, just as they are to the resources available or to the cultural demands that are placed upon them. Customarily, they are the structures made by the indigenous people whose buildings, like those of the Malays or the Yapese, are the result of centuries of evolution, checks and balances, and successive minor adjustments. Such 'generalized adaptations to a fairly well-defined area' were not achieved, as Reyner Banham believed, 'only at the cost of human and social inconvenience'. On the contrary, it was human and social convenience that was important, achieved sometimes only at the cost of a measure of climatic comfort. He was correct in his belief that some vernacular buildings may still be insufficient to deal with particularly adverse conditions, but he did not acknowledge, in his conclusion, that this was 'especially true where the local type is applied too rigidly, for reasons of ancestral custom, status seeking or commercial inertia', was just as true of his own cultural background.

For it is their cultural, rather than their climatic, appropriateness that accounts for the longevity of architectural traditions. This is underlined by the colonists and settlers whose building types and environments often perpetuated the traditions that they left behind, rather than developed afresh in response to new conditions. The suburban environment of the British family in Ghana and the houses of the Arab-Swahili builders off the Kenya coast, have this in common. It may even account for the climatic unsuitability of the houses of the Asante who, though long a rain forest people, have origins

**Figure 7.9**
An air-conditioner on the upper level of an Arab village house. Qatif, Saudi Arabia.

that lie in the hot and dry savannah. What then, is to be made of attempts to find appropriate 'comfort conditions' in hot, humid climates? The tropical world offers literally hundreds of examples of building traditions that are suited to their steaming environments, and which afford adequate measures of comfort appropriate to the cultural demands of their respective societies. But they are seldom suited to the technological, time-dominated, televisual, temperature-sensitive culture that now seeks to learn from them.

Demands that we place upon the building in the interests of our concepts of comfort are heavily conditioned by the nature of our culture. Were this to change and to adapt to the climate, many of the difficulties would disappear. But this is unlikely for, as we have seen, the tenacity of our cultural inheritance is such that we will continue to strive for an impossible resolution. Design in the hot, humid zones requires of the architect an understanding not only of the practicalities of climate modification, but of the far more subtle, intangible, but fundamental cultural imperatives that direct the pursuit of comfort. In the final analysis, the problem is not a question of 'comfort conditions' but one of *comfort conditioning*.

## References


Banham, P.R. (1969). *The Architecture of the Well-Tempered Environment.* London: Architectural Press, pp. 18–19, 286.

Domenig, G. (1980). *Tektonik im Primitiven Dachbau.* Zurich: ETH.

Donley-Reid, L. (1990). A structuring structure: The Swahili house. In: Kent, S. (ed.). *Domestic Architecture and the Use of Space.* Cambridge University Press.

Fitch, J.M. and Branch, D.P. Primitive architecture. *Scientific American* **202**, 133–44.

Frankowski, E. (n.d.) Carta representive de los palafitos yn graneros sobre estacas en la actualidad. *Com de Invest. Paleont. Y Prehist.* Mem 188. Lam X111.

Ghaidan, U. (1975). *Lamu: A Study of the Swahili Town.* East African Literature Bureau, Nairobi, Kenya.

Gibbs, P. (1987). *Building a Malay House.* Oxford University Press.

Hunter-Anderson, R.L. (1983). *Traditional Yapese Settlement Patterns: An Ethno-Archaeological Approach.* Guam: Pacific Studies Institute.

Lewcock, R. and Brans, G. (1975). The boat as an architectural symbol. In: Oliver, P. (ed.). *Shelter, Sign and Symbol.* London: Barrie and Jenkins.

Lim, J.Y. (1987). *The Malay House: Rediscovering Malaysia's Indigenous Shelter System.* Institut Masyarakat.

Morgan, W.N. (1988). *Prehistoric Architecture in Micronesia.* Austin: University of Texas Press, pp. 30–56.

Waterson, R. (1990). *The Living House: An Anthropology of Architecture in South-East Asia.* Oxford University Press, pp. 78–85.

# PART III

# TRADITION AND TRANSMISSION

# 8

# Vernacular know-how (1982)

When I was invited to speak on vernacular technology, I must admit that I felt that another theme would have been closer to my personal interests. For me, the problems of why societies have determined the forms of building that they use seem far more challenging, and ultimately more important, than the questions of how. Nevertheless, the invitation prompted me to focus on those aspects of the subject which relate to vernacular technology. Use of the term begs the question of what we mean by 'vernacular', but this will be discussed elsewhere. I will therefore merely state that for me, vernacular architecture – or shelter – embraces the entire field of tribal, folk, peasant, popular and informal sector urban building. The anthropology of shelter has a multitude of aspects, of which those which come within the scope of technology are clearly important.

Although I understand that in Turkish the equivalent for 'technology' is broad in meaning, in English it usually has fairly limited applications. The word comes from the Greek *tekhnologia* and means 'that branch of knowledge that treats of the arts' (*tekhnë* – art) which in application refers to 'the science of the industrial arts'. It has a second, less familiar definition in English which particularly appeals to me: 'the ethnological study of development of arts'. But in usage in architecture and engineering it is customary to speak of technology as the building methods used (Newby, 1982). I presume that a broader, rather than a narrower definition is anticipated here, so, using a vernacular term to identify the subject I shall use the word 'know-how' in this short discussion. I wish to discuss some of the problems of vernacular know-how which I perceive, rather than give a comforting list of its successes. Among these are the issues of access to knowledge; the passing on of information and skills, and those that arise from specialization. I am interested in the vernacular use of means for the transformation of energy and their limitations; and in the questions of vernacular building efficiency and performance, including the compromises that may have to be made. The introduction of 'modern', or basically nonvernacular, materials raises problems of our own perceptions, as well as those in the societies that are now encountering them.

Know-how is the faculty of knowing; cognition, if you prefer. It has to do with knowledge, with awareness, understanding, even intuition. In practice, within the context of vernacular architecture it embraces what is known and what is inherited about the dwelling, building or settlement; it includes the collective wisdom and experience of the society concerned, and the norms that have become accepted by the group as being appropriate to their built environment. It is also to do with the inherited knowledge of the natural environment of climate, topography, seasonal variation, natural hazard, suitability of site. Inevitably this spills over into the values of the society and how they may affect, through belief, observance, ritual, and respect for ancestors or deities, what might be seen as more practical considerations to those outside the group.

Within the compass of know-how is knowledge of natural, material resources and how they may be utilized, nurtured or replaced. The working of such materials for the purposes of building, whether for practical or symbolic roles as applied to construction, cladding or decoration, is as much a part of it as is the making and selection of tools with which to effect the work. This aspect of know-how is intimately related to method or technique, and these in turn to skills, manual abilities, 'wrinkles' and specialized means which aid the maker to achieve his intentions. It is, of course, concerned with what we generally term 'technology'. As such, it is related to access to tools, contrivances, mechanical aids; and it is concerned with the transmission of skills and the educative processes whereby these abilities, this knowledge, are passed on from one generation, or by one group, to the next. This brief list does not exhaust the broad headings of vernacular know-how, but it does indicate perhaps, that vernacular technology is conceptually situated within a larger cognitive map or territory that constitutes the totality of building and settlement knowledge that is encompassed by a specific society.

Among some peoples much, if not all this knowledge is accessible to virtually all their members. In giving an illustration of this I will, as in other points that I wish to make, use a single example in some detail rather than hint at a number of them. It was possible for any members of a Paiute family in south-west Nevada to build a 'cattail' house from willow wands, sagebrush bark string and mattresses of

**Figure 8.1**
Tool-making blacksmith at work, forging sickles prior to harvest. Iran.

cattail leaves. Though it was often the work of the women in this hunter-gatherer society, it was not exclusively so. The knowledge that was required to build a grass house – gathering the poles for the framework before the willows came into leaf, but waiting until the grass in the river bottoms had grown tall before weaving the thatch bundles to cover the frame – was easily shared, or passed on to sons and daughters. 'Patched and repaired from year to year, abandoned when not needed, or burned when death occurred in them, shelters were mainly protection from the elements,' wrote Margaret Wheat (Wheat, 1967). Such a building process was easily learned, used available resources, produced a technologically unsophisticated dwelling which yet served its purpose, and was readily abandoned when it was no longer wanted. It was thus responsive to

**Figure 8.2**
A shelter of the Paiute type, with conical stick frame and cladding of bound cattail stalks. Nevada, USA.

the needs of a semi-nomadic people and represented little investment in time or property.

More settled peoples with agrarian economies, tend to build shelter of a rather more permanent nature. When settling a new site for their garden plots the Lambas of Zambia first built an *inkunka* village of conical, lean-to structures which served them during the first season's planting and raising of pumpkins, maize, wheat and sorghum. These were thatched and provided with bamboo doors before the seasonal rains came, while further temporary *ututungu* shelters were erected in the garden sites from which the crops could be protected. After the first season a permanent village of *intanda* dwellings was constructed, to a plan that was determined by the village headman and which precisely reflected the structure and

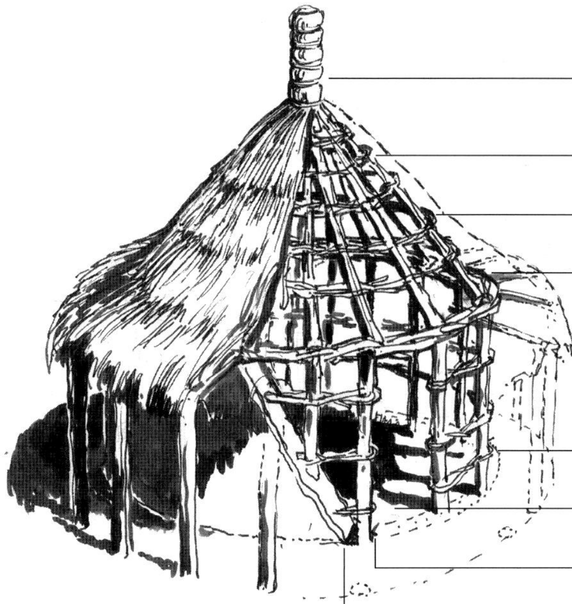


**Figure 8.3**
Lamba *intanda* (house), with named components. Zambia, Central Africa.

relationships of the clans. These houses were stoutly built of upright poles bound with *umusamba* withies and bark rope, being ringed at the eaves with a *kankasa* encircling belt of considerable strength, capable of withstanding the outward thrust of the four main *insonta*, or roofing poles, which constituted the main support for the roof structure. Further *insonta*, bound with encircling *ichiwango* withies, contributed to a tight, secure structure which was then thatched and capped with an ornamental, but rain resistant *sunsa* peak. The walls were rough plastered with mud, and this was followed by a fine *ukushingula* plaster, and a door, *ichiwi*, was made from bamboo.

Further stages, including the preparing of an earthen floor and the making of internal screens, sleeping platforms and the like, meant that the building of the permanent *intanda* was a deliberate process, with the roles of men and women carefully delineated.

Such detail of terms and names for processes and building elements threatens to be boring, but I have given them (in brief) because they illustrate the deliberate nature of the building procedure. From the marking out of the building site, *ukutala*, or the digging of the shallow *umufolwa* foundations, to the removal of the *ulupumpu* pole support used in the initial construction of the roof, or the beating of the *pamantila* hard surface of the dwelling floor, everything was known and named (Doke, 1931). This was a building sequence which was interlocked into the social structure and the cycle of the year's activities; know-how was shared by the precise identification of means and methods, and the naming of parts and processes. But, while it did not inhibit some measure of individualization of building details, for the most part it fixed the nature of building solutions to specific problems. The technology had been tested through experience over time, and while the patterns of life remained constant and little changing, the building type and technology remained constant also.

Specialization of roles in the building process frequently relates to the complexity of the undertakings. It may reflect the associations of meaning in symbolism, custom or rite, which may exercise control over the materials used, or the necessary preparation required to participate in some aspects of building. Often this was protected by the formation of guilds or craftsmen's organizations which required the membership, preceded by long apprenticeship, of an aspiring craftsman who learned the skills and mysteries of his craft, and safeguarded it against interlopers. Along with this kind of closed shop was the development of specialized language and terminology which helped to make the know-how of the craft still more esoteric. In the English Cotswolds, stone was excavated which could be split into roofing slates. They were graded as to size, the largest and heaviest slates at the eaves, the lightest and smallest at the ridge-crest. The roofer's slates in the northwest of England were known as *Haghattees*, *Farwells*, *Chilts* and even *Rogue-Why-Winkest-Thous* and *Jenny-Why-Gettest-Thous*; other names, hardly less bizarre, were used elsewhere (Anon. n.d.). As with the slates, so with the tools for working them: the slater's *saxe* or billhook, his *pick* and his *claw* – finely shaped instruments with which he deftly cut and split the stone (Batsford and Fry, 1938; Clifton-Taylor, 1972). Slaters are not thatchers, and the men who built the roof trusses that supported the thatched roofs were not thatchers either. Thatching too, is a specialized craft, the thatcher laying his *thraves*, or bundles of *yelmed* or *gabbled* and combed straw, in *strakes* or layers. He fixes them with *spics*, *tangs*, *sparrods* or *brotches*, as the hazel spars are called, aligning the butt ends of the straw with his *beetle*, repairing the battens with his *shingling*-hammer and fixing the *thraves* adroitly with his thatching needle. The thatcher's craft is still a flourishing one in Britain and is jealously protected (Hartley, 1939).

It is likely that, in many parts of England, such specialization in the technology of roofing has been distinct for many centuries. It is therefore at the furthest removed from the kind of vernacular where

**Figure 8.4**
Thatching a roof, with layers of yealms, or sheaves of reeds. Horizontal battens and short ladder sections enable free movement on the roof. Dartmoor, Devon, UK.

all the necessary skills and know-how are accessible to an individual and his family. In fact, specialization is even more marked than that, for while the Paiute might collect his own *tói* (cattail) leaves, the slater did not even quarry and cut his own stone slates; this was the province of the quarrymen. Specialization in the vernacular undoubtedly enriches the technology as each craftsman passes on what he learns, and adds to the store of know-how. Progress in the solution of technical problems would seem to be assured, but it is offset by the basic conservatism of traditional craftsmen. And by the fact that weaknesses and difficulties in building technology are not necessarily perceived as problems to be overcome, but as limitations within which the craftsman works.

It is by no means clear whether or not this is the reason for the technological simplicity of the means of production in vernacular architecture. Technology, in the sense in which it is used in Britain, is dependent on the conversion of energy into power. At its most basic, this means the employment of the converted energy of consumed foods into muscle power or unassisted manual technology. The next stage involves the use of tools, which direct muscular energy in specific ways, and which may augment it: hammers, chisels, saws and levers, for example. Major transformation in technology comes with the use of contrivances and machines, like pulleys and block-and-tackle devices, though these still use human energy to set them in motion, usually aided by gravity. Animal power, harnessed to such contrivances, like the Arab *noria* or endless chain of buckets for raising water, or more simply, the horse and cart, greatly

**Figure 8.5**
A *noria* of Arab origin, drawing water from a well with buckets on a chain, the wheel mechanism operated by a blind-folded horse. Ballearic Islands, 1950s.

assisted man's technological range; while the conversion of natural energy, in the form of wind or water power through windmills and watermills, marked notable advances in man's technological resources. But what has been long termed the Industrial Revolution of the late eighteenth century, saw dramatic advances in the conversion of energy with the harnessing of steam. If we disregard subsequent growth in engine technology and the extensive applications of electric power and energy converted from fossil fuels, we

**Figure 8.6**
La Pichora, a Spanish windmill adapted to drive a water-raising *noria*. Mercia, Spain.

can still note that vernacular architecture the world over has made surprisingly little use of techniques for converting energy.

For the most part, vernacular shelter employs direct muscle power, and, through the use of tools, muscle-assisted power, for most building production. Even mechanical contrivances of the block-and-tackle kind seem rather rarely used within the traditions, suggesting that in Europe, at any rate, the know-how available to the crafts guilds employed on the building of cathedrals or palaces was not readily applied to more humble domestic shelter. Animal power has been used mainly for the transporting of heavy materials – elephants in India, donkeys in Europe – but although wind and water have been harnessed for a thousand years, their energy has rarely been used to assist the vernacular builder. There are water-powered sawmills in the United States, and wind-powered sawmills in Holland, but even these seem to depend on working parts that were factory-made. Today, of course, the cement mixer is to be found on every western building site, and one may occasionally see stone slates being raised to roof level by an elevator powered by an electric generator. But the cement mixer is hardly a vernacular machine, and only the wealthy can afford a slate roof in England today.

It is curious that in the matter of building their houses or granaries, people are less inclined to be inventive in the technology employed than in raising water or grinding corn: the *shadouf* seems not to have been adapted to lifting mud bricks, nor the mill for pulverizing the earth to make them. The reasons must be partly due to the degree of necessity for survival that these activities represent when compared with building; partly to the fixed nature of the more advanced technological machines, when compared with the distribution of houses within settlements; partly related to the scale of the building operation, and partly to the climate under which technological innovation thrives. It is interesting to note, for example, how the advances were made in the vernacular technology of windmills: from the fixed windshaft of the Cretan mill and the adaptable sails of the Greek mill, to the complex development of brake wheel and wallower, 'great spur' wheel and stone nuts of the French, Dutch and English mills, within their revolving post-mill constructions, or with their revolving caps. Tiller beams and tail poles made the turning of the mill caps by muscle power possible, but the invention, possibly in East Anglia, of the fantail as a servomechanism, was a technological innovation that may not have come from within the vernacular. Without doubt, the invention of Meikle's shutter sails in 1772, and the introduction of Cubitt's

**Figure 8.7**
Mundsley mill, a tower mill with a Cubitt 'spider' to adjust the sails, and a fan-tail servomechanism, that turns the cap and sails into the wind. Norfolk, UK.

'spider' mechanism for controlling them in 1807, were mechanical inventions that were products of the Industrial Revolution and not of the vernacular (Freese, 1971). They were the result of deliberate designs arising from addressing specifically identified technical problems; a conceptualizing of a problem and its solution which, I suspect, occurs only rarely in vernacular traditions.

This brings us to the question of vernacular efficiency, or the technology of building performance. What I have suggested so far, is that vernacular know-how is of different kinds according to the nature and complexity of the society concerned, its economy, its resources and its architectural aspirations. I have argued, in effect, that the vernacular builder's know-how becomes more detailed and exclusive with specialization, and that this should lead to technological innovation. To some extent it does, but conservatism in both means and methods, coupled with an unwillingness or disinterest in using more advanced technological resources, and a thought process which is disinclined to isolate problems in order to find specific solutions, have together retarded progress. How valid is this, in the light of the successes of vernacular architecture? We all know how well adobe walls can moderate the transmission of the sun's heat, acting as a heat store that will keep the interiors of buildings in the Middle East or North Africa warm at night yet, through the process of the cooling off of the walls, cool during the day. We know, because Hassan Fathy explained it. Fathy brilliantly discovered and demonstrated for us the method of working of Sudanese vault builders, who can construct earth-brick parabolic barrel vaults by an inclined layer method, that does not require formwork and centering (Fathy, 1973). We know how efficient the windscoops of Iraq are – although we may not be certain whether they originated within the vernacular tradition, or were borrowed by it (Roaf, 1982). Innumerable other instances of vernacular know-how could be cited which support the view that, by some strange alchemy, by some undetected processes of trial and error, or by some D'Arcy Thompson-esque evolution of growth and form, the 'right' solutions have been arrived at (Thompson, 1961).

We may nurture romantic notions about the technological qualities, even the superiority, of vernacular architecture but we shall learn little, and do little useful service in the advancement of building, if we are not also aware of the weaknesses, even the failures. In many societies house structure and technology is the result of a trade-off against other factors, the limitations or disadvantages of their built form being accommodated within the pattern of life. I was aware of this in northern Ghana, where for most of the year the beautiful, sculptural forms of the Gurunsi mud-walled dwellings are ideally suited to the climate. But there are heavy rains for a couple of weeks in August during which life is extremely uncomfortable: roofs fall in, and the footings of the walls are damaged or penetrated by splash-back from the rains. This necessitates extensive rethatching with elephant grass, and repairs to the cracked and eroded walls. In the rain forest regions there are other problems. Traditional houses among the Ibo are well constructed, with roofs that are built independently of the 'swish', or rammed mud-ball walls. The light and resilient roofs are well suited to a region which has high winds, but they are low and steep-pitched from the eaves, to reduce the effects of wind pressure. The roofs are covered with *awmu* palm-leaf mats, called *atani*, which are tied to the *offolaw* palm-frond

**Figure 8.8**
Gurunsi compound, its granaries rethatched with elephant grass. Rain damage is repaired with boiled plantain stalk juices and locust bean pods. Nangodi, north Ghana.

rafters with plaited string. They are skilfully made with the shiny side of the palm leaf uppermost to reject rainwater, and they are laid with considerable overlap to provide a dense cover. Tests of similar roofs on *wakuti* houses of the Swahili in Kenya have shown them to be thermally extremely effective in bringing down the internal temperature. But they are breeding grounds for mosquitoes and wood-boring insects, they are subject to attacks by white ants and are susceptible to dry rot. The bamboo mats of the leaves of *ngwaw* palm, used to repair the roofs, need frequent replacement but the smoke from fires in the dwelling helps to preserve them and keep down the insects, even if it hardly contributes to internal comfort conditions.

In many parts of the world corrugated iron has totally replaced thatch of palm or grass, and pitched roofs with iron cladding have appeared where conical or flat roofs were once to be found. Regarded as ugly and evidence of the damaging influence of western technology by enthusiasts of vernacular architecture, its trade-off value for many peoples is often disregarded. Manufacture of corrugated iron sheeting commenced in the first half of the nineteenth century, and it was widely used in the export of prefabricated buildings during the colonial period. As a cladding material it has had a long history, and rusty or deteriorated sheets generally found their way to indigenous communities, where they were rapidly reused. Whole towns in Latin America, Africa and the east were roofed in corrugated iron sheeting, and it has gradually become, in spite of the condemnation of visitors, and love of traditional vernacular architecture by some of them, a ubiquitous element in the modern vernacular. Corrugated iron sheeting may not always be lovely to look at, but it has many virtues. It is cheap to transport and suffers hardly any damage in transit; it is easily stacked when the gauge of the corrugations is identical in the sheets; it does not require skill to handle it when it is exported and imported. On site, sheet iron is light to handle, it is affixed to building frames with galvanized nails and little difficulty, and it requires only a moderately light construction to take its weight. Once in position it casts off rainwater by virtue of its section and, with adequate overlap of sheets, it is relatively impervious to the creeping action of water. Seams at the ridges and roof hips can be covered with standard ridging and it is speedily erected, and hence cheap to employ. It is strong, yet flexible, and can take up roof irregularities. And if, in the event of severe tropical storms or hurricanes, it is torn off the roof, it can be speedily replaced. Galvanized or coated with a zinc chloride flux it comes in sheets which range from 5 to 12 feet in length and to various gauges. From the point of view of the vernacular builder it is far more durable than thatch, less subject to damage than many roof materials, far lighter than layered earth and requires far less timber to be purchased, felled or worked.

There are, naturally, disadvantages. Corrugated iron is subject to rust when the galvanizing is damaged, or when the roofing screws or spring-head nails used to secure it, are not used with lead washers. It can be extremely hot, and being very thin, transmits the heat rapidly to the interior of the building, heating up the air in the roof space. But it breeds no insects and requires relatively little maintenance – although it would benefit from painting at intervals with a bituminous coating, a treatment that it seldom gets in the vernacular. Yet, it may be argued, it has been ruinous in many cultures. Australian aborigines who once lived in improvised 'humpies' made from found natural materials have taken to using corrugated iron, apparently to their detriment. But is it? They use the sheets of iron as they used the sheets of stringy bark torn off trees, as light membranes that offered shade but did not close the shelter with walls. For them the material is as durable, if not more so, than bark, and for the conservationist the reduced damage to the trees is a bonus. More inconvenient are the corrugated iron houses, with sheets affixed to rectilinear timber scantling framing, and with side walls of sheet iron also, which some resettlement agencies have provided. Australia nevertheless, has a long history of corrugated iron that has been well used. The suburban vernacular of a city like Brisbane offers literally thousands of examples of corrugated iron

**Figure 8.9**
Old cabins re-roofed in corrugated iron sheeting. New sheets reflect sunlight and reduce solar heat gain. Beechworth, New South Wales, Australia.

sheeting used with imagination, simplicity and know-how. The iron is maintained by occasional painting or is kept in a glistening, heat-reflecting condition when the material used has been zinc coated. Parapet gutters, valley gutters, edge rolling and a variety of ventilating ridges and onion-shaped revolving ventilators are available to cope with the vagaries of the climate (Sharp, 1946). The discrimination with which this basic, fairly modern, material is used by the anonymous Australian builders, parallels that of traditional builders in other cultures.

Vernacular know-how is not a single phenomenon and vernacular technology cannot be studied in general terms. It is inextricably bound up with the specific nature of the cultures which employ its countless forms. To understand the full implications of the technologies used, it is necessary to consider them in relation to their cultural contexts, as well as in terms of their efficiency or performance. In the modern world, vernacular traditions are fast disappearing or are subject to accelerating social change. Vernacular know-how in the past has been developed, as far as we know, over long periods of time (admittedly, there has been little research to confirm this statement). Vernacular know-how is not automatically appropriate to any innovation that is introduced, as the many examples of dangerously fabricated and barely reinforced concrete structures clearly indicate. Concrete frames with little or no reinforcement, or with lengths of rod stuck in the top of a still wet concrete pier in simulation of reinforcement, has been observed in situations, such as post-earthquake reconstruction, where new technologies have been hastily introduced. Adequate training has not been given to the new builders and, in particular, no confirmation has been obtained that they understand the structural principles underlying the use of reinforced concrete. Vernacular builders depend on the authority of tradition, and cope with problems pragmatically on the basis of experience; where know-how of post-and-lintel structures has been acquired in the use of timber, this is applied to concrete beams, that appear to be essentially the same.

The fundamental nature of this conceptual process has its benefits; it accounts for instance, for the variety in vernacular architecture of a specific tradition, which yet displays remarkable homogeneity. The widely known Greek vernaculars of Hydra, Paros or Santorini are the outcome of a tradition of forms and a technology to build them, firmly based on the heritage of centuries. Their subtle but lively variability, which so belies the frequently applied adjective 'cubic', is the result of a multitude of pragmatic design decisions made in response to personal need, undulating terrain or division of the patrimony, for which the builder's know-how has the answers in a multitude of alternative moves. This pragmatism also accounts for the use of old motor car tyres, packing cases or the rusting corrugated iron, in the hastily constructed shelters in the *bidonvilles* of cities in the developing world. Urban living demands labour all the year round; there is no time for building and maintenance. Shanty settlement dwellers cannot dig materials from the land or cut withies from saplings, as they might have done in the villages. They acquire a new know-how: obtaining waste materials from the city itself with which to make lamps, cookers, rope – and their houses. Eventually, more elegant solutions to the problems of building in the city periphery will evolve, differentiation of skills may appear, know-how will be expanded and passed on to subsequent generations. With the possible growth in literacy, problem isolation and the conceptualizing of solutions may become commonplace. But if it does, will the resultant forms of shelter still be 'vernacular'? There are many who do not view the shelter of the *barriadas* of Peru or the *favelas* of Brazil as vernacular architecture, but as a debasement of skills and traditions. However, it seems likely that we may be witnessing the processes of emergent vernacular and the acquisition of new know-how, as successive waves of migrants to the city learn to cope with it. Evidence of this is abundant in the *geçekondus* in Ankara. Others view with dismay the use of 'modern' materials in vernacular architecture, but the vernacular builder is a wise one who chooses to use concrete blocks, if by doing so he saves his time and effort for earning money to support his family.

**Figure 8.10**
Shanties built by migrants to a new settlement, using waste materials. Most have a rectangular plan, but some retain the rural cylindrical form with thatched roof. Mathare Valley, Nairobi, Kenya.

An incipient romanticism pervades much enthusiasm for vernacular architecture which is based on a belief that it is, by definition, superior to modern architecture. A similar attitude is shared by those who advocate the use of traditional materials. Their advocacy is based on love and respect, but this can cloud judgement. Professor Kiyosi Seike, for example, has made an eloquent argument in favour of wood for building in his captivating study of Japanese joinery. 'Even white cedar, which is considered weak among wood, has a tensile strength about four times as great as that of steel and its compression force is about six times as great as that of concrete', he writes. 'Only in its vulnerability to insect attack is wood inferior to steel, concrete or stone'. Kiyosi Seike argues that 'even in a fire, wood construction is actually safer than steel-frame construction, since steel is a very good conductor of heat, bending like soft taffy at 800° C' (Seike, 1977). But of course, there are spans that steel can achieve that are impossible in wood, there are loads that steel can take, rigidity of structures that steel construction can offer, and building heights that can be attained by its use, that are simply impracticable in timber. Wood can be worked with simple tools, but so in a sense, can steel construction. The pros and cons cannot be evaluated lightly: steel production consumes fossil fuels and water, but the acquisition of wood consumes forests. In other words, until we know the basis of the criteria that we are using, we are in no position to make valid judgements as to which material, or indeed which building type, is 'better' than another.

Some claim that vernacular methods, materials, buildings or know-how are 'better' because they have a respect for them and wish to see their merits recognized. Many who work in this field

**Figure 8.11**
Corner bracketing in a village temple, requires complex joints from the carpenter. Some examples date from the eighth century. Ogimachi, Shirakawa-Go, Japan.

are aware that vernacular architecture and the means whereby it has been built, are under threat in a great many societies. We have witnessed the thoughtless destruction of many traditional buildings, the censure of architects and planners who wish to 'modernize', and the arrogance of those who are wedded to the idea that western building forms and technology are applicable in all climates and to all cultures. Inappropriate housing has been mindlessly inflicted upon countless numbers of people in the name of modernity; traditional skills are in decline but western building types and technologies reflect wealth and status. In the eyes of many, vernacular architecture is 'backward' and 'undeveloped'.

For most of us who appreciate it, therefore, recognition of the vernacular has an emotional, subjective element. Frequently we hear, or we ourselves ask, 'what can we learn from vernacular architecture;

what has it to teach *us*?' We ask the question in respect, and hope to profit by the knowledge we may gain. Instead of thrusting our architectural solutions on a vernacular community we seek solutions to some of our architectural and social problems by studying it. It is right that we should, for there is very much to learn. But, I would contend, there is an uncomfortable measure of self-interest in the question 'what has it to teach *us*?' Our concern should not stop there, with the borrowing of know-how. So what role have we to play? What use are we to the development of, or mere recognition of their know-how? It is a truism to state, but true for all that, that these are changing times. Exposure to the media, to urban values and urban hardware, even to the visits of researchers in regional traditions, contribute to the conflicts of standards with which a vernacular society has to cope. There is much to shake its confidence and little to support its own value systems. With the confusion that all this represents, traditional know-how is easily discarded. Yet it is clear that there is a world shortage of housing, that the materials, the skills, the financial expenditure necessary to meet it by 'modern' means, simply does not exist. It is also evident, though by no means always acknowledged, that western methods of building in industrialized countries with temperate climates, are often quite inappropriate to the needs of other cultures in very different climates. The technological merits of vernacular traditions do need to be studied and understood, the extent of vernacular know-how does demand to be examined and recognized. But little is gained by romanticism or special pleading, and nothing is gained by overlooking the limitations, the defects, the structural and climatic failures of vernacular means while striving to document the successes.

I have concentrated upon the problems that are posed by the nature of vernacular know-how, and not on the achievements. This is because I firmly believe that comprehending them is also very necessary. We have the training and the objectivity to make such a balanced evaluation possible, and with the knowledge gained we have better arguments for sustaining and assisting the use of traditional technology. We can apply ourselves to the problematic areas and advise on improvements, or remedial measures, when they seem necessary. In themselves, these are fraught with problems which are cultural, but they too must be understood. We have, moreover, the special advantage of access to communication and the know-how of varied cultures. We are in a position, as the traditional builder often is not, of seeing his building types in the context of others built by comparable cultures in similar physical or economic conditions. With the knowledge to which we have access and with the advantages of mobility, comparative data and the means of information exchange, we are in a position to assist in the sharing of technological know-how. For those who are facing the difficult adjustments necessary in a period of cultural change; for those who have been subjected to fragmentary exposure to modern technology but who are still deprived of the basic necessities of shelter and services; for the victims of natural and man-made disasters who have seen their homes disintegrate; for those who are ciphers in a statistical survey and are numbers to be housed in a planning scheme; for all these and more, we should surely have much of value to offer.

## References


Anon. (n.d.) Craftsmen's inventories of the sixteenth and seventeenth centuries. *Lincolnshire Historian* 11, 6, 17–18.

Batsford, H. and Fry, C. (1938). *The English Cottage*. London: Batsford, pp. 165–67.

Clifton-Taylor, A. (1972). *The Pattern of English Building*. London: Faber and Faber, pp. 163–73, includes Welsh slater's terms.

Doke, C.M. (1931). *The Lambas of Northern Rhodesia. A Study of their Customs and Beliefs*. London: George G. Harrap.

Fathy, H. (1973). *Architecture for the Poor*. University of Chicago Press.

Freese, S. (1971). *Windmills and Millwrighting*. Newton Abbott: David and Charles.

Hartley, D. (1939). *Made in England*. London: Eyre, Methuen Ltd.

Newby, F. (1982). *The Engineers* (Exhibition Catalogue). London: Architectural Association.

Roaf, S. (1982). 'Wind catchers', Chapter 13. In: Beazley, E. and Harverson, M. (eds) *Living with the Desert: Working Buildings of the Iranian Plateau*. Warminster: Aris and Phillips.

Seike, K. (1977). *The Art of Japanese Joinery*. New York: Weatherhill/Tankosha.

Sharp, W.W. (1946). *Australian Methods of Building Construction*. Sydney: Angus and Robertson, Sydney (Chapter 13).

Thompson, d'A. (1917, 1961). *On Growth and Form* (J.T. Bonner, ed.), Cambridge University Press (Chapters 8 and 9).

Wheat, M. (1967). *Survival Arts of the Primitive Paiutes*. Reno: University of Nevada Press, pp. 103–11.

# 9

# Earth as a building material today (1983)

In the unlikely high-tech setting of the Centre Pompidou, an exhibition was held at the close of 1981 which may have marked a new era in the recognition of traditional building materials. Entitled *Des Architectures de Terre ou l'Avenir d'une Tradition Millénaire* it was organized by Jean Dethier with the aid of teams of designers, historians, draughtsmen, model-makers, display builders and producers of the *produits culturels* designed to accompany the exhibition, whose names filled three pages of the lavishly produced catalogue. It was intended that the exhibition should be rehoused in prestigious locations in different countries for the subsequent 5 years, and it was the fervent wish of Dethier and his organizing team that it would promote a renaissance in earth building.

*Des Architectures de Terre* placed great emphasis on the beauty of earth and mud building with seductive photographs of examples from many parts of the world. They were mounted on the backs of panels, made somewhat incongruously from fibreglass, which so strenuously emphasized the decorative nature of some buildings in this material as to create a gingerbread house, Noddy-land imagery. Fortunately, the moulded panels could not detract from the impressive quality of the examples illustrated, although they did reflect the partiality of Jean Dethier for the aesthetic appeal of his subject in such sections as 'De L'Ornamentation. . . ', 'De La Sensualité. . . ', 'Du Confort des Architectures de Terre' (Dethier, 1982). The first half of the exhibition was devoted to traditional building, claiming an ancestry of 10 000 years to the building of Jericho and the Tower of Babel. Stunning examples of earth building in the Sahara, the Middle East, Latin America, China and India, with a sprinkling from Europe and North America, underlined the universality of the employment of the material. But the second half

**Figure 9.1**
The exhibition *Des Architectures du Terre* installed at the Centre Pompidou, Paris, France, 1981.

of the exhibition, rather unconvincingly presented as a large architectural drawing office, displayed beneath innumerable anglepoise lamps the designs of a number of architects who are now using earth as a structural material, especially in North Africa and the United States. At times, the links between the two sections of the exhibition seemed rather slender; the marked change in presentation had a symbolic significance that was not intended by the organizers. Nevertheless, the examples shown, which numbered well in excess of 200, presented an appealing, even glamorous image which characterized what may be seen as the romantic view of architecture in earth.

Some months earlier, in May 1981, an 'International Workshop on Earthen Buildings in Seismic Areas' was held in Albuquerque, New Mexico. Largely funded by the National Science Foundation of Washington DC, it was supported and accommodated by the University of New Mexico at Albuquerque and organized by the Dallas-based concern INTERTECT, which specialized in housing in disaster-prone regions. Of the aesthetics of earth building there was hardly a mention. If the exhibition at the Centre Pompidou focussed on the visual qualities of such architecture, the conference in New Mexico brought its weaknesses into sharp relief. Earth construction is highly vulnerable to certain natural hazards, and being a material with considerable mass and weight, it can be lethal when it collapses. Of all the natural disasters to which it is prone, earth building is probably most affected by earthquakes. The unpredictable nature of seismic movement, and the extraordinary speed and course of earthquake shocks, subject mud walls to violent movement. Effects of 'humping action' which occur when shocks are felt in different directions simultaneously or in rapid succession, create movement in the walls which cause the roofs to fall in. In a series of papers remarkable for their number and sometimes, technical complexity, authorities on earthquakes, engineers, architects and representatives of international agencies described the results of seismic action on towns and villages of mud construction. They listed the extent of the casualties, showed slides of the devastation and in a number of instances, described the problems of conducting research into safe methods of building in earth.

The problems are considerable. If the technology of earth construction might be simple, the technology for testing it is complicated and expensive. Methods of reinforcement of existing buildings, techniques for anchoring ceilings and roofs to side and end walls, tests on types of cracking and failure resulting from particular stresses exerted on simple structures were described in detail. Unblessed with advanced technological aids to research, some contributors described intermediate solutions, such as the railroad flatcars and length of track which were used to test the effects of shocks on the simulated ground (the flat-car bed) on which mud houses had been specially constructed. But how could anyone be sure that the shocks exerted by these means were comparable to those experienced in an earthquake? Even the ingenious engineers at Roorki, India, where these experiments were conducted, could not answer that. Few conventionally built structures are proof against earthquakes and masonry or rubble stone walls can be as potentially dangerous as earthen ones. But mud-built structures are susceptible to other hazards, particularly flood and torrential rainfall which may weaken foundations or wash away walls, altogether. In dry climates they are still subject to erosion and the attacks of termites or other insects. Lime and salts can also attack mud walls and rodents, birds and domestic animals such as goats, can all contribute to damage. Such issues were not discussed at the Albuquerque workshop, which was essentially devoted to earthquake hazard; nevertheless, they must be added to the list of weaknesses which were unmentioned in the Paris exhibition, but which must be recognized if the 'earth renaissance' is ever to be a reality.

In fact, for much of the world the renaissance of earth as a building material is a meaningless concept, in that mud construction, in one of its forms, is still the customary method of building. But the influence of western architecture, and the status given in the developing countries to the use of modern materials has led to widespread

**Figure 9.2**
'Borrow pits' are designated areas from which city residents can obtain desertic soil to build houses. Kano, northern Nigeria.

dismissal of the old methods. Concrete, steel frame construction and plate glass have all acquired prestige, even if they are expensive, unnecessarily used and climatically inappropriate. Standards for building based on western models are frequently invoked to justify the use of imported materials and the rejection of traditional ones, while the areas of potential failure in earth building mentioned above, are cited in support of policies of demolition. In such circumstances, the merits of mud architecture are overlooked. These merits extend far beyond the aesthetic qualities illustrated at the Centre Pompidou. In the first place, earth, soil or mud is cheap to obtain; virtually without cost of itself, it may be obtained on or near the site of building, in theory at least. Building in mud can be labour-intensive and does not require sophisticated techniques, special equipment, or more than a modest level of training in building skills. This means that it is accessible to the unskilled and the poor, so that self-help building is possible among people who are employed in agriculture or other rural occupations. Unlike timber, it is not a renewable material, but it is in vast and ready supply. Moreover, it can be recycled so that even sun-dried earth bricks that have broken or cracked, may be broken down and mixed for use again.

Mud is a compression material; that is, it can take a considerable amount of vertical pressure and additional weight in the form of extra floors, timber joists, wood roofs and often, several storeys. It has little or no tensile strength, however, and this means that it is not a good spanning material in the way that a timber beam, or even

**Figure 9.3**
Roof domes of adobe bricks covering routes of the bazaar at Isfahan, Iran.

a stone slab, might be. Various ingenious solutions to this problem have been developed among indigenous societies where the use of mud has been known for generations, even for many centuries. Successions of finely-wrought domes of sun-dried bricks are built to span bazaar routes in Iran; high parabolic mud brick domes with earthen steps on the exterior surface for use during maintenance, were constructed by the Mousgoum people of Cameroun. These might seem to be universal solutions to the technical problems of spanning spaces with mud bricks, but soils are not consistent in their composition and every soil type used for building demands techniques best suited to it (Argawal, 1981). Reinforcement is one way in which soils are given greater strength and resilience. Wattle-and-daub, the traditional English wall cladding system makes use of the tensile strength and lightness of the interwoven wattles and the capacity of the clay daub to fill all interstices. Clay does not bond well with wood however, and some clays will dry and detach from wood framing. The wattle provides a texture in depth which gives plenty of 'key' to the clay. Similar uses of wood, withies and bark are to be found in many parts of the world. Earth that might be washed away in tropical rainstorms is used with wood in many types of Sub-Saharan African shelter, rings of posts, interlaced wands and branches or meshes of trimmed sticks providing the framework for screen walls that are then plastered with mud. Deep eaves to thatched roofs protect the walls from the washing of heavy rains. Even so, such methods are not necessarily proof against splash-

**Figure 9.4**
Earthen parabolic domes of the Mousgoum, Cameroun, photographed by Marc Allegret in 1912.

back at ground level, nor resistant to termites. Some peoples mix cow dung with the mud which helps make it more resistant. The Maasai of Kenya, whose dwellings appear to be mud plastered are in fact, entirely plastered with cow dung which effectively reduces their vulnerability to wood-boring insects.

Changes have taken place in the methods of earth construction used by various societies, often through the influence of contiguous peoples. So the timber-framed and mud-plastered walls of the Asante were replaced by 'swish', a technique of building first introduced in the Ghanaian forest a century ago. The red lateritic soils are compacted in balls which are laid in courses of approximately half a metre in height, each being permitted to dry before a subsequent course is laid. The strong walls so made, support roofs of timber framing traditionally covered with thatch. Further north, in the savannah regions, clay lump is also used, the Hausa employing *tabale*, or pear-shaped bricks of puddled mud, laid in courses and bonded with mortar of mud and horse dung. These walls are plastered with a preparation of mud and an extract of the pod of the locust bean, to provide a smooth, durable surface. With the aid sometimes of reed reinforcement, relief decorations may be modelled on the facades of the Hausa dwellings and sculpted into decorative and symbolic devices. In recent years the influence of mud brick building from the Saharan fringe has been felt among the Hausa who have adopted techniques which are to be found

**Figure 9.5**
Freshly moulded mud bricks being laid out for drying in the sun. Mali.

in North Africa. Sun-dried bricks approximately 30 cm square, or in other proportions but similar mass are laid in courses and plastered over. Bricks of this type are also extensively used in Egypt, the Sudan and the Middle East. Adobe, the sun-dried brick, is one of the most ubiquitous of mud building methods, its Arabic root indicating the source of the technique. It was widely adopted in Spain and brought to the Americas by the Conquistadores and their successors; today it is to be found extensively in Latin America. In the south-western United States, American Indian sedentary peoples living in pueblos, have used adobe for several centuries (probably pre-Conquest), with sun-dried bricks made of puddled mud. Today, these are shaped in wooden frames that ensure standardized blocks of about 40 × 20 × 10 cm. Adobe, which requires a consistency of rather more sand than clay, the clay binding the sand particles in the block, is ideally met by the soil conditions of New Mexico, Arizona and the state of Mexico.

Another method of mud building which is widely employed is that of rammed earth, or *pisé de terre*. Used in countries as far apart as France, Morocco, India and China, rammed earth walling is constructed by the use of wooden formwork in the form of box-sides (but not top or base), in which the earth is 'rammed' or tamped until it is compacted. Stones and pebbles are normally mixed with the moist soil, which is allowed to dry before the wood frame is placed on the completed layer. The process is then repeated, in the making of the next wall section. Such walls of compacted *pisé* can be extremely durable. Cob walling, the traditional form of mud construction used

**Figure 9.6**
Cob walling with a light mud plaster and lime-wash, and a 'good hat and shoes' (thatched roof and bituminous paint at ground level). Aston, south Devon, UK.

in Devonshire, has a high proportion of fine and coarse sands, some 20 per cent of clay and an aggregate of small stones. In some parts of Devon this occurs naturally, with no further admixture, the 'shillet', or shale and clay soil being ideal for the purpose. The method of building is somewhat similar to that of rammed earth, though wooden shuttering is not used; instead, after shaping a layer of cob, the builders 'tread down' the layer to compact it, and shave down the irregularities to obtain a suitable wall surface. With, in the oft-quoted Devon adage, 'a good hat and a good pair of shoes', or in other words, a good thatched roof to cast off the heavy Devon rains and a black, bituminous paint at ground level to combat splashback, a cob wall can last for centuries (Williams-Ellis, 1919).

As everyone who has lived in an English cob house knows, it is 'warm in winter and cool in summer'. The thermal properties of earthen building are particularly agreeable, and especially suited to hot climates. Earth walls are not so much insulators as climate moderators: they tend to equalize temperatures. Hot tropical sun beating on mud walls inevitably heats them up, but the transfer of heat through the walls is relatively slow. By nightfall, when the air temperature often drops considerably, the warmth has penetrated the room, making it comfortable at night. The walls act as storage heaters gradually surrendering their warmth to the interior. By daytime the process is reversed; the interior is cool and remains so, until the building is again heated by the sun and the warmth transmitted by the end of the day. In climates where ventilation is nonetheless important, other climate modifiers are introduced, such as the *mushrabiyya*, or latticework screens of Egypt and other Middle Eastern countries. Large vessels of water may be used as humidifiers standing in the air flow, and various forms of wind scoops, constructed of mud bricks, are employed to direct cool air into the interiors and promote circulation.

Although the forms of earthen building employed in various parts of the world today are by no means exhausted in this summary, in fact their diversity is scarcely indicated, sufficient examples have been cited to demonstrate a number of significant points. First, mud construction in one form or another is used in countries throughout the world. No one knows how many earthen buildings are currently in use, but in India alone estimates run as high as 80 million dwellings. There is no doubt that considerably more than half of all Indian houses are mud-built. While the African continent is less densely populated, millions of mud dwellings, not to mention mosques, public buildings and even palaces, exist. Combined with wood, saplings, branches, straw mats and other natural materials, many more millions may be included in the total. In the Middle East, in many parts of the Far East and extensively in China, earth building is predominant, while in Central and South America adobe construction is employed in millions more.

A second significant factor is that earth building is directly related to the availability of suitable soils. Ideal are the tropical red soils, lateritic soils or latosols which occur throughout Sub-Saharan Africa west of the Rift Valley and north of the Zambezi. These also occur in much of the Indian subcontinent, China and the Far East, as well as Latin America and the south-east United States. Forest cover over some of these areas, and over the strongly leached, and paradoxically, less fertile soils of the Congo and the Amazon basins, may mean that available timbers and broad leaves take precedence over mud for building. The next principal soil type, the desertic soils, occurs in areas which have little rainfall. Broken rock and sand is an important constituent of this type, which is found in the North American south west, the Sahara and much of North Africa, and throughout the Middle East into Central Asia and Mongolia. The podzolic and grassland soils of Canada and the northern United States, most of Europe and Russia and parts of East Africa and south-eastern South America are also sometimes used for building. Acidic, and found beneath forests in the northern hemisphere, they are less widely used than the timbers they support. Though these generalizations hold good in broad terms local soil variations may account for differences in building type – like the highly localized parabolic domes of the Mousgoum, mentioned earlier, which cannot be built by related peoples only a score of miles away because the consistency of the local clays is not capable of supporting such structures.

Thirdly, mud construction is environmentally suited to the living conditions of hundreds of millions of people in the world. In the arid climates of the North African and Middle Eastern states in particular, where desertic soils prove ideal for building by adobe or sun-dried bricks, the thermal properties of the houses and mosques are very benign. Heat transmitted on the roofs of such buildings may be deflected by combined timber and mud layering, often with additional brush or leaf layers to act as further insulation. The flat roofs are much used by peoples of these regions for drying fruits and for sleeping out of doors. Further protection from the effects of the relentless sun is afforded in these and other tropical regions by building with shared walls, reducing the number of external surfaces, and by winding narrow, shaded lanes between blocks of houses. In forest regions, the combination of mud with timber allows differentiation of walls and roofs, permitting air flow at eaves level. Other climate modifiers abound. A fourth point, of vital importance to the developing world, is that mud, clay, earth or desert soil is abundantly available. With techniques that have been developed to suit the peculiarities of the differing soil qualities, and which have been refined in use over centuries, methods of building exist which exploit their potential. Building may be undertaken on the site where the raw material is found, excavated, mixed and worked,

**Figure 9.7**
Flat roofs of the Dogon town of Sanga, are used for the drying of millet and other crops. Narrow lanes provide effective shading. Bandiagara plateau, Mali.

cutting both importation and transportation costs to zero. As the techniques do not necessarily require advanced learned skills, but a sound knowledge of local traditions, earthen houses can be built by self-help labour. Even if labour differentiation is to be found in some societies which use earth extensively, this is often the work of local builders or of self-building families who thus fit into the balance of indigenous economies. In countless societies, mud building today represents virtually no-cost housing: costing neither paid labour nor purchased materials.

However, there is a fifth issue, which the Albuquerque conference emphasized and which cannot be overlooked. Mud construction is extremely vulnerable to earthquakes and flood. Collapse of load-bearing walls, or of roofs constructed of heavy materials, can cause frightening loss of life as it has done in Turkey, Iran and China in recent years. Adobe bricks weigh around a quarter of a hundred-weight each; a cube foot weighs a hundredweight. The lethal mass of a falling wall on sleeping occupants or of a dislodged timber roof supporting a mud platform can be imagined. Extensive research is being conducted to devise means whereby adobe and earth buildings can be made more safe. Welded steel wire frames within poured mud walls, wooden ring beams to tie in the walls, diagonal corner timbers and rod ties at corner junctions all contribute to safety. But they may also add to the cost, and for those building a low-cost house in a minimal developing world economy, this is a crucial factor. Research programmes in Mexico, Turkey, India, China and elsewhere have been addressing these still largely intractable problems. Assuming that they may be solved for the seismic regions of the world, and bearing in mind that vast areas where mud is used are not subject to seismic risk (most of Africa, for instance) what is the state of earth-building today, and what are its prospects for the future?

Building in earth throughout much of the globe today, is a fact; there is no disputing that it is among the most common of all building materials and in terms of the contribution it makes to the total building stock, it exceeds stone and very probably, timber. It is, however, associated strongly in the bureaucratic mind with 'under-development'. Its very prevalence in the countries of the developing world makes it suspect among those who have set their sights on industrialization. That the importation of cement, steel and other 'modern' building materials is costly is often disregarded because their image is more sophisticated. This is not a minor matter; in all parts of the world where mud is employed there is a fascination for steel, concrete and glass in the western model. Economic necessity, rather than a change of image, might ensure the survival of earthen building, but changing patterns of life-style, increasing urbanization and rural depletion all contribute to a lessening of the knowledge of the necessary skills, and a reduction in the time available for building: seasonal agriculture permits lay-off periods for building and maintenance, but the production schedules of factories do not. As image is so important, it is possible that a change in attitude to earth building in the west could ultimately be of greatest benefit in ensuring its continuation in the future. It has not lacked support, altogether. Apart from the publications of the eighteenth century French architect Francois Cointeraux, who was committed to *pisé de terre*, there have been several advocates of earth architecture (Cointeraux, 1793). In the twentieth century, the British architect-eccentric Clough Williams-Ellis published his *Cottage Building in Cob, Pise, Chalk and Clay* in 1920. Written as a proposed solution to the chronic shortage of housing after the First World War, when six billion bricks were needed to build houses for the working class alone, it was reprinted after the Second World War with a similar purpose. In neither case were its sober and pragmatic recommendations acted upon, even though the successful buildings by Ernest Gimson and designs by Sir Edwin Lutyens were included (Williams-Ellis, 1947). More successful, was the building of New Gourna in Upper Egypt under the direction of the eminent Egyptian architect, Hassan Fathy, between 1946 and 1950 (Fathy, 1973). Designed to house some 900 families, using local labour and earth construction, developing crafts and trades to offset the loss of income from tomb robbing (which had been the Gournis' principal source of money), and training young craftsmen in techniques of dome building and the making of new domestic equipment like a mud brick *kachelofen*, Hassan Fathy was motivated by immense personal conviction. New Gourna was not an unqualified success: bureaucratic opposition and local reluctance could not be wholly overcome; nevertheless it was still a remarkable achievement. Fathy went on to build a large co-operative agricultural college at Baris, in the oasis town of Kharga, Egypt, using the inclined vault system to create forms that were at once traditional and wholly suited to modern demands.

In the United States, there has been a resurgence of adobe building which ranges from self-build, low-cost adobe dwellings in New Mexico and Arizona, to a mosque designed by Hassan Fathy at Abiquiu, and to luxury homes in the pueblo style built on the *Bosque*, in the Rio Grande valley, and costing upwards of a quarter of a million dollars. The latter do not make much of an

**Figure 9.8**
Entrance and health centre house of the Medical Centre at Mopti, Mali, designed by Andre Ravereau, 1976. It won an Aga Khan Award for Architecture, 1983.

argument for economy, but the designs of adobe buildings by architects like William Lumpkins or John MacGowan, with their emphasis on employing passive solar energy, are strong indications of the potential of earthen architecture today. New methods of stabilizing adobe and mud with small admixtures of cement or asphalt are helping builders to overcome the problems of erosion from wind or rain (Doat and Houben, 1979). Soil-cement blocks are extremely durable, providing a building material which seems to meet developing aspirations while being made at very low cost. The Medical

**Figure 9.9**
The clinic of the Medical Centre, after recent structural repairs and 'modernizing'. Mopti, Mali.

Centre at Mopti, designed for the Assistance Médicale de Mali by Andre Ravereau and completed in 1976, was a recipient of an Aga Khan Award for Architecture (Holod and Rastorfer, 1983). The jury praised it for responding 'with great sympathy both to the local culture and to the sensitive surroundings. The design takes into account local traditions and practices, and makes effective use of local materials and techniques of construction'. Such recognition of a building which was of mud brick construction, with some parts of the walls and roof structure of cement-stabilized earth, may do much to overcome resistance to earth building. Nevertheless, it is ironic that the oldest and most widely used of building materials should now have to depend on such advocacy, when the world's expanding multibillion population needs it more than ever.

## References

*Adobe Today* (1980s journal). Old Albuquerque Station, New Mexico.

Argawal, A. (1981). *Mud, Mud: The Potential for Earth-Based Materials for Third World Housing*. London: Earthscan Publications.

Cointeraux, F. (1793). *Schule der Lanbaukunst*. Hildberg-haussen, Germany.

Dethier, J. (1982). *Down to Earth. Mud Architecture: An Old Idea, a New Future*. London: Thames and Hudson.

Doat, P. and Houben, H. (eds). (1979). *Construire en Terre*. CRATerre, Editions Paris: Alternatives et Paralleles.

Fathy, H. (1973). *Architecture for the Poor*. University of Chicago Press.

Holod, R. and Rastorfer, D. (eds). (1983). Mopti Medical Centre, Mopti, 1976. In: *Architecture and Community: Building in the Islamic World Today*. Aga Khan Award for Architecture. New York: Aperture.

Williams-Ellis, C. (1919, revised edn 1947). *Building in Cob, Pise and Stabilized Earth*. London: Country Life.

## Additional references

Norton, J. (1997). *Building with Earth. A Handbook*. Intermediate Technology Publications.

# 10

# Handed down architecture: Tradition and transmission (1989)

Since the early 1970s we have seen the gradual adoption of the adjective 'traditional' to describe buildings that have previously been termed 'primitive', 'folk', 'indigenous' or 'vernacular'. *Traditional Domestic Architecture of Japan* by Teiji Itoh (1972), Susan Denyer's *African Traditional Architecture* (1978), *Traditional Architecture of Afghanistan* by Hallett and Samizay (1980), Friedrich Schwerdtfeger's *Traditional Housing in African Cities* (1982) or Anita and Viera Larsson's *Traditional Tswana Architecture* (1984) are cases in point; to these we can add books by Lewcock and Freeth (1978), Kaj Blegvad Andersen (1977) and others. (We might also note the broad acceptance of 'architecture' to describe buildings in which architects as designers played no part, but that is another matter.) Implicit in the titles and the texts is the assumption that we are agreed on what 'traditional' means in terms of architecture; there is little in the way of explanation of its use and application in these works. 'Tradition' is defined in *The Concise Oxford Dictionary* as 'opinion or belief or custom handed down from ancestors to posterity'; as 'doctrine supposed to have divine authority but not committed to writing'; and as 'artistic or literary principles based on accumulated experience or continuous usage' (1954). The problem with these definitions, insofar as they are relevant to architecture or to the uses to which buildings are put, is that they are as applicable to a Mayan temple or a Gothic cathedral as they are to any of the kinds of building represented in the books mentioned above. We may observe though, that belief, custom, doctrine or principles refer to concepts *about* the 'traditional' ('pertaining to tradition') rather than to material artefacts.

**Figure 10.1**
A traditional Iban Dyak longhouse, raised on piles, and with *bileks*, or domestic units, fronting on to shared spaces covered by a common roof. Sarawak, Borneo island.

tradition and custom. 'The object and characteristic of "traditions"', he wrote, 'is invariance. The past, real or invented, to which they refer imposes, fixed (normally formalized) practices, such as repetition. "Custom" ... does not preclude innovation and change up to a point ... (it) cannot afford to be invariant because even in "traditional" societies life is not so' (Hobsbawm and Ranger, 1983). Stated in semiological terms, tradition as interpreted here is the rule system, the *langue*, while custom is the manner in which it was practised or exercised, the *parole*. It can be argued that there can be no change without tradition; that tradition provides the matrix within which any changes may be introduced. Even so, the rate of change may be virtually imperceptible, as small innovations and modifications are tried, repeated and proved to be effective and gradually incorporated into customary practice, or are found wanting and

**Figure 10.2**
A modern Iban longhouse with areas corresponding with the *bileks* identified by different colours and access ladders. Brunei, Borneo.

dropped. The deliberate solution of problems encountered in specific construction contexts and the devising of skills to meet them, occur in every part of the world. As Malinowski demonstrated many years ago, all societies change, however slowly (Malinowski, 1945).

Yet, if some changes are brought about by subtle influence or modest innovation, others may be sudden and brutal. Military conquest may bring in its wake dramatic changes which may lead to the colonization of building styles. One need go no further for examples than the pervasive Turkish architecture in Albania, or the presence of Venetian houses on Greek islands. There may be change as a result of religious conversion, such as the adoption of North African plans and forms by Islamized West Africa. Change may be induced by edict, Henry VIII's requirement that timber houses should be built with box frames so that more trees could be saved for the building of the fleet, being one such instance. Or it may be the result of the deliberate initiation of a new technology, like the introduction by the British in the Sudan of fired bricks, using the clamp kiln.

**Figure 10.3**
Diffusion: A Toba Batak house which has the characteristic saddle roof. Northern Sumatra, Indonesia (see also Figures 3.5 and 7.6).

While such forms of induced change may be effected by conflicting with local traditional practices, eventually they are likely to become accepted traditions in themselves.

Isolation notwithstanding, the processes of borrowing and adaptation by contiguous societies, of elements which are acceptable or seem appropriate to their needs, may be traced in many cultures. They may be of a purely practical or structural nature, or they may be of symbolic or decorative import; sometimes a combination of both, like the distribution of 'saddle' roof structures in south-west Asia (Domenig, 1980). 'Culture is transmitted geographically as well as chronologically, in space as well as in time, by contagion as well as by repetition' wrote A.L. Kroeber, 'the spread in area is generally called *diffusion*, as the internal handling through time is called *tradition*'. Kroeber, in fact, placed less importance than some other writers on the *traditum*. 'The terms "social inheritance", or "tradition" put the emphasis on how culture is acquired rather than what it consists of'. Culture, he argued, 'consists of conditioned or learned activities (plus the manufactured results of these); and the idea of learning brings us back again to what is socially transmitted, what is received from tradition, what is "acquired by man as a member of societies." So perhaps *how it comes to be* is really more distinctive of culture than what it is' (Kroeber, 1923).

Definitions of 'tradition' have much in common. 'Generally speaking, "tradition" covers the total cultural heritage handed down from one generation to the next', summarized Kazimierz Dobrowolski (1958) when writing on peasant culture in southern Poland. Like other writers, including some quoted above, he used the phrase 'handed down' to describe the process whereby the continuity of tradition is maintained. It is persistently used to describe the process whereby tradition is maintained – there is hardly any definition of 'tradition' in which it does not appear – 'handing down' is almost always used metaphorically. With the exception of certain ritual contexts, such as the transfer of a symbol of office or rule, a sceptre perhaps, to a new political or spiritual leader, or the giving of a trousseau or dowry where parents may pass on family heirlooms, little is literally 'handed down'. Even here, 'handed on' might be a better term. Yet, if the metaphor is an overworked one and often thoughtlessly applied, there is general agreement that a fundamental characteristic of tradition is that it is *transmitted* from one group to another, or from an individual to another. Usually, the process is assumed to have a temporal, rather than a spatial dimension, and to be diachronic rather than synchronic. Diffusion apart, the transmission of a tradition, or *traditum*, is most often seen to be from its guardians to their successors.

If transmission is of the essence of tradition, it would seem imperative that its nature is given serious attention. 'In all the great cultural undertakings of the human race, the oral transmission of tradition plays a great role', Edward Shils observed. 'In the production of material objects such as sculptures, paintings, and buildings, the instruction of the novice must to a large extent be oral, even though observation and empathy also provide guidance, as do written manuals, drawings, and models' (Shils, 1981). But Shils had far less to say on the subject of oral transmission than he had on transmission through texts, and less to say on the traditions of the common people than he had on the esoteric knowledge of priesthoods and intellectual elites. With his concern for the culture of the peasantry, Kazimierz Dobrowolski gave more attention to the processes of transmission, noting that the passing of the social heritage by speech or other stimuli, which are received by the sense of hearing, or which are visually perceived demonstrations of actions and objects, always involves direct human contact. Transmission media of a mechanical character, including print, musical scores and phonographs, relieve the producers and receivers of the cultural content from such contact and establish only an indirect and impersonal relationship. Observing that 'traditional culture' is customarily used by ethnographers to mean 'cultural contents and values *which are transmitted orally*', he noted the conservatism and stabilizing 'propensity for the preservation and maintenance of the existing social order', within peasant traditional culture. The past 'supplies a pattern for living and provides a model for human action'. Oral transmission, in his view, had a limited capacity for cultural transfer from one generation to its successors, affecting the quantity and quality of what was passed on. This resulted in a decline in the public memory, opening the way for the slow processes of change and replacement, older usages falling irrevocably into the 'limbo of social oblivion'.

Against this loss of folk memory, peasant craftsmen had their own defences. The village carpenters of Podhale used neither drawn plans nor written calculations: 'their entire technological knowledge was based exclusively on memory and was reduced to the repetition, in practical action, of a few basic models ... a larger, two-roomed house, and a smaller one having one room only, with certain variants which consisted of adding summer-rooms and stores (*kamora*)'. The family likenesses between artefacts and buildings so frequently noted and admired in the architecture of preliterate societies, is thus seen as the outcome of the need for the survival of a technological tradition and a control against change. Dobrowolski concluded that there was a relative paucity of different examples of material culture when these were compared with the highly developed system of behavioural patterns. 'On the one hand we have a limited number of such material arrangements as types of houses, plans of the interior, furniture, dress, ornaments, etc., and on the other, a great number of highly differentiated social situations, each demanding a special, customarily prescribed form of conduct' (Dobrowolski, 1958). Though some may not agree with this view, Dobrowolski's analysis of the effectiveness, strengths and limitations of the transmission of tradition in peasant societies is a key text in an inadequately studied field. Oral transmission was of the essence of peasant traditional culture in Dobrowolski's discussion; and it may also be seen to be a distinguishing characteristic of most traditional societies. Yet, in spite of the large number of volumes and articles on such peoples and their culture, the nature, kinds and extent of oral transmission – or indeed any other form of transmission – has been seldom researched in any depth.

In spite of the fact that there is an increasing literature on 'oral history' (there is an Oral History Association in the United States, and an Oral History Society in Britain), the bulk of the material gathered and discussed has been the result of oral transmission between interviewer and interviewee. Its purpose is the documentation of the culture of the nonliterate, which 'offers a challenge to the accepted myths of history, to the authoritarian judgement inherent in its tradition. It provides a means for a radical transformation of history', Paul Thompson wrote, claiming that 'oral history gives history back to the people in their own words. And in giving a past, it also helps them towards a future of their own making' (Thompson, 1978). It is a proud claim, but a dubious one. Oral history is not about oral transmission *within* a culture, where history does not need to be 'given back'. It is through internal oral transmission that the people move towards a future of their own making, and not through documentation by scholars. Even when they describe their techniques of building to specialists in vernacular architecture, craftsmen may use neither the means nor the terminology that they employ when instructing a novice. Oral and other forms of transmission of tradition within cultures have vehicles about which we know little. The Belgian historian and anthropologist Jan Vansina is singular in having devoted a complete work to the subject. Even he is largely concerned with oral traditions as historical sources, and is interested in the reliability of 'historical information that can be derived from oral testimonies' (Vansina, 1961). Perhaps for this reason he does not make a clear enough distinction between transmission among members of a society, and transmission from informant within a society to external interviewer. Nevertheless, the extent of his fieldwork and the breadth of his study make it a valuable guide to the processes of oral transmission.

Important sections of Vansina's work identify many of the characteristics of oral transmission: the chain of transmission, the structure of testimony, esoteric traditions and mnemonic devices; and many of the problems – failure of memory, the personality of the informant, the bearing of cultural values on informant and testimony. But these are factors which may differ in diverse contexts. Overriding them are the vehicles used to communicate testimony. Vansina proposes a typology based on criteria that include the purpose, significance, form and manner of transmission. He divides oral tradition into five categories: *Formulae, Poetry, Lists, Tales* and *Commentaries*, some having subcategories (official and private roles for poetry; historical, didactic, artistic and personal subcategories for tales); each category has a number of types. If his list does not encompass all that might be employed in the passing on of traditions in the making or use of buildings, it is sufficiently relevant to warrant summarizing. *Formulae* consist of stereotyped phrases which may contain archaic elements, but which are transmitted with accuracy. They include titles, slogans, didactic formulae such as proverbs or riddles, and ritual formulae such as spells or oaths. *Poetry* also has fixed forms but the form and content have, in the values of the society, artistic merit. Historical songs and poems (whether accurate or idealized records), panegyric poetry often incorporating stereotypical phrases, and religious poetry in the form of prayer, hymns or dogmatic texts, all have official functions. Personal poetry, such as laments, may be of a private nature. *Lists* of place names may record migration routes, or may be used to defend land rights, while lists of personal names include genealogies. *Tales* are narratives characterized by prose composition. They may recount the general history of a people, the local history of a community, or family history. Myths are didactic tales, of a religious character and with a moral purpose, whereas aetiological myths explain origins in other terms. Vansina identifies as subtypes, local legends, tales accounting for natural phenomena, popular etymologies, and stories about cultural traits. Tales told for artistic merit form a separate category, while personal recollections constitute another. Finally, *commentaries* are supplementary information to other data, or are transmitted in a particular context. Legal precedents, explanatory commentaries and occasional comments given as brief observations or answers, fall within this category. As Vansina acknowledged, his categorization was a 'rough outline', but it served to emphasize the 'diversity of types which exist, and to show that each type has its own usefulness, and provides one particular kind of information only' (Vansina, 1961). These types often have distinct structures and sequences. They do not constitute all the means of oral transmission used or available but rather, those that are in themselves, traditions. A few examples must suffice to illustrate the relevance of some of these types of oral transmission to the processes whereby buildings 'come to be' or are used.

Although Jan Vansina's draft of a typology of oral transmission was compiled with anthropological, and particularly, historical purposes in view, it offers a framework on which a typology related to the workings of tradition in architecture might be directed. By

**Figure 10.4**
Houses in a small Fijian village. All houses stand on family sites occupied by successive generations, bordering the communal and ceremonial ground. Fiji Island.



applying some examples of oral transmission with architectural significance to his typology, its applicability and its shortcomings may be observed. For this reason I propose to follow his sequence, giving examples within each category, and some, if not all, of his types. As noted above, *formulae* is the first category, with 'titles' the initial type. House names might be a suitable architectural equivalent of the latter. 'The name of the house (*inoa paito*) remains; the names of individual men (*inoa tanata*) disappear' said the people of Tikopia. The inhabitants of the island gave their houses permanent names, such as Ratia or Niukapu, which were related to the names of kinship groups. When a house collapsed its name remained associated with the site and a new house would bear it. Lying somewhere between an honorific title and a place name, such an identification of a house site was, in Raymond Firth's words, 'a valuable mechanism for the preservation of social continuity' (Firth, 1957). The permanence of the site and the transitory nature of the family has a corresponding sentiment in the Maori slogan 'The home is permanent, the man flits'.

In many societies, 'didactic formulae' such as proverbs, aphorisms and sayings, draw upon building to point a moral. 'Never think a home is yours until you have made one yourself' said the Winnebago, while the Yoruba of Nigeria favoured gradualism with the proverb: 'If you are not able to build a house at once, you first build a shed'. In Ethiopia, the Gurage warn that 'you cannot build a house for last year's summer'. Sayings directed to the craftsman himself have many counterparts to the English aphorism that 'a bad workman always blames his tools'. But if the meaning here is clear enough, proverbs and sayings may often be deliberately obscure, as one Swahili pithily explained. 'When they do not want a person to understand, they use a double meaning, saying for example, "If you pass elephant's dung you will split your anus," meaning, if you see someone build a fine house, and you want one like it but have not the money to build it, you will steal and get into trouble. That is what it means' (Allen, 1981). 'Ritual formulae' in particular, may be couched in oblique or esoteric language, fully known and learned only by the initiated. They may be used in religious or magic rites associated with, for example the selection of sites, the dedication of house posts or the blessing of the dwelling. The efficacy of the ritual is usually considered to be dependent on the precise repetition of the incantations and rites of the ceremonial. For instance, among the Lao Song of Thailand, the builder of a new house celebrates its completion with the *sen phi* ceremony to the ancestors, with appropriate rituals, recitations from the scriptures, blessings and consecration. With the *liang phra*, the ritual 'feeding of the monks' he gains *tham bun ban*, 'merit making in the house', with which he seeks to ensure the security of the dwelling (Pedersen, 1982).

In Vansina's classification, *poetry* embraces types which may often overlap, both with the functions of ritual and within the category itself. He does not accommodate song in his classification, though many kinds of poem are sung, just as formulae may be chanted. Apart from revealing the values of a society towards the building, they may be instructive of the processes of making it. A song cycle translated from the Riradjingo of the Goulburn Island, north-eastern Arnhem Land, described the raising of stilt houses:

> Erecting forked sticks and rafters, posts for the floor, making the roof of the hut like a sea-eagle's nest:
>
> They are always there, at the billabong of three goose eggs, at the wide expanse of water . . .

> As they build, they think of the monsoon rains – rain and wind from the west, clouds spreading over the billabong . . .
> They cover the sides of the hut, placing rails on forked sticks.
> We saw the heaving chests of the builders, calling invocations for the clouds rising in the west . . .
> Making the door of the hut, preparing it within . . .
> They think of the coming rain, and the west wind . . . wind bringing the rain, spreading over the country.
> Carefully, therefore, prepare the hut, with its roof and its posts . . .
> (Berndt, 1976)

Other songs speak of living in the dwelling, of happiness, domesticity or sometimes, of the struggle for shelter. 'The Rain-man's Praise Song of Himself' was noted among the Aadonga of Angola:

> No house is ever too thick-built
> To keep me, the rain, from getting in.
> I am well-known to huts and roofs,
> A grandson of Never-Been-There.
> I am mother of the finest grasses,
> Father of green field everywhere.
> My arrows do not miss their aim,
> They strike the owner of huts.
> I am a terror to clay walls and the architecture of termites . . .
> (Pettinen, 1926)

*Lists* follow poems. Locations on migration routes and place names may have some relevance to the study of traditional architecture, providing information that may indicate patterns of diffusion and influence. But within popular culture they can have other functional purposes. The stone roofs of the Cotswold houses in England are clad with thin flat slabs, or 'tiles', split by frost and drilled to take wooden pegs. As a young 'slatter' or roof-maker, Gilbert Peachey of the village of Chadworth, when aged fourteen, started to 'pick up the rubbish and sort all the tiles out . . . when you sort a few thousand out to go on a roof you very soon learn the names of the measurements but you never finish learning the tiling itself'. Like other apprentices to the craft he learned the list of traditional dimensions on the 'slatter's rule', starting with the smallest: 'short-cocks, middle cocks and long-cocks; short cuttings, long cuttings; muffeties; bachelors; short nines and long nines; short whippets and long whippets; short elevens and long elevens; short becks and long becks. . . .' the numerals indicating the introduction of imperial measurements (Peachey, c. 1970). Lists of measurements may also be learned by heart, and systems other than metric

**Figure 10.5**
Stack of thin Cotswold stone tiles with drilled holes for hanging. Irregular shapes will be covered by successive layers, exposed leading edges being trimmed square.

and imperial have persisted until recently, among them the Swahili units:

| | |
|---|---|
| *shibiri* | A hand-span from thumb-tip to fourth fingertip |
| *dhiraa* | A cubit or half a yard. Also called *mkono* |
| *pima* | Four *dhiraa* or a fathom |
| *jora* | Sixty *dhiraa* or a bolt of cloth |

More recently, imperial measurements have their Swahili equivalents, the *inchi, futi, yadi* and the *maili* (mile) (Zaslavsky, 1973).

Both the methods of building and the values associated with it may be present in *tales* told after dark. Through them the young may be prepared for their future roles, as well as being entertained by stories. The 'Glaistig Lianachan', a local folk tale from Lochaber in the Scottish Highlands, for example, tells of Big Black Gillie MacCuaraig who was abducted by mythical Glaistig at a river ford. To secure her freedom she promised him 'a big house, well-built, into which spells of fire, or water, or arrow of iron could not penetrate and that he would get it dry, sheltered, and with a blessing upon him against armed men and the fairies' – all in a single night. With a loud scream she summoned the fairies to her aid. As Mrs Ryan, born Clementine MacDonell of Keppoch retold the legend: 'they brought flags and stones from the Fall of Clainaigh, and they were passing them from hand to hand. And on the inch they were cutting cabers and the taobhan – the long rafters, smooth and flat from the Wood of Caoranach. And she was saying without a pause, "One stone on the top of two stones. Two stones on the top of one stone, sharp sticks, turves, wattle, pins from every tree but the wild cherry." And in the graying of the day, there was turf over the ridge and smoke out of it . . . ' When the Glaistig denied Big Black Gillie her freedom she put a curse on him 'that he should wither like the bracken and grow old like the rushes . . . and he should have no sons in his own place. And it is still said in that country that this curse came true indeed' (Grant, 1961).

If the purpose of the aetiological myth is to account for the origin of phenomena and may therefore refer to non-historical time, it may still be revealing of values related to quite specific aspects of building – even to the unlikely theme of the origin of the 'privy'. According to one Maori aetiological myth the first *heketua*, or latrine, was made by Mauima, the eldest of the ancestral culture heroes, the Maui brothers. Hunting for his sister he learned from one Rehua that she was held on the island of Motutapu. Turning himself into Rupe, a pigeon, he rescued her and bore her to Rehua's village, which was polluted by excrement as its people were too lazy to clean it. Unaided, Rupe cleaned the village and, as the verse-myth explained,

> Also made by him
> Was the latrine for disposing
> Of the filth.
> Also erected was the post
> For the hand hold,
> The name of that post
> Being the Post-of-Whaitiri.
> And all was finished.

The myth goes on to describe how Kaitangata, the son of Rehua, saw the latrine, which was built on the edge of a cliff, and decided to try it out. 'When he reached the side of that cross beam, he lifted one of his feet onto that cross beam and squatted.' Stretching out his hand he grasped the Post-of-Whaitiri and strained back, 'thinking vainly that it was firm, but no, the post pulled up, that man fell, was killed immediately, and did not recover.' As he fell his blood stained the sky, and thereafter a red streak in the sky was called *Ka tuhi Kaitangata*. Many Maoris concluded that Rupe deliberately loosened the post so that Kaitangata would be killed, as a punishment to Rehua because his people failed to help clean their village (Buck, 1950).

The final category, *commentaries*, includes legal statements, explanations and brief comments. These, Vansina argues, have a legal or didactic purpose and are therefore invaluable microtraditions. Such accounts, though frequently noted by researchers, are usually reworked for subsequent incorporation in a paper. A description given by a Portland quarryman, Harry Hounsell, while splitting a large rock prior to breaking it up for building stone, is an example:

> Well, we're trying to ream this rock off the bed, a piece of rock of about two hundred tons, approximately. Well, the process is puttin' in pig placers, that's pieces of cast steel about inch and a half thick, fifteen inches long and about six inches wide. And you work your placers up under the rock, what you call on the risin'. Well after you got your placers in you fix your pigs in, nice and tight. Then you knock these wedges in and the wedges is about fifteen inches long and two inches wide and they're tapered down to a very sharp – taper. Well you might have five placers under this rock here, now, and you knock all your wedges in. And you have a chant – somebody give you a chant for to keep in time.

**Figure 10.6**
Evidence of the early splitting of granite rocks by the placer and wedges method, found in numerous locations on Dartmoor, Devon, UK.

> The rock must be struck altogether, not one after the other, for to get your weight behind your wedges, what they call reamin' your rock out before you start cuttin' out.

And the quarrymen returned to work, with Harry Hounsell leading them with a work-chant (Hounsell, 1954).

In considering these examples of oral transmission in the frame of Jan Vansina's typology, I am very much aware that some have been driven in like Harry Hounsell's wedges; they were not a natural fit. In part, this is due to the typology itself, which lays emphasis on formulaic oral transmission and does not include informal or spontaneous observations and narratives. This limitation, which places a low premium on creativity, also omits any kinds of mutual exchange or argument. Even in the notes to the final category, which includes brief comments, he stresses their formulaic nature. Though I have included examples of song to illustrate the categories, in fact he makes no reference to song as such, but only to poetry. Ballads, folk song, popular verse, children's rhymes are among the kinds of oral tradition which find no place among the types – even though many are highly formulaic in structure and have proven longevity. These omissions notwithstanding, the typology has been useful in demonstrating some of the kinds of oral transmission that throw light on aspects of popular involvement in architecture. It also reveals, if incidentally, a number of other facets of the subject. Among these is the question of the identities of the transmitters and the receivers of the 'testimonies'. Unfortunately, many of the sources of the examples cited are by no means clear on this point, and it cannot be assumed that these are evidence of oral transmission in process. In some instances they may have been heard and noted in the act of transmission; in others they may have been heard and subsequently repeated at the interviewer's request, and in still others they may be the record of direct oral transmission between informant and interviewer.

Traditions are reputedly 'handed on' from 'generation to generation', but the nature of the generation is seldom identified. A generation may be considered as the average period that elapses before children are in a position to replace their parents. Three to five generations might span a century. It is sometimes considered that it takes three generations to establish a tradition, though members of a club will know that a 'tradition' can be accepted in a cycle of three meetings. Elders to youth, priests to initiates, fathers to sons, mothers to daughters, masters to apprentices, craftsmen to novices, children to their juniors – the generations who transmit traditions differ according to their age, gender, role and function. The occasion of transmission is significant: some traditions are passed in secret, some in formal circumstances, some in anger, some in affection. They may be a part of ritual, as a means towards the acquisition of skills, as entertainment, as learning through play, as socialization within the family and the community. The kind of the society, its cultural identity and location may all affect both the nature of the traditions transmitted and the importance placed upon them by its members. It is perhaps worth drawing attention to the fact that the examples cited above were recorded in tribal, folk, peasant and popular communities (acknowledging that in the present context these terms are unqualified). The contexts included day labour, house-building, tale-telling and ceremonial, among others.

All the foregoing discussion has been in relation to oral transmission, but many of the circumstances indicated apply equally to other forms of transmission: mimicry, mime, acting, dance, music, play, gesture, painting, carving, modelling and model-making being among the kinds of non-verbal communication which carry and sustain traditions. Many of these have direct bearing upon architecture, in building, decoration, occupation and use. Whatever the means of communication and the social circumstances in which it takes place, it is the message which is of ultimate importance, and this is related to the specific purpose for which it is intended. In architecture this involves a great many issues, too many to

**Figure 10.7**
Transmission between carpenters and their young apprentices by demonstration and traditions of oral instruction. Nanjing region, China.

detail here. But we are aware that they include the physical environment and site, natural resources and the nature of the economy. They involve settlement pattern and orientation, location and spatial organization, social structure and family type, territory and inheritance.

Structural systems, preparation of materials, construction methods, skills and technologies are fundamental to building. But the cycle of the seasons, age and gender, concepts of public and private space, the proprieties of behavioural norms can all be reflected in occupation and utility, while religion and belief, symbols and signification may be implicit in the use of space or explicit in detail and ornament. All are defined or influenced by tradition and are subject to change, however subtle (Oliver, 1987, 2003). It would seem obvious, therefore, that the nature, purpose and content of oral and non-verbal forms of transmission would be fundamental to the study of 'traditional architecture'. Yet such is not the case. In spite of the vast quantity of studies of vernacular buildings, measured, drawn in plan, section and elevation, described in technical detail; in spite of the fewer, but still numerous studies of their use and the occasional analyses of their symbolism, the verbatim record of the transmission of the traditions in the processes involved is exceptionally rare (McAllester, 1980; Blier, 1987). With the partial exception of the account of the Lao Song ritual, none of the examples cited above was specifically recorded to illumine the transmission of tradition in building.

In a sense it can be argued that there is no such thing as a 'traditional building', no larger field of 'traditional architecture'. There are only buildings which embody traditions. I would argue that this most neglected area of study is also the most pressing, and ultimately, the most important. As yet I offer no general theory to encompass it, believing that the paucity of research does not justify it. But this may be a step towards that end.

## References

Allen, J. (1903, trans. 1981). *The Customs of the Swahili People*. Berkeley: University of California Press, p. 289.

Berndt, R. (1976). Three faces of love. *Traditional Aboriginal Song-Poetry*. Melbourne: Thomas Nelson.

Blier, S. (1987). *The Anatomy of Architecture: Ontology and Metaphor in Batammaliba Architectural Expression*. New York: Cambridge University Press.

Buck, Sir P. (1950). *The Coming of the Maori*. Maori Purposes Fund Board. Wellington: Whitcombe and Tombs.
Denyer, S. (1978). *African Traditional Architecture*. London: Heinemann.
Dobrowolski, K. (1958). Peasant traditional culture. In: Shanin, T. (ed.). *Peasants and Peasant Societies*. Harmondsworth: Penguin Books.
Domenig, G. (1980). *Tektonic im Primitiven Dachbau*. Zurich: ETH.
Firth, R. (1936, 1957). *We, The Tikopia*. London: George Allen & Unwin, pp. 82–87.
Grant, I. (1961). *Highland Folk Ways*. London: Routledge & Kegan Paul, pp. 147–49.
Hallet, S.I. and Samizay, R. (1980). *Traditional Architecture of Afghanistan*. New York: Garland.
Hobsbawm, E. and Ranger, R. (1983). *The Invention of Tradition*. Cambridge University Press, p. 2.
Hounsell, H. (Interview with Peter Kennedy). (1954). *Knock, Ream and Bash: Work Chants and Stoneworkers' Shanties*. Folktracks, FSC-30-203.
Itoh, T. (1972). *Traditional Domestic Architecture of Japan*. New York: Weatherhill.
Kroeber, A. (1923, 1963). *Anthropology: Culture Patterns and Processes*. Harcourt Brace and Wold, p. 219.
McAllester, D. and McAllester, S. (1980). *Hogans: Navajo Houses and Songs*. Middleton, Conn: Weslyan University Press.
Malinowski, B. (1945, 1965). *The Dynamics of Culture Change*. Yale University Press.
Oliver, P. (2003). *Dwellings: The House Across the World*. Oxford: Phaidon Press.
Peachey, G. (Interview with Turner, J. c. 1970). *Cotswold Craftsmen*. Saydisc SDL247.
Pedersen, L. (1982). The influence of the spirit world on the habitation of the Lao Song dam, Thailand. In: Izikowitz, K.-G. and Sorensen, P. (eds). *The House in East and South-East Asia, Anthropological and Architectural Aspects*. Scandinavian Institute of Asian Studies, monograph No. 30, Curzon Press, pp. 119–22.
Pettinen, A. (1926). Sagen und Myther der Anadonga. Reprinted in Trask, W. (trans. 1969). *The Unwritten Song*, Vol. 1. London: Jonathan Cape.
Redfield, R. (1956). Letter in Singer, *ibid*, p. 10.
Schwerdtfeger, F. W. (1982). *Traditional Housing in African Cities*. Chichester: John Wiley.
Shils, E. (1981). *Tradition*. London: Faber & Faber, p. 12.
Singer, M. (1972). *When a Great Tradition Modernises*. New York: Praeger, p. 4.
Thompson, P. (1978). *The Voice of the Past: Oral History*. Oxford University Press, p. 226.
Vansina, J. (1961, 1965). *Oral Tradition: A Study in Historical Methodology*. London: Routledge & Kegan Paul, pp. 1–18.
Weber, M. (1947). *The Theory of Social and Economic Organisation*. London: Collier-Macmillan, p. 341.
Zaslavsky, C. (1973). *Africa Counts: Number and Pattern in African Culture*. Westport: Laurence Hill, pp. 88–89.

# 11

# Technology transfer: A vernacular view (2003)

Before any discussion of the means involved, the necessity for technological transfer and whether it is related to building construction or to materials, services, installations and methods could, and in my opinion should, be debated. Implicit in the phrase is the assumption that the technology of the west (especially Europe and North America) should be passed to cultures and countries of the one-time 'Third World', now the 'Developing World'. In this term is built a further assumption: that 'development' is technological, rather than for instance, educational or social. It is important, I believe, that we question our own terms, our sense of priorities and our perception of the 'need' for technological transfer. Is the transfer to be one-way only, even though concepts and devices, from the zero to the astrolabe, the wheel and the windmill to the pointed arch and the bungalow, were the inventions of the east transmitted to the west? We may rightly be critical of the arrogance of former attempts at technological transfer made without consideration of the cultures affected. But, we should also be prepared to criticize the presumption that we in the west have the 'answers', which we wish to transfer to the 'primitive' or 'retarded', the 'backward' or 'developing'.

A related question, which is also uncomfortable but needs to be addressed, concerns the desire to ascertain what the basis may be for a recipient community's reluctance to admit introduced technologies. We seek to understand indigenous cultural values, in order that any obstructions to the acceptance of innovations can be overcome. Is the desire to defeat such resistance, which will doubtless be interpreted as ignorance or prejudice, justified? Of course, we will argue that it is; that the advantages of certain western advanced technologies should be for the 'benefit' of everyone. Knowing indeed, how beneficial they are, we should find the means

**Figure 11.1**
Kits of tools hung on farmhouse wall, above a manual lathe and other implements of wood and iron. Eastern Slovenia.

to communicate them. In other words, whether a culture has the naiveté or the peculiarities of belief that makes the introduction of new technologies unacceptable, it is our responsibility to combat such resistance in their interests. Responsibility? Their interests? – or our self-interest? What drives our desire to make our innovations so intrusive? Is it altruism, the 'regard for others, as a principle of action' (Oxford English Dictionary)? Is it driven by a desire to dominate and to colonize, however masked or subconscious the desire might be? Or is it fundamentally commercial, with the marketing of products a major motivation, even if they are thought to be to the advantage of the recipients? Even if we deny that we have neither of the latter intentions in mind, our claims for 'altruism' still raise the question of the identity of the 'others' for whom we have 'regard'. It is not an idle query, for it highlights the problems of how those we believe to be in need of unfamiliar technologies are identified and how their requirements are ascertained, appraised and evaluated. These uncertainties and doubts come to mind as I consider the means, the processes and outcomes of introduced technologies or changes in practice in the past and in 'vernacular' communities. I feel that they should be given serious consideration by any and all who embark upon the intrusive and frequently uncalled-for transfer of technologies. Regrettably, the ethics of intervention are rarely, if ever discussed (Oliver, 2000).

What lessons may be learned and what good may come from such undertakings, are unknowable until the principles have become action and the results of the actions have been experienced. In this presentation I can only cite a few examples from the past and the present and, bearing in mind that they have often been poorly documented, if at all, draw some conclusions which are by no means infallible. Just where we might begin is in itself suspect, for the nature of technology may be said to begin with the flaking of flint and the carving of antlers, the transmission of which raises problems enough (Gamble, 1986). It is becoming increasingly evident that Palaeolithic hominids developed both the technologies and the cross-continental routes and contacts, for mammoth ivory from the Balkans is known to have been used by cave-dwellers in Iberia during the first Ice Age. Evident we may say, though irrelevant. But is it?

On a remote part of the west coast of the Cape York peninsula, Australia, lived an aboriginal people with a Palaeolithic economy, the Yir Yoront, who had few contacts with Europeans until the twentieth century. The skills, resources and techniques in making stone axes, which were their universal tools, were a male preserve, and the axes could only be borrowed by women or children, in accord with the rules of kinship. Apart from this, Yir Yoront social structure was not hierarchical; there were no chiefs, but patrilineal totemic clans defined status, roles, behaviours and values. The stone for the axes was obtained through a chain of trading partnerships from 400 miles to the south, the Yir Yoront providing in turn, hunting spears and spear-throwers, which gained value as they were passed along the trading chain. In 1915, an Anglican mission was established in the territory but the Yir Yoront had little to do with it until the 1930s, when the missionaries sought to raise aboriginal living standards, supplying them with useful and 'improving' articles, including a short-handled steel axe. Missionaries believed that the steel axe would be more efficient and save time, although in fact, it made little difference in use, and the time saved was spent in sleep. But it had a major impact on the social structure, for the working parties they introduced at the mission and on the cattle stations (with steel axes as rewards) were organized on a leader-and-group basis, contrary to the Yir Yoront non-hierarchical system. Welcomed by individuals in the tribe, the steel axes were given to women and young men, who no longer depended on the older men for them, upsetting the traditional roles and attitudes to possession. Trading relationships with other tribes to the south were permanently damaged. The social upheaval that resulted from the introduction of the axes brought the totemic myths into question, an effect that was probably appreciated by the missionaries, but which rapidly resulted in the collapse of Yir Yoront culture.

An American anthropologist witnessed, and subsequently reported on, the well-intentioned but destructive process of this simple example, which, nevertheless, is informative on a number of aspects of technology transfer (Sharp, 1952). There is little doubt that the replacing of stone axes with steel ones was well intentioned, but their introduction without respect for the values and social system of the recipients, was insensitive. We may note that many aborigines welcomed the new tools and were themselves unaware of the damage that could be done to the culture by their adoption, as well as by according with an alien structure of labour management and submitting to subordination. There was also a significant knock-on effect, with many communities suffering as a result of the breaking of the trading chain. It is not simply a matter of the transfer of a technology, but of the consequences of the means by which it is implemented. In this case it was partly one of altruism, but in spite of the restricted circumstances of a mission in a remote area, it was also one of the exercise of power. Power and domination, whether political, military, religious, ideological, educational or simply of technological superiority, plays a major part in the spread of knowledge between cultures. The more powerful imparts what it deems effective and withholds what may be ultimately to its disadvantage, while gaining what it may from the lesser or subjugated. We need go no further back than to the expansion of Augustine Rome, at which time the craftsman's tool-kit comprised hammer and chisels, saws and planes, and organizing templates, which were

**Figure 11.2**
A builder's yard and workshop has structures in wood, stone, brick and earth, and roofs of flat Roman-type tiles, and corrugated sheet iron. East Bohemia, Czech Republic.

**Figure 11.3**
Chinese tiled roof of fired clay with terminal end-tiles to repel rodents and nesting birds. Inverted tiles channel rainwater to the eaves. Nanjing, China.

dispersed throughout the Roman world (Derry and Williams, 1960). The kit of the craftsman of the early twentieth century in all of Europe, was virtually unchanged. The occupation of western Asia, North Africa and Europe meant that cultures under the dominion of Rome shared many of its inventions, from the use of tiles for roofing buildings, to the building of hypocaust systems where the climate warranted it (Singer *et al.*, 1954). Or was the influence in the reverse direction, with the tiled roofs and the kang hypocaust of the Chinese Han empire the source of these technological innovations? Debatable though these sources may be, there is no doubt as to the power of empire in dispersing technology, whether Ottoman or Arab, Iberian or French, British or American, or Soviet Russian. We should note that certain technologies were restricted to colonists and access to them only available within limits, for many of the subjugated and frequently enslaved cultures. I trust I am right in assuming that imperialism and conquest are not intended to be a part of any proposed programme of intervention. Nevertheless, it should be emphasized that western, especially American, technological hegemony is greatly resented in many parts of the world and attempts at technical 'improvement' may be regarded with suspicion, even with hostility.

While being in no way comparable in scale, the instance of the steel axe was, nevertheless, still one of power relations. It was a case of a deliberate technological introduction, but many, perhaps most instances of technological transmission may not have been so

**Figure 11.4**
Pivoted potter's kick-wheel in use in a rural village. Uttar Pradesh, India.

motivated. To what extent such inventions as the bow and arrow, the harpoon, the spear-thrower, the potter's wheel and the weaving loom were devised and carried by nomadic groups or were the products of autogenous, independent creation, we do not know. Based on the uneven archaeological evidence it is possible to hypothesize the passing on and sharing of traditions and technologies over the centuries. So for instance, the potter's wheel as a pivoted disc dating from 3000 BC was discovered at Ur. Wheel bearings for foot-wheels from Jericho are more than 4000 years old; Palestinian Arab potters were using the same system in the 1950s – and may be doing so still (Singer *et al.*, 1954). Such passing on of a technology we ascribe to 'tradition'. Unfortunately, the means of oral transmission have been little researched, but they include maxims and formulaic learning by rote, while non-verbal transmission involves demonstration, mimicry and practice in stages. Such temporal 'handing down' is most frequently from grandparents or parents to offspring, or from masters to apprentices, in guilds or crafts. Technology transfer will usually involve instruction which may, in due course, be passed on by oral or non-verbal means between generations. But this form of transmission over time is only achievable where there is a responsibility, or a willingness to learn from the elders; rarely will tradition be the vehicle by which most technological innovations will be introduced (Oliver, 1989).

More appropriate to our discussion is the subject of diffusion, or 'spreading abroad': the dissemination and assimilation of cultural phenomena. All cultures are hybrids to some extent and it could be argued that, like plants, they are the stronger for it. If the transmission of tradition is essentially diachronic, then diffusion is broadly synchronic (Oliver, 1991). It is spatial and geographic – though the passage of time has to be taken into consideration in many instances, including technologies: the invention, dispersal and acceptance of the plough, for example. First recorded in Egyptian tomb-painting, four millennia ago, it played a major part in the later stages of the agricultural revolution of the 'fertile crescent' which embraced Mesopotamia and Persia; but in the twentieth century there were still African tribes that would not accept the plough because iron was believed to corrupt the soil. There may also be practical reasons for the rejection of recently introduced technologies. In Anhui, China, as I have witnessed, ploughs drawn by water buffalo are extensively used in paddy fields, but mechanical tractors which have been introduced to draw the ploughs, become 'bogged down' and rendered useless (Oliver, 2000).

Regrettably, few anthropologists have studied the effects of diffusion, preferring to research discrete cultures. For the consideration of the means whereby technological innovations are accepted or rejected by vernacular cultures it is vitally important. We have already touched on some of the principal channels of influence, namely conquest, expansion of empire and colonization, but there are many others that are nonetheless related; the phases of establishment from exploration and pioneering to homesteading and immigration, whether in the United States and Canada, India, Australasia or southern Africa. Distinctions can be made between the colonists who abide by their traditions, representing power and exerting authority, and the settlers who retain some loyal values but seek a new life and new opportunities. Settlers are often more willing to converge, compromise and adapt, as exemplified in the adoption of Scandinavian and Central European log construction by English settlers in the United States, and the sharing of some building traditions by British and Boer settlers in South Africa (Lewcock, 1963). Later emigrants tend to bring much of their past culture with them and attach themselves to those who share similar culture traits. Yet influences are not simply one way; the dominant colonists may still learn from the autochthonous cultures, not least from their use of available materials and the building of climatically appropriate structures.

Movement of peoples is clearly significant, but so is the circulation of specialists, such as the medieval journeymen: craftsmen who were employed in the building of cathedrals and fortresses across Europe. In the process, details of joints and mouldings, stylistic

**Figure 11.5**
The post-and-console alternative to inclined brackets, supporting eaves or verandahs. Serbia.

features and forms, decorative elements and motifs were subtly diffused, even though the craftsmen prided themselves on meeting the requirements of their employers. Theirs was diffusion by contact, by the evidence of their practical skills and by the lasting influences of their completed craftwork. In the course of their travelling and sequential employment they also assimilated unfamiliar refinements of technique and method (Leeson, 1979). Borrowing from adjacent cultures is the most pervasive form of reflex diffusion; admiration, envy and the desire to emulate or excel resulting in the adoption or adaptation of processes and products, where they satisfy needs or values. The outcome of these forms of diffusion by contact between contiguous or related peoples, is the definition of the culture area, wherein substantial elements of cultural exchange are established

**Figure 11.6**
Example in Nepal of the possible diffusion of post-and-console. Bhaktapur.



while local identity is retained. This is evident for instance, in the vernacular architecture of the Slavic peoples of the Balkans with its identifiable regional traditions, but with correspondences in scale, structure and functions (Husa *et al.*, 1967).

How diffusion takes place has been one of the many bones of contention gnawed by anthropologists over the past century (Herskovits, 1963). I can only summarize here some aspects that I believe to be germane to the study of technological transfer. What I term 'intra-cultural diffusion' and what has been otherwise identified as 'primary' diffusion, is that which takes place 'in the country of origin'. This emphasis on the country, or nationality, is in my opinion, incorrect, for diffusion within a cultural complex, for instance the Akan peoples of West Africa, spreads across the rain forest regions of the Ivory Coast, Ghana and Togo (Oliver, 1964). 'Inter-cultural diffusion' on the other hand, extends beyond the definition of a single culture or culture complex, to others beyond, frequently displaying a greater degree of 'element transformation' or change, as it is accommodated. The 'rock in the pool' metaphor is often used to illustrate the centrifugal theory of such diffusion. When a rock is cast in the centre of a pool, the immediate area is most dramatically affected, but ripples spread outwards bringing with them strong waves of change. This is regarded as corresponding with a major, often urban, innovation at the cultural centre, with marginal folk survivals at the periphery of the widening circle with its faintly perceptible outer 'ripples'. The 'centrifugal' image is an oversimplification

**Figure 11.7**
The *tonkonan* or great ancestral house of the Toraja, is the dramatic eastern limit of the diffusion of the saddle-roof. Sulawesi, Indonesia (see also Figures 3.5, 7.6 and 10.3).

of course, with diffusion sometimes following a narrow channel of communication: quite literally, along trade routes or river valleys, in the many cases of the passing on of material artefacts. Thoroughly researched examples of architectural diffusion are few: a detailed study of the diffusion of the crossed-pole frame and saddle-roof ridge in South-East Asia is a notable exception. The diffusion route followed the island arc, challenging the centrifugal theory by culminating at its eastern limit with the most extreme form, the great roofs of the Toraja of Sulawesi (Domenig, 1980). Other characteristics of diffusion are observable in some regions: a 'leap-frog effect', for instance, as the nearest culture to a source may resist its influence but a culture beyond, may adopt it.

At this point it is important to emphasize that 'diffusion' generally refers to cultural or technological transmission that has been achieved, rather than to the possibility of doing so. In the past half-century or so, however, aural and visual media have dominated in the direct spreading of some cultural phenomena, such as various forms of popular music. They have also created an ever-widening circle of indirect influence, as in the promotion of images of advanced technologies. But it should be recognized that there is a negative aspect to this, such means provoking frustration as much as admiration, contempt as well as envy, depending on the cultural priorities of the peoples to whom the media are directed. Such responses also apply to the presence of tourists, or to fast food outlets and other invasive expressions of western commercial interests, however much they may, or may not contribute to the economies of the so-called developing countries. Resistance to change may be ascribed to 'tradition', 'custom' or 'conservatism', clichés of explanation which nevertheless acknowledge by implication, the persistence of cultural values over generations that are not readily compromised. Resistance is expressed when the innovation is uncongenial and fails to fit the accustomed patterns of utility or behaviour. Yet the problem remains that if most cultures are to some extent hybrids, what may be the circumstances that account for the acceptance of technological introductions? First, we have to recognize that any such introduction brings about a degree of social change (White, 1962). Sometimes, this is merely a change in habits, but when instruction or education of the young is involved there can be a marked social disruption within a matter of a few years. Clearly, circumstances differ and there are no rules, even if tendencies can sometimes be traced. Often the change is not one of sudden impact, but rather one of a succession of minor modifications in resources, processes and consumption – quite literally, in the case of food. This may be anticipated by reputation or by rumour: what has been termed the 'bow-wave' effect, indicating by its disturbance the craft that follows it.

Broadly speaking, we can identify some of the conditions under which the introduction of new ideas and of technologies may be admissible (Hetzler, 1970). Most important of these is necessity; the need for a resource or a means of delivering it, or making it available in order that life may continue and a culture survive. From the twelfth century desertion of the Chaco Canyon pueblos culture, to the famine in Afghanistan over eight centuries later, the loss of water and the incapacity to irrigate land and crops brought cultures to the point of collapse. 'Necessity', we say, 'is the mother of invention' and the most effective inventions are those made within the culture, rather than externally, when the resources and the means are available. When they are not, external assistance is welcome. Indigenous inventions are generally made to improve efficiency, and efficient solutions to persistent problems can be admissible. The popularity of boxes of matches across the world in the post-First World War years was contrary to expectations, for firelighting was frequently accompanied by ritual; that the matches were splinters of wood and corresponded to a degree with firesticks, appears to have made them acceptable. At another level of technology, the wristwatch has been remarkably successful: some ten million owners of wristwatches were estimated in India in 2000 AD. As a figure this is impressive – but it represents just 1 per cent of the population, which has exceeded a billion people, for a large proportion of whom the passing of minutes still has little significance. This, and the fact that they cost money, even at their present low prices, keeps the relative figure low. Efficiency is valued when it assists, when it saves time when time is at a premium, and when it protects against subsequent expenditure. As we have seen, however, there are other planes on which receptivity lies, the assumption of status through possession, among them. Pride of possession is related, but diminishes in time, as the distinction becomes less evident, or the rare becomes commonplace. Association with a donor, or prestige attached to the receipt of a superior tool, can also have its temporary appeal, but is as likely to create envy or dissatisfaction among others in the group. Awareness of necessity, evident and improved utility, economic feasibility and cultural compatibility are among the principal factors which most influence the acceptability of an innovation.

There is probably no introduction to vernacular architecture from western technology that is more universally applied than corrugated, galvanized sheet metal, which meets most of these criteria. Not all – it is climatically often uncomfortable, but it keeps the rain out even if it is noisy; corrugated iron is cheap, easy to fix, more durable than thatch, and comes in sheets of sufficient pliability to fit most roof forms. It can easily be replaced and like the kerosene can roof tiles and the *bidons*, or flattened oil drum modular wall units, is used with ingenuity by the world's poor. This is not to say that I recommend its aesthetic. Often therefore, recycling and further use of a redundant technology may be preferable to the

**Figure 11.8**
*Bidons*, or sheets of metal claimed from split and flattened oil drums, as well as the tops and bases, are used for building in squatter settlements.

costly purchase of new resources or devices. Consider the volume of worn-out vehicle tyres, such as I have seen used in many countries as fuel in kilns, as weights on grass silos, as boundary markers, as playground features and as fend-offs on harbour walls. Others have been turned inside-out and used as waste-bins in the Philippines, or the inner-tubes have been cut in strips and used to repair tubular steel chairs, as in Kenya. It may be of interest that of all items of modern design traceable to the early masters of the Modern movement, the most ubiquitous in my experience, is the tubular steel chair (Oliver, 1964–2001).

So who transmits, who exchanges, how is diffusion or the introduction of technologies achieved? As we have seen, intracultural diffusion generally emanates from within a culture, perhaps from its seat of power or more sophisticated centre and spreading, with decreasing intensity and over a period of time, to its outer limits. Or it may occur between contiguous cultures, where language may not be a barrier and where environmental and social circumstances are sufficiently compatible to make the recognition of, desire for, and acceptance or mimicry of an innovation likely. It is broadly acknowledged that changes in technology are more rapidly assimilated by a cultural elite even if in some respects, they are more conservative. This is evident historically in, for instance, the use of fired brick in England by the Church and the aristocracy from late in the twelfth century. Under Flemish influence, brick became broadly popular in East Anglia, the peat-fired kilns of Hull making the Hanseatic city the first to be brick-built in Britain. Here the 'trickle-down' effect of technology from the higher status to the common people is evident, while regal use of brick for the palaces of Henry VIII assured its continued use among the rich (Lloyd, 1925). The example of brick demonstrates the 'horizontal' flow between members of groups within a class, and the 'vertical' movement between social strata. Typically, prestige and fashion were important, as was formerly the case with stone and later, stucco rendering. But brick was also cheaper to work than stone. Much later, kilns of the oval Bull's Trench type in which bricks are continuously fired, requiring manually moved chimneys, were introduced by the British to India. They partially replaced the clay-covered clamp kiln, which remains the preferred type among many brick producers in India and Nepal (Spence and Cook, 1983). Yet there were unanticipated problems. The British brought the clamp kiln to the Sudan, and built cone-and-cylinder 'African' houses for railroad employees, expecting to change the habit of building in unfired brick by their example. Neither the house-type, which was associated with southern Sudan and

**Figure 11.9**
Bull's Trench kiln. Oval in plan the trench facilitates continuous firing of bricks or tiles, the pair of high chimneys over the kiln being moved manually. North India.

inimical to the Muslim north, nor the decline in use of unfired brick, happened in the vernacular (Oliver, 1977). Fired brick was used for prestigious buildings, but with a consequent destruction of palm trees to fire the kilns, which created a major problem by the 1980s. In India and Nepal, the consumption of wood for the firing of the Bull's Trench kilns exacerbated the destruction of the forests that contributed to the flooding of the Ganges plain.

We are now considering 'intrusion' rather than 'diffusion'. Intrusion, the 'action of thrusting oneself in without right or welcome' or the 'encroachment on something possessed or enjoyed by another', is what many technological innovations and their introduction in alien circumstances, are really about. Specialists in the field prefer the term 'intervention' which is defined as 'the action of intervening,

**Figure 11.10**
A *pazawah*, or clamp kiln, may be covered in turves. It is built of bricks which will also be burnt in the firing process, so each kiln is dismantled after firing. North India.

"stepping in", or interfering in any affair so as to affect its course or issue'. To intervene is to 'interpose, to intercept, to come between, to prevent or to hinder' (Oxford English Dictionary). For most of us, such a definition does not include our motivations: our desire to make improvements to standards of living, to see the benefits of modernization as we perceive them, shared among all the peoples of the world. But we should not disassociate ourselves from the implications of such a position which places western technological innovations on a pinnacle of achievement to which others

**Figure 11.11**
Railroad employees' houses built to a culturally inappropriate design during the British mandate. Khartoum, Sudan.

are believed to aspire. No doubt, many interventionists believe that such advantages, from modern construction methods to information technology, are indispensable aids to development and are perplexed when a minor intrusion in an existing practice is not regarded with the same sense of value. Even relatively simple innovations are differently perceived by diverse cultures. Most of us would agree that improved sanitation is desirable in much of the world, although we are also aware that water-borne systems, including 'grey water', are wasteful of an urgently needed resource. Improved sanitation is welcomed, but if it involves a regular period of treatment, such as a composting apparatus may require, it may prove difficult to sustain. Reactions and responses to improved systems can differ markedly. When ceramic standing toilets were introduced to a Greek village, the people were proud to leave the doors of their newly constructed and plumbed outhouses open, so that others could be aware and envious of their sanitary installations. But they preferred to use their traditional 'privies' in private (Friedl, 1967).

These are minor examples, but they are illustrative of the cultural values which may help or hinder the acceptance, use and maintenance of a technological improvement introduced as an interventionist measure. Lest I should give the impression that the introduction of appropriate technologies is impossible, I would cite a well known but significant example of technology transfer. In southern Algeria, Niger and Chad, vernacular building is in adobe block, or in moulded clay. Roofs however, have had to be spanned, and as timber became scarce, this was mainly with palm trunks. Eventually, in this dry desert region, this resource too, was becoming scarce. A multinational team known as the Development Workshop, had formerly worked with the Egyptian architect, Hassan Fathy. Based on his rediscovery of the Nubian vault system of building earth vaults without using wooden formwork, the workshop team devised a 'woodless construction' programme which included a training scheme for builders in this 'new' technology. Working with the communities, they introduced the Nubian vault system to these regions. The method was adopted; it did not impede or influence the plans of houses and settlements and it solved the problem of using local materials to span the structures. It was a model of successful technology transfer, rather than intrusion (Cain *et al.*, 1976). So too, has been the work of the architects and labourers of the Barefoot College of Tilonia, Rajasthan, who have used scrap materials and discarded items of agricultural hardware to make houses with geodesic domed roofs for the homeless of the region (Merrick, 2001).

**Figure 11.12**
Houses in the village of Ollantaytambo follow a grid plan, being erected in clay on the foundations and low walls of an ancient Inca settlement. Peru.

Belief systems, language, gender differentiation, child labour exploitation and a great many other cultural factors may compound the problems of intrusive alien technologies, which may also have many biophysical aspects. Climate constraints and variables, such as monsoon periods, hurricanes and natural hazards, and difficulties of access to fresh or clean water when this is still denied the populace, are just a few among the many environmental and resource difficulties that confront the interventionist. But even so, it is still the cultures that reside with them and have resolved ways of living that go far to meet their spiritual, spatial, social, domestic, economic, technical and architectural needs, which have to be understood, nurtured and sustained throughout the process and into the future. It is not possible to discuss here the implications of the cultural factors that can be in conflict with technological intervention, although the mismatch between the provision of post-disaster houses in Turkey and the structure of the Anatolian family (Aysan and Oliver, 1987) (see Chapter 14) is indicative. Sociospatial issues are as important, many cultures organizing their settlement patterns according to belief and rule systems such as the Japanese *hogaku*, or the Indian *vastu-sastras*, of which only the popularized versions of *feng shui* are widely known, if largely misunderstood. Innumerable cultures reflect their ancestry, clans, lineages, age-sets and phratry divisions in their settlements in ways that are not immediately perceptible but are, nonetheless, meaningful. The layout of service lines in militaristic grid patterns on the grounds of efficiency, is frequently advocated in the west. But such grid plans can be in direct conflict with traditional sociospatial customs to the extent that they can be culturally destructive or are rejected by the recipient communities.

What then can be done to meet these cultural differences, and is there any future for the scale of technological change to vernacular traditions in architecture, that some would believe is necessary in the developing world? Fundamental to any partial answer to this question is understanding the nature of the cultures concerned: their values, their social systems, their economies, their resources, their responses to their environments and the embodiment of much of these in their settlements and dwellings. Of these, responses of cultures and their buildings to the environments and to the generalities of the climates where they live are the most readily analysed scientifically, and are the most extensively documented (Givoni, 1969). Anthropologists can tell us much more about the intangible abstractions of cultures, while their respective social, functionalist, cultural, economic and other emphases must be recognized. For the purposes of the present discussion the work of theorists and researchers in the field of social change can be valuable, even if the built environment is the aspect that has received the least attention (Steward, 1955). So one may ask, where can we turn for the information that we need and guidance on how we may proceed? This problem I felt had to be met, in part, in the compilation of a multidisciplinary *Encyclopedia of Vernacular Architecture of the World* (Oliver, 1997). In my view awareness of technological introductions that may make life more fulfilling, less stressful and less dependent on meagre resources, is important. Preferably, this may be done by way of demonstrations or marginal examples which do not seriously impinge upon the culture, until the benefits, the economic implications and the possible disadvantages are realized and understood. These need not intrude on its vernacular architecture to any great extent, but rather they should support it. Vernacular technologies are rarely environmentally or resource damaging, and only in those situations where resources are threatened or exhausted, need alternatives be introduced. Primary attention should be given to services, such as fresh water – through desalination plants, if necessary – and to sanitation, waste disposal and electricity supply. Replacement of threatened materials by others that are renewable, should be combined with transmission on their use in construction, and on their sustainability in the future.

Technology transfer that facilitates the solution of a problem confronting a culture could be undertaken, but not with the intention of achieving an objective that satisfies, favours or benefits the transmitting technologists rather than the recipients. The need for technological change or modification must be recognized and preferably expressed by the recipient culture with whom, and with whose indigenous knowledge, any changes may be introduced. A facilitating role rather than an interventionist one is, I believe, essential. Sustainability through independence, rather than dependence, is vital. The freedom must be ensured for intracultural and intercultural diffusion to take place, for traditions to be passed on, and for social change to occur in the forms and at the rate that meet cultural norms. By such means and with these safeguards, the vernacular architectural traditions that have developed and adapted over time, and with which their builders and users identify, can continue to evolve or redirect. With appropriate support they may help present and future generations to meet the massive demands for housing that the growth of the world's population in the forthcoming decades will create.

## References


Aysan, Y. and Oliver, P. (1987). *Housing and Culture After Earthquakes. A Guide for Future Policy Making on Housing in Seismic Areas.* Oxford Polytechnic for Overseas Development Administration.

Cain, A., Afshar, F. and Norton, J. (1976). *Indigenous Building and the Third World.* Teheran: Development Workshop.

Derry, T.K. and Williams, T.I. (1960). *A Short History of Technology.* Oxford: Clarendon Press.

Domenig, G. (1980). *Tektonik im Primitiven Dachbau.* Zurich: ETH.

Friedl, E. (1967). *Vasilika.* New York: Holt, Rinehart and Winston.

Gamble, C. (1986). *The Palaeolithic Settlement of Europe.* Cambridge University Press.

Givoni, B. (1969). *Man, Climate and Architecture.* Amsterdam: Elsevier Publishing.

Herskovits, M.J. (1963). Diffusion and Acculturation. In *Cultural Anthropology.* New York: Alfred A. Knopf (Chapter 25).

Hetzler, S.A. (1970). *Technological Growth and Social Change. Achieving Modernization.* London: Routledge & Kegan Paul.

Husa, V., Petran, J. and Subrtova, A. (1967). *Traditional Crafts and Skills. Life and Work in Mediaeval and Renaissance Times.* Prague and London: Paul Hamlyn.

ISVA (1998, 2002). *International Studies in Vernacular Architecture, Course Handbook.* Headington, Oxford: Centre for International Vernacular Architecture Studies. Oxford Brookes University, School of Architecture.

Kroeber, A.L and Kluckhohn, C. (1952). Culture: A critical review of concepts and definitions. Papers, Harvard University, Peabody Museum of American Archaeology and Ethnology. Vol. XL VII, No 1, pp.1–223.

Leeson, R.A. (1979). *Travelling Brothers. The Six Centuries' Road from Craft Fellowship to Trade Unionism.* London: George Allen & Unwin.

Lewcock, R. (1963). *Early Nineteenth Century Architecture in South Africa. A Study of Interaction Between Two Cultures*. Cape Town: A.L. Balkema.
Lloyd, N. (1925). *A History of English Brickwork*. London: H. Greville Montgomery.
Merrick, J. (2001). Bright stars in the east. *The Thursday Review*. London: The Independent, 25 October.
Oliver, P. (1986). Cultural factors in the acceptability of resettlement housing. In: Saile, D.G. (ed.). *Architecture in Cultural Change: Essays in Built Form and Culture Research*. University of Kansas.
Oliver, P. (2003). *Dwellings: The House Across the World*. Oxford: Phaidon (revised edn).
Oliver, P. (1989). Handed down architecture: Tradition and transmission. In: Bourdier, J.-P. and Al-Sayyad, N. (eds). *Dwellings, Settlement and Tradition: Cross-Cultural Perspectives*. Lanham, MD: University Press of America, pp. 53–75.
Oliver, P. (March, 1991). Transmitting technologies. In: *Mimar. Architecture in Development 38*, Construction Technologies issue, pp. 56–7.
Oliver, P. (ed.). (1997). *The Encyclopedia of Vernacular Architecture of the World*, 3 vols, Cambridge University Press.
Oliver, P. (2000). Ethics and vernacular architecture. In: Fox, W. (ed.) *Ethics and the Built Environment*. London: Routledge, pp. 115–126.
Oliver, P. (1964–2001). Field notes.
Oxford English Dictionary. 'Altruism' and other cited definitions are extracted from the *Shorter Oxford English Dictionary*. Oxford: The Clarendon Press.
Sharp, L. (1952). Steel axes for Stone Age Australians. In: Spicer, E.H. (ed.). *Human Problems in Technological Change*. New York: Russell Sage Foundation, pp. 69–90.
Singer, C., Holmyard, E.J. and Hall, A.R. (eds). (1954). *A History of Technology*, vol. 1. Oxford: Clarendon Press, pp. 198–204.
Spence, R.J.S. and Cook, D.J. (1983). *Building Materials in Developing Countries*. Chichester: John Wiley & Sons.
Steward, J.H. (1955). *Theory of Culture Change: The Methodology of Multilinear Evolution*. Urbana: University of Illinois Press (reprinted 1979).
White, L. Jr. (1962). *Medieval Technology and Social Change*. Oxford: Clarendon Press.

# PART IV

# CULTURES, DISASTERS AND DWELLINGS

# 12

# The cultural context of shelter provision (1978)

Of the examples of disasters discussed in conferences it seems that the majority are quantifiably massive: the floods in Bangladesh or Australia, the earthquakes in Guatemala or Peru. For the individuals and families in smaller-scale disasters, the loss of relatives or the destruction of homes is no less tragic because statistics reveal that the scale of the calamities that struck them are of lesser magnitude. So I will use as illustrations two statistically minor examples, from Cappadocia and north-west Sicily.

In the strange landscape of Cappadocia in Central Anatolia, thousands of peasants live in dwellings carved out of tufa rock pinnacles, formed from ancient deposits of lava dust. On exposure to air, the soft rock hardens so that the interiors have firm walls, while the stone from the carved voids makes a secondary building material. The interiors are not cave-like, but follow the rectilinear forms of an earlier tradition, so it is not surprising to see extensions, made from the quarried tufa blocks, of rectangular plan. Central Anatolia is earthquake-prone and the tufa pinnacles are unstable. When strong tremors affect the area the pinnacles can collapse, destroying the dwellings and causing loss of life. This happened at Cavusin, where scores of carved homes disintegrated in an avalanche of rock. A semicircular ridge of tufa remains and no doubt will collapse, some day in the future. But after evacuation, the inhabitants of Cavusin returned to the scree-slope and from the rubble of their former homes have built new dwellings, directly in the shadow of the still unstable ridge. Relief agencies lost patience with them and officials deplored the 'stupidity' of the peasants. Why should they want to build there again, contrary to all reason?

Gibellina is a small town in the western peninsula of Sicily. It is one of the towns, among them Menfi and Santa Margherita Belici, which

**Figure 12.1**
The curving cliff above the village of Cavusin, with earthquake and landslip rock debris near Avilcar in the landscape of tufa pinnacles. Cappadocia, Turkey.

**Figure 12.2**
Ruins of the small town of Gibellina, following an earthquake. North-west Sicily.

were destroyed by earthquake in 1968. A compact town of two- and three-storeyed buildings it was built of local stone; when the earthquake struck, the devastation was considerable. Fires followed and the ruins were dangerous; the villagers were resettled some distance away near another town. As a precaution against disaster in any future earthquake, the new settlement has been built on an immense concrete plinth approached by a flight of marble stairs. The noble stairway leads to concrete block-houses and, for a period, of galvanized iron huts of the 'Nissen' type which the occupants endeavoured to humanize with curtains, paint and wooden lean-to outbuildings. An atmosphere of numbed silence hung over the town. On the side of the concrete plinth, the local children were encouraged to paint pictures by their teacher. None of the paintings were of the town where they were now living, nor were they of the Sicilian countryside. Ingeniously using the textures of the concrete, all of them depicted the earthquake that destroyed Gibellina. What messages were these children's paintings communicating?

I sought to find out why the people of Cavusin built again by the threatening tufa wall, and why the children of Gibellina painted pictures of an event which they might have been expected to have wanted to forget. Some were realist and literal in terms of their depiction of specific incidents that lurked in the child's memory. Others were of the disaster seen from near or beyond its epicentre; still others were abstractions that conveyed the drama and the horror of the event. It was clear from the diversity of expression and the large dimensions of the murals, that the schoolchildren had been fortunate in their art teacher, who must have helped them in the past, to express themselves with confidence and a rare command of their paint brushes. Nevertheless, the imprint of the teacher was in no way evident in the paintings, which communicated the individuality of their responses to a common tragedy. The question remained, as to the underlying messages that the paintings conveyed, but it became apparent that the answer lay in the contexts of the shelter provision, which they inhabited following their respective disasters, and their relation to the cultural contexts of their former homes.

**Figure 12.3**
Children's paintings on the concrete plinth of the post-disaster settlement. Gibellina, Sicily.

This brief chapter was entitled 'the cultural context of shelter provision'. But there is never just one cultural context for the providing of shelter following a disaster – there are always at least two. They may not be the 'two cultures' of Sir Charles Snow's definition, but they are just as distinct: the haves and the have-nots, the powerful and the powerless, the relief organizations and the victims of disaster. They are thrown together by the unique and peculiar circumstances of a catastrophe, being obliged to relate in ways which would never occur in normal times. By far the majority of victims of disasters are the poor, while those who are engaged in the study of disasters, in the planning and implementation of relief and in the designing or building of appropriate shelter, are from the more privileged classes. Of the two cultural contexts in any disaster the most permanent is the one that has suffered; the most artificial the one that assumes control. To make the culture of relief work, roles are assigned – not without difficulties – procedures are drawn up, strategies implemented; a simulation of battle order passes for cultural cohesion.

For the relief bodies, organizations and agencies of the 'relief culture', as I will term it, their functions are clear: remove people from the danger areas and minister to their needs, bury the dead, search for the trapped, tend the sick, heal the wounded, comfort the shocked and bereaved. The relief culture provides supplies of food and water, takes precautions against contamination, exerts controls to fight disease and epidemics, establishes regular supply routes for medicines, consumables, clothing, blankets. Further, agents of the relief culture salvage, or direct the salvaging of materials, erect temporary shelter, find alternative accommodation, rebuild repairable dwellings, plan and build new ones that may afford protection against further disasters, or the ravages of climatic extremes. The tenuous threads that hold the relief culture together are scarcely strong enough to accommodate the plethora of assistants that may arrive in the 'convergence behaviour' of would-be participants, not to mention the representatives of the media.

Disasters very rarely occur in the cultural context of the relief culture, whose context is essentially post-disaster. They occur indiscriminately in the cultural contexts of different societies, special in kind to every disaster but central to it, inescapably bound up in it, who are obliged to survive in some form or other, after the whole operation is over. Like the doctor who only sees his patient when he is ill and never in the full bloom of health, the relief culture witnesses the victim culture in an unrepresentative state – at its weakest, most helpless, least effective. The 'victim culture', as I will term what Marks and Fritz have called 'the community of sufferers' (Marks and Fritz, 1954) is the indigenous culture under stress; it has the constituent elements of the indigenous culture, but these are often distorted, impaired or malfunctioning in the unique circumstances of the disaster. In the post-disaster period, the victim culture is always the most disadvantaged, always the recipient of aid. Both relief culture and victim culture are, to a greater or lesser extent, dependent on the circumstances and scale of the disaster, which are invariably untypical, even unique. At the time of impact, the indigenous culture (the culture that has been subject to the disaster) suffers stresses that change its state to a victim culture. Immediately after the disaster it is in a transformed state, but it is also subject to the additional strains of accepting the alien, but in itself untypical, relief culture to direct the solution of its problems. It is therefore prone to a double trauma: the traumatic experience of the disaster and the trauma of having an external body assume responsibility for its welfare and for its shelter, a humiliating experience which in itself can do irreparable damage to the cohesion of its social system.

In Allen Barton's definition a social system is a 'collectivity of human beings whose interaction maintains itself in identifiable patterns over relatively long periods of time' (Barton, 1969). He perceives disasters as part of the larger category of 'collective stress situations' which occur when 'many members of a social system fail to receive expected conditions of life from that system'. Such collective stress situations he broadly defines as 'external' arising from sources outside the social system, such as 'large unfavourable changes in the environment of the system', and 'internal' in the form of 'massive social disorganization.' I would contend that whereas the disaster itself clearly falls within the former group of unfavourable changes in the environment of the system, the relief culture and its operations exert both internal and external pressures. When decisions are made on the form, construction and permanence of shelter provision by the relief culture, the conditions are created for the continued exertion of internal pressures. During the relief operation, the traditional, local systems of organization are likely to be rejected in favour of the systems familiar to and exercised by the relief culture. A victim culture is made aware of the failure of its local, traditional, indigenous systems to either anticipate the disaster or be able to cope with it when it happens. Depending on the kind and location of the social system such an awareness may lead to loss of faith in traditional leadership and hierarchies of social or religious order, making the distressed community still more prone to external influence. Though it is generally the aim of the relief

**Figure 12.4**
Post-disaster metal housing occupied by the victims of the Gibellina earthquake, overlooked by the ruined buildings.

culture to assist the victim culture to return to a state of normalcy as speedily as possible, it is a rare community that is not permanently damaged to some extent by the effects of the disaster and its aftermath.

A major source of disruption is the capacity of the relief culture to summon resources out of the range of the indigenous culture. Where circumstances permit, relief bodies will bring medical aid, road and airborne transportation, using field communications and employing advanced technologies whenever they can. Bearing in mind it is those in conditions of extreme poverty that are hit hardest, this marshalling of resources is in striking contrast to the victim culture's own meagre means. Transference of allegiance, or submission to the greater authority of the more powerful relief culture, may follow. They are generally willing participants in the relief operations but, in their willingness to be directed and dragooned to meet the ends of relief, they are inevitably loosening the ties to the traditional culture. The victims who hinder the operation, who seem dazed or inept, or who return to danger areas to salvage or rebuild, are also trying to piece together the remnants of their traditional culture, or are failing to make sense of the external and internal stress situations to which they have been subjected. When the relief culture withdraws, alienation from some aspects of the traditional culture, disruption in the social system, the blaming of victims and the finding of scapegoats may ensue, symptoms of the damage done at a psychosocial level (Chomsky, 1968).

If we examine the reports of relief organizations, we are soon aware that they are largely concerned with the measurable and the quantifiable. However much attention and concern has been given to the sick, the shocked and the shelterless, the reports express the work of the relief bodies very largely in graphs, charts and statistics. The numbers of deaths, buildings destroyed, people rehabilitated; the quantities of food distributed, goods moved, transports involved; the total costs to region or nation, to the relief organizations or the insurance companies are tabulated in terms that may describe the human predicament in columns of figures. So an important study of disaster economics proposes the development of 'a theoretical analysis of behaviour following natural disasters... using basic concepts of economic and statistical analysis' (Dacy and Kunreuther, 1969). By virtue of the urgency of the situation, relief bodies seldom have time or opportunity for more than the most superficial perceptions of the indigenous culture, or to ascertain the transformations that have taken place as a result of the impact. Both in their own operations and in their dealings with the victim culture which has been subjected to the collective stress situation, the relief culture and its agencies must deal with problems as they find them. To borrow a term from linguistics they can only be concerned with the 'surface structures' of society. Such surface structures are further compromised when they are reduced to statistical terms, but even in the emergency they can only be the manifestations of a culture at the immediately observable level. Often however, the fragments of material culture, the idiosyncracies of human behaviour do no more than hint at the complex of interpersonal relationships and social organization that lie beneath the surface, and which constitute what may be termed the 'deep structures' of a social system. Whether they are codes of behaviour, forms of education, observances of mysteries and rites, myths and beliefs, calendrical cycles, devotions to deities and ancestral spirits, relations between the sexes, the generations, the living, the dead and the yet unborn, they give meaning to the externals of the surface structures (Levi-Strauss, 1968). Together they express the world view of a culture and its value systems.

As we have seen, the victim culture is the indigenous culture transformed by disaster; some vestiges of that transformation may always remain, but a society that is able to return to its indigenous state, as far as possible over a short period of time, is probably going to suffer less permanent damage. Relief bodies have seldom the time, nor generally the awareness to be concerned with the deep structures; their approach is essentially pragmatic. And so, when the relief operation is over and the damaged surface structures are patched up, the deep structures may remain seriously impaired. Disillusion and fragmentation may be the result, expressed in splits within the community at worst, or, in the human need to repair the damage, a return to what appear to be the vulnerable circumstances that made the community disaster-prone initially. Turning to the examples of Cavusin and Gibellina, we may see some evidence of this. The rebuilding of the houses of Cavusin close to the original collapse, can be seen not as bovine stupidity but a powerful motivation to associate as quickly as possible with the traditional roots of the community. By building on their inherited ancestral lands, the inhabitants of Cavusin were attempting to restore the traditional patterns of their social system and to mend the damage to the deep structures which displacement had caused. As for the paintings by the children of Gibellina, they can be interpreted as cathartic expressions which enabled them to come to terms with the horror of the catastrophe. While they performed this function, the paintings were more significant: they were symbolic of the event that destroyed not only their houses but also their homes; that reduced to ruins their community as well as their town. In the interests of their safety, they were not permitted to return to, or even to enter, the piles of debris and stone which had been their home environment, which could be seen from the concrete plinth on whose safe, but inhospitable form they were obliged to stay.

A town is made of buildings, but a community is made of people; a house is a structure, but a home is much more. The distinctions are

**Figure 12.5**
Rebuilding of houses below the rockfall. Cavusin, Turkey.

**Figure 12.6**
Example of children's paintings. Gibellina, Sicily.

**Figure 12.7**
Adjacent paintings by the children of Gibellina.

not trivial, nor are they sentimental or romantic: they are fundamental to the understanding of the difference between the provision of shelter which serves to protect and the creation of domestic environments that express the deep structures of society. To draw again upon linguistic terminology it may be said that the 'house' is denotative, whereas 'home' is connotative; the house or 'small dwelling' describes the structure whereas the home is symbolic of the lives spent within it. The home is connotative of the deep structures of a social system and how these are reflected in the family's relationship to the domestic space it occupies. In indigenous cultures, the bond between the deep structures of society and their expression in house form is very close. This is why the study of vernacular architecture and shelter is important, and accordingly, why it has bearing on shelter provision in disaster situations. Here we are confronted with a basic problem, for the concept of 'shelter provision' is alien to a large proportion of the world's social systems.

Dwellings are not 'provided for', they are 'built by'. External agencies do not contrive housing solutions for indigenous cultures, the latter resolve their own over long periods of time. Changes do take place, and they are invariably indicative of social change also. They are matters of choice even if they are indicative of social upheaval; ideally, they are not the product of provision. In the west, and in the countries of the world that have developed on western lines, there is an increasing tendency to 'provide' housing. Not however, without considerable problems of stress arising; provision has worked best when opportunities for choice have also been provided. In the disaster-prone regions of Asia, Africa, the Middle East, Central and South America, the majority of the populations determine their own shelter forms and embody their values within them. It is precisely these peoples for whom shelter solutions may be designed.

One of the advantages of the temporary structure is that it matches the temporary nature of the post-disaster period. At least in theory; just as the post-disaster periods are sometimes long term in their effect, so too are temporary shelters likely to become long term in their use. As the 'temporary' has a way of becoming semipermanent, so semipermanent shelter is likely to last indefinitely. The arguments in favour of providing more secure shelters than merely temporary ones are considerable, nonetheless. Concerns of the designers will inevitably be concentrated on low-cost, impact and quake-resistant, impermeable small dwellings with adequate facilities for cooking, sanitation, hygiene and family living that may accord with World Health Organisation or other recommendations, if not with Parker-Morris standards. They will be concerned with surface structures in more ways than one. Yet, there are inherent problems in the designing of disaster-resistant, permanent dwellings. To the designer a small, low-cost shelter is a specific type of artefact whose materials and construction can be specified, whose performance can be measured and whose costs can be totalled. Within the peculiar constraints of economic stringency and the extremes of environmental disturbance, design solutions may not be easily arrived at, but they are feasible. One can imagine a design for a mass-produced small dwelling that meets this brief, obtaining international funding for its development. Conceivably, the right design could satisfy most physical demands, but whether it could meet most cultural requirements is altogether, another matter. Collectively, cultures do not lend themselves to the design approach; one cannot write a brief for a shelter type that meets the needs of all cultures; it is doubtful if one could effectively define the shelter needs of even one social system that would give expression to its deep structures. Permanent shelter can potentially shape a community in a way that is destructive to its integrity as a whole, and inimical to the expectations of a family, as a unit.

It may be argued that disaster victims often appear to prefer shelter that follows the rectangular plans and pitched roof types of western forms. Merely to accept this as proof of their universal desirability would be to recognize the surface structures only, of their responses. The underlying reasons may be various: they may indicate the tendency of victim cultures to imitate the artefacts of the relief culture on whom they depend; they may appear to be 'urban' and 'modern' and hence relate to the assumed values of western culture and its apparent roots in urbanization; they may simply indicate the limited availability of building materials that necessitates the use of *bidons* (galvanized iron sheets); they may be following the guidance of relief agencies in the construction of shelters, or they may negatively express the victim culture's disillusion with the indigenous capacity to cope with a major disaster. Whether some, or all, of these apply, if the shelter type does not serve the deeper needs of the society it may ultimately contribute to social disruption or change, lacking the strength of support of evolution within the deep structures of the social system.

Literature on the provision of shelter in disaster areas is still thin, while the volume of anthropological studies related to recovery that considers shelter, is scarcely more substantial. It seems to me of paramount importance that in future disasters, thorough studies on these themes are made, in association with anthropologists who themselves have experience of shelter in the afflicted communities. This is not as simple as it may sound – anthropologists have been seriously neglectful of the study of architecture of all types and scales. As a matter of urgency, I consider that a directory of architects, anthropologists and others who have worked, or are working, in the disaster-prone areas, be drawn up and kept up to date, extending into the less vulnerable areas as files become more complete. A resource list of those who are able to advise on the initial stages of resettlement, and who can observe and monitor progress, adaptations, successes and failures over extended periods, is also necessary. From such co-operation between anthropologists and designers, sufficient data might be obtained that would give guidelines on how to proceed. I am personally of the opinion that support and service systems capable of being adapted to a wide variety of building types, conditions and materials would constitute the most fruitful line of research.

Any proposals for permanent shelter provision in disaster areas should be advanced, in my view, with extreme caution. But conceivably, solutions could be found that may provide a framework for homes as well as houses, and which may enable the deep structures of social systems to be expressed through them, in ways that may satisfy the needs of many cultures. The cultural contexts of shelter provision in disasters are complex and in the ultimate sense, incompatible. But one can but hope that, with informed research and sensitive design, the gap between the relief culture, the victim culture and the indigenous culture can be effectively narrowed.

## References

Barton, A.H. (1969). *Communities in Disaster*. Garden City, NJ: Doubleday.
Chomsky, N. (1968). *Language and Mind*. New York: Harcourt Brace Jovanovich.
Dacy, D.C. and Kunreuther, H. (1969). *The Economics of Natural Disasters*. New York: Free Press.
Levi-Strauss, C. (1968). *Structural Anthropology*. Allen Lane.
Marks, E.S. and Fritz, C.E. (1954). *Human Reactions in Disaster Situations*. Chicago: National Opinion Research Center.

# 13

# Earthen housing and cultures in seismic areas (1984)

For a year, I was staying in a favoured part of Berkeley on the well-timbered slopes above the university, during which there was a minor earthquake at Coalinga, half-way between San Francisco and Los Angeles. While there I took the opportunity to question a number of my acquaintances, architects, professors and retired professionals, as to their attitudes to the risk of a major earthquake recurring in the area. Jokey responses, even a curious kind of glee at residing close to, or virtually on the fault lines, greeted every enquiry. It was pointed out to me with wry irony that most Berkeley schools had been sited on flat ground which masked dangerous faults. An expatriate Englishman, long resident in California, shrugged his shoulders and said 'If your number's on it . . . ', using the fatalistic phrase employed during the Second World War, by Londoners threatened by the silent menace of the V2s.

Not an unfamiliar attitude to those living in California, no doubt. But I could not help but wonder how these sophisticated, highly intelligent and, by developing world standards, fabulously wealthy architects and educationalists, could so readily screen the scale of the danger from their conscious thoughts. After the bitter cold of Wisconsin which I had just left, and living in the lush, sun-soaked environment of the San Francisco Bay area, I found myself rapidly slipping into the same frame of mind; if I'd stayed longer I would have soon joined them in their disregard of the earthquake risk. That there is some anxiety in California is not in question, but the fact that it had taken so long for any serious action to be taken was indicative of the many forces at work in shaping attitudes and policies. In Berkeley, there were some 11 000 brick buildings which constituted

**Figure 13.1**
One of a number of faults that follow the coastal range of mountains that edges the San Andreas tectonic Plate, California and are parallel with the Pacific Plate.

a serious hazard; to reinforce them or to replace them would cost the Bay area a billion dollars in the values of the 1980s; in Los Angeles, the number was some 9000, the figure currently quoted for making them safe being proportionately large. According to a seismologist at the University of Berkeley there was a high probability within the next decade of a major earthquake of 1906 proportions, but the Geological Survey in Washington disagreed – not in 50 years, the chief seismologist argued (Cooke, 1981). So time passed, although the fact that rebuilding and reinforcing might create jobs for building contractors and engineers, could eventually provide the clinching argument for them to go ahead.

In the San Francisco Bay area, the cultural context is exceptional: the costs implied are high, but in scale with one of the richest regions in the world. What of the poorer countries where earthquake risks are as great and buildings as vulnerable? When even wealthy, literate, capitalist California cannot face the reality of earthquake hazard, is there any ground for surprise that in other cultures, with different values, marginal economies, rural populations and earth houses, perceptions of risk and measures to combat it are rare? Perceptions and anticipations of hazard and the measures that could be taken to minimize dangers, are intimately bound up with cultural factors that colour attitudes. To consider the problem of earthen housing in seismic areas solely as a technical one, is to disregard those aspects of culture and society which may, or may not make acceptable any measures to alter building forms or modify existing types, to render them safer. Such cultural factors operate at many levels; if simple technical guidelines might be drawn up for all builders of earthen structures, no such general guidelines can be drafted that can apply to all cultures. The interplay of hierarchies, beliefs, kinship patterns, economy, customs and mores is extremely complex and special to each culture, so that the dangers of oversimplification are considerable. Yet some measure of generalization can be made with regard to the distribution of certain traits, which may assist in the understanding of the cultural implications of building.

Any discussion of the cultural context of earthen building in regions of high seismic risk must obviously demand that the regions of seismic risk, the distribution of soils suitable for adobe or earthen building, and the pattern of such building, are identified. Seismic regions of the land mass (which are not the only ones to have serious cultural implications), are normally identified in terms of earth structure and fault lines. But a simplified map which considers their location in delimiting lines of longitude and latitude enables cultural factors in those areas to be discussed on a comparative basis. A swathe drawn across the northern hemisphere between latitude 20°N and 40°N encompasses a large proportion of the affected regions. However, the highest concentrations of earthquake activity in Central and South America occur in the Equatorial belt 0°–20°N, while earthquake regions of the Philippines, Malaysia and Melanesia fall within the 0°–20°S belt. Longitudinal extensions of these swathes between 60°W and 80°W, and between 90°E and 120°E, together contain a substantial proportion of the remaining areas at risk. Extensions in the northern hemisphere complete a configuration which, for the present purposes, I will refer to as the 'quake belts', to distinguish them from any more scientifically defined seismic zones.

An important geophysical factor related to earthen building is, of course, the nature of the soils. The lateritic and ferralitic red earths are among the most suitable for mass walling. They occur extensively through Sub-Saharan Africa, being the predominant types in most regions west of the rift valley – but these are of low seismic risk. They also occur in South America and in South-East Asia. The fertile podzolic soils of North America, Europe and Russia also provide useful building material though their fertility produces timber which is extensively used in these regions. The quake belts are largely comprised of mountain soils which, in the valleys, are suitable for building but which are frequently combined with stone or rock. The quake belts also include a wide band of desert soils spreading across North Africa and the Middle East. Desertic soils in arid regions are often ideal for building and are fertile when water

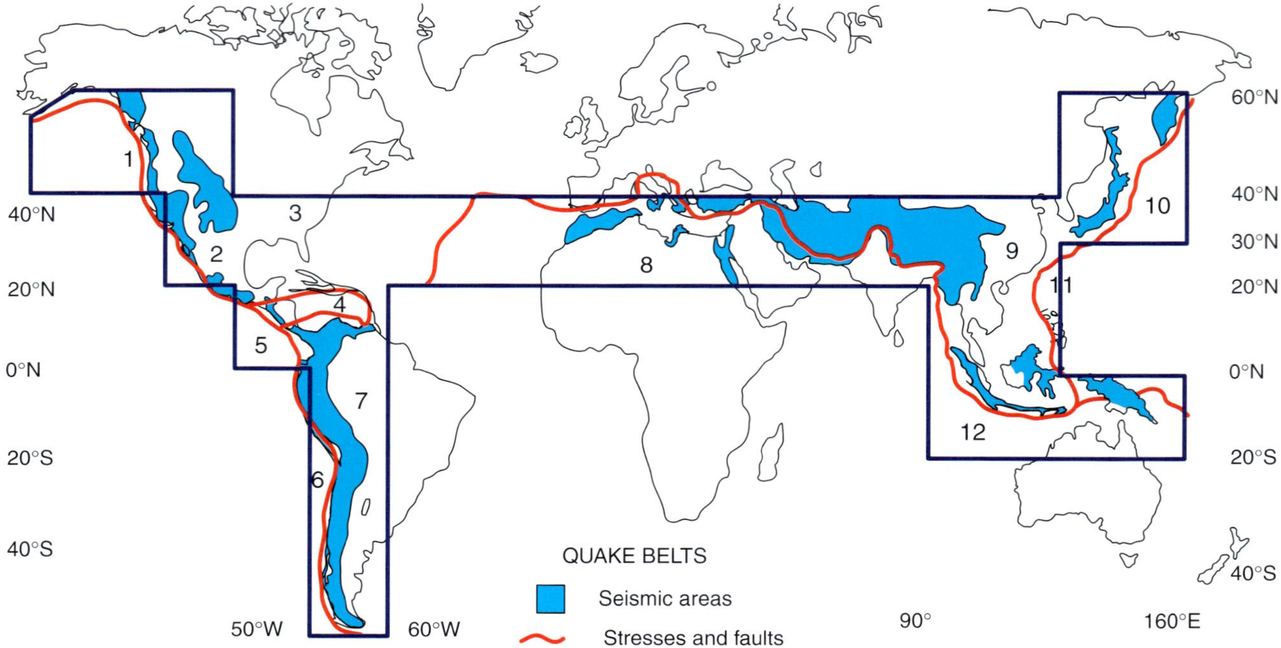


Tectonic Plates: areas in the Quake Belts

1 Garda Plate
2 San Andreas Plate
3 North American Plate
4 Caribbean Plate
5 Cocos Plate
6 Nazca Plate
7 South American Plate
8 Africa Plate
9 Euro-Asian Plate
10 Pacific Plate
11 Philippine Plate
12 Indo-Australian Plate

**Figure 13.2**
Map of the quake belts including seismic areas, tectonic plates, stresses and faults as they affect the areas defined in the belts.

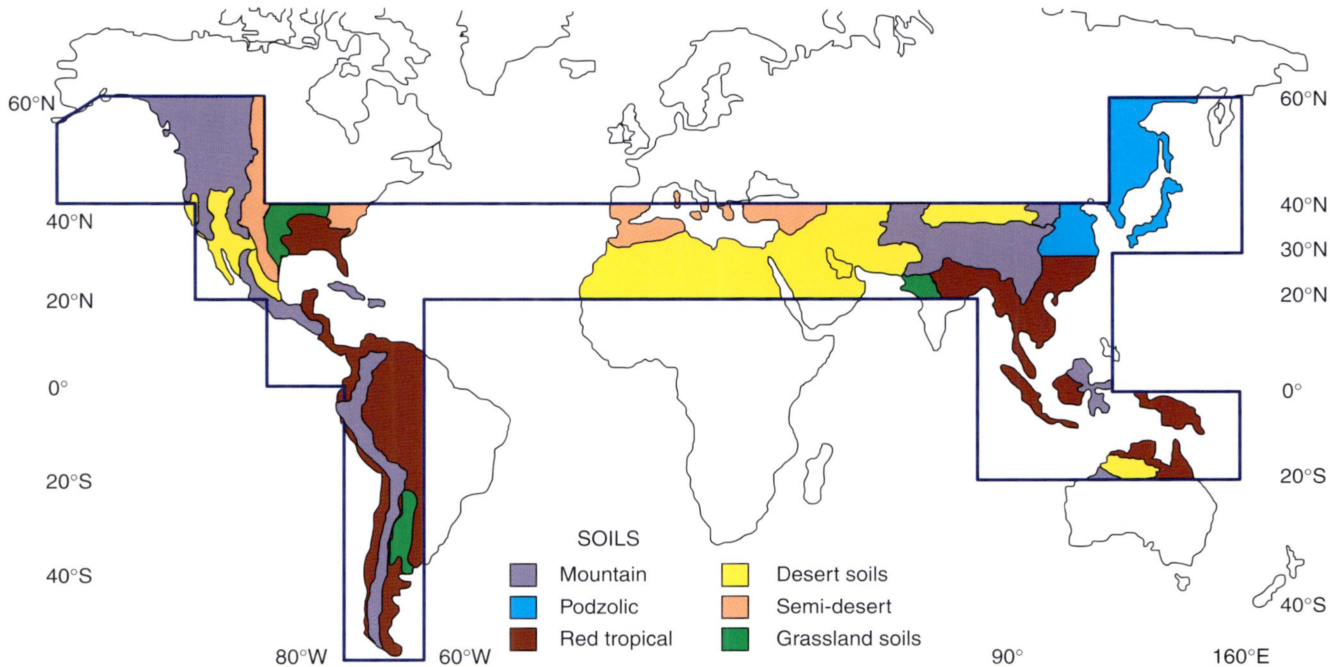


**Figure 13.3**
Map of soils in quake belts: includes the red tropical, montane, podzolic, desertic, semi-desert and grassland soils relating to quake belts.

for irrigation is in sufficient supply. But others are sandy and less suitable, both for construction and for agriculture. When soils are compared with other environmental factors, such as climatic regions and vegetation – a number of correspondences may be seen. North Africa and the Middle East are hot and arid with no forest growths; desert regions are also found in areas of low rainfall and generally dry conditions in the south-west United States and Mexico, and along the western seaboard of South America. On the other hand, the tropical rain forests with year-round high temperatures in Central America, much of the Indian subcontinent and throughout South-East Asia and Malaysia correspond closely to the distribution of red tropical soils. This helps to explain one of the apparent anomalies of the distribution of earthen construction in the quake belts: in spite of the suitability of the red soils to earth-building their coincidence with areas of high temperature, high rainfall and high humidity demands that in much of South America and throughout South-East Asia, light frame constructions, and screen or lattice walls which permit the passage of air but retain privacy, are extensively used. In some tropical areas which also have readily available saplings and leaves for building materials – Yucatan, for instance – frame structures are used with daubed clays to produce combined wood and mud constructions.

Although this chapter is about 'earthen housing' in seismic areas, precise definition of the term remains elusive. Presumably, 'earthen' includes all buildings made of unfired clays, and as such, embraces those constructed of sun-dried brick, adobe block, rammed earth, west African 'swish', clay lump, *pisé de terre* and Devon cob. How much earth or clay must be present for a building to be 'earthen'? Does the term include those that are constructed of both stone and clay, or made of stone bonded with clay? Does it include those that are timber constructed, but earth covered? And are the wattle-and-daub, pole-and-daga, stick-frame and mud, dwellings of Central America or Malaysia, considered as 'earthen'? To compound the difficulties, in some areas of the world, two, three or even more of these construction systems exist side by side, even following the same morphology. It need hardly be pointed out, but should be remembered, that bricks that are not sun-dried are generally also 'earthen', but are of 'kiln-fired' or 'burnt' clay. These problems of definition are exposed when one attempts to compile a map of earthen building. In tentatively offering such a sketch map, I am acutely aware of the lack of detailed or even, of generalized information, as well as of the problems of definition outlined above. Here I have indicated only those areas where adobe, rammed earth

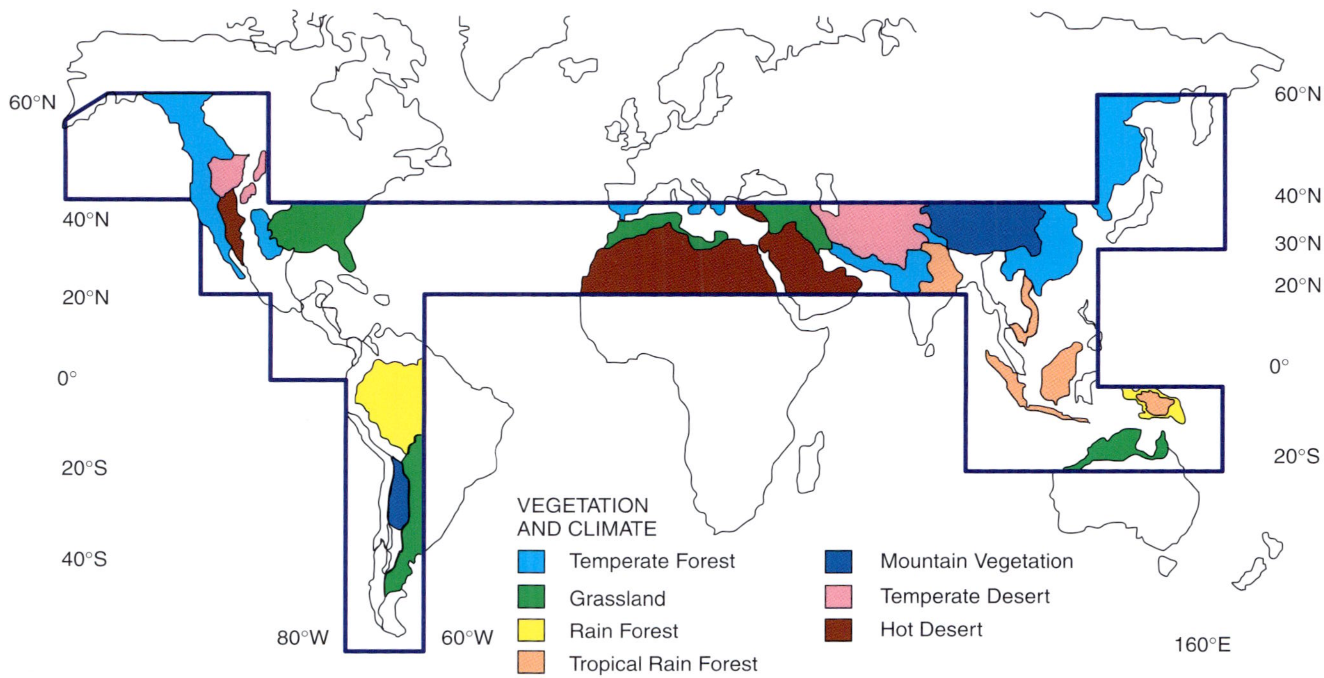


**Figure 13.4**
Map of vegetation and climate which includes the temperate deserts and hot deserts, grassland regions, rain forests and tropical rain forests, temperate forests and hot deserts and mountain vegetation, relating to quake belts.

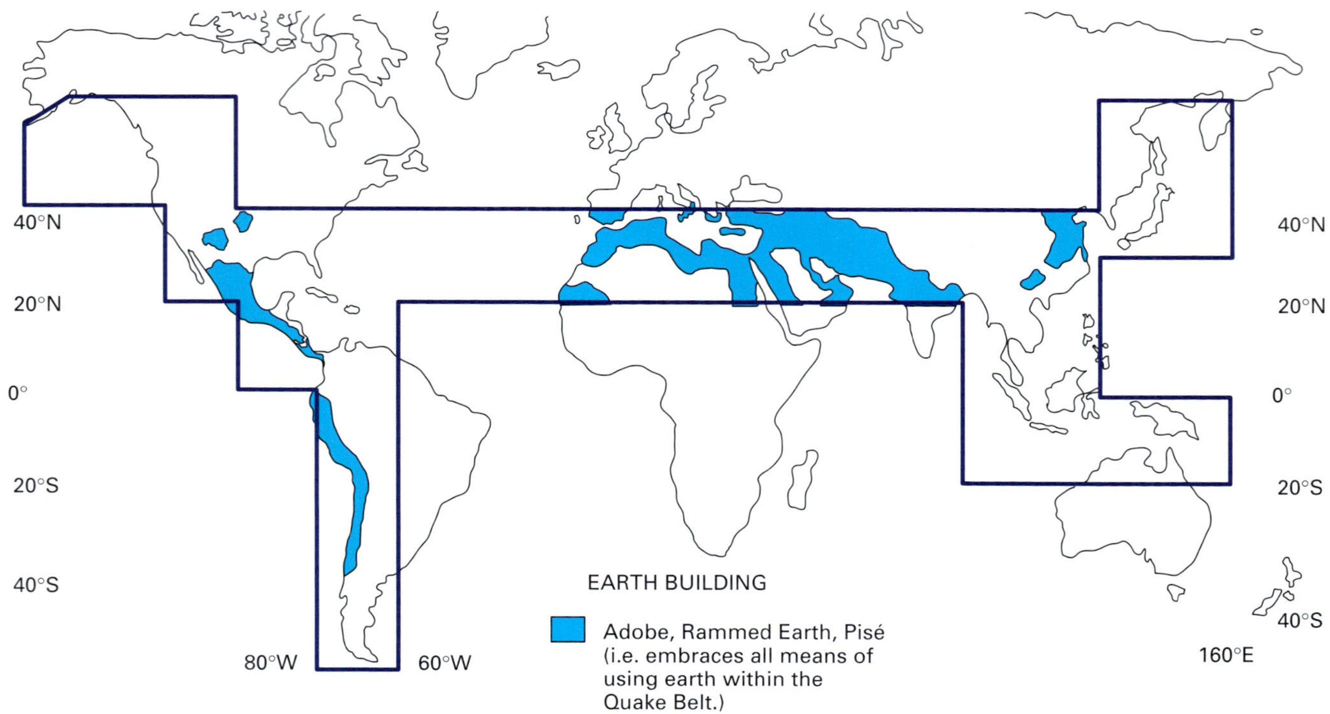


**Figure 13.5**
Map of earthen building in the seismic areas, embracing adobe, rammed earth, and *pisé de terre*, within the quake belts.

or clay are used as load-bearing material, sometimes in association with stone. Timber is generally employed in the roof structures but in many parts of the Middle East where there is little wood, barrel vaults or domes have been used. Some buildings are single cells, round or rectangular in plan but in other areas, Yemen and Morocco, for example, multi-storeyed buildings are constructed. More refined maps would show these distinctions and might identify the diversity of house types within a comparatively small area. This, it is intended, a map in the proposed *Atlas of Vernacular Architecture*, will do.

From one point of view perhaps, the relationship of building types to materials and climate accounts for their diversity. Yet housing is a cultural expression, not a geophysical or environmental fact; it is a response to the physical and the environmental but not determined by them, being articulated through the forms appropriate to the values of a specific culture. But what is culture? Tylor's 1874 definition of 'that complex whole which includes knowledge, belief, art, morals, law, custom, and any capabilities and habits acquired by man as a member of society' is still valid (Tylor, 1874). Julian Steward believed that there would be no great disagreement with the bare statement 'that culture consists of learned modes of behaviour that are socially transmitted from one generation to the next and from one society or individual to another' (Steward, 1955). The singularity of each culture within the universality of culture in mankind was one of the paradoxes which Melville Herskovits summarized: 'Culture is universal in man's experience yet each local or regional manifestation of it is unique. Culture is stable, yet it is also dynamic, and manifests continuous and constant change; culture fills and largely determines the course of our lives, yet rarely intrudes into conscious thought' (Herskovits, 1963).

The sheer diversity of peoples and the complex of cultures even within a single 'nation' has led many anthropologists to attempt larger classifications or groupings that may assist in identifying comparable cultural characteristics or traits. One such trait is language.

Extensive population shifts have occurred in relatively recent historical times, but broad linguistic groupings can still be identified. Language and culture are not one and the same, as the widespread use of Spanish, French or English among indigenous peoples in various parts of the world indicates; nevertheless, the current uses of language give some important clues to cultural identification. So we find that the linguistic map overlaid on the quake belts reveals a widespread distribution of Arabic and Berber-Arabic-speaking peoples in the central band which abuts the Iranian cluster, that includes

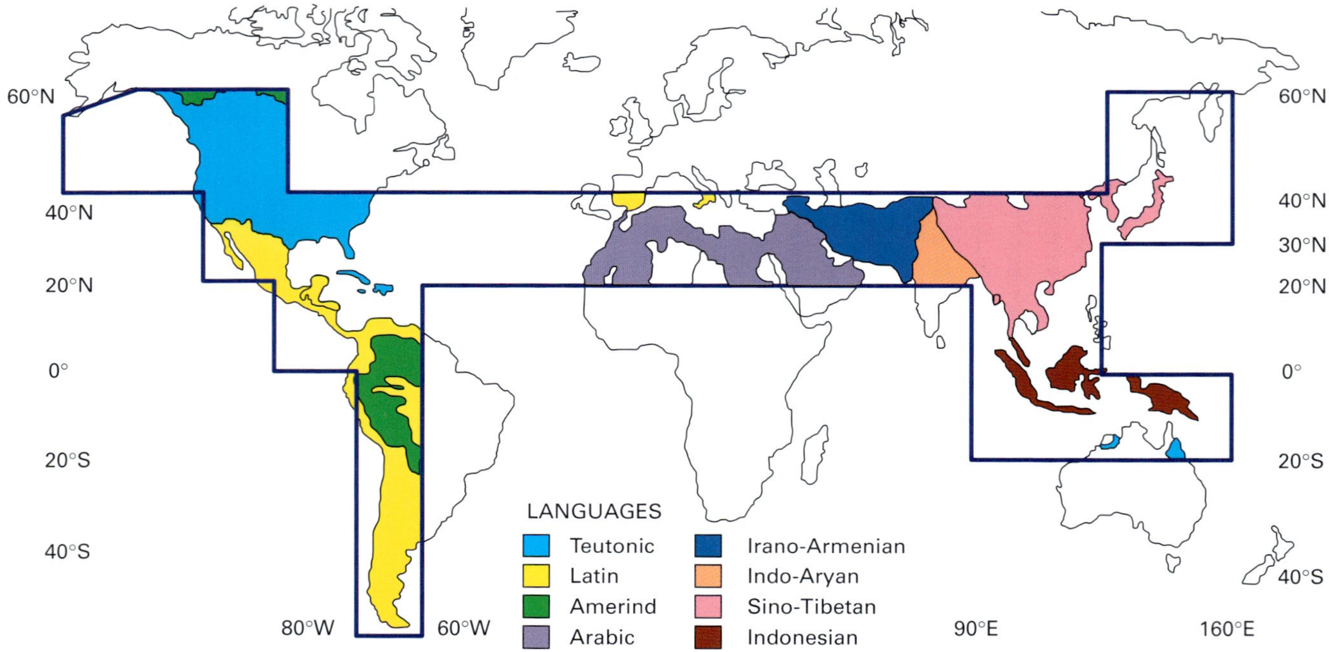


**Figure 13.6**
Linguistic map, indicating Teutonic, Latin, Amerindian; Arabic, Irano-Armenian and Indo-Aryan; Sino-Japanese and Tibetan; and Indonesian, spoken in the quake belts.

Armenian, Kurdish, Pushtu and Baluch. Indo-Aryan-speaking peoples, southern Mongoloids, Malaysians and Melanesians form other major linguistic groups in Asia. In the Americas, Spanish predominates in much of the quake belts where, among indigenous peoples, Indian dialects including Mayan and Quechua, are still spoken. While indicating admixtures and extensive cultural exchanges these linguistic clusters still reveal cultural groups that are broadly identifiable and largely homogeneous. A glance at the linguistic map shows that Arabic, Iran-Armenian or Chinese are each extensively used in seismic zones. English may be spoken in most of the countries embraced in the quake belts by the educated elites, but its use is unsatisfactory when it comes to the implementation of modification proposals at village level. Parallel maps of literacy rates, or of education opportunities, among the total populace of nations would only reinforce the impression of cultural bias, or as some would see it, 'cultural colonialism'.

Language is an important index not only of culture, but of culture change. Its transmission as a result of conquest or influence is comparable to that of religion. Here too, a marked separation of the prevalent faiths likely to be represented among readers – Christian Protestant, Roman Catholic or Jewish – is widely at variance with those of the remaining earthquake belts. A substantial part of the populations of the quake belts are of the Islamic faith. All of North Africa, virtually all of the Middle East and Malaysia are Muslim, while much of the Indian subcontinent has a substantial Muslim minority. Buddhism and Hinduism account for much of the remaining major religions in the belts, while there are pockets of animism in each of the continents. Language and religion are cultural traits which need have no physical tangible manifestation. As an example of the relationship between culture and the environment, agriculture is a significant indicator. Here we find that across a considerable expanse of the dry land regions, nomadic herdsmen utilize the thin pastures. The irrigated dry land areas sustain subsistence agriculture and in the regions where oriental rice farming prevails are to be found largely rural populations with peasant economies. The landholdings of large ranch owners do not necessarily imply high standards of living and income for those engaged in cattle or sheep ranching in the Americas. Again, however, a clear cultural distinction between the western hemisphere and the east is evident, the latter being further subdivided by different forms of native subsistence farming.

A score of cultural traits could be mapped at this generalized level to give a clearer profile of the cultural complexes that may be

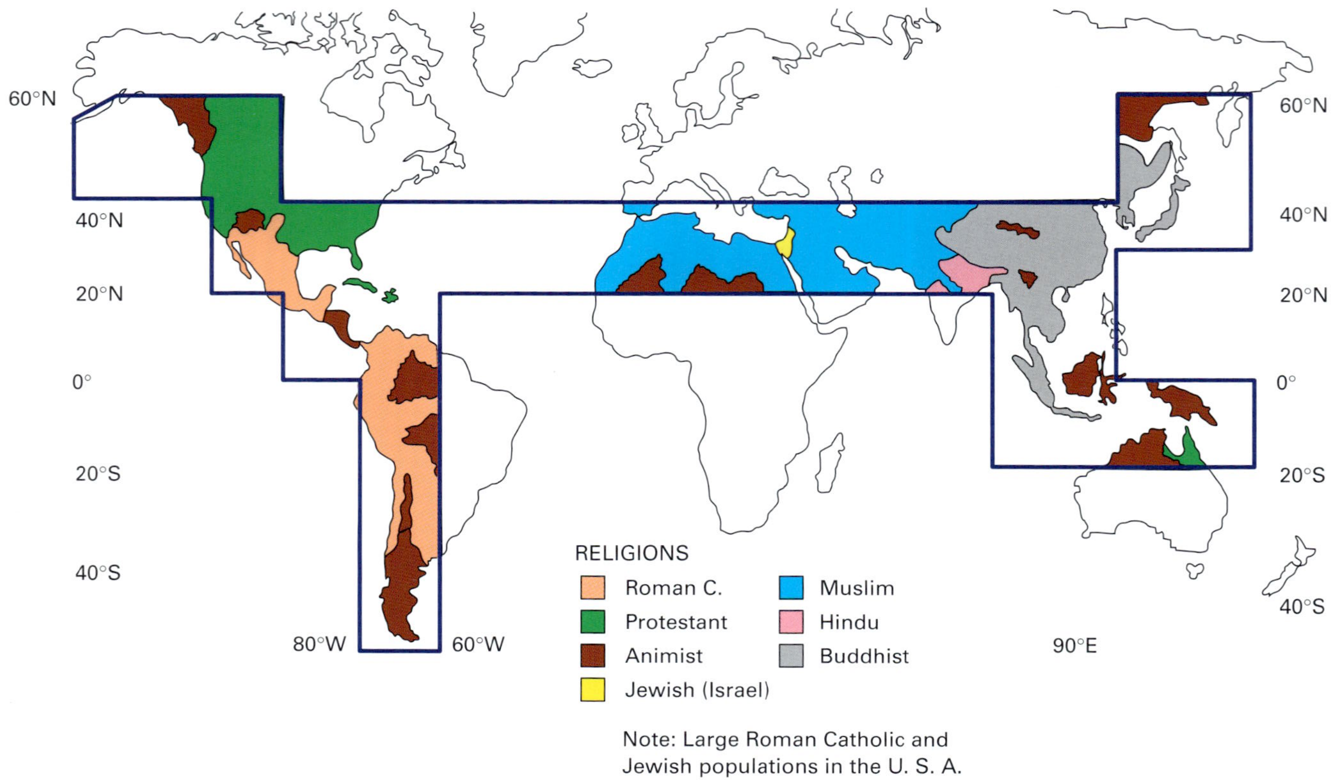


**Figure 13.7**
Map of religions: Roman Catholic Christian, Protestant Christian, Muslim, Hindu, Buddhist, Jewish and Animist, where practised in relation to the quake belts.

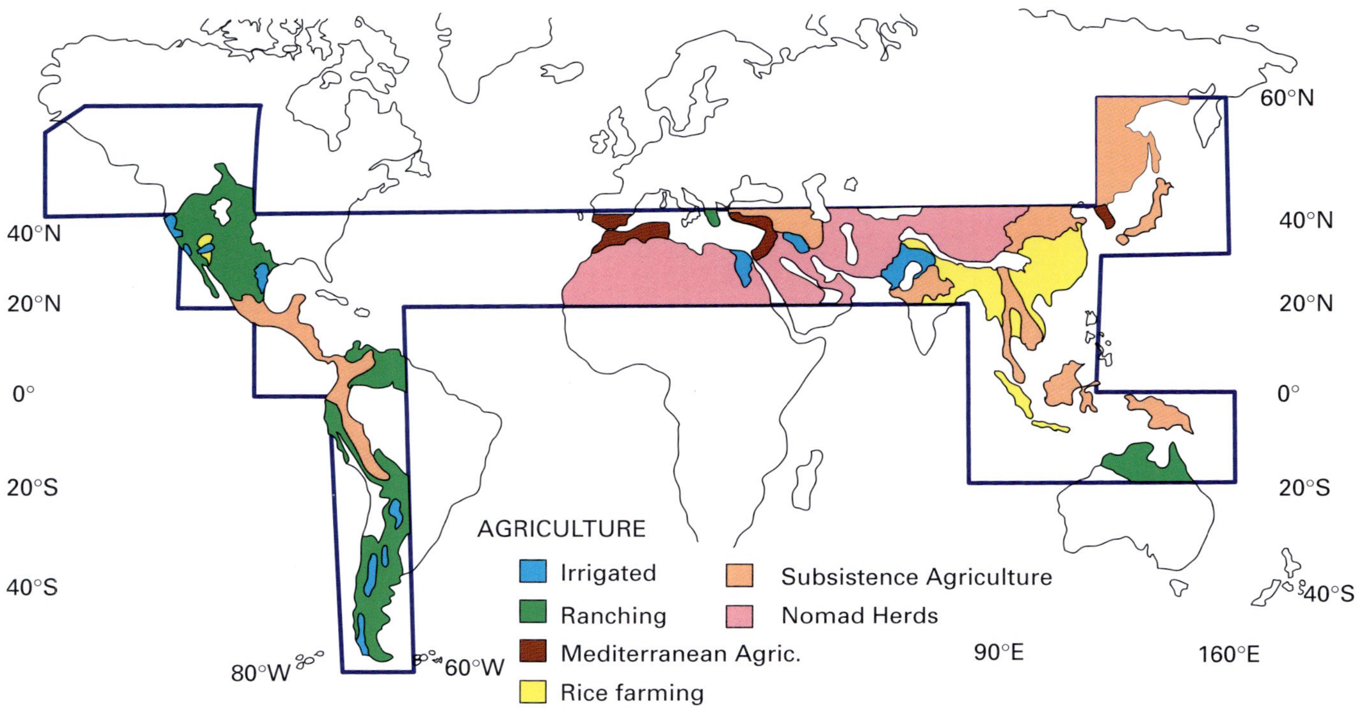


**Figure 13.8**
Agriculture and economy: Subsistance agriculture, Mediterranean agriculture; irrigated and rice farming, nomadic pastoral and ranching, within the quake belts.

found within the quake belts. Political institutions, types of trade, forms of social organization, class structures, land tenure, technologies, ceremonials and so on could be mapped, their relationships giving a fuller understanding of the complexes of culture traits which may be found in a region. From such a profile, deductions could be made on their bearing upon attitudes to disaster and disaster relief, housing modifications, new forms of housing, the acquisition of skills, etc. Though this is, in my view, an essential undertaking, space and time does not permit further examples here. Can anything be gleaned from the few maps illustrated? Perhaps this can be best viewed from the position of western architects or engineers, the seismic area building experts (SABE), who have proposals for change in housing earthen building methods. Linguistically, the SABEs will find themselves unable to share verbal communication with the people most affected, but only with the educated and the town-bred. If the SABEs are Spanish-speaking they will have the advantage of direct communication through the quake belts of the Americas, but even here the limitations of language comprehension, both for the understanding of abstract ideas and of technological innovations, may present linguistic and other problems.

The SABEs are unlikely to share the same religious beliefs as the people that they address. The major religions, as observed in the quake belts, are largely determinist. Followers of the orthodox doctrine of the Muslim theologian Al-Berkevi, 'that all that has been and all that will be was decreed in eternity and written on the preserved tablet', have their Christian counterpart. St. Thomas Aquinas's Augustinian pronouncement, that 'it is manifest that whatever is of grace is the effect of predestination', still has innumerable adherents among Roman Catholics. For the poor and illiterate peasants, the esoteric arguments concerning free will, responsibility and predestination are remote; they are more likely to content themselves with a fatalistic 'As Allah wills' or 'God moves in mysterious ways . . . '. As human beings, they may react to a disaster with similar fear and stress as their counterparts in other, more sophisticated societies. But their resignation and belief in divine intervention or retribution, may be paralleled by a reluctance to accept measures which would seem to attempt to frustrate God's intentions. Animistic peoples would be far more inclined to propitiate the enraged spirits (Sorokin, 1942; Lachman and Bonk, 1960).

Economically, rural people in the quake belts are largely nomadic-pastoralists or they are rural cultivators or peasants. Many nomadic peoples follow set routes for the seasonal pasturing of their herds leaving their womenfolk, children and elders in permanent, usually mud-built villages. Although the problems of seismic risk may not apply to their tented settlements, they are just as applicable to the more settled home bases as they are to the peasant villages. There are several peasant ecotypes that employ different cultivation methods such as swidden, fallowing or hydraulic systems. Structurally, they may differ but, generally speaking, peasant communities tend to be tightly knit and to comprise extended families which are linked by complex kinship ties, and which have ritualized or ceremonial calendars that reinforce the social structure and the cycle of the working year.

Symbols which underline their belief system and express family and community ties to the value systems of the culture are important. Frequently these are associated with the lands worked by their forefathers and with their buildings, which play significant parts in the rites of passage through birth, marriage, death and burial. In general, peasant society is traditional, conservative, moralistic, unquestioning and uncommitted to change and innovation. Peasant communities that are linked to the market networks are frequently suspicious of external authority, or of members of alien societies. For the SABE arriving with an endorsement of intentions from a central authority and armed with proposals for new methods of building, the resiting of houses, or proposals for new and safer 'designs', the outlook is not promising.

Such observations as these, I am all too well aware, are dangerously stereotypical. They are generalizations which give no indication of the variables that are to be found in the multiplicity of cultures embraced by these broad headings and summarily shaded areas. Cultural mapping is concerned with the comparability of traits at the macroscale; its evidence may assist in heightening awareness for certain kinds of cultural attitudes and behaviour patterns, but only as a preparation for the encounters at the microscale. If anthropologists have their disagreements over the traits to be identified, 'cultural area' mapping, such as that undertaken by G.M. Murdock for his *Ethnographic Atlas*, could be of considerable assistance to the well-briefed SABE. For the specific examples of cultural context and response to housing modification or building in seismic areas, we should be able to turn to case studies based on recent events. During the period 1950–1975, there were over 50 major earthquakes in the quake belts, claiming around 150 000 lives and a toll of five million victims. It would not be unreasonable to expect a substantial literature on the cultural responses to the measures taken following these disasters, and the programmes for housing or house modification that were implemented. Such was not the case;

the literature on the cultural contexts of disaster housing generally is woefully inadequate – to the extent that in the 200 page UNDRO report on *Housing in Disaster-Prone Countries* not a single reference is made to cultural issues (Roth, 1959). On the other hand, a considerable amount of attention has been paid by many writers to the effects on victims of stress, induced by disasters, whose psychological disorders and problems have been frequently discussed (Sinha, 1952; Fogelman and Parenton, 1959).

Much of the available writing on the psychological impact has concentrated on disasters in the west, particularly in North America, so that the effects of Hurricane Audrey, the Oregon cyclone of 1962, tornadoes in Waco and San Angelo and the earthquake at Anchorage, Alaska, etc., have been extensively documented. Undoubtedly, this is of great value, but it *is* culture-bound. The reasons are not hard to seek: the centres of much disaster research are in the United States, access to the disaster areas is fairly simple, the language of many researchers is English. Communication with the victims is more readily possible, they are culturally more inclined to accept in-depth questioning from psychologists, perhaps even viewing this as a therapeutic activity in itself. Insofar as human responses at the psychological level are similar, general conclusions may be drawn of some validity for application in other cultures. Nevertheless, human responses are also shaped by culture, and little attention appears to have been paid to the role of cultural mores in conditioning responses to stress situations. In a previous paper, I endeavoured

**Figure 13.9**
Earthquake damage at Coalinga under inspection, 1983. A minor quake, like the Oakland earthquake, it was a warning of the vulnerability of the California region.

to differentiate between the relief culture, with its fragile structure, its apparent authority and command of skills, resources and money, and the victim culture (Chapter 12). The victim culture is at its most vulnerable, being subject to disorientation and demoralization by its failure to cope through its existing social mechanisms with the magnitude of a disaster and being forced to be dependent on a temporary, but authoritarian, organization which has a clearly defined purpose to bring aid to the victims. As recovery from disaster is manifest, cultural factors take over; the lack of animosity that researchers have noted in immediate post-disaster situations may be followed by resentment at the behaviour of officials, and antipathy to aid and relief organizations (Dirks, 1979). Cultural responses have been observed in the rejection of certain foods offered during relief or in the unacceptability of types of clothing and other articles of a more culturally defined nature; illogical in the terms of the relief culture, but nevertheless inadmissible in terms of the victim culture. Rejection behaviour may be ascribed to psychological disturbance, but may also be perceived as an expression resulting from cultural incompatibility.

As the recovery period progresses, cultural characteristics related to family and community structure and behaviour, to hierarchies and law, to territory and even to housing may be seen to operate. After disasters, most societies wish to return to the *status quo* as early as possible, and express this in a desire to rebuild on the traditional, if obviously vulnerable sites. Nevertheless, the impact of the disaster, and the likewise disastrous impact, in cultural terms, of the temporary assumption of responsibility by relief organizations, leave their scars and bring about culture change at a more rapid rate. No culture is unscathed or unchanged, either by disaster or by disaster relief. In the specific context of vernacular architecture, it is the introduction of methods of building modification, the adaptation of existing technologies and structures, propositions as to the alteration of plan types and sites of buildings and other means of making more safe the earthen building in seismic areas, that have particular cultural implications. Houses, we have noted, are the focus of a large part of man's cultural activity and carry considerable symbolic associations, both in their organization and in their form (Rapoport, 1969; Oliver, 1977a, 1977b). Their importance differs in emphasis with different societies and the anthropomorphic associations of one house type cannot be assumed for others; the significance of the location of an entrance may have different meaning in one culture than another; the areas of security or privacy, those assigned to women or children, to men or important visitors, to particular domestic functions, shrines and ritual observances are of varying degrees of significance. In the face of seismic risk are such factors of any importance? Indeed they are – for the perception of a risk that may manifest itself once in a lifetime is of a low order to the users, compared with the daily, even hourly observance of cultural mores within the home.

Modifications of building techniques and technology, introductions of new methods of building to make adobe and earthen structures safe, or safer, against seismic disturbance can be seen as essentially a part of the process of culture change. But any such innovations are representative of *induced* change rather than of indigenous change from *within* the culture. Housing innovations which are not the result of evolution, individual discovery or invention within a culture, may be seen as representative of the most common form of innovation, resulting from diffusion. However, the emphasis in *diffusion* is on *borrowing* rather than on the acceptance of an externally imposed, or proposed, innovation. As Kroeber pointed out, 'items of culture that are isolated, not much woven into a pattern, and therefore relatively neutral in their functioning, and yet of an indubitable practical value, are least likely to encounter resistances to their diffusion: matches, for instance' (Kroeber, 1948). But housing is essentially woven into the cultural pattern and far more subject to rejection.

Extended culture contact provides the most fertile ground for the borrowing of culture traits, but few SABEs have the time, the money or the patience to consider it. If, as I would recommend, documentation of the processes of acceptance, experimentation or rejection of an innovation is carefully made, SABEs must be prepared for the diffusion (and rejection) of some of their own culture traits, which were not on the programme of housing modification. These too, should be monitored, as they may provide useful clues to the means for successful information transfer, and to the long-term adoption of a trait. The introduction of modifications to buildings, let alone of proposals to replace an existing building type with another designed by an SABE team, should be recognized as being potentially damaging to a culture. Once the immediate dangers are over and the perception of risk has receded, a culture is likely to reject such innovations even if they initially accepted them and, in defence, to turn to established norms of building. In many instances, 'rational' proposals have been made for building modification – the substitution of a lighter-weight pitched roof of lamina for a heavy, timbered and mud-surfaced flat roof for example, have failed, for the simple reason that the flat roofs are used for other purposes – drying fruit, storing millet, even sleeping upon. A western observer who perceives such uses as 'illogical' in the face of seismic risk, does not place his scale of values on the same axis, or with the same weighting as does the community that he advises. Even suggestions as to the resiting of houses so that escape corridors exist between them, or to ensure that the collapsing walls of one do not bring danger to another, may be inimical to a spatial organization that reflects the social and family interactions of a given culture. They may be rejected because they interfere with such social interaction, or they may be accepted – perhaps under the force of law and the implementation of 'codes' – to the ultimate detriment of the social fabric.

Although building modifications such as these, may be more modest than some of the wholesale alterations to plan form and building method proposed in the past, it is unlikely that they will come singly. Building innovations, unlike matches, are in fact, rarely introduced solely, and in neat packs. Modified building techniques employing, for example, the use of cross-braced cables, requires the learning of new building skills, the introduction of new materials, a method of demonstration, or an educational package for instruction. Posters, booklets, film and videos may be employed, each bringing with it, in subtle ways, innovations in communication and exposure to new technologies and values. The introduction of any element may have, almost certainly will have, a chain reaction which may be instrumental in bringing about profound culture change. And it may also inhibit the initiative of the culture to meet a newly perceived risk in its own way. In a carefully documented study of the Canadian 'High-Aid' housing programme at San Andres Itzapa, Guatemala following the 1976 earthquake, Chris M. Rosene recorded both the advantages and the disadvantages of the programme which left the people 'as surprised by the arrival of Canadian aid as they were by the earthquake. To them it had no rationale; no history, no cause – it *must* have been preordained'. The writer concluded that it was 'in itself a social shock which destroyed the possibility for them to find their own solution . . . while it helped promote the social reform movement in the town, it restricted the movement by orienting it towards outside solutions. . . . In the final analysis the people of San Andres were no better prepared than they were before to find their own solutions to the problems which faced them' (Rosene, 1976). It would be valuable to know now, years later, just what remains of the 'High Aid' programme, and what the long-term effects have been upon the people of San Andres Itzapa.

It is certain that any measures introduced are unlikely to persist if they are culturally unacceptable. Acceptability may depend on many things, but it may be made more possible by coupling the innovation seen necessary by the SABE, with a need perceived and expressed by the populace. A low ceiling that inhibits the storage of cereals and generates smoke nuisance is unlikely to be accepted, however much it reduces the problems of deflection aggravated by height. But a roof system which contributes to safety whilst improving the conditions of cereal preservation and storage and which channels away internal domestic smoke without encouraging parasites, is more likely to succeed. In the perception of the community, the advantages of a changed roofing system may be immediate; to the SABE team the primary intention of safety in seismic areas may be achieved by riding on the back of the other, explicit advantage. It is indeed, largely a matter of perception of immediate need. In one of the few apparently authenticated examples of indigenous housing developed consciously to meet the threat of earthquakes, that of the Greek island of Lefkas on the Adriatic, Demetrius Porphyrios noted that 'the overwhelmingly crucial factor in this environment is not just the threat but the actuality of periodically recurring earthquakes. Their destructiveness was so widespread and so devastating that it forced the inhabitants to evolve special building methods so that the buildings – and they themselves – might survive' (Porphyrios, 1976). In this rare example, an earthquake-resistant building type was 'developed and highly perfected' over 'long traditional practice' as a direct result of the perception, from within the culture, of the extent of risk.

Whereas the people of San Andres had no say in the new housing in which they were to make their homes, the people of Lefkas had exclusive control. Both, it is safe to assume, were accustomed to building their own houses; the essential difference was one of the perception of risk, such that the Lefkians were obliged to develop an appropriate building type, which they did, and which has endured. The first responsibility of western SABEs is not, in my view, to provide solutions, but to aid the perception of risk. If building solutions or new construction techniques are proposed, it is not satisfactory to expect the endangered society to provide the labour force for the building of a house type not of their own devising. The participation of the members of a community must be actively encouraged at all stages; not only in the building but in the decision-making related to site disposition, form, internal layout, roof system, construction and the development of new skills as well. Only through this kind of participation, which demands the end of architects' schemes for universally applied 'disaster housing', can the accommodation of cultural issues important to the people concerned be achieved and some chance of success in the long term, be attained. All of which necessitates measures of long-term commitment, patience, knowledge and understanding of different value systems and priorities, which are by no means shared by all who have an interest in shelter in seismic areas. Given preparedness and willingness to advise, to promote and participate in, but not to define or dictate the building solutions, by no means the least of the problems confronting the SABE relates to communication.

Childrens' party games in which whispered messages or line drawings are passed secretly along a line, reveal the distortions of meaning that may occur in a closely linked group of culturally similar individuals; experience of misunderstandings in chains of command or in management–union negotiations are familiar to many of us. Between people who are culturally very dissimilar, with quite different expectations of the means of conveying information, the manners and modes of address: of vocal emphasis, of gestures, body language, grimaces and impassiveness, opportunities abound for confusion and misunderstanding on both sides. Formal and polite languages, appropriate modes of respect or authority, indelicate usages and codified or symbolic references, may all seem to be irrelevant to the SABE intent on passing on a simple technological process, in view of the seriousness of seismic risk. But to the recipient of advice, they may be more important than the content, at that time. Fugelsang's work on communication (1973) has been augmented by occasional articles by Bowers (1980) and Ressler (1979). They offer good advice on graphic communication in disaster housing contexts and give evidence of communication interpretation. The issues related to strip cartoon montage, graphic ambiguity, religious sanctions against figurative depiction, pictorial depth perception, geometric illusion have been the subject of extensive research, some of it well summarized by Hudson (1967). In some contexts, for example on the Indian subcontinent, where film is widely available, other more sophisticated media may communicate information more effectively. But even here, extraneous detail, unaccustomed dress and behaviour patterns depicted on the screen, may distract attention, creating further cultural barriers to communication of the message (Kuppuswamy, 1976).

Where greater experience in the recognition of messages through mass media is to be found, more complex systems may be used. This generally applies in the city, where some familiarity with advanced technologies and communication techniques is evident among the majority of the population. In the cities too, are to be found the technological innovations which have still to reach the villages, or to have been generally accepted in them. Those who have moved to the cities and have built their homes in the peri-urban communities and squatter settlements, have already chosen to have a stake in modern society. In this sense, they are more open to innovation and have already experienced aspects of cultural change. To some extent the degree of change may be illusory; the 'folk-urban continuum' of which Redfield wrote (1941), has many and varied levels in different cultures. Linkages with rural communities, strong emotional and social ties, the persistence of traditional customs and observances, and the evidence of rural mores within the urban environment, have been detailed by many anthropologists and in numerous countries (Singer, 1972). The acquisition of contemporary gadgets is not by any means, a sign of total cultural transformation.

While the security of the traditional framework has been in part disengaged, the urban dweller in an earthquake-prone Third World city may still be employing largely traditional methods of building. Mapping the degree of urbanization in the quake belts raises the problem of how much adobe building there is in the cities. Selecting four Iranian cities, Reza Razani reported that only a little over 4 per cent of Teheran's buildings were of adobe and wood, while over 70 per cent of those in Isfahan were of these materials (Razani, 1978). Clearly, much more needs to be known about this, and of the values and processes whereby adobe buildings are retained or replaced. In the early *gecekondus* of Ankara there was extensive use of adobe,

**Figure 13.10**
*Gecekondus*, or squatter housing in Ankara and Istanbul. Originally of adobe and now often of concrete block, they are still vulnerable to seismic shock. Ankara, Turkey.

but as Geoffrey Payne has shown, the adobe houses have been largely replaced by houses built of concrete blocks. The patterns of house forms have changed in response to the 'reduction of Islamic customs in domestic life which gave women more freedom . . . the reduction of family size and the emigration and subsequent return of workers in western Europe which exposed them to new life-styles and forms of building which many sought to emulate on their return' (Payne, 1980). It is important to realize that urban living in the Third World means a total commitment to a cash economy. Innovations that are not seen to have immediate benefit are likely to be converted into cash, while the slack periods in the farming year when village building traditionally takes place, do not exist in the city. The immediate benefits that may accrue are more likely to appeal than the unspecific, long-term possible advantages of an untried, but assuredly seismic-safe building. Although the fact that Ankara is prone to severe earthquake damage is not in question among many seismologists, the perception of this is no more shared among the populace of the *gecekondus*, than it is recognized as an imminent risk by the residents of Berkeley. Moreover, the changes in building type within the *gecekondus*, have arisen from changes within the culture of the communities themselves, and have not been imposed by agencies from outside.

Nevertheless, the potential for change and the acceptability of innovations is greater in the cities than in the villages, and SABEs who are concerned with seismic risk may be advised to direct their attention to urban settlements that are especially vulnerable. Here as elsewhere, the necessity to involve the participation of the community in the decision-making is of fundamental importance; the opportunities for effective communication may be greater but the independence of the newly urbanized may not make the process more effective. Given that a programme of building modification is achieved through demonstration and participation, the possibilities of slow but effective information transfer back to the villages, are real. The threads that link the rural communities with the cities are also the communication channels by which elements of urban living are transmitted to the more conservative peasant cultures. That this is an instrument of culture change is undeniable, and the introduction of technological innovations in building types will contribute to the dissolution of traditional ways of life. But the changes will be assimilated from within, and at the speed most acceptable to the communities concerned. To the engineer or architect with a ready-made solution and little time to spare, the process may be impossibly slow – but it is more likely to succeed in the long

**Figure 13.11**
The concrete and brick mosque at Gediz, 15 years after its destruction in the Emet and Gediz earthquake of 1970. Kütahya Province, Turkey.

term than any imposition of unenforceable building codes, or the introduction of unwanted new techniques for building.

Of course, the urgency recognized by SABEs, whether or not they are perceived by rural or urban communities, may be considered by some to be justification enough for draconian measures. Certainly, there will be many circumstances where persuasive argument, good communications, the participation of wise leaders and far-sighted household heads, or even the provision of demonstrably better levels of housing may make such introductions effective and permanent. In all instances, detailed records and careful and repeated return studies should be made, so that the nature of successful or failed overtures is fully documented. So far, there is little precedent. Snarr and Brown observed that 'systematic user evaluation of permanent housing built for disaster victims in the Third World is unknown to these authors. Such evaluations may exist as in-house documents, but we even doubt this' (Snarr, Brown, 1980). Anthropologists have been giving more attention to disaster studies. William I. Torry has written persuasively on the role that they can and should play in disaster research (Torry, 1979), although he stops short of the issues central to this paper, namely the important contribution that the anthropologist can make to teams concerned with the problems of resiting, rebuilding or rendering safe the earthen buildings prone to seismic risk.

Profound changes in housing have formerly taken place in some parts of the quake belts, with the introduction of adobe building itself. Although adobe was present among some pre-Conquest societies, its use in Central and South America was considerably extended by the Spanish. The Spanish *adobe*, however, derives from the Arabic *atob* (sun-dried brick), and was previously an importation, during the occupation of Spain by the Moors. Such housing innovations were brought with much pain and duress. Hopefully, the new changes planned for adobe housing will be introduced in a more enlightened and humane climate; but if there is not to be further unnecessary social distress and disruption it will be with full regard to the cultural contexts.

## References


Bowers, J. (1980). Some thoughts on communication. *Disasters* 4(1), 22.

Cooke, A. (1981). Letter from America. BBC Radio Four, 14 March.

Dirks, R. (1979). Relief-induced agonism. *Disasters* 3(2), 195.

Fogelman, C.W. and Parenton, V.J. (1959). Disaster and aftermath: Selected aspects of individual and group behaviour in critical situations. *Social Forces* 38, 129.

Fugelsang, G. (1973). *Applied Communication in Developing Countries.* Uppsala: Dag Hammerskjold Foundation.

Gauchet, U.P. and Schodek, D.L. (1977). *Housing in Disaster-Prone Countries: A Codification and Vulnerability Analysis.* Harvard University Press for UNDRO.

Herskovits, M. (1963). *Cultural Anthropology.* New York: Alfred A. Knopf, p. 306.

Hudson, W. (1967). The problem of pictorial perception among unacculturated groups. *International Journal of Psychology* 2, 90.

Kroeber, A.L. (1948, 1963). *Anthropology: Culture Patterns and Processes.* New York: Harcourt Brace.

Kuppuswamy, B. (1976). *Communication and Social Development in India.* New Delhi: Sterling Publishers.

Lachman, R. and Bonk, W.J. (1960). Behavior and beliefs during the recent volcanic eruption at Kapoho, Hawaii. *Science* 131, 1095.

Oliver, P. (ed.). (1977a). *Shelter, Sign and Symbol.* New York: Overlook Press, p. 7.

Oliver, P. (1977b). The cultural context of shelter provision. *Disasters* 2, 2/3.

Payne, G. (1980). The Gecekondus of Ankara. *Process Architecture* 15.

Porphyrios, D.T.G. (1976). Traditional earthquake-resistant construction on a Greek island. *Society of Architectural Historians Journal* 30(1), 31.

Rapoport, A. (1969). *House Form and Culture.* New Jersey: Prentice-Hall, pp. 40, 74.

Razani, R. (1978). Seismic protection of unreinforced masonry and adobe low-cost housing in less-developed countries: Policy issues and design criteria. *Disasters* 2, (2/3).

Redfield, R. (1941). *The Folk Culture of Yucatan.* University of Chicago Press.

Ressler, E.M. (1979). Development of educational materials following the Andhra Pradesh cyclone. *Disasters* 3(3).

Rosene, C.M. (1976). *San Andres Itzapa, Guatemala: the Impact of High-Aid Housing Program*. Emergency Shelter Study Phase 1. INTERTECT for UNDRO, Dallas, Texas.
Roth, R. (1959). Cross-cultural perspectives on disaster response. *American Behavioral Scientist* 13(3), 440.
Singer, M. (1972). *When a Great Tradition Modernizes*. New York: Praeger.
Sinha, D. (1952). Behaviour in a catastrophic situation: A psychological study of reports and rumours. *British Journal of Psychology* 43, 200.
Snarr, N. and Brown, L. (1980). User satisfaction with permanent post-disaster housing. Two years after Hurricane Fiji in Honduras. *Disasters* 4(1).
Sorokin, P.A. (1942). *Man and Society in Calamity*. New York: E.P. Dutton.
Steward, J. (1955). *Theory of Culture Change*. University of Illinois Press, p. 44.
Torry, W.I. (1979). Anthropology and disaster research. *Disasters* 3(1), 43.
Tylor, Sir E.B. (1874). *Primitive Culture*. Boston: Estes and Lauriat, Vol. 1, p. 1.

# 14

# Factors affecting the acceptability of resettlement housing (1984)

There are probably no vernacular contexts that are not subject to processes of change, though the rates, degree and nature of such change may vary considerably depending on the agents that occasion them. Change brought about by the slow introduction of alternative materials – corrugated iron instead of thatch, for example – may affect the aesthetic qualities of an indigenous African architecture, and may make it microclimatically less agreeable. One could argue that in terms of economy or even the cycle of annual house repair, such a change in technology would have serious implications. But in many respects it may not influence the cultural mores or value systems to any appreciable extent. On the other hand, the total resettlement of a nomadic or hunter-gatherer people may have profound effects, leading to the disruption, even the dissolution, of its culture. A measure of this kind could be motivated by a number of reasons – the more 'efficient' use of land resources, the appropriation of lands to 'open up' a region, the political desire to stabilize the population, and so on. There are other circumstances where housing resettlement and relocation is necessary on humanitarian grounds, such as in the immediate aftermath of a major disaster, whether it is following hurricane damage in Jamaica, floods in Andra Pradesh or earthquakes in Turkey. It is the latter context in which our shelter and settlements team was working, an aspect of which I wish to discuss.

Turkey is subject to earthquakes, being situated in a highly seismic region of the Middle East. A great deal is known of the seismicity of the region and Turkey's Earthquake Research Institute and its Building Research Institute have substantial records based on research in the laboratory, and experience in hazard prediction, rescue, emergency relief and recovery. One of the country's more remarkable achievements has been the provision of housing for those who have suffered building loss in an earthquake; only in villages or towns where fewer than 10 per cent of the dwellings have been affected is there no housing replacement; otherwise, houses built to government specification, or provided in the form of government prefabricated units, is used to replace those lost. This is unique in earthquake-prone areas and is a considerable drain on the resources of a far from wealthy country. One implication of this rehousing is that new settlements are established, sometimes on locations a few miles from the former sites on what is believed to be safer ground. Another is that the enormous costs of such a programme have led to the standardization of designs and units. A long, rectangular country, Turkey is bordered by the Black Sea to the north, the Aegean to the west and much of the south, and by Iran, a thousand miles to the east. Across this great area of some 300 000 square miles, there are peoples of many differing ethnic groups and cultures; hence, the standardized house types provided in post-earthquake situations are supplied to peoples who are of differing origins, language groups and culture traits. While housing provision to stricken communities is received with gratitude in the aftermath of a disaster, the long-term implications of the adoption of the introduction of a new building type, new techniques of building and new settlement forms are not understood. In fact, these effects have not been studied in post-disaster housing contexts in other countries apart from Turkey. Although some studies of the short-term effects of rehousing in immediate recovery periods exist, no analysis has been made of the acceptability of the houses in cultural terms, or of their success or failure over an extended period of time after the post-emergency responses had worn off.

On 27 March 1970, a major earthquake, 7.1 on the Richter scale, occurred mainly affecting the Gediz and Emet regions of Kütahya Province in Western Anatolia. The town of Gediz was severely damaged and further ravaged by fire, while in the adjacent regions over 300 villages were destroyed or damaged. More than a thousand people lost their lives and 17 000 homes were lost or seriously affected: as many as 50 000 people were rendered homeless. Massive post-earthquake relief and recovery measures were

**Figure 14.1**
Earthquake damage of a *bagdadi* (wood and earth) house, with nailed joints, Eski (Old) Muhipler. Wood houses did not collapse as readily as stone or adobe structures. Kütahya Province, Turkey.

taken, aided by international agencies. Some of these published reports on the work, in Sweden, the United States, Great Britain and Turkey (Krimgold, 1974; Germen, 1978). Though few of these reports received more than limited circulation, in total they amount to a comprehensive coverage of the relief measures, which included the provision of immediate emergency shelter and longer-term housing replacement and resettlement. Some forms of emergency shelter, notably the Bayer Corporation's domes of spun polystyrene formed *in situ*, which were provided for relief at the village of Akcaalan, have received some attention, partly perhaps, because of their novelty (Ozkan, 1972). More prosaic standardized housing as supplied by the government, although contractor-built to government designs, has not been the subject of study, even though this represents the bulk of the housing provision. Not all of it, because Akcaalan itself was the site of two-storey housing projects, based on British 'new town' prototypes, while the town of Yeni (New) Gediz, built 7 km from the stricken town had several house and apartment types. These were intended to accommodate urban dwellers from the old town of Gediz, as well as new arrivals to the region.

In conducting our research into the 'Cultural Aspects of Housing in Seismic Areas', the Oxford team studied a number of facets of the problem. Here I wish to concentrate on the impact of rehousing on former village communities. The study was intended to be a long-term appraisal of the success or otherwise, of housing provision following the disaster, which had occurred some 14 years before our arrival. Permission was given to study villages in the

**Figure 14.2**
Bayer domes provided as emergency housing were fragile and inconvenient, but later used as stores in the 'new town' of Akcaalan.

Gediz subregion, which had the immediate effects of providing a 10 per cent sample; of the 300 villages, nine-tenths were located in the Emet subregion. Our team was handicapped by a lack of basic information; no anthropological or sociological studies had ever been conducted in the specific region; there were no ethnographic descriptions of its peoples and their cultures, no histories of the settlement and development of the area (Pierce, 1965; Stirling, 1965; Wolf, 1966). Maps were not available, as this was a militarily restricted area; village plans similarly, were not accessible, beyond cadastral maps of the new housing settlements. The team was fortunate in having the help of two research students of the Middle East Technical University, Ali Günoven (1977) and Fusun Ceylan (1983) who had recently been studying the vernacular architecture of one or two of the villages in the area. But apart from these very localized studies there was no published material on the local building types, or their use. Considerable time had to be spent by the team therefore, in establishing not only the vernacular architecture forms that existed in the stricken villages, but also the vernacular context, by which I mean the cultural context, in which they were used, in order that the processes of assimilation, adaptation or change that may have occurred in rehousing could be understood.

Obviously, this is too complex a subject to be examined in detail here and the vernacular context must be crudely summarized. The people of the Gediz region villages were peasant farmers with a mixed arable and animal-rearing economy. In this, as in other aspects which I am summarizing, there had been many changes in the twentieth century. Robert Redfield's description of the 'peasant society' which 'exists by virtue of the traditional moral solidarity to be found in any isolated folk society'; in which 'kinship relationships are still of first importance, the ends of living are implicit and strongly felt' was as applicable to the Gediz region villages as was his rider that 'certain elements' of urban life were assimilated: 'a trading spirit, money, formal and personal controls, whether economic or political'. Theirs was a style of living which was 'a balanced adjustment between moral order and technical order . . . where the influence of the city has spread, but not very rapidly' (Redfield, 1953). It is not an inadequate sketch of Gediz village circumstances. The moral order in this region of an officially secular state was essentially Islamic; kinship relations among patrilineal people with a 'partible inheritance' system were, as might be expected, within an extended family structure. These were land-owning peasants engaged in the market economy, with New Gediz the focus for that market and its regional administrative system penetrating their lives through the institutionalized election of village leaders, the *muhtars*. Modern technology had been accommodated where it could be an aid to farming: every family aspired to own a tractor. Sited in a well-cultivated and irrigated country on the slopes of snow-capped mountains, the villages, on first acquaintance, seemed relatively prosperous. Houses in the customary vernacular are large – I use the word 'customary' rather than 'traditional', for the age of the building forms and methods, and the changes that have taken place in local building practice are undocumented. Timber framed, with stone or adobe infill, or with lath and plaster walls in the system known as *bagdadi*, the houses were two-storeyed under tiled, hipped roofs. The ground floor was used for storage and for the wintering of the animals, whose body heat helped to keep the domestic quarters above warm.

Access to the living spaces was by a broad ladder, or in the better built houses by steps, either inside the house or external and attached. The access opened on to a large communal space, the *salon* (or in some villages, the *sofa*) where outdoor shoes were left and where much of the preparation and cooking of vegetables was done. In this space there was room for the storage of articles, sacks of grain and utensils. Off the *salon*, a grand term for a roughly plastered hall, were rooms, usually four in number, in each of which lived a unit of the extended family. The elderly patriarch and his wife might live in one, the eldest son, his wife and children in another; other sons and members of the family including unmarried daughters, in the remainder. Between the living spaces, and opposite the

**Figure 14.3**
A traditional Küahya house, in which animals and stores are kept on the ground floor and living spaces for extended families are on the floor above.

entrance, was a kitchen, while on the transverse axis at the side walls there were usually two closets. One was for storage, the other, on the opposite side of the house, was in the form of a medieval garderobe. A latrine, a mere hole in the floor and vessels for ablutions, was situated above the animal dung-heap. Faeces were mixed with animal dung and the combined manure used to enrich the soil. In each room there was a fireplace in the centre of an outside wall, though it was sometimes replaced by a metal stove bought from its maker in Gediz, on which water in a tinware pot was kept hot for brewing *cai*. To the left of the fireplace was a recess used for ablutions, rather in the manner of a bidet, while to the right was a further recess for the storage of bedding. Around the room was a bench seat, or *sedir*; store-bought rugs or linoleum lined the floor.

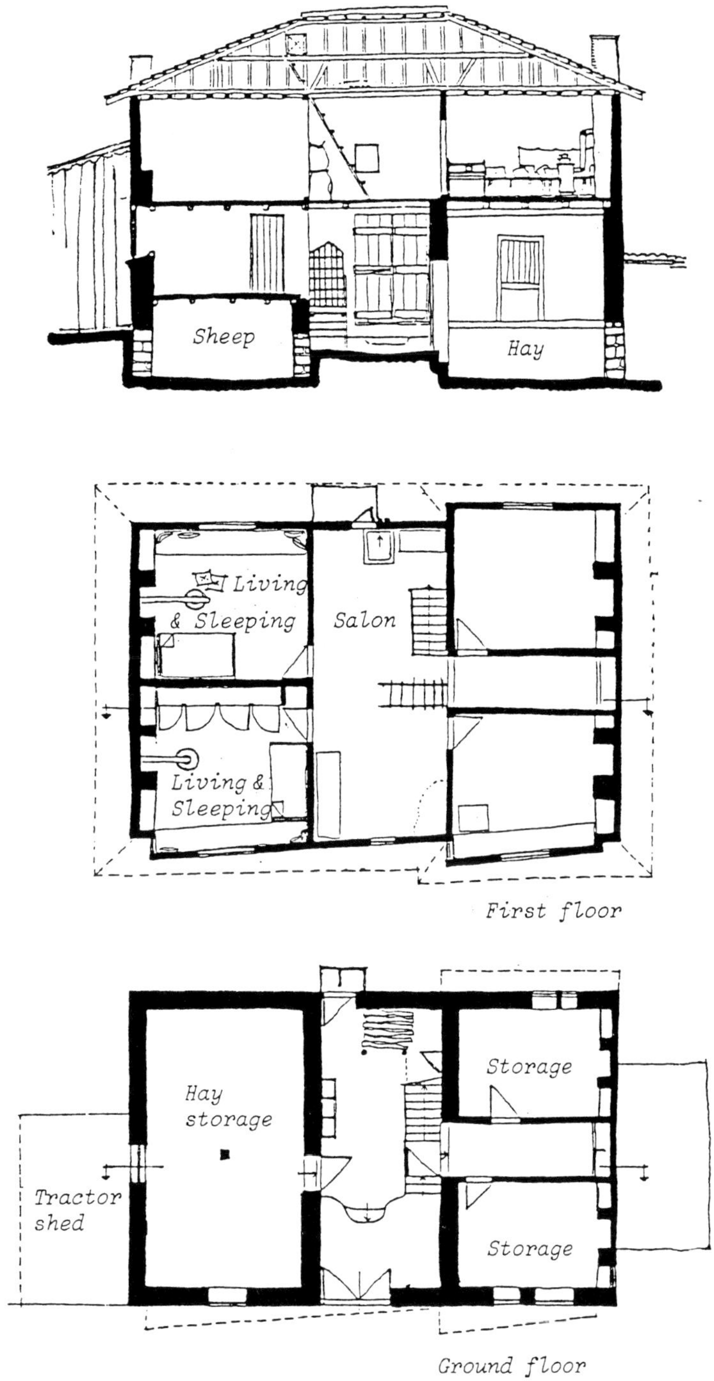


**Figure 14.4**
Plan of the ground and upper floors of a traditional house, showing the communal *salon* (termed *sofa* in other regions) and rooms for families and stores. Hay storage is used for housing cattle in winter.

**Figure 14.5**
Interior of the *salon* on the upper floor, where meals are held. Doors are kept shut.

There was usually a steel-framed bed piled with blankets and down covers; there may also be a simple chair. On the walls were pegs for working clothes and a broken mirror; a tractor advertisement or an out-of-date calendar was likely to be the only decoration. The simplicity of the interiors and the poverty of the furnishings revealed that the scale of the houses was deceptive; these were poor peasants whose annual cash income in the 1980s might be £200 ($300) per family. A family of six full-grown able-bodied men, who prided themselves on their ability to work hard, would need 7 years, if prices remained stable, to buy the tractor that was their ambition. Some of the houses and indeed, whole villages, were better built than others; the house builders of Erdoğmus were locally famed for their superior craftsmanship. There are morphological differences of minor kinds; the balconies to be found on some houses, the outbuildings attached to others. But, in general, these descriptions apply to houses still standing – and there are many of them – in villages like Hoçalar and Catak on the Emet fringe, or Erdoğmus and Sazkoy closer to Gediz.

When the disaster occurred, entire villages were destroyed, like Kayakoy, though generally the destruction was seldom total. Where the debris was excessive or access difficult, villages were relocated and new settlements built, like Gökler or Yunuslar. Where there was partial damage and rebuilding within the village was possible, a new section of government-provided houses was built adjacent to the surviving buildings, as at Dört Değirmen or Gömele. Within 3 weeks, the major decisions as to relocation were made

**Figure 14.6**
Row of uninhabited, government-provided, post-disaster houses, Kiranköy village.

and the contract units had been built and upwards of 50 000 people had been rehoused. Housing programmes continued as New Gediz itself began to grow – the initial population to be accommodated in 1970 was 7500, since when the town population more than doubled in a decade. In providing essential accommodation for many thousands of people in a disaster-struck country it was, by any standards, a notable achievement (Mitchell, 1971; Ministry of Rehousing and Resettlement, 1970). To the team, on its initial field trips, the disparity between the form of the settlements and scale of the houses within the vernacular context and those provided by the state was hugely apparent. Regular rows of single-storey, pitched-roofed houses faced each other across bleak streets on grid plans, contrasting with the closely knit, organic plans of the villages clustered on their hills or in their valleys. Eloquent evidence of the inappropriateness of the new settlements was to be seen in the rows of houses at Kiranköy, standing empty as the day they were completed, with beyond them, the corrugated iron minaret of the prefabricated mosque. Or there was the village of Yunuslar, resited closer to the main road with all the apparent advantages of improved communications and access to incoming goods from Kütahya, 2 hours away by road. It too, stood abandoned, the plaster falling off the walls of the silent boxes.

So it seemed, the failure of the government houses was self-evident – except for the fact that large numbers of houses were clearly in use. At Dört Değirmen they appeared to be used as barns and storage spaces rather than as houses, and this seemed

**Figure 14.7**
Extensions made to a government house, to conceal the external access to the toilet and shower, Gökler village.

reasonable in a village which still had standing a good proportion of its housing stock. But there were settlements which challenged these simplistic interpretations – like Örenköy, where the remains of the original village were now totally obliterated by scrub. On a hillside, a new settlement of government houses ran around the contour; in front of it, across a road, was a row of barns apparently built in the vernacular form. Higher than the government houses were several new buildings in concrete of considerable size now being completed. What did this indicate? Or again, there was the new Gökler, now sited across a gorge from the old largely demolished town. Yeni Gökler has an arid, unlovely square, lined on one side with single-storeyed shops; beyond is a grid of streets with government houses; a planner's design. But the houses are far from being abandoned. Extensions are to be found on the sides of the dwellings and sometimes in the front. Bread ovens under wooden shelters are attached to some; in the yard of others are further extensions in concrete block. A few villages have two-storeyed houses rising above the government houses. Again, there is Yeni Muhipler; the large planned layout with wide streets and open public spaces where the rows of houses have a distinctly suburban appearance. But the houses have barns and stables built behind them and most seem to support on their plots a variety of market crops and vegetables, even poplar trees. There are new houses in Yeni Muhipler too, concrete and rendered, with balconies and tiled roofs. But at Eski Muhipler, the old village a few kilometres away, there are some new extensions built in the vernacular tradition, among the scattered houses still standing; signs of families who had returned to their old village, when they were permitted to do so a dozen years after the earthquake.

What were we to make of the conflicting evidence? Did the relief houses disregard cultural values or not? Were they unacceptable, as seemed the case in Kiranköy, or suitable only as barns, as at Dört Değirmen; or were they, after all, acceptable housing as seemed to be the case at Yeni (New) Muhipler or Gökler? Was there an overriding principle that could account for these disparities? What did the large, new houses indicate – unexpected wealth or unbelievable thrift? And why were they so large? These and many other questions the team sought to answer. To deal with the latter problem first: the large, two-storeyed houses we ascertained, had been built with money sent home by 'guest workers' in Germany. The Turkish Government had recognized that getting money in circulation is one of the necessary steps towards post-disaster recovery, and one member from each family that had lost property in the earthquake was permitted to 'jump the queue' and get employment as a menial worker in Germany. The pay was exploitative by German standards but by rural Turkish standards it meant, with hard work and rigorous living, unanticipated wealth. Savings accrued were usually sent home and invested in the building of a new house, to a design that was acceptable to the planning officers in Gediz and Kütahya, and in modern materials (reinforced concrete) more capable of withstanding an earthquake of similar magnitude. The Turkish guest worker programme was just one of the additional elements that helped to

**Figure 14.8**
Beside a standard post-disaster unit a large house had been built with money sent from Germany by *gasterbeiter* (guest worker) relatives.

confound our simple conclusions as to vernacular context and process. By living frugally in Berlin the *gasterbeiter* (guest worker) was able to send money home. In the Gediz area, a bus service between the villages and the town was paid for by the accumulated money that the workers had provided, and in Eski Muhipler a remarkable, large mosque had been erected to replace the small, prefabricated mosque at its side.

In contrast with this optimistic investment in new building there were the empty villages; why had they remained abandoned for so long? At Kiranköy, it transpired, four families had settled; the remainder had chosen to rebuild in the ruins of their old village. The settlers thought that the latter were 'crazy'. The site had not been selected arbitrarily by the planners – it had been chosen by the villagers and was on their own land. But first attempts at settling revealed that there was little water on the new plateau location, and no trees on the windswept site to provide timber for building extensions. Compared with its exposed position and lack of resources, the old village was preferred by the majority and the *muhtar* was successful in persuading the government to provide it with services. At the totally demolished village of Orenköy on the other hand, the new houses built nearby had similar access to amenities and to farmland. The sites provided were too small to build outbuildings and byres for the animals, so these had been built across the road at the limits of the pastures. Above, the new houses were being built by guest worker money. In Dört Değirmen, the government houses had been made into stores and barns, and the families lived with other members of their extended families and gradually rebuilt their own houses. But in some cases the government houses had been occupied and extended, some families owning two properties in consequence.

A word should be said here on the matter of title to the houses. They were provided at a cost price in 1970 of 20 000 TL each, and families agreed to pay back the cost over 20 years. Few showed signs of doing so, and the government showed little sign of collecting the money. Meanwhile, the town of New Gediz had expanded for, as is often the case, recovery has brought a new prosperity and attracted people to the area. Villagers in Dört Değirmen found that their government houses were becoming useful property investments – which, with plot included, changed hands 15 years later, at 15 times the 1970 price. At Yeni Muhipler on the other hand, the houses had been adapted and extended to suit the expanding needs of the families. At Gökler there was less space; the plots were smaller and with the extensions the houses were soon almost in contact with their neighbours. Gökler, which was soon to be a municipality, was originally a large village and the occupations of the residents of new Gökler reflected this; they required smallholdings less and were engaged in mining, truck driving and in more urban employment. In Yeni (New) Muhipler, where there was more land allocated, houses had larger plots which the newly resettled villagers had turned into smallholdings. They were able to enlarge their houses or build byres and still have room for the growing of flax and fruit, or young saplings as potential building material. Living close to Eski (Old) Muhipler, the dwellers in the new settlement maintained the links with their old village and continued with small-scale village cultivation, even though Yeni Muhipler is on the fringe of Gediz and was being incorporated into the Municipality.

These various factors accounted for the differences between the responses of the respective villages to the provision of government houses. But they did not explain why, and in what ways, and for what reasons, the government houses were adapted, nor what changes in life-style had taken place in the process of transition from the vernacular context. Before discussing these aspects it is necessary to consider what was provided in the government plan. The basic houses consisted of four rooms with no hall or corridor, but with interconnecting doors. Windows were generally large, permitting adequate internal lighting and electricity for artificial lighting was provided. Water was piped to one room, which served as a small kitchenette supplied with a concrete sink. Cooking was generally done here on bottled gas stoves or rings. Adjacent was a latrine situated over a cesspit; no flushing system and no removal of effluent with water was installed. Built on concrete bases, the houses were of light timber-framed construction with a thin wall of single bricks; internal partitions were of brick. The whole structure was under a tiled low-pitched roof, except for the kitchenette and latrine which were covered by an outshut roof.

As has been noted, this was a conservative community with strong moral codes related to Islamic law. Protection of the women from other men, comparative seclusion of the women and general family privacy were valued highly. For a male to enter a house occupied only by women without the presence of the male head, and without his express invitation, would be unthinkable. When, in the vernacular context, a visitor comes, the women might retreat to one of the family rooms. If permitted to enter, the visitor was expected to remove shoes and to sit and talk in the salon without entering one of the family rooms. Social exchanges between the men normally took place away from the house at the village tea-house – *cayhane* – or

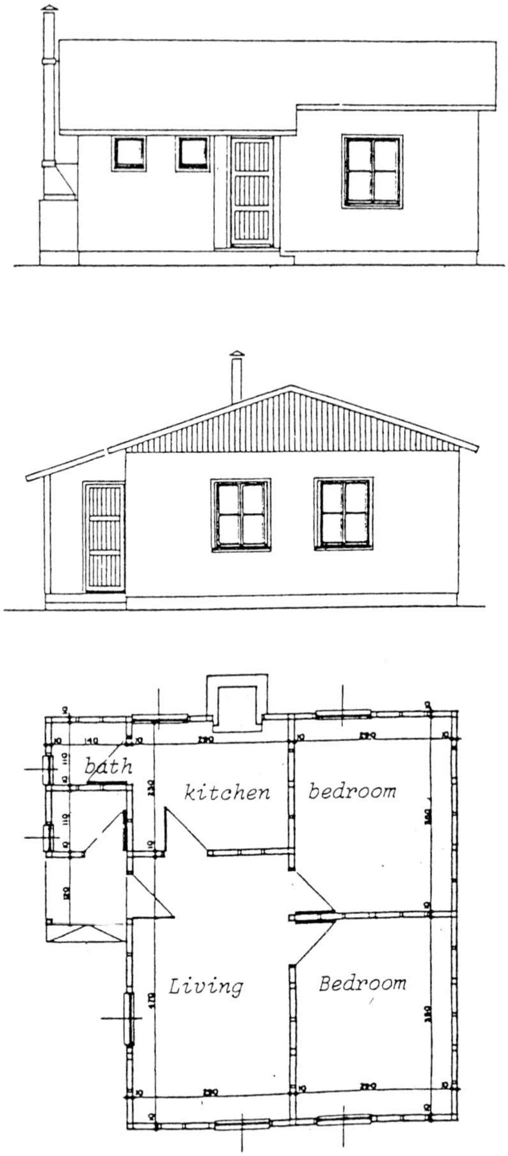


**Figure 14.9**
Plan and elevations of the government postdisaster house, as provided.

'village room'; social visiting by the women took place in the houses. To preserve the privacy expected at the entrance, and to provide a space where shoes may be removed and left, as well as a buffer zone between the outside and the domestic spaces, virtually every family extended the government house by first introducing a closed-in porch or corridor from the side wall of the kitchenette to the front of the building. The new corridor did not provide a *salon* or function as one. Most families attempted to use one room as a *salon* but in

**Figure 14.10**
Extensions to a government house, creating a smallholding farm, where space permitted this.

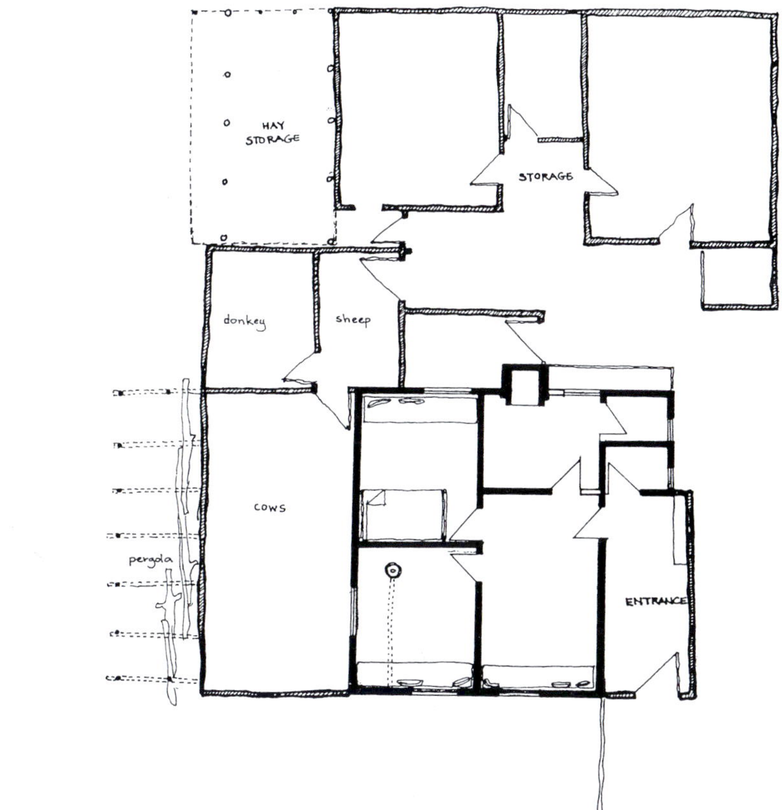


**Figure 14.11**
Plan of an extended government house, with provision for cattle, sheep, horse and storage.

**Figure 14.12**
Interior of main room in the post-disaster government house. Occupants were obliged to have their room used for access to the others.

so doing, they reduced the number of habitable spaces. It became apparent that the government plan was designed for the nuclear family of parents and children, and as such would offer sufficient rooms for a family to be adequately accommodated. The trend towards the nuclear family, evident in a city like Ankara, was encouraged by the government as being, in effect, modern and western. But in the villages of the Gediz region the families were extended, and even in the small government houses, the parents, and one or two sons with their families, would expect to live jointly. Inevitably, this led to overcrowding but more important to the occupants, it led to intrusions on desired privacy. Access to the rooms furthest from the main entrance was through another room, which was intended to be used for living purposes. The customary vernacular cruciform plan had permitted some insulation from domestic sounds or conversation between living units; in the government plan house the thin walls and the lack of any such sound baffle, meant that every noise was heard by other occupants, a source of distress to all. Similarly, access to the latrine within the house could only be gained by passing through other living spaces, again causing embarrassment. This was exacerbated by the fact that the door to the latrine was external, and its use evident outside. This could only be screened by the building of the enclosed corridor, mentioned above, and virtually all families felt obliged to build one.

There were many other problems for the occupants of the new housing. In the vernacular context the house had a fireplace in each room or, when this had been replaced by a stove, a stove in each room. The government houses had only one stove, intended to heat the whole house, which was situated in the first room. This became the *salon* when there was room to spare for the purpose, but on privacy grounds doors could not be left open to the other living units to circulate hot warm air. The rooms were too small, and the installation of stoves too complicated and expensive, for the placing of a stove in each room – though some families did just this. Much of the repositioning of doors, the building of extensions and the relocation of latrines or kitchenettes had revolved around these problems of living, encountered by extended families of perhaps ten or a dozen people including children, in houses meant for nuclear families of four or five.

In providing houses for families who had lost homes in the earthquake, the government built a house for each biological family unit; thus, a vernacular house which accommodated four family units would be replaced by four separate dwellings, each on its own plot. In the interests of fair allocation, plots were not chosen, but received after 'drawing from a hat'. While this avoided the risk of preferential selection it resulted in many extended families being divided over considerable distances. For many families it was better either to live with relatives in a house that had survived the earthquake until a new or extended building could be constructed, or, where this was impossible, or where re-occupation was not permitted as the structures were unsafe, the whole extended family attempted to take up residence in one government house. This left a residue of unoccupied houses, a lack of 'take-up' which gave the impression of overprovision and often led to the use of the houses for storage or as byres, rather than as dwellings. From the point of view of the village families, the new houses were 'too small'. Faced with the reality of squeezing a large family into a small house, many extended families accepted the nucleated structure enforced by the scale of accommodation, but maintained their traditional ties. As more than one family head said, '70 square metres is the proper size for a house' and when they had acquired sufficient capital from sons in Germany they set to building one. In a number of villages, such as Yeni Kiranköy, these matters of congestion and discomfort, coupled with a failure to consider the necessary access to water for the settlement, meant that virtually all government houses were left unoccupied.

There were many other aspects which made the houses unsatisfactory for the occupants: hard and bitterly cold concrete floors for a people that ate sitting on the floor and on which most of its women and children spent much of their time. Another was poor ventilation, which could not be alleviated without creating draughts. Condensation is a problem on thin walls that offer little protection from either the bitter cold of the winter or the extreme heat of summer. But these were tough people, whose vernacular houses were lacking in material comforts, and were not especially well constructed. Comfort was not a serious issue with them and the harsh rigours of a peasant way of life inured them to much that western city-dwellers would find difficult to tolerate. But if 'the well-tempered environment' was a concept with little meaning in this context, the culture-tempered environment was one that was of paramount importance. The houses that they built traditionally were not notable for their aesthetic qualities, their craftsmanship, their attention to detail or even, beyond the generous proportions, their quality of space. But they did meet the cultural needs and values of the society. All the adaptations, or modifications to their government-provided houses were means to this end, although for many extended families the problem of maintaining their living proximity while protecting their privacy, was not possible without compromise and the building of extensions.

Within the houses in the vernacular context, in the houses provided by the government and in the houses which are being built with guest-worker income, there was a notable unity in their adaptation in terms of furniture and the use of space. The government houses may have been small, and the individual living units within them minute, but the room that served as a *salon* was still surrounded on two sides by a *sedir*, covered with bright, striped rugs and cloths; the floor was still where meals were taken around a large salver that served everyone, from which each member of the household took food in the prescribed order. The beds in the living rooms might now take up most of the space, but the clothes still hung from pegs, the stove still heated the tinware vessels. On the wall, the mirror may have a scene painted upon it, the calendar still displays a tractor; superficially, there was little significant difference beyond the evidence of congestion and the lack of closet space. There were a few new items of furniture, most notably the buffet in highly polished plastic laminate of imitation wood with glazed doors, protecting the collection of objects on the glass shelves within. These were usually tea sets, one or two plates, photographs of sons and families in Germany, plastic flowers, a gewgaw or two. There might be a large blue screen for magnifying a television image but it was a symbol; there was no television behind it. The buffet was the modern equivalent of the dowry chest, its drawers filled with spotless, starched

**Figure 14.13**
Main room of a government house with a 'buffet' or cabinet acting as a dowry chest.



linen; its slick, shiny surface confidently announcing the value placed on its traditional role as dowry.

Outside, the arrangement of the government houses contrasted most markedly with that of the houses in the vernacular context. To the planners, the rows of houses lined a modern street. This could have been embarrassing for the people, whose sense of propriety is such that overlooking the windows of another house or being so overlooked, is unacceptable. Where there were wide streets, designed for the cars they would never own, these kept them sufficiently apart from such violations. Where houses were close together and roads were narrower, many houses had windows partially boarded up against the eyes of passers-by. The urban planner's notion of street design runs counter to common practice, even in a village like Dört Değirmen, where the houses appear to be arranged in rows along the contour. In fact, the ways through the village are as much uphill and down, as they are lateral, but in all cases within the vernacular context the houses face south on a southern slope. There are no rear windows, so houses situated below have no openings facing those above. But in the small government settlement the houses face across the street so that half of them do not have the benefit of the sun and, closer together than in New Muhipler, they overlook each other – another factor that contributed to their being used to house animals rather than families.

Kütahya Province, like all of Western Anatolia, was undergoing change, subject to the forces that were set in motion by Kemal Ataturk a lifetime before. Social change may be, in Julian Steward's formulation, a complex and continuing process of multilinear evolution (Steward, 1955), but the processes already taking place were interrupted with brutal suddenness by the catastrophe of the Gediz earthquake, and vastly accelerated with the secondary impact of the recovery programme and new development that followed it. No society is the same after an earthquake and may have been assailed by more pressures to change than a peasant community might be expected to withstand (Lerner, 1958). For the villages in the Gediz region, they had been subject to considerable resettlement, not to mention the drawing off of much of their youth to have contact with another country, another culture and another set of material values, as had Gediz with the guest worker programme in Germany and Switzerland. Nevertheless, over 14 years the people of

**Figure 14.14**
Self-building reconstruction of houses, Eski Muhipler, near Gediz, Kütahya Province, Turkey.

*A neighbourhood of the resettlement village of New Muhipler, 1971*

*A neighbourhood of the resettlement village of New Muhipler, 1984*

**Figure 14.15**
Settlement plan of part of Yeni (New) Muhipler, as allocated in 1970 under official direction, and as extended and utilized by occupiers when surveyed in 1983.

the Gediz villages responded resourcefully to the opportunities and changes that confronted them. The catalytic forces of their 'reward-awareness' had not been simply opposed, as Egbert de Vries suggests, by the inhibiting 'fear of risk taking' (de Vries, 1961). But in the face of the onslaught of social, technological, educational and economic changes that they had had to meet, in addition to those of habitat and settlement, there had been a resolute dependence on cultural constancy, which helped them to cope. This persistence of the vernacular context in the processes of change found expression in the adaptation of their government houses to meet their needs, and in their aspirations for new houses that were 'modern', built in reinforced concrete, which yet satisfied the same cultural conditions.

That all this has implications for the design of new dwelling types in the future, should Turkey continue with its programme and policy of housing replacement and resettlement for earthquake victims, would seem inescapable. But for those who are concerned with the relationship of built form and culture the lessons are salutary, warning against making judgements on visual evidence alone. There is no facile relationship to be made between architectural 'quality' and cultural values; our aesthetic preferences, or prejudices, are not a reliable measure of what is important within the vernacular context. Ultimately, the principal qualities that should be the guiding principles in the design of post-disaster settlements and dwellings, must be those of the affected communities. Training in the ascertaining of these in the post disaster period is necessary for members of the relief cultures. Constructive dialogues between designers and communities are essential for the acceptability of post-disaster housing; community participation may also contribute to the alleviation of the double trauma, for the disaster victims.

## References

Ceylan, F. (1983). *Evaluation of Post-Earthquake Long-Term Housing in Rural Areas of Turkey*. Case study, Geziz. Middle East Technical University (METU).

De Vries, E. (1961). *Man in Rapid Social Change*. SCM Press, London.

Germen, A. (1978). *The Gediz Earthquake: Reconstruction Between 1970 and 1977*. METU Press, Ankara.

Günoven, A. (1977). *Earthquake-Disaster Related Activities in Turkey with Special Reference to the 1970 Gediz Earthquake*. Unpublished. Master's Thesis, METU, Ankara.

Krimgold, F. (1974). *The Role of International Aid for Pre-Disaster Planning in Developing Countries*. Stockholm, KTH: Avdelningen fur Arkitektur.

Lerner, D. (1958). Turkey. In: *The Passing of Traditional Society*. New York: The Free Press (Chapter 5).
Murdoch, G. P. (1967) *Ethnographic Atlas*. Pittsburgh: University of Pittsburgh Press.
Ministry of Rehousing and Resettlement. (1970). *Report on the Gediz Earthquake*. Government of Turkey, Ankara.
Mitchell, W.A. (1971). Reconstruction After the Gediz Earthquake of 1970. *The Geographical Review: Symposium on Gediz Earthquake*. Association of Civil Engineers.
Ozkan, S. (1972). Roam home to a dome. *Architectural Design*. London, April.
Pierce, J.E. (1965). *Life in a Turkish Village*. New York: Holt, Rinehart and Winston.
Redfield, R. (1953). *The Primitive World and its Transformations*. Cornell University Press.
Steward, J.H. (1955). *The Theory of Culture Change*. University of Illinois Press.
Stirling, P. (1965). *Turkish Village*. London: Weidenfeld.
Wolf, R.E. (1966). *Peasants*. Englewood Cliffs, NJ: Prentice-Hall.

# 15

# Rebirth of a Rajput village (1992)

As a concept, the notion of 'development' being a process of transition from a predominately peasant economy to an industrialized one, is of relatively recent date. The process of industrialization has been one which has taken place at intermittent rates, and in a wide variety of cultural contexts, for the last two centuries. Such processes, whether under colonial rule, or in the post-colonial period of independence of nations, have sometimes had unexpected consequences. So for instance, India, often regarded as the epitome of a vast country with a peasant economy, is in fact the tenth largest industrialized country in the world. Economic development, marked by growth in income per capita, was experienced by a number of the newly independent countries in the post-Second World War years. Bolstered by the support of countries with advanced technologies in the power blocs of both the east and the west, the newly 'developing countries' nevertheless encountered many complex problems as they became increasingly dependent on the International Monetary Fund, and the 'aid' of the major powers.

In the 1970s, the definition of development shifted from an emphasis on income per head to the elimination of poverty and unemployment. In the struggle to reduce poverty and inequality, and to provide basic services, loans from the International Bank for Reconstruction and Development – the World Bank – were used to support the supply of water to improve sanitation, and to upgrade housing, among many other applications. The World Bank, essentially administered by the wealthy nations, imposed and still imposes its conditions on the projects it finances, and in effect, intervenes to ensure that they are met. While there may be good economic reasons for doing so, external intervention has become a commonplace of development. It has meant the frequent, if often misguided, involvement of planners and architects from 'advanced nations' in housing, resettlement projects and disaster relief.

Just when the term 'intervention' entered the language of development is uncertain; perhaps in the late 1970s or early 1980s. It is always instructive to ascertain what the terms we use actually mean. 'Intervention' derives from the Latin *inter* and *venire*, literally 'to come between', while the *Concise Oxford* definition runs 'Come in as something extraneous; occur in the meantime; (of person or thing) come between, interfere, so as to prevent or modify result, etc.' Somehow, the term has acquired benign associations in the decades of its recent currency, but the dictionary definition is a salutary reminder of the intrusive nature of architectural design intervention in development contexts.

Among the diverse situations in which such architectural intervention occurs, the most dramatic, most immediate and most widely sanctioned, is that of post-disaster housing. Some forms of slow-onset disaster, such as desertification, drought and famine, do not have immediate housing implications, although in the long term, migration as a result of such disasters, as in Ethiopia and Sudan, may lead to resettlement problems. Impact and rapid-onset disasters, such as earthquakes, avalanches, hurricanes and floods may create considerable housing problems, as the massive earthquakes in Armenia and Gilan province, Iran, or the recurrent floods in Bangladesh have tragically emphasized. Immediate responses to housing needs in disasters like these, may include the despatch of tents and polythene sheeting for temporary shelter. It has become a standard exercise in schools of architecture to 'design an emergency shelter', and in 1990 the International Union of Architects (UIA/IUA) proposed an international competition for the design of such temporary, prefabricated or rapidly assembled units, which could be flown in immediately a disaster occurs. To architects this seems a desirable demonstration of their potential to contribute to the solution of world problems, and they have been displeased when they have encountered resistance. The issues cannot be dealt with here; sufficient to say that temporary shelters always become permanent ones, but as they are designed for short-term use they rapidly deteriorate, exacerbating housing difficulties. In cases where they have been designed for long-term use, the very nature of mass solutions capable of being delivered rapidly to any notional place on earth where a disaster occurs, militates against their appropriateness to any specific geographical or cultural context.

In Ankara (1987), I discussed in some detail the damaging effects of housing and settlement design by absentee architects, which did not take into consideration the sociocultural requirements of the communities for whom they were built. Well-intentioned, and in many ways admirable, though the post-disaster housing provision may have been, it largely failed because the architect-engineers had their own design programme and paid no attention to the cultural values of the victims of the earthquake. Theirs was an intervention that sadly met the dictionary definition: they came in 'as something extraneous' and interfered with the close relationship between a peasant society and its dwelling, preventing the desired result of achieving culturally appropriate post-disaster housing (Aysan and Oliver, 1987). Intervention of the kind exemplified by the Gediz case is predicated on the belief that the victims of a disaster should be provided with housing, as they may be provided with medicines, blankets or food. But First World housing is largely based on the concept of the dwelling as consumer product and marketable commodity; the separation of owner and builder is assumed. Consequently, designers with this background are confident that mass housing which meets the physical needs of the members of any community can be designed by the pragmatic synthesis of the available site, practical structural considerations, internal space minima, provision of basic utilities, cost of materials and labour, and the meeting of legal requirements. From such a position the cultural dimension is of no significance, and the intended owners of the building play no part in its design or construction (Davis, 1978, 1981).

So extensive has this mode of design intervention become that little attention has been paid to the capacity of stricken communities to cope with their own recovery, or to rebuild after a disaster. In particular, the motivation to invest in new building the values of the pre-disaster tradition has been virtually ignored. An opportunity to make such a study presented itself unexpectedly in 1989, when I was in Pakistan. I had been invited by the faculty of the School of Architecture of the National College of Arts in Lahore to present a series of lecture-seminars on the anthropology of architecture. After principles, theories and methodologies had been examined in some detail, it was clearly necessary that fieldwork should follow. Members of the group had knowledge of a number of villages which were considered for detailed study. Among them, Assistant Professor Mrs Yasmin Cheema mentioned a village of considerable interest, Jubbo, some 10 miles beyond the city limits of Lahore, which had been the subject of a study she had conducted with a staff team the previous year. Unfortunately, the village had been totally destroyed by the flood waters of the Ravi river, the following September. 'What happened to the inhabitants?', I asked. No one knew, but

**Figure 15.1**
The village of Jubbo on a small rise of land above the waters of the river system. Village, Lahore state, Pakistan.

presumably they had been absorbed into the city or rehoused. I had a hunch, however, after learning more about the village, that the site would be well worth revisiting. Preliminary reconaissance revealed that indeed, the villagers were still there. We decided to study the post-disaster recovery of Jubbo.

Jubbo was a Rajput village. Innocuous though the phrase may be, it is by no means easy to explain. The Rajputs are a proud people who are distributed across northern and central India and Pakistan, from Rajputana to Bihar state. Their name, Rajput, means 'son of a Raja', indicating a superior caste status. Traditionally, Rajput males were soldiers or merchants; they had a distaste for manual work, and those that were high-caste farmers were considered by the British during the long years of the British Raj, to be intelligent but idle, and poor at husbandry. They were frequently compared unfavourably with the industrious Jats, another and frequently contiguous high caste, who were and are dedicated farmers. Today, the Rajputs are not tied to one religion; there are Muslim, Hindu and Jain Rajputs, and they are so numerous as often to be regarded as distinct peoples. Some two million Rajputs lived in the former British administrative region of Punjab which extended beyond its present limits. Known as 'The Land of the Five Rivers', the fertile alluvial plain is watered by the Jhelum, Chenab, Ravi, Beas and Sutlej rivers which have their headwaters in Kashmir, Kangra and the hill states on the slopes of the Himalayas. Further to the southwest, a web of canals, built by the British, increased the potential farmlands to

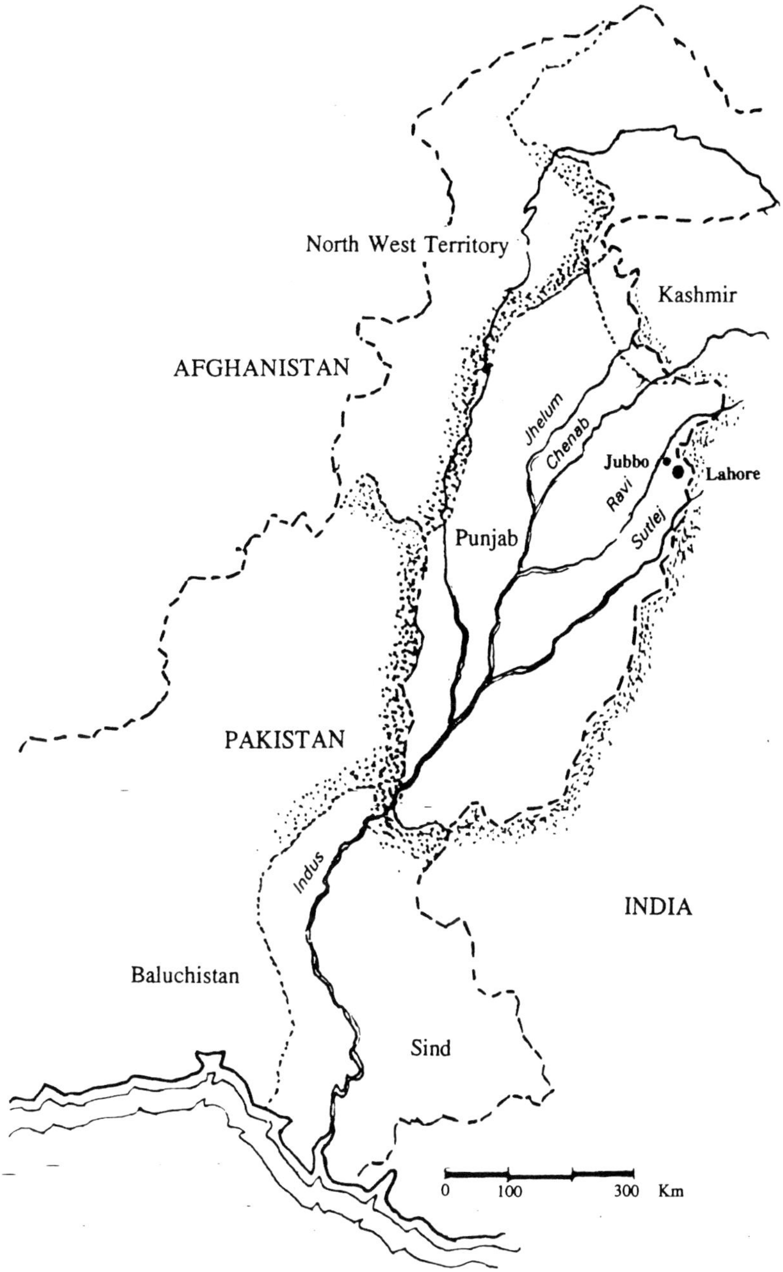


**Figure 15.2**
Map of the 'Land of Five Rivers', showing the Sutlej, Ravi and other tributaries to the Indus.

sustain densities of up to a thousand people to the square mile (Darling, 1949; Sherring, 1948).

When the partition of India and Pakistan came, following independence and the subsequent civil war, the frontier between the two states separated the nearby cities of Amritsar and Lahore, bisecting

**Figure 15.3**
Plan of the village of Jubbo, indicating the dwelling complexes and the house of the Zemindar (Z), the Mosque (M) and the *tawala* cattle yards (T).

the redesignated state of Punjab. Many Rajputs moved back to India, but large numbers remained in Pakistan, some to become urbanized, others to continue their former way of life. Pakistan is united by its devotion to Islam, but ethnically it is far from homogeneous; some 32 distinct languages are spoken by its peoples, and there are innumerable dialects. Up to nine-tenths of the population in most of its states are farmers (Smith, 1955). The villagers of Jubbo are among them. They trace their origins to a Rajput prince who gave his name to the village, and who settled his clan close to the River Ravi during the rule of the Sikh, Ranjeet Singh. 'He who neighbours a river is neither hungry nor thirsty,' runs the proverb; Prince Jubbo chose a long, low and slightly inclined hill with its adjacent land partially screened by trees. In time, the village of Jubbo attracted sailors and fishermen on the Ravi river, who settled in the vicinity, the population eventually numbering some 2000. But the frequent floods and the change of course of the Ravi drove many people away; by the time it was studied in 1988 there were about 200 inhabitants in the village, two-thirds of them children.

In the course of 150 years, the Rajputs had clearly overcome their reputed distaste for farming; they bred numerous heavy-horned buffalo and other cattle, kept goats, and farmed the nearby lands. At the time of the survey there were some nine extended families in the village, each farming a smallholding of approximately five acres. Cereals were grown, but sugar cane was an important crop, thriving in the well-irrigated fields, the heat and humidity. The village sold milk and marketed its crop surplus, with the family income averaging some 3000 rupees a month. The National College of Arts team who studied the village gained much information from the *zemindar* or village head, who, as one of only two adults in the village to have ever attended school, negotiated sales and also acted as intercessionary between the government revenue collector, the *dehsildar*, and the village. The nine extended families lived in *katchi abadis*, or mud-built houses, single-storeyed and flat-roofed; the low-lying village presented a simple profile in its position on the inclined hillsite. There were no windows but the groups of small rooms (*kanra*) opened on to a *vera* or family courtyard. A few had open-sided loggias (*baranda*) facing the *vera*, with columns and arches. Some of the columns, moulded over discarded pots, had an abacus-like form, while the interiors of the loggias were often painted in deep earth colours.

Three extended families, members of one clan, lived in a *hatta*, or joint compound, which opened on to a shared courtyard. The *kanra*

**Figure 15.4**
Detail of a Jubbo house showing a *baranda* or loggia facing the *vera* or family courtyard.

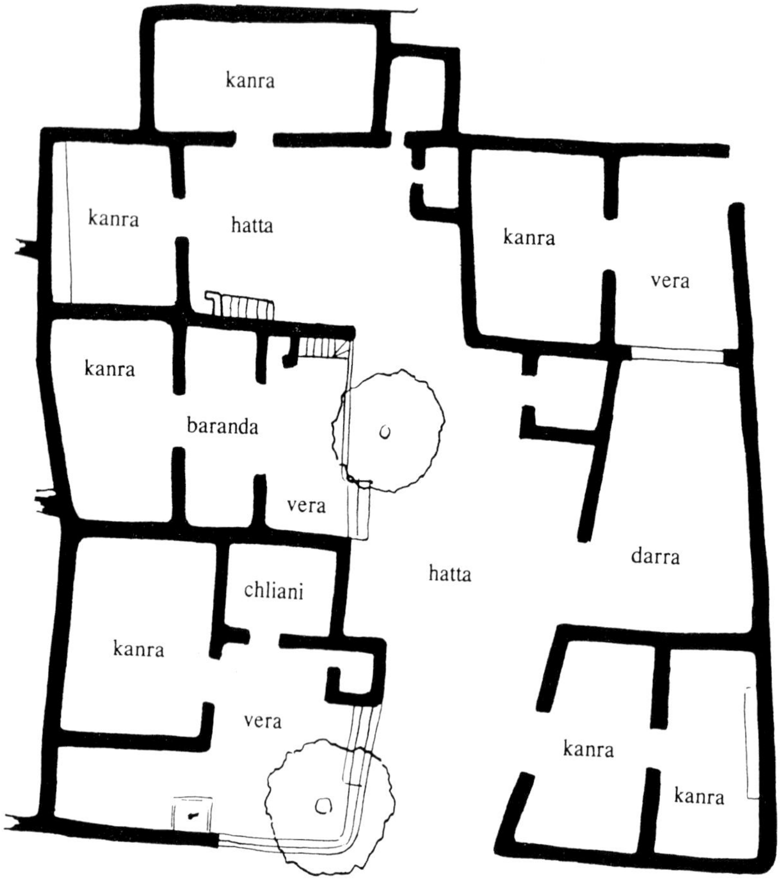


**Figure 15.5**
Plan of a traditional Rajput house in Jubbo (corner site, south of the mosque), of which there are innumerable variants.

would be used for sleeping when the weather was cool enough but, during the oppressive heat of summer, villagers slept on the roofs, which were mud-plastered over logs; there was sufficient timber available for this. Inside, the *kanra* would be kept immaculately clean, the mud and dung-plastered floor swept and polished, the few possessions stowed in chests. Except, that is, for china, glassware and mirrors, which would be displayed on shelves, their reflectivity aiding the illumination by candlelight. The wall opposite the entrance usually had a moulded relief of a tree, of birds or a figure. Outside, there was a *chliani*, or kitchen and ablutions place for the women off each vera; food preparation and cooking would be done there. The mud-built ovens, fired by use, would be decorated in relief. Water was obtained from wells, with three hand pumps and a motor pump which had an unauthorized electrical connection. Comprehending the social structure proved difficult. While three families lived in the joint compounds, the males of the other six had separate houses of their own. Not all the household heads were male; two were women, who also owned their houses. Marriage was largely endogamous within the village, but residence was patrilocal, the married sons living with their parents. Maintaining the dwellings was the work of the women, who did not observe *purdah* and who were free to move as they chose, though they might retire to a *kanra* when the men had visitors. Uneducated but intelligent, several of the men serviced tractors for other villages. About one in five of the children went to school; generally they helped with the care of the animals, crushed the sugar cane or helped in the house. The cattle were kept tethered for much of the time, in a *darra* (byre), or the *tawala*, the cattle yard at the top of the rise, and taken to the Ravi to drink and to be washed (Cheema, 1988).

'To go and live by a river is to place a babe in a witch's lap', runs another Punjab proverb. It was the river which wrought havoc for the village. Abnormally heavy rains in the Himalayas caused flooding in the five rivers region, on a scale unprecedented for 70 years. Commencing on the 28th September 1988, the floods totally inundated 17 of the 21 districts of the Punjab. The Ravi rose 3 metres in the first 2 days, and continued to rise. By the 9th October, the Red Crescent was reporting that as many as three million people were rendered homeless. Counting the cost a month after the flood began, it was evident that 50 000 cattle had been drowned, 300 000 acres of cotton and 200 000 acres of rice were totally destroyed. 40 000 km of the canal and irrigation network were damaged, 14 bridges, 28 hospitals and 6500 schools were destroyed. 4000 villages were severely affected and over 900 people were reported killed, though the eventual toll was certainly higher. On Jubbo's hill the swirling waters washed away the footings of the lower houses, causing them to collapse. Remembering former floods, Jubbo's older inhabitants untethered the animals and made their way as best they could to the *bund*, the high protective levee that surrounded Lahore. It had been strengthened after several breaches had been caused by a previous, though less severe, flood in 1972. The *bund* held, and refugees from the *kucca abadi* villages between it and the river gathered on the levee (LICROSS, 1988). When the floods subsided, only three single-cell *pucca* (brick-built) buildings in Jubbo remained standing. After the emergency relief phase was over the city offered a site for the Jubbo villagers on the urban side of the *bund*, but this they refused, choosing to return to their hillsite. The reasons for their refusal related to their strong associations with their ancestral lands, and fear of being absorbed into the city; they preferred their

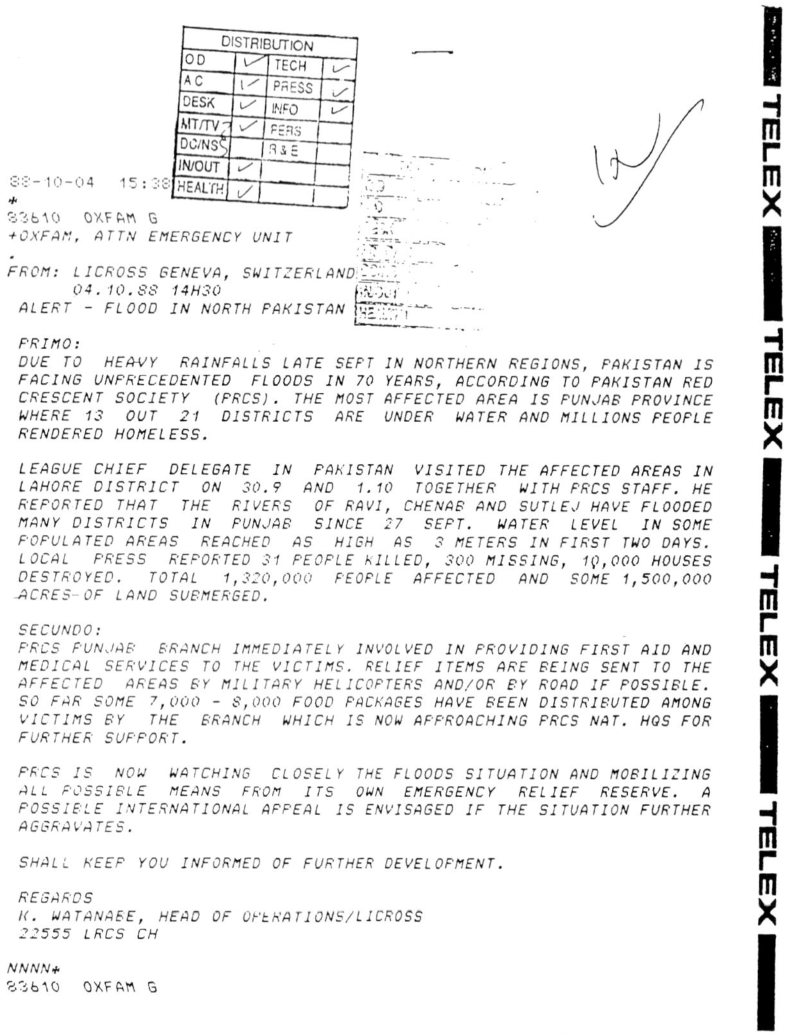

| DISTRIBUTION | | | |
|---|---|---|---|
| OD | ✓ | TECH | ✓ |
| AC | ✓ | PRESS | ✓ |
| DESK | ✓ | INFO | ✓ |
| MT/TV | ✓ | PERS | |
| DC/NS | | R & E | |
| IN/OUT | ✓ | | |
| HEALTH | ✓ | | |

88-10-04 15:38

83610 OXFAM G
+OXFAM, ATTN EMERGENCY UNIT

FROM: LICROSS GENEVA, SWITZERLAND
04.10.88 14H30
ALERT - FLOOD IN NORTH PAKISTAN

PRIMO:
DUE TO HEAVY RAINFALLS LATE SEPT IN NORTHERN REGIONS, PAKISTAN IS FACING UNPRECEDENTED FLOODS IN 70 YEARS, ACCORDING TO PAKISTAN RED CRESCENT SOCIETY (PRCS). THE MOST AFFECTED AREA IS PUNJAB PROVINCE WHERE 13 OUT 21 DISTRICTS ARE UNDER WATER AND MILLIONS PEOPLE RENDERED HOMELESS.

LEAGUE CHIEF DELEGATE IN PAKISTAN VISITED THE AFFECTED AREAS IN LAHORE DISTRICT ON 30.9 AND 1.10 TOGETHER WITH PRCS STAFF. HE REPORTED THAT THE RIVERS OF RAVI, CHENAB AND SUTLEJ HAVE FLOODED MANY DISTRICTS IN PUNJAB SINCE 27 SEPT. WATER LEVEL IN SOME POPULATED AREAS REACHED AS HIGH AS 3 METERS IN FIRST TWO DAYS. LOCAL PRESS REPORTED 31 PEOPLE KILLED, 300 MISSING, 10,000 HOUSES DESTROYED. TOTAL 1,320,000 PEOPLE AFFECTED AND SOME 1,500,000 ACRES OF LAND SUBMERGED.

SECUNDO:
PRCS PUNJAB BRANCH IMMEDIATELY INVOLVED IN PROVIDING FIRST AID AND MEDICAL SERVICES TO THE VICTIMS. RELIEF ITEMS ARE BEING SENT TO THE AFFECTED AREAS BY MILITARY HELICOPTERS AND/OR BY ROAD IF POSSIBLE. SO FAR SOME 7,000 - 8,000 FOOD PACKAGES HAVE BEEN DISTRIBUTED AMONG VICTIMS BY THE BRANCH WHICH IS NOW APPROACHING PRCS NAT. HQS FOR FURTHER SUPPORT.

PRCS IS NOW WATCHING CLOSELY THE FLOODS SITUATION AND MOBILIZING ALL POSSIBLE MEANS FROM ITS OWN EMERGENCY RELIEF RESERVE. A POSSIBLE INTERNATIONAL APPEAL IS ENVISAGED IF THE SITUATION FURTHER AGGRAVATES.

SHALL KEEP YOU INFORMED OF FURTHER DEVELOPMENT.

REGARDS
K. WATANABE, HEAD OF OPERATIONS/LICROSS
22555 LRCS CH

NNNN+
83610 OXFAM G

TELEX TELEX TELEX TELEX

**Figure 15.6**
Telex appeal to Oxfam (4 October 1988) from LICROSS, Geneva, Switzerland, indicating the extent of devastation in the previous week.

independence and, led by the *zemindar,* proceeded to rebuild. It was the rebuilt village of Jubbo which we visited 4 months later.

Between the *bund* and the village site, the terrain is flat but rough; bullock cart or jeep are the only practical means of transport. There are groves of acacia trees on the way, but within the vicinity of the village itself, the fields were cultivated and fresh-green. On the slight incline of the hill, probably not more than 20 metres at its highest point, the low-lying village seemed complete and timeless; in fact, it was still in the final stages of being rebuilt. A member of the faculty had already established contact; on our arrival the adults were dignified and reserved, but welcoming. While some of the team redrew the village plan and compared it with the former

88-10-09 13:09
Msg 201 Title: 88-10-09 12:54

*
83610 OXFAM G
+OXFAM, ATTN EMERGENCY UNIT
.
FROM: LICROSS GENEVA, SWITZERLAND
09.10.88 10H45

| DISTRIBUTION | | | |
|---|---|---|---|
| OD | ✓ | TECH | ✓ |
| AC | | PRESS | ✓ |
| DESK | ✓ | INFO | ✓ |
| M/TV | ✓ | PERS | |
| BC/NS | | R & E | |
| IN/OUT | | | |
| HEALTH | ✓ | | |

A P P E A L - PAKISTAN FLOODS

FURTHER OUR ALERT 4.10.88 ON FLOODS SITUATION IN NORTHERN PAKISTAN PRCS HAS NOW REQUESTED ASSISTANCE FOR:
CHF: 3.6 MILLION

WITH FOLLOWING DETAILS:
PRIMO- GENERAL SITUATION
THE FLOODS WHICH HAS SUBMERGED 16 OUT OF 21 DISTRICTS OF THE PUNJAB PROVINCE ARE UNPRECEDENTED. THOUSAND OF KUCHA HOUSES (MUD HOUSES) AND MOST OF BRICK HOUSES HAVE BEEN WASHED AWAY RENDERING MILLIONS OF PEOPLE HOMELESS. ABOUT 25000 HEADS OF CATTLE HAVE BEEN KILLED AND ALL POULTRY FARMS IN THE AFFECTED AREA DESTROYED. ABOUT 3.7 MILLIONS ACRES OF CULTIVATED/CULTURABLE LAND IS UNDER WATER AND THE STANDING CROP INCLUDING RICE, COTTON AND FODDER HAS BEEN DESTROYED.

STATISTICS ON CASUALTIES STILL NOT AVAILABLE BUT IS ESTIMATED THAT HUNDREDS PEOPLE KILLED AND APPROX 3 MILLION RENDERED HOMELESS NEEDING URGENT HELP.

SECUNDO - GOVT. ACTION
EVACUATION OF VICTIMS TO SAFER PLACES, SUPPLY OF FOOD AND RELIEF GOODS AND MEDICAL AID.

TERTIO - RED CROSS RELIEF ACTIVITIES
THE PRCS WHICH IS ALREADY COMMITTED TO ASSIST HUGE NUMBER OF AFGHAN REFUGEES IN THE COUNTRY, IS DOING ITS BEST TO RELIEVE THE SUFFERINGS OF THE VICTIMS BY DISTRIBUTING/AIR DROPPINGS OF FOOD PACKS, PROVISION OF CLOTHINGS INCLUDING BLANKETS, SUPPLY OF TENTS AND FIRST AID. IT WOULD BE A COLOSSAL WORK IN DAYS/WEEKS TO COME KEEPING IN VIEW THE FAST APPROACHING WINTER AND DANGER OF EPIDEMIC.

QUARTO - NEEDS
DUE TO MAGNITUDE OF DISASTER AND LIMTED RESOURCE AVAILABLE TO THE SOCIETY, PRCS IS REQUESTING INTERNATIONAL ASSISTANCE AS FOLLOWS:

| ITEMS | QTY | RS(MILLION) | CHF EQV. (THOUSAND) |
|---|---|---|---|
| TENTS | 5000 | 12 | 1.080 |
| BLANKETS/QUILTS | 50.000 | 10 | 900 |
| KHADOR CLOTH | 200.000 MTR. | 3 | 270 |
| COOKING UTENSILS INCLUDING KEROSENE OIL | 10.000 | 4 | 360 |
| DRY FOOD(RICE, PORCHED GRAINS,GUR, TEA, FLOUR, SUGAR ETC. | | 4 | 360 |
| MEDECINE | | 2 | 180 |
| (A) ORS | | | |
| (B) ANTIMALARIALS | | | |
| (C) ANTIBIOTICS | | | |
| (D) ANTHELMENTHICS | | | |
| (E) MICELLANEOUS, INCLUDING WATER PURIFICATION TABLETS ETC. | | | |

**Figure 15.7**
Further telex to Oxfam (9 October 1988) estimating that three million people had been rendered homeless by the floods.

plan of 1988, others interviewed Niamat, the *zemindar*, and the inhabitants of many of the houses. Some of the children noisily crushed sugar cane, while a few followed us and indicated where different extended families lived. All but two of the families had returned to the village. One had retained contact with the promise of eventual return, and the other had apparently decided to settle in the city. Even so, the village respected their homesite in case, after all, they chose to come back. With the fields well cultivated,

**Figure 15.8**
The *bund*, or protective levee surrounding Lahore, on which some refugees camped, and which defined the city's limits.

**Figure 15.9**
Children crushing sugar cane, helped by young adults, Jubbo.

the village appeared to be prosperous, and in some respects it had profited by its shrewdness at the time of the disaster. Other villages had not untethered their animals as the waters rose, fearing that they might lose them; consequently, many cattle drowned. Jubbo's villagers found that there was a larger market for their milk, and a demand for the calves they bred. It was clear, however, that the *zemindar*'s land, which had been protected by trees, had retained more of its topsoil; the families on the lowest part of the slope had lost much of theirs to the floodwaters. They were somewhat disadvantaged and there was evidence of a social, if not subcaste distinction related to elevation, perhaps reflecting the length of their ancestral claim to their homesites.

To a remarkable degree the village was as it had been studied before the flood. Each family had identified its home site and proceeded to rebuild on it, generally to the identical plan. Here and there, a few changes could be noted; a room built on an open space, a *vada* or storehouse constructed near the *chliani*. But these were minor rather than significant alterations. The women did much of the mass construction of the mud walls, though the men built the roofs and usually did the plastering. Children, watching intently as they learned the techniques, prepared the mud for the walling and the plaster. Inside the houses the floors were already hard and polished and many walls were painted. Newly made shelves hung on the walls and dishes and mirrors were again on display. A bicycle or a sewing machine might stand beside the wall with the beds, but there were few signs of modernity beyond a light bulb in some of the rooms. Refusal to accept the offer of a new village site had placed the community virtually beyond official recognition, but a concession had been made with the provision of poled electricity. The loggias were simpler than they had been formerly, but the beautiful forms of the earlier columns and arches had not been arrived at overnight; in due time, no doubt they will be enriched. As it is, in the *chliani* the hearths and ovens were surrounded with zigzag fire symbols moulded in the mud surfaces. One woman, building a

**Figure 15.10**
Jubbo children learn and help where they can, as their families continue to work on rebuilding.

**Figure 15.11**
Interior of a rebuilt dwelling in which mirrors and small objects were installed to replace those lost in the flood.

new hearth while we observed, commenced to mould the symbolic motifs when the structure had barely risen a foot in height. Within her *kanra* the centre of the wall facing the entrance was moulded in the form of the Tree of Life, symbol of fertility – and, it might be said, of the rebirth of the Rajput village of Jubbo (Oliver and Cheema, 1989).

All this may suggest that, with the exception of the welcome supply of electric light, the inhabitants could effectively rebuild their village without any aid whatsoever. But this would be an oversimplification. Partly due to the perspicacity of the *zemindar*, partly perhaps, to good fortune, not a single human life in Jubbo was lost to the flood. The picture might have been very different if several adults had been drowned, as occurred in other villages. Again, Jubbo's renewal was made possible by the survival of their cattle;

**Figure 15.12**
Modelling the roots of the Tree of Life, symbolizing rebirth, was a vital early stage in the rebuilding of a *chliani*, or kitchen.

if the animals had drowned, economic recovery would have been difficult. They would have benefitted from help in the clearing of debris from their wells, and the removal of the tangle of fallen trees, but most important of all, they needed help with the reconstruction of their buildings. The houses of Jubbo are as vulnerable now as they were before the flood, for the bond between wall and ground is no more secure than it was before. Both are the same material – earth – which is resistant enough to seasonal rains, with routine maintenance. But in a future flood of similar proportions walls and ground will liquify. Unstabilized, the walls will collapse, and there will be no support for the roof timbers. Such a disaster taking place at night can result in the deaths of countless people, as roof timbers fall in on the occupants. This is a problem that is not easily solved, but research is being undertaken in several countries to find ways of stabilizing earthen houses against flood damage. Although this is difficult even when building new houses, 'retrofit', or the installation of strengthening materials in existing houses, is more so. Walls and roofing materials need to be secured, corners need to be made resistant to damage, and strong footings which can support the building and not dissolve under water pressure, are required. The task of finding means of effecting such retrofit measures is formidable; it is often easier to rebuild with more secure systems in place.

Even if solutions are found and proved to be workable, in a region like Punjab the peasants have no cash to meet the cost. When hard-pressed government agencies and urban administrations are expected to bring relief, there is generally an expectation of a trade-off – like the proposed absorption of the inhabitants of Jubbo within the city of Lahore. When international financing bodies are involved, the trade-off is likely to be more demanding and the intervention in the functioning of a rural culture still more intrusive. Simplistic solutions of rehousing to pattern-book plans without reference to the specific cultures affected, are commonplace. But people who have traditionally built their own homes to meet their particular cultural needs do not readily accept, or adapt to, such housing provision. These observations are necessarily sweeping; in practice every case is different, not only because environmental and economic conditions are highly variable, but because every culture is distinct, and because every administration or financing agency has differing targets. There is a role for the designer/engineer in the housing of disaster victims and in safeguarding houses against future tragedies. Yet such projects can only be successful with the participation of the victim communities, by aiding them in achieving their housing objectives while giving greater assurance of safer housing in the future. Interference in the process by housing 'provision' can divest a culture of the ability, let alone the right, to house itself, creating a more dependent culture in so doing. It is time that 'intervention' was deleted from the vocabulary of development and post-disaster housing.

## References

Aysan, Y. and Oliver, P. (1987). *Housing and Culture After Earthquakes: A Guide for Future Policy Making on Housing in Seismic Areas*. Oxford Polytechnic, for the Overseas Development Administration.

Cheema, Y. (1988). Jubbo: Case study of a Punjabi village. Survey and field notes, presented in an exhibition at the National College of Arts, Lahore, Pakistan, 1988.

Darling, Sir M. (1949). *The Punjab Peasant in Prosperity and Debt*, 4th edn. Lahore.

Davis, I. (1978). *Shelter After Disaster*. Oxford Polytechnic Press.

Davis, I. (ed.). (1981). *Disasters and the Small Dwelling*. Oxford: Pergamon Press.

LICROSS (League of Red Cross and Red Crescent Societies). (1988). Statistics and Telexes. Courtesy Oxfam Emergencies Unit, Summertown, Oxford.

Oliver, P. (1987). Cultural aspects of housing in seismic areas. In: Erdik, M.O. (ed.). *Earthen and Low-Strength Masonry Buildings in Seismic Areas*. Conference Proceedings, METU, Ankara.

Oliver, P. and Cheema, Y. (1989). Field notes, compiled with survey team. Department of Architecture, National College of Arts, Lahore.
Sherring, M.A. cited in Cox, O.C. (1948). *Caste, Class and Race*. Doubleday, p. 28.
Smith, M.W. (1955). Social structure in the Punjab. In: Srinivas, M.N. (ed.). *India's Villages*. London: J.K. Publishers.

# PART V

# CONSERVATION AND CONTINUITY

# 16

# Conserving the vernacular in developing countries (1986)

As I explained in Chapter 14, with an Oxford-based project team I conducted research into the cultural implications of housing in seismic areas. Gediz in Kütahya province, Turkey has been the focus of the study where an earthquake in 1970 destroyed or seriously damaged over 300 villages. Some villages escaped undamaged and it was possible to compare the local vernacular buildings in them with those that had been affected by the earthquake, and to study the successes and failures of the government rehousing and resettlement programmes. On the first field trip to the region, I saw many of the large, timber-framed houses standing in their villages which were surrounded by the pastures and forests of this mountainous area, and drew some initial conclusions as to their age. I noticed the stone or adobe block infill between the timber framing of many of the houses and the lath and mud daub *bagdadi* walls of others; regarded the crumbling balconies, the dust-clad timber lintels and the sagging roofs of some of the buildings; saw the bow-framed carts with solid wheels, looking like ancient chariots standing beside the ground level barns. From these clues I deduced that this was an old society using venerable technologies and that their houses were 150, perhaps even 200 years old.

Returning for a more detailed survey a while later, I noticed with some surprise that the timbers were not jointed where they were exposed where the mud plaster had fallen off, but were joined with massive nails. I wondered whether this was customary, or a crude repair, and just how long the houses had been built this way. It turned out that there had been an earlier earthquake in 1942 and that the government had supplied six-inch nails to facilitate

**Figure 16.1**
Partial collapse in the earthquake of a nailed *bagdadi* house, Gediz, Turkey.

a speedy rebuilding operation. Nails had been expensive and this was a practical form of assistance. But it meant, if they were used ubiquitously, that the houses were much more recent than I thought. Indeed they were: hardly a village was more then 80 years old and, in the villages that we studied intensively, most, if not all, of the houses had been built within the previous 40 years. The construction of the buildings was quite crude and contributed to their short life. A relatively recent practice of wintering the animals in the ground-floor barns had helped warm the living quarters in the upper floor of each house but had created a steamy, humid condition which had caused timbers to rot quickly. These were poor peasants and their lands and houses were among their few possessions; nevertheless, they had no interest in maintaining their houses and if they began to break up or walls to fall out, many were disinclined to do anything about the deterioration.

This puzzled me, as it did the rest of the team. In one village we witnessed the rapid dismantling of one large house. It was of the customary plan of four corner rooms separated by a large *salon* where visitors were met and stores were kept, with a byre and storerooms below. Not, it would seem, an easy building to destroy, or one that merited it. But the villagers who were knocking away the adobe and cleaning the long poles of the frame were swift in the demolition job. We enquired why they were engaged in what seemed to us such wilful destruction, to be told that the house was being replanned to accommodate other members of the family. To the villagers of the Gediz region, any male family head with the help of his sons and the women and children could dismantle and build a house. Building a house was a task that everyone learned to do, they said. It was clear that if a house was beyond its useful life it was replaced by a new one, using, where possible, the materials of the former. Rotting timber often meant that it was not practicable to build with all the previous house materials, but most families had a grove of poplar trees to provide wood for such eventuality, and the earth all around provided the material for adobe or daub. In fact, the matter was more complex than this, as we found in later field-work. There were local builders who brought specialized skills to the work of house construction, and there were villages, like Erdogmus, which had a reputation for good quality building. But even so, it

**Figure 16.2**
Family dismantling their house, in order to reclaim the materials for the construction of another dwelling. Eski Muhipler, Turkey.

was evident that this was a society whose houses gave the illusion of gently decaying longevity, but which was committed to a far more impermanent notion of the dwelling. This could be attributed to the threat of earthquakes but, as in other communities prone to seismic activity, the fear of such disasters was less significant than the fear of failing crops or low prices. To the people of the Gediz villages, the way of life and the social interior spaces of the houses was more important than the durability of their fabric. Government-provided houses, though smaller, were slowly adapted to meet traditional spatial requirements, while money sent home by 'guest' workers in Germany was being used to build modern concrete houses which would accommodate, inevitably, certain traditional modes of living.

From such an example, it can be seen that it is representative of a society where the conservation of the vernacular is an almost meaningless concept. Buildings are not conserved; they are rarely even maintained. Customary western attitudes to the preservation of the building only apply for its useful life. As it happens, some 200 miles away, somewhat similar houses have been preserved. They are examples of fine craftsmanship and attention to detail of a kind which is not to be found in Gediz. The internal arrangements and use of space is very similar, but these houses, largely built in the nineteenth century, adorn the town of Safranbolu on a major commercial route between Europe and Asia. Fine, three-storey houses they were built largely by merchants, especially those of the Baglar district with its summer-houses and orchards. Though the feudal artisan sector Cukur might compare with Gediz, the much-admired Baglar houses are sophisticated, immensely attractive, surviving in a museum town which crosses the 'polite threshold' to a self-conscious style.

Conservation is frequently seen as a technological problem and it is true that the preservation of old materials, the keeping of venerable buildings in good repair is a technical matter. But fundamentally, conservation is a cultural problem. To the villagers of the Gediz area the conservation of their houses is not an issue and the identification of an example for the purposes of keeping it for posterity, would not come within their cultural concepts. The conservation of the houses of Safranbolu is not a cultural concept of its original occupants either, but one which relates to the urban values of an educated sector of the nation, generally living far from the town (Sózen, Eruzun, 1992). The two places encapsulate many of the cultural considerations that affect the conservation of the vernacular. Except for those instances where a building or complex of great

**Figure 16.3**
Machu Picchu, the Andean Inca town. The gables of pitched-roof houses are still to be seen. Peru.

quality has been abandoned by a society, or where a long-forgotten people has left silent reminders of a once flourishing architecture, all conservation takes place within a cultural context. Machu Picchu in the remote Peruvian Andes, Suryavraman II's vast Khmer temple of Angkor Wat or the elliptical walls of Great Zimbabwe were left unoccupied centuries ago. Their conservation to recent times was the result of accident, isolation or merely climate, but the cultures that had produced them had long since disappeared. When their respective merits were recognized and the processes of conserving them for the future begun, it was in a different cultural context from the one that was responsible for each of them. In this sense all conservation that is the product of man's efforts is the expression of cultural values; there is no question but that the process of conservation once initiated has deep cultural implications.

What those implications are may be different in differing circumstances. Sometimes they are related to a sense of history and respect for the achievements of a vanished people; more often they are related to a sense of ancestry, real or imagined, with which the conservers associate themselves. Conservation is very often a symbolic act, demonstrating pride and values to the present and the future. Whatever the motivation, the future plays a large part in it. Conservation is rarely solely for the present; most frequently it is justified, and financial support sought for it, in the name of 'our children, and our children's children'. In European countries and countries where European mores have been widely adopted or where the inhabitants have strong links with, or descent from

Europe, the concept of conservation is largely taken for granted. In Britain, we may embark on the preservation of, say, Hadrian's Wall with no serious argument about the merit of doing so. Though it has no bearing upon the lives of any specific community its symbolic value as a part of our history, let alone its believed intrinsic value as a monument to man's endeavour in itself, is enough to justify the activity. Of course, there is no general agreement on what is to be conserved. The rape of the city of Bath in the post-war years, the reckless demolition of Georgian terraces in London or the destruction of buildings in the Victorian suburb of north Oxford in the early 1960s would be far less likely today. Now north Oxford is a 'conservation area' and residents deplore the sweeping away of Wilkinson's Victorian piles in order that faceless halls of residence could be built. The activities of conservation societies and local amenity groups have considerably changed attitudes. It is highly unlikely that the Templeton carpet factory in Glasgow with its 'Paduan Gothic with Guelfic battlements' would have survived, had not attitudes to Victorian eccentricity changed; it is now preserved and used as offices and workshops.

Exactly what should be conserved is often a matter of dispute, but the concept of conservation is not held in question. Now Londoners look back aghast at the loss of the Euston Arch, the Coal Exchange or the Firestone factory, victims of bureaucratic spite or developer's avarice. The Firestone factory was deliberately destroyed over a weekend in the knowledge that a preservation order was being sought and likely to be applied the following Monday; the iron ball of the demolition crew swung first at the ornamental Art Deco entrance to ensure that the jewel in its crown was the first to go, making any stay of the process of destruction fruitless. The effect though, was a rapid growth in appreciation of Art Deco architecture. Firestone might have been lost, but others will not be so easily sacrificed. All these examples are, in one way or another, large in scale and, whether admired or not, they are recognizably monumental. These are not vernacular buildings, but architect-designed ones. Their plans may exist, their histories can be ascertained and they have advocates in the design professions to extol their merits (Fielden, 1982). But what of the vernacular buildings? Until recently, the conservation of English vernacular houses was a hit-and-miss affair, affected by a variety of factors. A building might be saved, like Anne Hathaway's house in Stratford-upon-Avon, for its historic associations – in this case with Shakespeare. It might be conserved because of an outstanding feature – exquisite pargetting perhaps, on an East Anglian house, or elaborate timberwork on a Cheshire

**Figure 16.4**
The early sixteenth century thatched house of Anne Hathaway, wife of William Shakespeare, formerly Hewlands Farm, near Stratford-upon-Avon, Warwickshire.

one. But often it was the private interest and enthusiasm of an owner which saved a house from being swept away in the enthusiasm for new housing estates. The listing of 'minor' buildings of the vernacular has scarcely begun (Bowyer, 1980).

Western cultural values place considerable importance on the building as object, reflecting an interest in it as commodity. For Europeans the building is a subject of investment; if its monetary value declines it is likely to be sacrificed so that the site can be built upon once more and its potential realized. Even the owner of the small domestic house shares the same sense of material value, expecting his house to appreciate in worth, eventually to be sold at a profit. He has no difficulty in perceiving the conspicuous wealth displayed in a mansion, a country house or place and is likely to equate architectural importance with size and grandeur. Admittedly, the issue is more complicated or we would not be regretting the extensive destruction of English country houses over the post-war decades. The explanation that they were 'uneconomic' was often excuse enough for their destruction, creating a conflict in material and cultural values which has sometimes remained unresolved. When the building has powerful symbolic associations – York Minster, or one of a number of cathedrals for example, there is no serious doubt that the building should be conserved even though substantial sums have to be raised to make this possible. Vernacular buildings, though often worth only a fraction by comparison, have

**Figure 16.5**
House and garden, of the respected Japanese poet Mukai Kyorai, died 1753. Rakushisha, Japan.

often been conserved more for their associations, like Wordsworth's Dove Cottage, than for their merit as buildings.

In many non-western countries, the monetary value of a building may not be rated highly, and may certainly not be a reason for its conservation. Symbolic value is likely to be of far greater importance. Restoration of the Imperial Palace at Katsura in Japan took place in the seventeenth century, and Chu-Soin and Shin-Shoin, like many other palaces, villas and shrines have been conserved with almost obsessional attention to detail. Conservation of mosques and shrines of particular quality and sacred significance is widely practised in Islamic countries, though sometimes, as in many instances of Imamzadeh in Iran, the dates in the tilework are often misleading. Frequently the dates are those of the process of conservation

**Figure 16.6**
Sheikh Lutfullah Mosque, on the great Maidan of Isfahan, Iran, commenced in 1603 by Shah Abbas in honour of his father-in-law. The portal was retiled in the 1940s.

rather than of the time of building (Godard, 1965). Often, restoration is accompanied by embellishment which may be more lavish than the original form. The mosque of Sheikh Lutfullah in the Maidan at Isfahan has a richly decorated, recessed façade before the entrance *iwan*, but this is a twentieth century addition; the original Safavid building was simple and austere outside, so that the dramatic effect of the internal tilework was the more surprising.

Religious significance is a major reason for conservation in countries that otherwise may be reluctant to expend money and labour on buildings. But rising nationalism also plays a considerable part, with buildings of importance in a country's history meriting attention for their value as symbols of struggle or nationhood. Perhaps the only non-European building to be restored to something like its original condition in Khartoum, is the Mahdi's house at Omdurman. It is now a museum and shrine to the memory of the Mahdi and his lieutenant and successor, the Khalifa Abdullah. Relics and battle-torn garments from the massacre of the Dervishes by Kitchener are displayed in unostentatious surroundings and gain in their emotional impact. Here the symbolic importance of the mud-brick and plastered house might be thought to outweigh its importance as an architectural structure, though in fact, it was the only two-storeyed house in nineteenth century Omdurman. In Khartoum, the old colonial buildings of the British presence have been well preserved on the whole: in the 1970s they housed branches of the civil service (Ellen, 1996). But in many countries buildings of the

**Figure 16.7**
The Omdurman house of the Mahdi, who defeated the Egyptians at El Obeid late in 1883, and General Gordon a year later. He died in 1885 and his house is a museum in his memory. Khartoum, Sudan.

colonial past survive more because of their solid original construction than for their merit. Sometimes, external agencies have been instrumental in the conservation of buildings, or have been influential in saving them. The writings of A.W. Lawrence drew attention to the many slave castles on Ghana's coast (Lawrence, 1963). They could have been unwanted symbols of a people's subjugation but instead, Cape Coast, Dixcove, Elmina and other castles were restored and made into government rest houses or museums. But the slavers' houses built by the Portuguese that stand almost in the shadow of Dixcove had no advocates and they were allowed to fall into disrepair. With no-one to indicate their architectural interest, these reminders of Ghana's unhappy past were poor candidates for conservation.

Where the scale of the architecture, the richness of its detail or its demonstrable symbolic value, correspond in some way with that of the west, there has been a basis for recommending conservation. The World Heritage list reflects western cultural attitudes in identifying 'great monuments' in urgent need of protection. One may not argue with the concern for the buildings listed, but the concept of the 'great monument' runs counter to the values of many societies, as in fact, does the very idea of conservation itself. Though the mosques of Mopti and Djenné (also declared a World Heritage Site), the Oba's palace at Benin, the palace of the Kubaka of Buganda and Great Zimbabwe itself were of a scale and quality that could be described as monumental, monumentality is not a characteristic of

**Figure 16.8**
Dixcove Castle, Ghana coast. Such castles were built by the Portuguese, Dutch, Danish and English in the sixteenth and seventeenth centuries. Most were used in the trade in gold, copra and slaves.

most African architecture. Hundreds of societies do not differentiate between the architecture of shrine or leader from the houses of the ordinary people. Hierarchies, belief systems and other values were often expressed in ritual, dress, dance or modes of behaviour which were far less physically evident, though no less significant. This is not restricted to Africa; the ancient 'Sky City' of Acoma situated on its lone rock in the New Mexican desert, has been inhabited continuously by pueblo Indians for hundreds of years. Its walls

**Figure 16.9**
The Great Mosque at Djenné, Mali overlooks a large market. The third in this site and in the regional tradition it was built under French colonial direction, 1907–1911.

**Figure 16.10**
View from Acoma, the 'Sky City' situated on a *mesa* rock. Destroyed by the Spanish in 1583 it was rebuilt in stone, bonded with mud. New Mexico, USA.

crumble, houses fall in, old mica windows are broken. It would be relatively easy to stabilize the ancient structures and preserve them for posterity, but this extremely uncompetitive society would regard such 'improvement' with disfavour. This is a people which is culturally disinterested in the conservation of building fabric, but wholly dedicated to the conservation of its ritual life. Buildings may collapse and perhaps, be replaced or subject to minimal repairs. Yet, in this ageless, static society there is no special significance attached to the quality of its buildings, only to the rituals that take place in some of them.

So, we have here a conflict of values related to the idea of interrupting the proceeds of gradual decline in the life of a building and repairing, restoring and making it permanent.

In other instances the concept of conservation not only conflicts with values, it runs counter to the way of life. For example, the simplest *kua* of the Kalahari bushmen is, by definition, impermanent; a day or two after the Bushman family unit has departed the site, there is little trace of its brief presence remaining (Marshall, 1976). This is even more the case with certain groups of Fulani in West Africa, who build reed shelters that are rapidly erected and just as rapidly demolished: they are essentially temporary. Other Fulani use and reuse the shells of mud-walled, cylindrical houses which are re-roofed during occupancy, but which are left empty for long periods while they continue to move their cattle. Many other peoples are using houses which are poised between semipermanent and ephemeral.

To conserve the buildings in one state or the other would be to fail to acknowledge their changing state according to the seasonal requirements of their builders. In these instances, the process of decay might be arrested without undue damage to the cultural patterns of the societies concerned – though I advance that thought with caution. But there are societies for whom the destruction of a building is a cultural necessity. Huts built for the *abakwetha*, or initiates into manhood in the *rite de passage* of the Xhosa are ritually burned to the ground, consuming the belongings of the boys now entering manhood; their past life burns with the hut. Conservation of the ritual hut may be of anthropological, even architectural interest, but it would run counter to the values of the Xhosa (Elliott, 1970).

If the *abakwetha*'s hut might be a structure of minor quality by most criteria, quality is not a necessary criterion for preservation. Singularity, or merely the fact that a building may be one of the last of its kind, might be reason enough. In England in the nineteenth century, squatter's rights permitted houses to be built on common land, though legislation was soon found to support their being swept away. Today, only a few examples survive; not notable as buildings in themselves, but significant survivals of working class history. Buildings of modest or undistinguished character with little to commend them as architecture can easily be overlooked. It is to the credit of the Avoncroft Museum at Bromsgrove that a crude brick structure that contained a nail-maker's workshop was preserved before this once-familiar Midlands building had disappeared altogether. Sometimes, it is not the merit of the building as a whole that seems to argue for its conservation, but rather the decorations on it. There are houses in Rothweil or Colmar which wear their polychrome-like embroidered vestments. Conservation of such rich external details can lead to absurdities such as the house of Anne Bodley in Totnes High Street with its splendid Tudor decoration of which only the façade remains. The conservation order applied to the street-front only; inside, one sees only the slick plasticized interior of a modern bank. Perhaps the sculptured fronts of many Hausa buildings in Kano and Zaria might be less easily prised from the main structures, but many observers have noted some evidence of declining interest in these moulded decorations and have advocated their protection. To the Hausa these often witty decorations, which include Roman knots, Islamic devices, but also bicycles, rifles and automobiles in some examples, are indications of the wealth and success as traders of the owners of the houses. Their topicality is part of their character: replacement of old decorations with new ones ensures that designs remain up to date. Their cost – often

**Figure 16.11**
The homesteads and *lelapas* (walled yards) of the southern Ndebele are repainted annually by the women to designs that reflect local textiles and other motifs. Pretoria region, South Africa.

equivalent to the cost of building the house itself – is some inhibition on rapid change.

Among the Ndebele of Southern Africa, house decorations have a shorter life. Each year the women redecorate the interiors, sculpting buffets and sideboards complete with ornaments in clay, painted in strong colours. On the exteriors, the walls of the *lelapas*, or forecourts, are painted with geometric motifs, some abstract, some hinting at houses, license plates, razor blades or other sources of motifs. These stylized, black-bordered designs have a boldness and harmony which some enthusiasts for contemporary tribal art would like to see preserved. Yet, fixing a design in time would run counter to the cycle of annual renewal which is part of Ndebele custom. Still more ephemeral are the linear rice drawings on the houses of Orissa, drawn during the Hindu festival of Laxshmi, the goddess of wealth. Beautiful though these Indian decorations are, they are washed off each day, to be replaced by new ones as the festival proceeds. This lack of concern for durability is occasioned by the religious nature of the rice paintings, but to westerners unaccustomed to such temporary paintings on walls, the loss of them leaves a feeling of discomfort. As has been shown, the attitudes to architecture in many cultures are very different from those in western countries, and may be quite unlike those shared by the signatories to the Venice Charter. With the thrust towards development, it is apparent that many Third World countries are discarding traditional values and assimilating western ones. This might suggest that values related to conservation will be adopted also, but the values that attract are associated with modern technology, commerce, communications and urbanization; values concerned with the cultural heritage are likely only to be acquired slowly. Conservation of the traditional old quarters of cities may be possible where urban culture is long established, as is the case in some Islamic countries, but even in some of these, including parts of Saudi Arabia, the drive towards modernization has generated a disregard for old buildings, many of which having been permitted to collapse or decay. Here, the use of adobe block is regarded as an indicator of poverty and retarded development. To a certain extent, belated recognition of the loss of the material culture has stemmed the rate of destruction, with conservation measures being introduced in Jeddah, and elsewhere. But in many instances the vernacular inheritance may seem increasingly irrelevant and the site values of old houses occupying prime situations in the city may be more compelling than any arguments concerning conservation of historic buildings.

Such problems of site value are by no means confined to developing countries: countless fine examples of English vernacular have been demolished for just such reasons. Yet many have also been saved, with conservation groups, local history societies and museums being instrumental in drawing attention to their importance. Often this has meant removal from the original site and re-erection elsewhere. As land has to be obtained for re-erection the new site is often in an open-air museum set aside for this purpose. Such museums of building were established in Scandinavia and a number were located in northern and eastern Europe in subsequent years. The open-air museum was slower in developing in Britain, but the Welsh Folk Life Museum at St. Fagan's, the Weald and Downland at Singleton in Sussex, and the Avoncroft Museum in Warwickshire are now notable collections. There is something akin to putting old workhorses to graze in the same field in this process, and these are still museums, even if very large ones. But some old ones, like Frielandmuseet at Lyngsby, have farmhouses that have stood on their relocation sites for 50 years and which seem totally accommodated to their surroundings. Inside, there is a certain 'Flying Dutchman' eeriness in the interiors, which appear to have been suddenly vacated.

Removal of the buildings and rebuilding them, or having new ones built, may be one solution to the problem of conservation of the vernacular in developing countries or tribal regions. But this too, may be an unacceptable measure. Modernizing peoples are often ashamed of their traditional dwellings and are sensitive to the curiosity or condescension that visitors can display. And there are other problems, as 'Bomas of Kenya' illustrates. This open-air reserve outside Nairobi has examples of many compounds representing peoples like the Kikuyu, the Kuria or the Pokot. Several of them have been built by veteran members of the tribes, and some are convincingly displayed. But there are others that are inappropriately sited, having surroundings that are very different from their authentic contexts. Again, compromises have been made: the Maasai houses have mud 'conning towers' to admit light to their interiors – useful for visitors but incorrect in the windowless Maasai *enkang*. And, as is so often the case with conserved buildings, compounds and groups of buildings, whether in an open-air museum or on its original site, the *bomas* are unnaturally clean. The desire to conserve in pristine condition, to scrub, polish, paint and sanitize for the visitor and tourist, common from Warwick to Williamsburg, even creeps in here.

Reconstruction may be the only way in which some traditional buildings can be conserved. Yet, if this is so, it must be done with accuracy and integrity. To use the wrong techniques, incorrect dimension and 'improved' conditions is to be as damaging as to lose the buildings to termites or tractors. At the Museum of British Columbia in Victoria, Vancouver Island, a Haida longhouse has been reconstructed – but to half scale. The internal spaces, the mass of the building have been unacceptably altered. Not only that: the timbers have been sawn, not split, the joints effected with modern

**Figure 16.12**
Constructed at reduced scale this Haida longhouse was painted by Mungo Martin who depicted a *tseekis*, or rock cod. Thunderbird Park, Victoria, Vancouver Island.

iron bolts. It may succeed as a tourist attraction, but as evidence of Haida material culture it fails. Clearly, traditional methods were not used in reconstructing the building, which serves to emphasize that, if there is to be a future for conservation, we need to conserve the technology and the methods of building, the skills and the 'wrinkles' as well as the structures themselves.

I am aware that this discussion raises more problems than can be readily answered, but this is partly due to the fact that cultures and their respective values are different; a solution to a conservation problem may seem totally appropriate in one context, but it may be quite unacceptable in another. In spite of World Heritage approaches which list monumental buildings and ignore modest ones, which place emphasis on the special and not on the representative, and which seek global proposals and international decisions, ultimately every instance has to be considered on its own merits, and in its own cultural situation. I am of the opinion that in the long run, most societies will look back with respect and pride to their indigenous architecture, but that this will take time. Meanwhile, it is necessary for informed enthusiasts, museum directors, local conservation societies or (though many do not see this as part of their remit) schools of architecture, to take the lead. Many already have, and have particularly devoted their attention to the many serious technical problems involved.

And what of the houses of Kütahya Province, with which this discussion commenced? They are, as I have said, by no means exceptional as buildings. They are not richly decorated, they are not put together with refined skill. In the use of concrete blocks, they reveal the introduction of relatively recent changes in technology, while the deterioration brought about by the wintering of animals discloses a change of use. As buildings they do not appear to be valued symbolically, nor are they maintained and repaired. When a new house is wanted, or an old one ceases to suit requirements, old materials are recycled with little fuss. They have no advocates, they do not appeal to nationalistic or religious pride, and interest in them is perceived by their owners as morbid fascination with their extreme poverty. They present in an extreme case a summary of many of the problems of the conservation of the vernacular when it is not obviously special, or singular. There is no easy answer to the problems they pose. But it does seem that recognition and respect for their way of life, sensitivity to their culture and less draconian measures in resettlement, such as occurred after the earthquake, would help to restore the self-confidence and pride that some have lost. Among the families of the affected villages there are some who have set about rebuilding, who have gone back to their old sites and are re-using buildings that survived the earthquakes in defiance of the plans to relocate them. Given support and assistance with materials and money rather than prefabricated house units they could be encouraged to build safely, well and for the future.

Conservation becomes necessary when a tradition dies, and it often dies because of neglect, disregard, or the active antipathy of those with whom power resides. When there is a serious concern for the nature of different cultures and their building, 'conservation' becomes less of an issue. Cultural conservation, with room to change or not, as the society wishes, is what matters; the conservation of buildings is most significant when it stems from self-esteem within a culture and not from the somewhat patronizing recommendations and measures taken by those outside it. Too often, measures to conserve seek to freeze a vernacular building, a village or a cultural landscape in time, rather than to sustain its life. This may be with the intent to preserve intact an aspect or unique feature of the architectural heritage, or increasingly, it may be motivated to promote tourism. The former may isolate its chosen examples for the appreciation of the paying visitor, which may ensure that the entire structure of the buildings concerned may be repaired, restored and maintained for the public at large, but may not necessarily be in the interests of the specific community. The latter intent, with tourist appeal as a significant aspect of its overall objective, may permit continued occupation but will frequently concentrate on external conditions and the restoration or assumed

**Figure 16.13**
As a World Heritage Site, Acoma is in process of 'restoration' using adobe blocks and modern details. Apart from tourism, it is now mainly used for ceremonials.

improvement of visual appearances. Representation of the affected communities is customarily nominal, seeking professional, political and legal engagement rather than the active participation of the people. Ultimately, however, cultural values and active community involvement will determine the quality and relevance of the conservation of the vernacular – but this has serious implications for all concerned.

## Addendum

Since this paper was written, the village of Acoma has been declared a World Heritage Site, and many of its buildings have been subject to reconstruction, but with adobe block rather than with the traditional mix of stone and mud. A road to the top of the mesa now serves the visitor, and conducted tours are arranged. Except for the observance of traditional rites and dances, the village is now virtually deserted, with the Acoma people living in Acomita and McCalls settlements on the desertic plain.

## References


Bowyer, J. (1980). *Vernacular Building Conservation*. London: Architectural Press.

Ellen, N. (1996). *African Architecture. Evolution and Transformation*. New York: McGraw Hill, pp. 154–158.

Elliott, A. (1970). *The Magic World of the Xhosa*. Cape Town: Collins, pp. 83–95.

Fielden, B.M. (1982). *Conservation of Historic Buildings*. Oxford: Butterworth-Heinemann.

Godard, A. (1965). *The Art of Iran*. London: George Allen & Unwin, Chapter 10.

Lawrence, A.W. (1963). *Trade Castles and Forts of West Africa*. London: Jonathan Cape.

Marshall, L. (1976). *The !Kung of Nyae Nyae* [sic]. Cambridge, Mass: Harvard University Press.

Sözen, M. and Eruzun, C. (1992) *Anatolian Vernacular Houses*. Istanbul: Creative Yayincilik ve Tanitim Ltd.


## Additional references


Facey, W. (1997). *Back to Earth. Adobe Building in Saudi Arabia*. Riyadh: Al-Turuth, with the London Centre for Arab Studies.

Minge, W.A. (1976, revised edition 1991). *Acoma. Pueblo in the Sky*. Albuquerque: University of New Mexico Press.

Ozkose, A. (1999). Renovation and conservation activities in Yoruk village from past and present. In: Dr Can Mehmet Hersek *et al.* (eds). *Safranbolu*

*Yoruk Koyu. Geleneksel Yasam Bicimi Ve Evleri* (Safranbolu Yoruk Koyu. Traditional Lifestyle and Houses). Istanbul: Emlak Bankasi, Creative Yayincilik Ltd.

White, L.A. (1932). *The Acoma Indians.* 47th Annual Report of the Bureau of American Ethnology, 1929–1930. Washington DC: Smithsonian Institution. Reprinted 1974, with colour illustrations. Glorieta, New Mexico: The Rio Grande Press, Inc.

# 17

# Re-presenting and representing the vernacular: The open-air museum (2001)

'History', the car manufacturer Henry Ford is reputed to have said, 'History is bunk.' Bunk, or bunkum means verbal rubbish, tinged with deception. What he actually said was 'History is bunk, as it is taught in schools'. His concern was genuine, and he founded the Henry Ford Museum and Greenfield Village near Dearborn, Michigan to introduce Americans to the material facts of their history (Zook, 1971). But he could be cavalier in his methods. Wishing to demonstrate that many American families came from rural England, in the mid-1920s he tried to purchase a row of Cotswold cottages to transport and rebuild in his open-air museum of Greenfield. Alarmed at the impending demolition of Arlington Row, Bibury, the local community alerted the Gloucestershire Archaeological Trust who succeeded in saving the row. In 1929, it was bought by the Royal Society of Arts and 20 years later it was given to the National Trust for safe keeping. Even though he had failed to transport Arlington Row, Ford bought a Cotswold house and blacksmith's forge from another village, and had all 500 tonnes of stone and timber shipped to Michigan. Whether Americans learned much more of their history as a result is open to question, even if, by default, Bibury was the richer for having saved the row (National Trust notice).

Henry Ford's Greenfield collection demonstrates how a single influential, affluent and motivated person, with a certain perception of history, can arrange for the location, demolition, transfer and re-erection of a collection of buildings (in Greenfield, about a hundred) ostensibly for the benefit of present and future

**Figure 17.2**
Farm buildings, including the granary store, in the Maihaugen Museum. Many farms in the eighteenth century had more than 15 buildings, including house, stables and byres, barns, stores for crops, wash-house and smithy. Lillehammer, Norway.

display folk architecture and how Finnish people lived' (Ailonen and Kinnunen, 1983). His purpose was at least in part nationalistic, symbolically using the museum to distance Finland from its Russian and Swedish neighbours. The site, which was part of a public park, was rented from the city of Helsinki by a newly formed company in 1911; two years after it was acquired by the state and operated as a national museum under the auspices of the National Archaeological Commission (later, the National Board of Antiquities). Others were

**Figure 17.3**
Niemela tenant farm from Konginkangas, the first buildings to be brought in 1909 to the Seurasaari open-air museum, on a coastal site near Helsinki, Finland.

**Figure 18.2**
Proportions of windows and other details of the modest buildings at the Shaker village, New Lebanon, New York State.

not be made by Believers.' Section IX of the Laws also gave guidelines on the colours of buildings. 'The meeting houses should be painted white without, and of a bluish shade within. Houses and shops, should be as near uniform in color, as is consistent; but it is advisable to have shops of a little darker shade than dwelling houses... Barns and back buildings, as wood houses, etc. if painted at all, should be of a dark hue, either red, or brown, lead color, or something of the kind, unless they front the road, or command a sightly aspect, and then they should be of a very light color' (Andrews, 1953).

Thus, there was a fair measure of freedom within the bounds of propriety, and as appropriate to function. 'All work', wrote Father Joseph Meacham in the 1790s, 'ought to be faithfully and well done, but plain and without superfluity. All things ought to be made according to their order and use'. There were many alternative ways to achieve this end. Some buildings were timber framed and clad; others were of brick or, at Enfield, New Hampshire, even of granite. Enfield was the home of Moses Johnson who, at the age of 33 and already an experienced carpenter, was given the task of designing and building the Mount Lebanon meeting-house. Shaker dances often became ecstatic and abandoned and the celebrants required unimpeded spaces. Johnson's solution was to span the principal meeting room, which was over 78 feet long and more than 63 feet wide, with seven great curved trusses of radial prince-post construction. The curved principal rafters which supported the tongue-and-groove boarded, tin-covered roof were of four layers

**Figure 17.4**
A timber-framed, wattle-and-daub (later, some brick infill) farmhouse of a subsistence smallholding, with byres, pigsties and privy, from Krawinkel, South Limburg in the condition as when obtained. Nederlands Openluchtmuseum, Arnhem.

adopted, like the Nederlands Openluchtmuseum, Arnhem, which was founded by a small private group in 1912 and opened in 1918, operating independently for 30 years until the state assumed overall responsibility in 1941. Its declared purpose was to 'present a picture of the daily life of ordinary people in this country as it was in the past and has developed in the course of time'. In producing a 100-page guide they 'concentrated on the social and economic background rather than overburdening the visitor with technical terms or local names, or giving detailed accounts of the past history of the buildings, which in any case have mostly found their way to the museum more or less by chance' (Anon, Arnhem, 1993). The museums grew in number, and many in size, between the wars, with Muzeul Satulut in Bucharest, Romania which opened in 1939, eventually displaying well over 300 buildings. Open-air museums proliferated after the Second World War, Norway establishing an association to unite more than a hundred in that country. Typical is the Trondelag Folkemuseum, Sverresborg, Trondheim which was privately founded in 1913. Staffed voluntarily and subsisting on private funds and later by grants, it has retained its independent status. By 1980 the Polish historian of the skansen movement, Jerzy Czajkowski, could write that 'there are approximately 500 big and small, ready or being built, skansen museums in Europe at present' (Czajkowski, 1981).

Skansen, village museum, Freilichtmuseum, Openluchtmuseum, musée de plein air, open-air museum – whatever the term used, they all conserve buildings within outdoor museum compounds. Or so it appeared to me, until notices of a Freilichtmuseum near

Stadthagen in north Germany led to a park inhabited by full-size concrete dinosaurs. There is no agreement on terms and often, little on what is preserved, how buildings are relocated and restored, what form the museum may take, and even why they are assembled. This may be regarded as inevitable, bearing in mind the vast range of terrains, resources, materials, periods, traditions, functions and building types which may be considered to merit preservation. During the past century, the incursions made into the rural landscapes of countries in all continents have been of a scale which is almost beyond measure. The expansion of cities, the growth of suburbs, the migration of peoples, the construction of superhighways, the decline of small agricultural economies and the growth of agribusiness are among the manifold factors which have contributed to the irreparably changed face of the world's rural landscapes. Such a summary may be platitudinous but it is undeniable, nonetheless. Victims of such physical changes have been countless fields, farmlands and forests, among which were untold rural buildings, sometimes of considerable age, that have been lost forever. Sometimes, this has been virtually unnoticed, as farm properties fall to the auctioneer's hammer along with the farmlands. In certain instances their destruction has been part of deliberate policies, motivated by industrial greed or political ideologies, of which the planned programme of village elimination and 'rural systemization' of the Ceaucescu regime in Romania is the most notorious (Giurescu, 1989). Their loss has been paralleled by the destruction of innumerable urban buildings of all kinds and often, of considerable quality, that have obstructed industrial or commercial expansion and the exploitation of land values in high-rise development.

If the safeguarding of certain examples of architecture has been assured through the efforts of individuals and conservation groups since early in the century, the period following the Second World War has witnessed a redoubling of efforts to do so. The 'listing' and grading of buildings, devising of heritage trails, establishment of eco-museums, declaration of World Heritage Sites and other measures have been taken to ensure the protection of significant buildings. Some of these are of archaeological importance, others are of unquestioned architectural merit: singular buildings, whose scale, architectural quality, prominence in their urban or landscape context, historic record and in most cases, religious significance are justification enough for their conservation. Yet, many buildings are conserved for their historic associations rather than their intrinsic value as architecture. It is its function as a national symbol and the home of the first president of the Union, George Washington, that is the primary reason for the preservation of the seventeenth century Virginian mansion, Mount Vernon. Its conservation might be argued on aesthetic grounds, but this could not be said of the modest homestead at Johnson City near Fredericksburg, Texas. Yet the conservation of the Sam Early Johnson log house, the reconstructed birthplace and the restored boyhood home of Lyndon Johnson, whose memory is preserved with the building while emphasizing his rural background, could be as readily justified as their being examples of regional, vernacular architecture.

Distinguished from free-standing chateaux, churches and country houses, monasteries and mosques, by their rural and largely domestic character, the majority of open-air museums display examples of what may be termed in their publications as 'regional', 'folk', 'traditional', 'peasant' or 'vernacular' architecture. Such assemblies were suggested as early as 1790 and a number of precursors date from the nineteenth century. Admittedly, some consisted of only a few structures, as was the case with the buildings relocated on the Bygødy peninsula, Norway on the orders of King Oscar II in the 1880s, but a few were larger. Among these was the ethnographic village of 24 houses, a church and several farm buildings from the Carpathian basin, which were re-erected in 1896 as part of the Hungarian Millenary Exhibition. Dismantled the following year, the village nevertheless inspired the formation of a number of open-air museums in Hungary, a life-time later.

It remains uncertain at what date and to what location the term 'open-air' museum was first applied, though it has been in international use since the 1950s. The vagueness of the term means that it can embrace a variety of situations, although it is generally employed to identify a museum of buildings, located in a territory often approximately equivalent to that of a provincial zoo. The unifying concept of the 'open-air' museum refers to the dispersal of the buildings within the territory, and not to the inherent nature of the exhibits themselves. This permits the display, not only of domestic buildings, but of cart-sheds, hayricks and farm outbuildings, and unique structures such as the chainmaker's shop at Bromsgrove (England) or the water-powered laundry at Arnhem (The Netherlands). Certain such complexes could be on open access but for the purposes of this discussion the 'open-air museum' is defined as one in which diverse buildings have been relocated in a physically, if artificially determined landscape setting, to which access is gained by payment of an entrance fee. Encompassed within the concept are village museums, such as Old Sturbridge village, Massachusetts; folk artefact collections, like the Welsh Folk

**Figure 17.5**
Most European museums feature farm buildings, but some include other types. This brick chainmakers' workshop in which a row of blacksmiths simultaneously forged links in a chain is in the collection of the Avoncroft Museum, Bromsgrove, UK.

Museum, St Fagans; museums of building, such as Avoncroft near Bromsgrove, England; ethnographic museums, for instance the Park Etnograficzny, W. Sanoku, Poland; heritage centres like the Isle of Arran Heritage Museum, among several other, more or less synonymous, designations.

Within its territorial confines the open-air museum may conform to one of a small number of specific types. In much of Europe, the term 'park museum' denotes one which has buildings dispersed at intervals that are sufficiently distant as to preserve their distinct

**Figure 17.6**
Freilichtumuseum, Cloppenburg, Lower Saxony with its massive brick and timber Hofenlage 'Hoffmann'.

identities, whether in function, period, method of construction or region of origin; the Niedersachsisches Freilichtmuseum at Cloppenburg, north Germany is a representative example. By contrast, a 'village museum' is applicable to those where a number of buildings have been clustered in village form, simulating for instance, the relationship of domestic buildings to church, windmill, smithy and village green, as at the provincial open-air museum, Bokrijk in Flanders, Belgium. Their disposition may depend upon the intentions of the museum authorities. The last-named was founded within the Bokrijk provincial domain in 1958, with its objectives 'based on culture, nature and recreation'. Commenting that 'earlier open-air museums erected their buildings with little thought to their actual inter-relationship', the 'museum village' of Bokrijk was constructed so that 'visitors feel that they are stepping into the past and entering a snapshot of life in former times' (Laenen, n.d.). It is unusual, in that it includes a simulated Brabant 'old town', comprising buildings transferred or partially reconstructed from Antwerp, around the 'Antwerp Square', with additional streets of buildings from Leuven and Diest. Future plans include clusters of urban buildings from Limburg and Flanders. A regional approach to the organization of the open-air museum is particularly evident in the national collections, that seek to illustrate the local or provincial traditions within the frontiers of a country. Such is the Swiss open-air museum at Ballenberg near Brienz, founded in 1978, where some 80 farmsteads from all cantons are 'arranged in 13 architectural units, on the basis of their regional origin'. Approximately 80 hectares are devoted to buildings in clearings and routes between them, in a total area close to 200 hectares consisting mainly of forest. Here, the visitor can 'discover a realistic representation of the peasant style of living. Ballenberg does not just consist of ancient dwellings that have been rebuilt, but represents a vivid reconstruction of rural Switzerland of the past centuries. Truly a dream . . .' (Melli and Gschwend, 1987).

Founded earlier, in 1967, but still far from completion, the Hungarian open-air museum in Szentendre, near Budapest, was more ambitious, with a master plan that 'envisaged the relocation of about 300 buildings to the museum for re-erection in nine groups, each representing a region in Hungary within 46 hectares'. The regional grouping, of which four are complete, 'shows the pattern of settlement characteristic of each region' and with furniture and demonstrations of customs, gives visitors 'a comprehensive picture of life in the villages and market towns of Hungary in a defined segment of time'. While the director of the museum at Szentendre is committed to the authenticity of the depiction of the chosen periods, he also emphasizes that 'authenticity also means authenticity of material and structure. The buildings chosen are usually not exhibited in the form they were found. They have to be restored to the form, material and structure they had at the time to be represented' (Cseri and Füzes, 1997). Smaller museums may also opt for the 'village' structure, either by arranging the component buildings that they have acquired in a village format, and obtaining others that would complete the notional ensemble, or by assembling from scratch the representative buildings necessary to create the preconceived village considered to be typical of its locale. Old Sturbridge Village, 'a bit of past history come to life', is pre-eminently such a museum. Albert and Cheney Wells of Southbridge, Massachusetts, purchased a tract of some 250 acres on which stood just two buildings. Relocating and re-erecting over 30 buildings, including several around a green, they opened the village in 1936. Private and nonprofit-making, it was 'chartered by the Commonwealth of Massachusetts to carry on its work of instructing and entertaining visitors, giving them a brief glimpse into rural New England that existed in 1800 or in 1820' (Chamberlain, 1969). More eclectic still is the Harold Warp Pioneer Village at Minden, Nebraska, the buildings drawn mainly from Nebraska, but their contents and exhibits chosen and purchased in the United States, Canada and Mexico, to illustrate 'Man's progress'. In spite of its name, a Nebraska village form is not simulated, the buildings being arranged in a cartwheel plan permitting the visitor to 'see everything, by walking less than one mile' (Harold Warp, n.d.).

Open-air museums whose stated intentions are fundamentally architectural, are fewer than might be expected. In England the Avoncroft Museum of Buildings was initiated by a group of people who endeavoured to prevent the demolition of an early timber-framed building in Bromsgrove. Although they were unsuccessful in this, they saved the framing timbers and re-erected the building on a 10-acre site in 1967. Other projects were commenced with the aim 'to encourage interest in buildings of architectural and historical value, where possible to prevent the demolition of such buildings when they are threatened, and to give advice on their restoration' (Anon, Avoncroft, 1973). Buildings that could not be restored *in situ* have been rebuilt at the museum, their value being the criterion for inclusion rather than their relationship to others within an ensemble. Of similar date and intention is the Weald and Downland Open Air Museum at Singleton, near Chichester, England. Founded by J.R. Armstrong MBE, in 1967 and opened 4 years later, its buildings range from a fine Wealden house to a man-operated tread-wheel.

**Figure 17.7**
Bayleaf, a 'Wealden' type house, with central hall open to the roof, and solars dividing the ends into two floors. Weald and Downland Museum, Singleton, UK.

Its founders aimed 'to establish a centre that could rescue representative examples of vernacular buildings from the south-east of England, and thereby to generate an increased public awareness of the built environment'. An introductory exhibition displays 'regional building materials and methods' and a collection has been gathered of 'artefacts representing the country crafts and industries, the building trades, and agriculture' (Harris, 1981).

Many museums serve a single function, preserving the architecture of a particular cultural or religious group, such as the Shaker Museum at Hancock, Massachusetts, or an industry or craft like that of the leatherworkers displayed at Das Museum im Lederhaus, Purgstall, Germany. Curators have differing perceptions of the purpose of the function of their respective museums, and of their clientele, and these influence the manner in which they present the architecture in their care. But, ask a director whether the museum is there to preserve buildings, to educate children, to inform the public, to communicate a past way of living, to aid architects, anthropologists or ethnologists in their work, the answer is invariably, 'all of these'. Museum directorates generally define their objectives in terms that reflect their personal views on quality, relevance, historic significance, status and architectural merit. To support them, they may have teams of ethnographers and architectural historians, engineers and technologists, and they may be subject to an administering institution or university. In 1966, an Association of European Open Air Museums was established, which has agreed standards of conservation, display, facilities and other common aspects of their work, though many museums do not subscribe to the organization (de Jong, 1997).

Like Italy and Spain, France came late to the idea of the open-air museum, but at Cuzals on the Célé river is to be found 'le plus beau Musée de Plein Air du Quercy, unique en France' (Anon. Cuzals, n.d.). It is of interest in a number of ways; for instance, it has a chateau on the site. Chateaux are common enough in France but this was different from most, rebuilding on a former site having been commenced in the 1920s and discontinued by the late 1930s. Its hydrological service system with a pumping station and gravity feed to the chateau, is restored in the museum. Other buildings include a farm, identified as having been built in 1910, and a reconstruction of a farmhouse from the pre-Napoleonic period. Examples of roof types and a row of stone walls, demonstrate different methods of construction. A collection of oil presses, another of tractors, a toy museum, a basket-making exhibit, physick garden, children's carousel, an apiary, a bakery and a 'museum of fire' have much that entertains, while having little sense of direction, or evidence of co-ordination. In 1998 two corbelled stone *cabanes* were being built by architectural students from La Villette, Paris – in an area where many dry-stone builders still live and work. Within its 50 hectares, Cuzals demonstrates both the successes of open-air museums and the problems confronting them.

As these examples have shown, the creation of an open-air museum is almost without exception, the result of a motivation on the part of an individual or of a group of people sharing a common concern or interest, to preserve a number of buildings for posterity. This means that the essential drive is one of a perceived need, but the distribution of the museums in different countries, their prevalance in some and virtual omission in others, indicate their uncoordinated establishment and development. Some have been adopted as national or as regional collections, but are subject to ideas of classification; only in Norway is it possible to see numerous local museums that together demonstrate the vernacular traditions of most of the country, permitting comparative study without undue preconditioned selection. In the majority of open-air museums the buildings on display have been obtained by the founder, the organization, the provincial or other authority to project an over-riding concept: of a presumed local tradition, the style of living in a favoured period, the values of a religious sect, the home of a memorialized individual, the labours of former workers, or some other historical construction. Statements of the founders, extracts from the charters or quotations from the published guides, reveal a pre-occupation with the visual image, often expressed in romantic terms: to create a 'picture-book', to 'present a picture', to enter a 'snapshot of former times'. The image is seldom of buildings alone but a 'comprehensive picture of life in the villages'. Though it is unusual to acknowledge that the resultant picture is 'truly a dream', the emphasis on the presentation of 'life' in the past is ubiquitous. But these constructed environments and picturesque images raise many issues that bring the validity of the open-air museum into question.

The issues are ones of presentation, re-presentation and representation. Rarely are buildings that have been presented to a museum, rescued from demolition, 'saved for the nation' or have 'found their way to the museum more or less by chance', in a state where they can be simply transported and re-erected. Removal of a building is not in itself a simple process, but one which may involve legal, contractual and planning approvals. If it is responsibly done, it requires detailed surveys and examination of condition, the drawing, recording and numbering of its component parts for disassembly and reassembly. In turn, the latter necessitates much physical but specialized work, and sensitivity and method in the sequences of dismantling, handling, transporting, storing and protection from damage or deterioration. Neither will the building be in a condition that permits straightforward re-erection. Extensive repairs may be required, materials considered inappropriate replaced (corrugated galvanized metal sheeting by thatch, for example), extraneous elements (add-ons or lean-tos) removed, and missing parts replaced or constructed. This is done in the name of 'authenticity', a concept of the authentic which, however, relates 'to the time to be represented', like the Japanese museum of buildings in which a representation of William Shakespeare's birthplace is declared to be 'more authentic' than the Stratford-upon-Avon house because its new construction is comparable with the state of the original in the sixteenth century. Such work cannot be undertaken lightly or spontaneously: it requires forethought and planning, selection and design decisions, professional skills in history, archaeology, architecture and building, and not inconsiderable investments of money, time and effort.

Some work may be done voluntarily but whatever the circumstances, the processes of re-erection and reconstruction are demanding and time-consuming. They also require explanation, though the terminology employed is not consistent and can be misleading. 'Erection' of a building and 're-erection' are often used synonymously, while 'reconstruction' may mean 'rebuilding' in one museum but largely obscure the fact that a 'structure' is a new simulation in another. The use of the term 'reconstruction' to mean 'new construction made to represent a former building' (such as the Napoleonic farmhouse at Cuzals) is now widely adopted, but less widely made known to the visitor. Similar ambiguities relate to 'repair' and 'renewal', to 'renovate' and 'restore', to 'reproduce' and 'reproduction', and notoriously, to 'preservation', 'conservation' and 'restoration'. Some or all of these terms are generally used in guides and museum handbooks, but a glossary that explains them, as distinct from one which gives historic or indigenous terms, is extremely rare. The looseness and ambiguity of the terminology assists museums in conveying their 'pictures' of 'life in past times' by laying a thin cloud of obscurity across the simulated villages and their furnished but lifeless buildings.

The buildings in an open-air museum cannot be casually obtained nor merely presented as they stand. Many are selected – or rejected – for what they are believed to represent within the chosen context and good, or if possible, excellent examples are sought. As such they are represented on specially selected sites and displayed as representative of the underlying theme of the museum. In forming part of a larger and more complex whole, their inter-relationship with other buildings may be invented rather than replicated in the process of re-presentation. Representation in the chosen context is dependent on an understanding of the building-producing- and-occupying culture in history, and its interpretation by the museum's curatorial management. How these are achieved and for what purpose, will depend on the message that is intended: no museum re-presentation or representation is value-free.

That the buildings are gathered within a compound is made explicit at the entrance to the open-air museum which, in the majority of instances, has a bureau and ticket office, administrative offices and gated access. These are necessary and often extensive but frequently, as for instance at the Nederlands Openluchtmuseum, Arnhem or the National Folk Museum, St. Fagan's, Wales, the offices of administration and conservators are placed close to the entrance. Apparently, this is to assure the visitor of the extent and intensity of the work involved in preserving the buildings, even if the conservator's premises are generally closed to the interested tourist. Their design appears to present a problem. Having failed to buy Independence Hall in Philadelphia, Henry Ford had it replicated for the entrance to Greenfield. The entrance at Frilandsmuseet, Lyngby, Denmark is of similar scale and palatial impressiveness, notwithstanding the museum's declared purpose 'to portray the

**Figure 17.8**
Entrance buildings to St Fagans Museum, Wales, which are used by the administrative staff, but do not convey the nature of the collection.

living conditions of the countryman' (Uldall, 1972). The forms and details of these entrance buildings emphasize the classical tradition rather than the vernacular, while the defensive walls of the museum compounds distance the visitors from the buildings and artefacts within, with a security that merits the term *skansen* (fort). That the contents represent the 'other', the peasant community of the past, could not be more emphatically expressed. The Niedersachsisches Freilichtmuseum at Cloppenburg, north Germany is one of the few to use a vernacular building, as the entrance to the museum. Albeit a large one, the Austellungshalle, 'Munchausen-Scheune' dating from 1561, is skilfully employed to allow the building to indicate the character of the museum without large notices or announcements. More inviting perhaps, but in an essentially modern group of buildings, the entrance to the Hungarian Open Air Museum, Szentendre is a veritable market of pavilions, shops, souvenir stalls and cafes. Beyond the entrance the visitor enters the invented environment and artificially constructed 'open-air' landscape of the museum. Few are geometrically planned, and many group the houses around an open space or 'green'. Often the arrangement of buildings appears to be determined, at least in part, by the circulation pattern prescribed for visitors and the convenient placing of restaurant or other facilities. In some museums, buildings may be clustered according to their affinity with others, in arrangements which can appear convincing but which are not necessarily accurate. Such was the case at Sirigoino open-air museum in Yugoslavia, where all the buildings of a simulated farm were placed in parallel on a sloping site and facing the same direction, even though the internally facing farm settlements located on contour patterns were clearly evident in the immediate locality.

Some collections are assembled *ad hoc* as buildings have been salvaged, bequeathed or made available, rather than by planned development. Often this has meant their relative isolation, as in the 'park' type of museum. Such serendipitous accumulation has its benefits but purposeful expansion depends on the potential availability of buildings considered important enough to save and restore. Both the clustering of unrelated buildings and the distant dispersal of others is to be seen at the Frilandsmuseet, Denmark. In many instances, a compromise is effected by creating the semblance of the village form of a region, which is linked by another with a path or roadway, symbolizing considerable physical distance. This is the case at Szentendre which however, has a group of houses from the Upper Tisza region nearest the entrance, selected in the Communist era to demonstrate by the contrast of their styles of living, the oppression of the serfs by the 'minor gentry', and of them in turn, by the nobility. Now made less blatant, it bears a revisionist message. Many fine buildings have been conserved in literally hundreds of museums, but when selection has been possible, museologists may bring professional criteria to exemplify, as in this case, a sociopolitical theme. But they may also bring criteria of quality, for example in craftsmanship, decoration, sheer size, or the uniqueness of the building concerned. While this can be meritorious in itself it can result in an overall distortion of the extent to which they are representative of buildings in their local context, emphasizing the special rather than the commonplace. In the early years of many museums, collecting was coloured by romanticism, as was the case at the Openluchtmuseum Bokrijk, Belgium founded in 1953 by the artist C. Wellens, who rebuilt the Wellenshoeve from Kempen 'in accordance with his own ideas', which included the addition of a dog-powered butter mill (Laenen, n.d.). This was a salutary warning to later curators who have been assiduous in their restoration, though they cluster them by their province or region rather than by their functional relationships.

Not least of the problems confronting museologists is one of period. There is a general archaeological tendency to restore a building as it was first constructed, without the additions, adaptations and appurtenances that have accrued over time. Only historic alterations, such as the insertion of a solar floor in an English hall house, are sometimes spared. This is done in the name of authenticity, and does not take into account the modification of buildings to meet changing needs and functions. Comparison of many photographs taken both before and after dismantling, transferral, conservation and re-erection, confirms the widespread practice, though there are numerous exceptions. A building may remain in largely unaltered form, even if the roofing thatch has been replaced by slates over several centuries. But interiors are more subject to change, not only in the removal or building of partitions and other minor alterations but also in the furniture, artefacts and furnishings utilized. Certain of these, such as wooden bowls or andirons and crooks, changed comparatively little in form, but ceramics, textiles, painted decorations, stoves and many items of household equipment are more period-specific. Curators may choose to keep the interiors vacant, as is occasionally the case, but though an empty room may hold the interest of an architect it can have little appeal for the general public. Usually, curators have to decide what period their recreated interior assumes. This is largely conditioned by what is available from the museum store – few buildings arrive with artefacts intact. Sometimes the reserves are considerable – Anders Sandveg left a legacy of 30 000 objects to Maihaugen, while Szentendre has 40 000 in store. Inevitably, most furnished interiors appear as stage sets for specific historical drama productions, undisturbed by any actors. Conscious of this, some museum directors have arranged tableau of wooden or waxwork figures, such as groups of purchasers and shopkeepers, schoolchildren and their teacher in a classroom. These and some 15 other period settings with characters in arrested action, are

**Figure 17.9**
A Norwegian farmhouse kitchen, with a chimney 'crane', baking pans, spinning wheel and other accoutrements. Trondelag Folkemuseum, Trondheim.

**Figure 17.10**
An embroiderer, wearing period costume, in one of the artisan's buildings that survived a major fire, in Turku, south-west Finland.

displayed at the Musée des Arts et Traditions Populaires, Wattrelos near Lille, northern France. Others have followed the lead of colonial Williamsburg and dressed some of their staff in period costume, a practice which brings with it further dimensions of the problem of representation, creating not only an artificial ambience but also fictitious characters to people it. Some measure of accuracy is introduced when the actors are involved in a craft or occupation, like firing pottery or baking cornbread, but such events are customarily to be seen at scheduled times only, perpetuating the impression of museum as theatre.

In the majority of museums, the buildings have been restored and, where necessary, rebuilt so that they have an ensured life of a few generations. Their crisp edges, tight bonds and joints, colour-washed walls, unimpaired brick and stonework, painted doors and sharp mouldings are often at variance with the condition of similar buildings standing beyond the museum enclosure. The exteriors bear no evidence of the dirt and damage of cattle, draught oxen and horses, of lurching loads and lumbering carts which leave their impressions on the buildings of working farms. Across the threshold, the interiors are usually immaculate, the tiled floors, the treen and pewterware, ceramics and hardware, plain and painted furniture, clean and polished. Devoid of mud and grease, they frequently present an idealized and antiseptic version of the peasant environment. This distancing from the hardship and not infrequently, the discomfort of rural life is made still more detached by the inhibitions against entering rooms or handling of objects. Suspended ropes, even glass walls and doors, separate the visitor from some of the living spaces which remain mute, inflexible and undisturbed. Even though the museum is not one of conventional glass cases, this curatorial fixation persists. Protection of the artefacts against damage or theft is, of course, the most readily offered reason, the objects in the Frilandsmuseet, Lyngby, for instance, being wired into position and alarmed. Moreover, there are serious problems of safety for both objects and visitors, as indicated by the fire at Arnhem in 1970, and even more drastically, the fire at the museum of Sanok, Poland in 1994, when 13 large buildings and 1400 exhibits were destroyed (Czajkowski, 1994). It is unusual for a museum to be the outcome of a disaster, but such is the case with the Buried Village of Te Wairoa, Rotorua, New Zealand, a museum of a Maori settlement which was engulfed by a volcanic eruption in 1886 and

**Figure 17.11**
Arawa Maori *whare* (dwellings) have been retrieved from the ash and lava from the eruption of Mount Tarawere in 1886 which buried the village of Te Wairoa near Rotorua, New Zealand. A tree has grown through the roof of this *whare*.

subsequently recovered, Pompei-like by excavation (Smith, n.d). It is one museum whose still emptiness is the essence of the site.

Departures from the hygienic standards shared by the majority of museums are rare. At Arnhem a single exhibit, a farmhouse from Krawinkel, has been re-erected as it was found: 'Beyond the smart facade, the old huddle of buildings, lean-tos and sheds remained unaltered' (Anon, Arnhem, 1993). But the smell of the fodder that once boiled in the fireplace is undetectable and even the dung-heap seems sanitized. Of listing walls, loose joints, peeling plaster and rotting timbers there is little to be seen; verisimilitude in representation does not extend that far. A more remarkable exception is the museum at Howick, New Zealand, an open-air museum which is a recreation of a 'fencible' (defendable) military settlement of the 1840s. Over 30 buildings have been recovered, largely due to the efforts of the Howick Historical Society and, as at Maihaugen, the initiative of a local dentist (Anon, Howick, 1995). He sought to keep every building in the condition in which it was obtained, with layers of soiled and peeling wallpaper and paint, broken and rusty locks, nails as wall hooks and splintered floorboards. The society was in conflict with regional authorities who, with the safety of visitors in mind, wished to avoid infection, contamination or minor injuries. Apparently, this was not considered to be a problem at Cuzals where the farmhouse, the cattle byre and the cowman's room within it, were left as they were found, in a welter of dishevelled clothing and bedding, with mud-caked boots and socks in the manure

**Figure 17.12**
Interior of cowman's bedroom in a reconstituted farm, circa 1910. Cuzals, Sauliac-sur Célé, Lot, France.

on the earth and cobble floors; the living presence of the former occupants was almost tangible. This is rarely the case: objects are displayed with the meanings and aesthetics of the twentieth and twenty-first centuries, with qualities of orderliness, cleanliness, purity and simplicity clearly apparent. Restoration of the buildings to their presumed genotypes, the precision and refinement of the skills applied to them, the undisturbed interiors with their ascetic frugality and perfection in the placement of artefacts, speak of the values projected on them rather than the values of their former inhabitants.

To take the visitor through their collection virtually every open-air museum publishes information. This may simply be in the popular twice-folded A4 leaflet form by which most museums attract browsers in hotel lobbies and information centres. Couched in phrases that evoke nostalgia and sentiment, awareness of history and above all, regional and national pride, they are published in their tens of thousands. Most museums publish a separate and more fully descriptive guide though they vary in the amount of information they carry. All buildings are numbered as if they were in a display case and in so presenting them a circulation route is implied. In most guides they are illustrated with photographs, now in colour and with current graphic styles, though less frequently with the perspectives, isometrics or other orthographic projections which formerly conveyed architectural information. The imagery employed indicates the museum's expectations of the market, which may now be larger than in the 1970s, when Arnhem succeeded in including

**Figure 17.13**
Examples of folded publicity leaflets which in some instances (e.g. the buried village) may include a map of the museum.

**Figure 17.14**
Guides to open-air museums, which frequently range from c. 50 to 150 pages.

photographs, sketches and plans in its guide. It claimed in excess of half a million visitors in 1990. Some museum guides use reproductions of prints, plans, sections and projections of selected buildings, and sometimes, pictures that record both the buildings *in situ* and after removal, as is the case with the guide to the Swiss open-air museum, Ballenberg (Melli *et al.*, 1987). The guide to the Australian House Museum, Geelong, Victoria, uses most of the above, though its drawings are sketch isometrics. Early photographs and reproductions of documents and media reports give it a distinctive character (Campbell, n.d.). Texts may range from the elementary to the informed, from a catalogue to a history, or a carefully edited combination of these. As few visitors read the guide in detail while entering buildings, a summary text is helpful. Inevitably, the approach varies with the type of museum and the expected clientele. Cover photographs tend to emphasize the bucolic, in lands where the sun always shines. The layout may be lively while the typography remains conventional, signifying both open-mindedness and seriousness of purpose. In some cases booklets or game sheets are available for children, with line drawings to colour, items to name or blank pages for their own drawings. More frequently these are issued to assist teachers with their classes; for school groups constitute the largest bodies of visitors to some museums – though coach parties of tourists are also numerous. The attention span of such groups is frequently brief, and many museums produce a basic map guide issued with the ticket to simplify the circuit.

To offset the impression that the simple guides can give, it is important for many museums to underpin their work with publication of their research. In part this is to establish their credibility with conventional museums, many of whom, after a century, still regarding open-air museums of building as dubious. Academic papers on archaeological surveys, on specific building types, technical problems, and socio-historical accounts are numerous. Some publish monographs like those of the Stichting Historisch Boerderij-Onnderzoek, the research wing of the museum at Arnhem, while others may have a regular publication, such as *Haz Ès Ember* – 'House and Man', the yearbook of the Hungarian open-air museum, Szentendre (Mjklos and Endre, 1997). Though some independent museums publish such studies, Old Sturbridge Village Museum producing its 'booklet series' since the 1950s, they are especially the productions of museums that have institutional, provincial or national interests behind them (Hamilton, 1964). This reflects both the economic and the academic bases of the museum. But it is also indicative of the motivation on the part of the latter to reinforce the regional and historical provenance of the buildings, promoting identification with former folk communities. Sometimes this is overtly expressed as, for instance, the Orkresne Vlastivedne Muzeum (the District Motherland Museum), Stara Lubovna, in the Slovak Republic (Stika and Langer, 1989).

In the corner of a display of agricultural equipment and close to the bakery at Cuzals, someone had posted a notice:

> QUELLES SONT LES DIFFERENCES ENTRE UNE ECÔLE, UNE PRISON, UN ZOO ET UN MUSÉE DE PLEIN AIR?

Freely translated, it read: 'What are the differences between a school, a prison, a zoo and an open-air museum?' (1998). Whether the question was written by a perplexed visitor, by a teacher for her class, by a doubting museum employee or a member of the management, I could not ascertain; Cuzals was hardly burdened by officials. Behind the rhetorical question, it seemed that there was a recognition of the didactic, idealistic, puritanical, contained, herded, classified, near extinct/surviving, wanted/unwanted, re-presented and represented features which are common to the forms and philosophies of all open-air museums.

The foregoing observations have been based on visits to open-air museums in over 20 countries and more than a dozen states, though for this chapter the examples cited have been more limited.

**Figure 17.15**
The formal garden centre of the Chinese Regional Architecture Museum, which is also the Ethnic Minorities Cultural Centre. Guilin.

After a century of existence, the nature and purpose of the circumscribed and gated museums of buildings need to be re-examined. They can, and often do, serve useful purposes but there is too little agreement on their functions, the basis of the selection of buildings, the degree to which they should attempt to evoke a sense of place and period, the planning of the environments in which they are sited, the movement and freedom of visitors. The nature and quality of the publications produced, the research which they permit or encourage, and the extent to which they serve local or national political interests are frequently constrained. This is evident at the museum of Chinese regional architecture at Guilin, whose imposing entrance, lined with the flags of many nations, underscores its propaganda role. The entrance building on its plinth approached by a full-width flight of steps, leads to a geometrically formal garden around which are newly built and austere versions in replica of the indigenous architecture of some of the peoples of south China, including the Dai and Hani. There has been no attempt at the relocation of existing traditional buildings, nor any evidence of how they are situated in their authentic contexts.

These and other issues become highlighted when the small but growing number of open-air museums in the industrializing and developing world are considered. The differences in quality and objective become readily apparent when the Museum of Traditional Nigerian Architecture at Jos is considered. This extensive and remarkable museum was the inspiration of Professor Zbigniew Dmochowski of Gdansk Technical University, Poland. His detailed research in the 1950s and 1960s led to his attempting to represent the diverse architecture of Nigeria's peoples on the 65-acre site. With a few exceptions, he chose less to preserve than to replicate, and greatly benefited by the employment of indigenous craftsmen to build the houses (Dmochowski, 1990). Although less thoroughly documented, Bomas of Kenya, a museum of traditional building near Nairobi, was also built by the members of tribal groups, the dwelling types being current, even if less monumental than many that were reconstructed at Jos. Both museums were created by motivated expatriates, but the village complex in the National Handicrafts and Handlooms Museum, Delhi, was built for the Asiad '72 Exhibition, and represents some 15 regions in India, the huts being 'built in facsimile with authentic construction by the villagers themselves. In every hut items of day-to-day life are displayed in order to receate the cultural contexts in which such objects were actually used' (Jyotindra Jain, 1989). The modest adminstrative building was designed by the Indian architect Charles Correa; more contentious is the regular plan to which the displayed huts and houses conform. Although construction by indigenous builders is less likely to misrepresent traditional structures, the Nicobarese builders at Delhi's village complex were obliged to reduce their traditional meeting house to an eighth of its customary volume. Such distortion of scale or quality was also evident at Taman Mini, Jakarta, where each Indonesian province was required to provide its own building to represent its region. Thus Bali built a typical domestic compound, while Central Sumatra chose the 'aristocratic' Minangkabau house,

**Figure 17.16**
A compound of dwellings and stores, built by Kikuyu for the Bomas of Kenya Museum.

**Figure 17.17**
A Nicobarese meeting house reduced to a fraction of its volume, National Handicrafts Museum, Delhi, India. The museum layout was designed by Charles Correa.

with its rich carving and painting, and its collection of regal wedding costume. Sulawesi was represented by the Toraja, who produce one of the most spectacular building types of any vernacular tradition. They had no need to embellish or exaggerate, though they did miniaturize their grave figures by building a rock shelter in perspective. But northern Sumatra, represented by the Batak Toba, built an immense and overscaled version of their domestic house, doubtless to rival other regions. Both the Indonesian Taman Mini and the Indian village complex are well patronized by their own nationals as well as by tourists. The management of the Delhi museum hope that the complex 'will symbolize the urgency for the preservation of rural technology and traditional aesthetic values in rapidly industrializing India' (Jyotindra Jain, 1989).

Already the small but growing number of open-air museums in industrializing countries are encountering the problems of re-presentation and representation; not necesarily the same problems as those in European museums, but clearly comparable. As their numbers increase issues of intention, of veracity, guidance and publication will become more problematic. Associations of museums may be instituted and advice based on the experience of a century in the west may be sought. Whether or not this is the case, the time is surely overdue for a serious reconsideration of the functions and forms of open-air museums. Many are deceptive, their invented, rather than authentic, environments being based on sentimentality, nostalgia and the falsification of 'life' in selected periods by sanitizing, insulating and idealizing the buildings and their contents. By rejecting the changes that have been wrought by generations, by deleting all references to the modifications and influences of subsequent periods, they fossilize them in mythical time. There is little doubt that many open-air museums are popular, and many are used for educative purposes as opportunities for schoolchildren to 'step into the past'. It may be argued that by so doing they bring history alive, and make future citizens aware of their heritage. It may also be contended that by preserving vernacular domestic and functional buildings they are helping to generate an understanding of regional architecture which will ensure respect for it in the future. Such was not the case in Romania however, where one of the most respected of museums and oldest of scientific academies concerned with conservation was powerless to prevent the destruction of whole villages in the name of progress. In fact, the open-air museum may be counterproductive in this respect (Giurescu, 1989). By saving 'representative' examples of the vernacular for contemplation in idealized surroundings they can relieve those intent on the destruction of such buildings in the world beyond the museum's walls of any responsibility to protect them. Again, by creating 'a picture' that associates vernacular buildings essentially with the past, they also isolate them from the modern world, an isolation which is emphasized by their enclosure within the museum confines. As many of the buildings are presented or selected for their uniqueness or special qualities of scale, craftsmanship or decoration, by implication they low-rate the simpler and less singular buildings which nevertheless contribute unspectacularly to their environmental contexts.

These considerations are important with regard to the European and North American open-air museums, whose continued existence in their current forms and serving their present purposes, is seriously open to question. They are even more important in the developing world where self- and community-built buildings based on vernacular traditions will continue to be essential if the housing demands of expanding populations are to be met in the twenty-first century. Rather than romantic depictions of old buildings with invented histories in spurious and contrived settings, vernacular architecture in the developing world needs respect and support, with encouragement for its continued use of renewable resources, passive climatic modifications, spatial organization based on social structures and scale according to need. Admittedly, this too is part of an agenda but it is one which, together with instruction in building skills where they are declining, and more forethought in the choice of building examples and their presentation, could give new purpose and relevance to the open-air building collections of the future.

## References

Ailonen, R and Kinnunen, R. (1983). *Seurasaari Open-Air Museum Vistor's Guide*. Helsinki: National Board of Antiquities.
Campbell, F. (n.d.). *Guide to the Australian House Museum*. Geelong, Victoria: Deakin University.
Chamberlain, A. (1969). *A Tour of Sturbridge Village*. New York: Hastings House.
Cseri, M. and Fuzes, E. (1997). *Hungarian Open-Air Museum, Szentendre*. Szentendre.
Czajkowski, J. (1981). An outline of Skansen Museology in Europe. In: Czajkowski, J. (ed.). *Open-Air Museums in Poland*. Poznan: Bibliotecka Muzeum Narodowego, Rolnictwa.
Czajkowski, J. (1994). *Park Enograficzny W. Sanoku W. Ognium*. Sierpien.
De Jong, A. (1997). Museological approach. In: Oliver, P. (ed.). *Encyclopedia of Vernacular Architecture of the World*. Cambridge University Press, pp. 49–52.
Dmochowski, Z.R. (1990). *An Introduction to Nigerian Traditional Architecture*, (3 vols). London, Lagos: Ethnographica and the National Commission for Museums and Monuments.
Giurescu, D.C. (1989). *The Razing of Romania's Past* (US/ICOMOS). London: Architecture and Technology Press, pp. 20–23.
Hamilton, E.P. (1964). *The Village Mill in New England*. Sturbridge, Mass: Old Sturbridge Inc.
Harris, R. (ed.). (1981). *Weald and Downland Open-Air Museum Guidebook*. Singleton, Sussex: Weald and Downland Museum.
Jyotindra Jain, C. (c. 1989). *National Handicrafts and Handlooms Museum*. Delhi, India: Crafts Museum.
Laenen, M. (n.d.). *Provincial Open-Air Museum, Bokrijk. Guide*. Brussels: Ludion-Lannoo.
Melli, D., Gschwend, M. and Schutt, C. (1987). *Guide to the Swiss Open-Air Museum, Ballenberg*. Brienz: Ballenberg.
Miklos, C. and Endre, F. (1997). *Haz Es Ember*, Yearbook No. 11. Szentendre: Hungarian Open-Air Museum.
National Trust. Information notice. Arlington Row, Bibury, Gloucester.
Stika, J. and Langer, J. (1989). *Ceskoslovenska Muzea V Pirode*. Oseveto Martin: Vydalon Vydavatewlstvo.
Uldall, K. (1972). *Frilandsmuseet: The Open-Air Museum, English Guide*. Lyngby, Denmark: Nordlundes Bogtrykkeri.
Valen-Sendstad, F. (n.d. late 1980s). *The Sandvig Collections: Guide to the Open-Air Museum*. Gjovik, Lillehammer.
Zook, N. (1971). *Museum Villages USA*. Mass: Barre Publishers.

## Anonymously authored museum guides cited:

*Avoncroft Museum of Buildings*. Avoncroft Museum, Bromsgrove. 1973.
*Buried Village of Te Wairoa*. Smith, Rotorua, NZ (n.d.).

*Cuzals: Musée de Plein Air du Quercy*. Sauliac-sur-Cele, Lot (n.d.).
*Harold Warp Pioneer Village*, Minden, Nebraska (n.d.).
*Howick Historical Village*, Howick and District Historical Society, 1995.
*Netherlands Open-Air Museum*, Arnhem, Nederlands: Openluchtmuseum, Arnhem (n.d.).

Phrases from guides listed are briefly quoted in the text.

# 18

# Perfect and plain: Shaker approaches to design (1990)

Recent preoccupations with the abstractions of Shaker belief, such as the meaning of the songs and poems of the believers, or the significance of the female interpersonal relationships in its community life, have drawn attention away from the artefacts which have so often formed the focus of interest in the past. To an extent they reflect the concerns of the present: through examining these abstract themes we may draw conclusions which have relevance to our times. But they also seek to combat the sterility of dialogue created by the concentration on rocking chairs and hatboxes, withdrawing the Shakers from the art galleries which seem destined to be their final homes, to rehabilitate them at the centre of the discourse on theology and community. Essential though this thrust in Shaker studies is, it would be just as imbalanced if the material culture of the Shakers were neglected in the process, to be regarded as of little importance when compared with the philosophical, social or religious issues. For the physical world of the United Society was a very real one; coping with it, rejoicing in it, designing for it, working and making within it was fundamental to the Shaker way of life and worship.

Of all the aspects of design to which the Shakers made a contribution, the layout of their communities has received least attention. This is partly due to the fact that in most villages the buildings were added as the need arose, and there was no master plan. In general, a linear street pattern was adopted, which was edged by wooden fences that defined the through route but which did not subdivide the land around the buildings in a manner that would suggest territorial claims. Sometimes, secondary and tertiary rows of buildings would be added behind those fronting the main route, either in parallel or at right angles. The effect was to create a sense of loose enclosures, of defined spaces through which however, there was no impediment to circulation, as can be seen in Joshua Bussell's 1845 plan of Alfred, Maine. It was customary for the 'families' to live in clusters within the village and these would frequently be indicated by a terminal building at right angles and a break in the street line before the next family was encountered. Lebanon, N.Y. and Hancock were of this pattern. In many instances, the church family at Watervliet being a notable example, the cluster of buildings embraced a partially enclosed 'yard', which might be open, apart from a fence, on one side. The yards were often well planted with trees, and trees lined many roads. The Shakers seem to have avoided the *ad hoc*, 'organic' growth characteristic of many English villages or the grouping of buildings around a church or village green, customary in eastern Britain, which was widely adopted in New England.

Order, rather than military precision, was expressed in the settlement plans, and the functions of the buildings were indicated by their relative sizes and locations. Barns, cattle sheds, wagon stores, shops, meeting houses and accommodation buildings were of sizes and scale appropriate to their functions. If the early builders were limited by their lack of money or tools, they replaced, improved or raised their buildings when they could afford to do so: by 1805, this process of rebuilding had been completed at New Lebanon. Shaker architecture was of varied quality but most of it derived from eighteenth century prototypes. A strong commitment to symmetry is evident in all the buildings, imparting a sense of balance and harmony even if, to the eye of Charles Dickens (1842) they were 'composed of many stories like English factories'. He was correct in his observation; the buildings did relate to what has been termed by J.M. Richards, 'the British functional tradition'. Implicit in this was the use of classical proportions which are most evident in the 2:1 and 5:3 (approximately 'golden mean') ratios employed in the fenestration. By no means all the builders seem to have had the same awareness of proportional systems, and the addition of window shutters marred quite a few façades. While the use of classical details persisted, especially in the mouldings of eaves and cornices, and to a lesser extent, mullions and door jambs, they were usually simplified. Plaster cavetto coving at the eaves protected the dwellings from draughts and the weather, but deep eaves without coving would be employed on barns. The Millennial Laws were clear on this point: 'Beadings, moldings and cornices, which are *merely for fancy* may

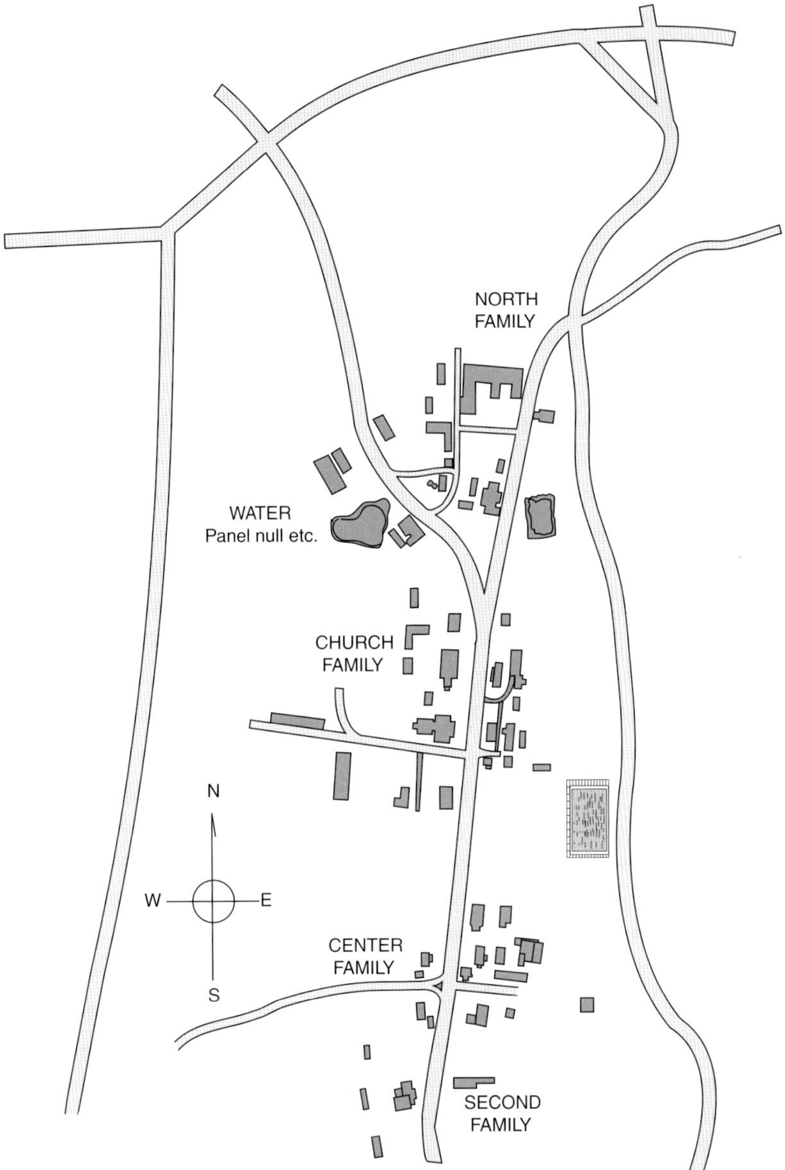


**Figure 18.1**
Part of the plan of the New Lebanon Shaker village, drawn from studies made by a WPA Historic Buildings Survey, 1939

**Figure 18.3**
New Lebanon Meeting House, designed and built by Moses Johnson in 1785.

of laminated planks. The radial prince posts secured the principal rafters, the tie beams and the suspended ceiling, the beam ends being supported by 10 × 14-inch posts, 17 feet high and capped by solid timber brackets (Lassiter, 1966). Inside the pale blue plastered and lime-washed auditorium, unobstructed by pillars, the slightly curved suspended ceiling barely hinted at the unique, ingenious construction above. So successful was Moses Johnson's meeting-house that he was to design and build nine others, culminating with the Sabbathday Lake building of 1794 (Nicoletta, 1995). Moses Johnson died, aged 90, in 1842.

We know of few other Shaker architects, but the work of Micajah Burnett (1791–1879) was exceptional. At the age of 22 he came from Virginia to Pleasant Hill, Kentucky where he realigned the settlement to an east–west axis and commenced the East family building. His many structures, built in wood, brick and stone were notable for their harmonious proportions and beautifully detailed interiors. The rails of the spiral and straight staircases, and the dark wood edging to the meeting of walls and the framing of openings, are drawn with clarity and elegance (Schiffer, 1979). If the construction of such buildings required excellent craftsmanship, they also demanded considerable management skills. As the work was mainly done by the Believers themselves, the costs could be reckoned largely in terms of time. Thus, the Church Family meeting house at Mount Lebanon has been estimated at $16 000, to which several other New England Shaker communities each contributed both labour and some $500 or more. The first mill built by Hancock's Church Family involved 2308 days of

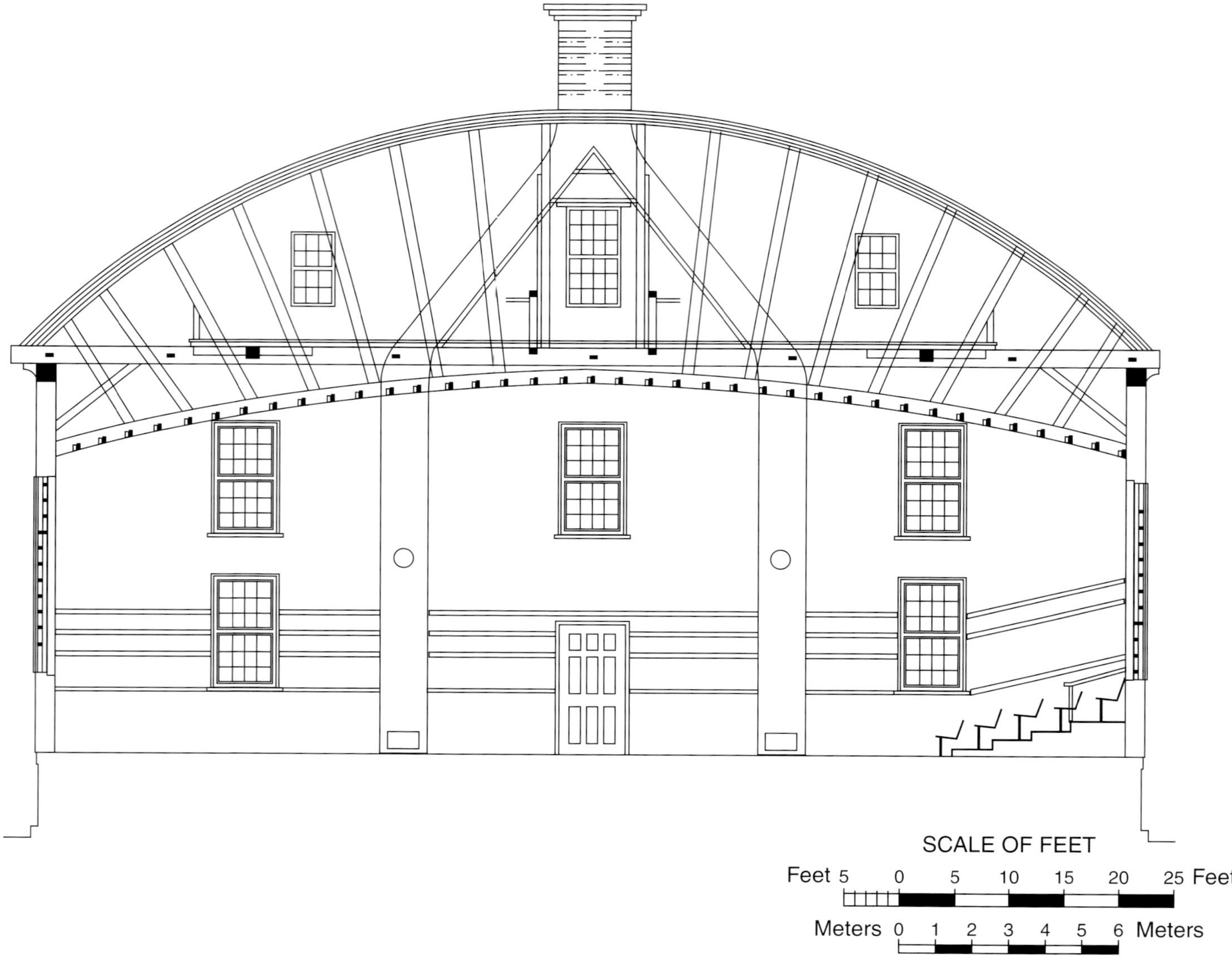


**Figure 18.4**
Section through the New Lebanon Meeting House indicating the laminated truss in the roof structure, and the method of spanning. Based on WPA Historic American Bulidings Survey drawings by A. H. Mosley, 1939.

**Figure 18.5**
Seven-storeyed (including the cellar) brick dwelling house built by the Church Family, Hancock, Massachusetts, and designed by Elder Deming, 1830.

work by the Brethren, some 22 days by the Sisters 'making bolts', ox-teams worked 355 days, presumably moving materials, and horses, 45 days. Other expenses amounted to exactly $2381. Elder William Deming gave an insight into the sheer scale of the quantities of materials prepared and worked for the same family's brick dwelling house which he designed and built for 94 people in 1830: 2326 feet of white hewn stone; some 900 feet of blue limestone, 350 000 bricks, 'and in 10 weeks from the placing of the first stone in the cellar, the house was neatly laid up, and the roof put on'. Including the loft levels, the dwelling house was seven storeys high. Its fittings included a 100 doors, 245 cupboard doors, 369 drawers – 'these we placed in the corners of the rooms and beside the chimneys' – and 3194 panes of glass in the 95 windows. In the

**Figure 18.6**
Interior of the Church Family dwelling, with separate doors for each gender.

cook room, there were 'two excellent ovens made on an improved plan which will bake four different settings at one heating', Elder Deming continued, allowing himself a touch of un-Shaker-like pride: 'the arch kettles are on a plan of my own invention, which proves to be the best ever seen around here'. Not only do these accounts reveal the scrupulous thriftiness of Shaker book-keeping, they also give indications of their policies to innovation (Ott, 1976).

In general, completely new design concepts did not extend to the overall planning of a building, although there are some exceptions,

**Figure 18.7**
Round Barn, Hancock, built in 1826 of stone, with timber internal structure. Interior reconstructed following a fire in 1884.

**Figure 18.8**
Interior of the Round Barn, showing cattle feeding floor. The cylindrical barn was probably the Shakers' most influential building.

most notably the Round Barn at Hancock. This was built in 1829 to a Shaker design, by hired masons who were paid $500 for the work. 270 feet in circumference and with walls 21 feet high and averaging 3 feet in thickness, it was designed to accommodate 52 head of cattle. Rafters, 53 feet in length, converged on the centre, but later a wide lantern and ventilating shaft was built to reduce the risks of spontaneous combustion. Trap-doors in the animal floor permitted the gathering of manure from below, but excavations for this facility undermined the walls and led to severe cracking. While the measure caused structural failure the basic intention to maximize efficiency was wholly expressive of the philosophy of Shaker design. Rooted in practicality, the ultimate objective was the achievement of perfection. 'Anything may, with strict propriety, be called perfect which perfectly answers the purpose for which it was designed' declared

Green and Wells in *A Summary View of the Millennial Church* (Green and Wells, 1823). Where an artefact or utility was seen to be short of 'perfection' within the experience and perceptions of the users, or where there was room for innovations that would increase efficiency, rather than simply ease the burdens of labour, Shaker inventiveness was stimulated. Sitting at her spinning wheel, Sister Tabitha Babbitt reflected on the possibility of making a saw with a revolving blade, which would greatly reduce the effort of sawing planks, then done by two-man crews in a saw-pit. Her invention, the circular saw, immediately took its established form of a disk with serrated edge and square spindle aperture. Water-powered, it was an invention that changed the lumber industry, not merely of the Shakers but of the whole world. Again in 1828, Brothers Henry Bennett and Amos Bisby invented a machine for making tongue-and-grooved boards, while other planing machines were adapted to make the finest poplar shavings for weaving into bonnets. Treadle jigsaws and lathes, and hand-levered mortising machines, were among the woodworking equipment made or adapted for Shaker workshops.

Several inventions were devised at Canterbury, New Hampshire, where the soil was poor and the Believers could not live solely by agriculture. Among their inventions was an electrostatic machine, reputedly of therapeutic use, which was devised as early as 1810 by Brother Thomas Corbett. A system of piped water was introduced by aqueducts, which in turn inspired another Brother to invent a water-powered cooling fan, with a faucet attached, which provided chilled water. Later, an improved washing machine was invented at Canterbury, and was one of the innovations on which the Shakers took out a patent. It was awarded the gold medal at the Philadelphia Centennial Exhibition of 1877. In general, they did not take out patents, believing that their devices should be available to all. They were not without influences themselves; while attending the Philadelphia show, some Brethren were impressed by Thonet bentwood furniture from Austria, and began to make their own on returning to their workshops. Modifications to existing equipment were often the result of deliberate problem-solving to meet perceived needs in agriculture, like the side-hill plough, designed to cope with the hill-slopes of New York State, or the rotary harrows, threshing machines, fertilizer spreaders, and the improved Maine mower from West Gloucester which, 'for ease of draft, durability, perfection and beauty of execution has never been surpassed, if equalled', as the sales publicity claimed. Other ideas related to textiles and laundry, from improved floor-looms and looms for weaving tapes, and a rotary clamp for turning chairs that were being seated

**Figure 18.9**
Built-in furniture was a Shaker ideal, as it did not interrupt space. Each member had limited possessions which could be kept in one drawer.

with the tapes, to silk-reeling machines and wheeled racks for specially designed drying rooms. There were multiple clothes presses and, at Sabbathday Lake, a press for making woven materials resistant to both wrinkles and water. Even the invention of the humble clothes pin is credited to the Shakers (Gordon, 1980).

While many of these inventions and improved technological items were marketed, sometimes providing thriving industries for the families who developed them, they inevitably brought the Believers in contact with the world and placed them in a competitive position with those whose values they had largely renounced. From very early in their history they had sold items of produce, and as they succeeded with the propagation and cultivation of herbs and plants for edible and medicinal purposes, they found a ready market for

**Figure 18.10**
Weaving loom in a room heated by the efficient Shaker iron stove, which also heated smoothing irons.

their products. Again, this led to innovations, including machines for packing herbs, and others for labelling herb boxes and seed packets. Some Brothers took up printing and produced the labels, although the Shakers seem to have used standard type founts and even, rather surprisingly, decorative stereotypes and borders. But probably they were most admired for their design and for the craftsmanship in their furniture, which was made for sale, as well as for their own use, right up to 1961. Much print has been set, numerous illustrations published and many exhibitions held, on Shaker furniture. Its attraction lies in its simplicity, in its colour, shape and form, and in the craftsmanship (Andrews, 1937). For architects and designers of the Modernist persuasion (approximately 1910–1970), it was a model of design which did not depend

**Figure 17.1**
Arlington Row, in the Cotswold village of Bibury is considered by some writers to have been a long barn, converted into cottages in the sixteenth century.

generations. A number of open-air museums started this way. Artur Hazelius in Sweden was responsible for assembling the buildings which, as 'Skansen' on Djugarden Island, Stockholm, opened in 1891. Hazelius believed that 'getting to know and falling in love with the past is the essential basis for all kinds of new production – a tree is the stronger the deeper are its roots' (Czajkowski, 1981). *Skansen* in Swedish means 'fort', and though the word referred to the former function of the site, it has symbolized the enclosed, contained character of the 'open-air' museum. Others soon followed, with the Lillehammer dentist, Anders Sandwig, building a collection which was adopted by the municipality and opened in Maihaugen in 1904. 'In my opinion Maihaugen should be a collection of homes, where it is possible to come close to the people who lived in them, to learn to know their way of life, their tastes, and their work,' Sandwig wrote, though he had more comprehensive ideas in mind. 'My aim is not merely to preserve a haphazard collection of old houses. No, I would like to include the whole parish, as a complete entity, in my picture-book' (Valen-Sendstad, n.d.).

Known henceforth as 'Skansens' in Scandinavia and eastern Europe, some 44 open-air museums had been established by the First World War, many at the instigation of passionate collectors, but others under museological or institutional, provincial or national auspices. The Seurasaari open-air museum for example, situated on Seurasaari Island near Helsinki, Finland, was founded in 1909 by Professor Axel Olai Heikel, whose declared aim was 'to collect typical buildings from the different regions of Finland in order to

# 17

# Re-presenting and representing the vernacular: The open-air museum (2001)

'History', the car manufacturer Henry Ford is reputed to have said, 'History is bunk.' Bunk, or bunkum means verbal rubbish, tinged with deception. What he actually said was 'History is bunk, as it is taught in schools'. His concern was genuine, and he founded the Henry Ford Museum and Greenfield Village near Dearborn, Michigan to introduce Americans to the material facts of their history (Zook, 1971). But he could be cavalier in his methods. Wishing to demonstrate that many American families came from rural England, in the mid-1920s he tried to purchase a row of Cotswold cottages to transport and rebuild in his open-air museum of Greenfield. Alarmed at the impending demolition of Arlington Row, Bibury, the local community alerted the Gloucestershire Archaeological Trust who succeeded in saving the row. In 1929, it was bought by the Royal Society of Arts and 20 years later it was given to the National Trust for safe keeping. Even though he had failed to transport Arlington Row, Ford bought a Cotswold house and blacksmith's forge from another village, and had all 500 tonnes of stone and timber shipped to Michigan. Whether Americans learned much more of their history as a result is open to question, even if, by default, Bibury was the richer for having saved the row (National Trust notice).

Henry Ford's Greenfield collection demonstrates how a single influential, affluent and motivated person, with a certain perception of history, can arrange for the location, demolition, transfer and re-erection of a collection of buildings (in Greenfield, about a hundred) ostensibly for the benefit of present and future upon, or require, superficial ornamentation but which gained its aesthetic appeal from satisfying its functional demands. This was not misplaced admiration: Shaker design principles were of this kind, although they arose from a moral conviction. 'Beauty rests on utility' ran one maxim. 'That which has in itself the highest uses possesses the greatest beauty,' stated another. But beauty for its own sake was deprecated. As Elder Frederick Evans told Charles Nordhoff, 'the beautiful, as you call it, is absurd and abnormal. It has no business with us. The divine man has no right to waste money upon what you would call beauty, in his house or his daily life, while there are people living in misery' (Nordhoff, 1875).

Where possible, Shakers preferred their furniture to be neatly stowed away when not in use. Some chairs were designed with low backs so that they could be placed beneath the table tops; peg rails for hats and cloaks were also used for hanging chairs and candle boards. Where furniture had legs it was designed to allow for cleaning around, and even side benches were designed with sweeping in mind. Built-in furniture, which was incorporated into purpose-designed recesses in the walls, included cupboards, stacks of shelves and drawers, even in some cases, bath-tubs. Beds were dimensioned for stacking after use; the first folding bed, possibly for children, was developed at South Union, Kentucky. Trundle beds for guest rooms were also used. Furniture related to work, included cobbler's benches and ironing tables, school desks and sewing 'desks', saddler's chairs and apple-paring benches. Many 'combination pieces' were made which served multiple functions. There were small items too: candle-holders, spit-boxes, hat-boxes and oval carriers, pestles and mortars. But the most numerous and most popular artefacts with the world, even before the close of the eighteenth century, were the ladder-back chairs, 'revolvers' (or revolving stools), and slender rocking chairs mushroom, lathe-turned hand grips. Many were seated with yarn strips, woven in a variety of colours and interlaced in more than 50 differing patterns, which arose however, from the nature of the chair seating process and not from 'superfluity' (Shea, 1941; Klankin 1972).

Chair seats were just one form of textile product; bed tapes were another. There was a vast range of textiles produced from the fine silks of Kentucky to the linens of the east. Every Shaker, male or female, had separate sets of garments for work, for regular use and for Sunday wear, and three sets of each of these for winter, summer and transitional seasons – nine sets of clothes in all. Bed linens, blankets, towels, stockings, gloves, table linen, kitchen cloths, horse blankets, hooked rugs, and splash cloths for washstands were among the textiles designed and made for daily use, as well as for sale to visitors. Producing the raw materials, designing the products, weaving the fabrics, making up and tailoring, washing and pressing (sometimes twice a week), represented a demanding investment of time, labour and devotion from the Sisters in the Shaker families. Perfection was not achieved without hard work. 'As we have received in obedience to our good Mother Ann's words – so we expect to receive,' wrote Elder William Deming to Elder Benjamin Youngs. 'Her precious words were these, "Your hands to work and your hearts to God and a blessing will attend you." This we have found true.' (Burns and Burns, 1987). The industry in Shaker life is apparent in every manifestation of its material culture, but so too, is the devotion of the Believers in their search for perfection. It could be argued that, in effect, the 'perfect' cannot be made *more* perfect, that there is no room for improvement once perfection is attained. It was a problem that worried the youthful Mary Antoinette (later, Eldress) Doolittle, who was answered by a comparison with the growing of corn. When the blade first appeared, it might be perfect in that state; but it was not the ultimate. 'First the blade, then the stalk, the ear, and the full corn in the ear' (Emlen 1987). Perfection was achieved at any one state. But this did not preclude change or development, and perfection at each succeeding state.

While there is much else that may be discussed concerning design among the Shakers which time and space do not permit, a word should be spared for the 'Spirit' paintings. 'Received' in visions or by inspiration, they were often presented to other Shakers as testimonies of love and faith. Being private gifts, they were never to be publicly displayed or sold, or to be hung as pictures on walls. Some were archetypal, the 'Tree of Life' or 'Tree of Paradise', being the most common. Others were more complex, with houses, mills and even machinery depicted, always symmetrically, among the symbols of flowers, moons, stars and angels. Where present, such motifs expressed the spiritual union of the artefact, made in the quest for perfection, with the perfection of the divine order. In planning, architecture, technology, furniture and textiles, this was the essence of the Shaker approach to design.

## References

Andrews, E.D. (1933, 1971). *The Community Industries of the Shakers*. New York State Museum Handbook, 15.

Andrews, E.D. (1953). *The People Called Shakers*. New York: Oxford University Press.
Andrews, E. and Andrews F. (1937). *Shaker Furniture*. Yale University Press.
Andrews, E. and Andrews, F.A. (1966). *Religion in Wood*. Bloomington: Indiana University Press.
Burns, A.S. and Burns, K. (1987). *The Shakers. Hands to Work, Hearts to God*. Aperture, Dickens, C. (1842).
Doolittle, Eldress M.A. quoted in Emlen, R.P. (1987). *Shaker Village Views*. University Press of New England.
Gordon, B. (1980). *Shaker Textile Arts*. New England: University Press.
Green, C. and Wells, S.Y. (1823). *A Summary View of the Millennial Church*. New York: Weed, Parsons and Co.
Klamkin, M. (1972). *Shaker Folk Art and Industries*. New York: Dodd, Mead & Company.
Lassiter, W.L. (1966). *Shaker Architecture* (WPA Project Drawings, 1029–41). New York: Vantage Press.
Millennial Laws, cited in Andrews (1953), pp. 249–289.
Nicolleta, J. (1996). Photography. In: Morgan, B. *The Architecture of the Shakers*. Woodstock, Vermont: The Countryman Press.
Nordhoff, C. (1875). The Shakers. In: *The Communistic Societies of The United States*. New York: Harper & Brothers, pp. 117–256.
Ott, J.H. (1976). *Hancock Shaker Village*. Shaker Community, Hancock, Mass.
Schiffer, H. (1979). *Shaker Architecture*. Exton, Pennsylvania: Schiffer Publishing.
Shea, J.G. (1941). *The American Shakers and Their Furniture*. New York: Van Nostrand Reinhold.

## Additional references

Pearson, E.R. and Neal, J. (1974). *The Shaker Image*. Boston, Mass: New York Graphic Society, with Shaker Community Inc., Hancock, Mass.
Rieman, T.D. (1995). *Shaker. The Art of Craftsmanship*. Alexandria, Virginia: Art Services International.
Stein, S.J. (1992). *The Shaker Experience in America. A History of the United Society of Believers*. New Haven: Yale University Press.

# PART VI

# SUBURBS AND SELF-BUILDERS

# 19

# Individualizing Dunroamin (1992)

In an article on the aesthetics of squatter settlements, Dr. Lisa Peattie noted that 'owner improvisation in England has its partisans', observing that 'there is even a book praising the suburban, semidetached style, entitled *Dun Roamin*' (Peattie, 1982). The fact that the title (and the author, the publisher and the date) was cited incorrectly, indicates that the book had not been so much as looked at. But that 'even' in the sentence is the give-away: the implication is that suburban houses do not merit attention. The remark is nothing exceptional; when *Beyond the Gates of Paris* by Francis Maspero, with photographs by Anailk Frantz, was published, a critic for *La Quinzaine Litteraire* wrote that it 'leads us into a land more exotic than the desert of the Tartars or Kafka's castle, a land which lies on our doorstep and which we've never seen' (Maspero, 1992). 'We' being, of course, the reviewer and presumably his readers too, on whom the juxtaposition of Kafka, Tartar and suburb would not have been lost. But such observations are merely recent examples of the persistent snobbery that has discoloured references to the suburbs in Europe, and particularly Britain, for more than a century. Contempt for the suburbs was expressed in the writings of Victorian and Edwardian authors like George Moore or T.W.H. Crossland – who regarded the 'suburbans' as 'low, inferior species'. But it was the later growth of the suburbs which inspired the bitterest invective. Between the world wars, half the housing stock of Great Britain was newly built, providing 'homes fit for heroes' (war veterans) and substantially replacing the Victorian slums. Remarkable though this housing revolution was, it had no supporters among intellectuals. To Cyril Connolly, the slums were 'the breeding-houses of crime, but the middle-class suburbs are incubators of apathy and delirium' (Davis, 1982).

Of the post-war suburban houses, two-thirds, or some 2 700 000, were built in the 1930s, typified by the semi-detached house and to a lesser extent, the seaside bungalow. This massive development of new housing provided open spaces, light, air and modern conveniences but, in the opinion of Graham Greene, the result was an 'empty, graceless, chromium world'. He was one of the privileged authors whose comfortable exclusivity was shattered by the suburban expansion which consumed farmland and landed estates, changing the face of Britain for ever (Carey, 1992). In the eyes of architects and planners, the suburbs represented not only the invasion of the countryside, but the obliteration of the distinction between town and country. In countless articles, books and radio programmes, the suburbs were subjected to an unceasing stream of abuse and vilification from the cognoscenti, who then had exclusive access to the media. At the fourth meeting of the International Congress of Modern Architecture (CIAM), dominated by Le Corbusier, the Athens Charter was drawn up, observing that 'the suburb is an urbanistic folly... it is one of the greatest evils of the century' (Davis, 1982). The British MARS group (Modern Architecture Research Society) thundered that 'the mad building of suburbs must stop – before it strangles the towns themselves' (Boumphrey and Cadbury, 1935). Its objections were based on what were purportedly rationalist grounds, while some architects regarded the suburban houses as 'ill-planned' and 'jerry-built'. The objections of most commentators were more emotional: the suburbs were 'hideous', a 'reproach to the city'. With the threat of a second world war looming in the late 1930s, the poet (later Poet Laureate) John Betjeman could entreat the Luftwaffe:

> Come friendly bombs, and fall on Slough;
> It isn't fit for humans now.
>
> Betjeman, 1937

Modernist architects referred to 'the crimes of our own century, the mock-Tudor suburbs' and deplored the 'blatant vulgarities' and 'primitive instincts' of their residents, whose escape from reality was 'individualistic, and at root, selfish'. The suburbs, they predicted in many publications, would become 'hot-beds of crime', the base of dissatisfaction and misery, while the 'semi' was the symbol of suburban values and taste that they deplored. Much of this propaganda was directed at the suburbs in order to advocate in their stead, the modernist high-rise housing blocks of flats, which, in the 1950s and 1960s were built throughout the country.

When the semi-detached houses of the suburbs are examined, the means become evident whereby individual identity was established, and the houses were made into homes. Built mainly between the two world wars, they still retain to a remarkable degree the characteristics and details which made them so successful for their original owners and purchasers. Changes of ownership by subsequent generations have not eclipsed these characteristics, but in many ways have enhanced them, demonstrating their capacity to accommodate re-invented personalization. As self-built housing has been largely inhibited in Britain, individual taste had to be exercised through choice. Estate developers always offered a choice of style in the semi-detached pairs of houses in their advertising. Many developers extended to the purchaser a number of alternatives of form which could be substantially augmented by further choices in materials, surface and texture, complemented by structural or applied details. Gables, gablets, oriel windows, porches, thresholds, square and faceted bays, roof ridge and suspended wall tiles, brick bonds and half-timbering, even regional features like the knapped flints on Sussex semis, all contributed to the range of choices that the houses afforded. As might be expected, these had their critics. 'The builder has merely taken certain features – such as sham half-timber, porch, mullions and leaded lights – and cheapened and debased them, using them only because they are good selling points', wrote Robert Furneaux Jordan, expressing his distaste but unable to grapple with the problem as to why they were good selling points. Uncertainty lingered. 'Whether, however, ill-designed, badly built mock Tudor is really popular or has gradually been made so by advertising and "keeping up with the Joneses" is a moot point', he added (Jordan, 1959). It was a debate in which he was not willing to engage. At the root of most objections to the suburban design was a dislike of its references to the past in British vernacular architecture. There were few precedents in the semi-detached house itself, but there were many in its details: in the use of gables, for instance, extensively employed in Tudor timber construction, or later, the insertion of dormer windows derived from the cottages of the Cotswolds and the stone belt. Such details, whether they provided additional space or, like the equally disliked porches, were effective baffles against external draughts, were considered at best as 'whimsical' and 'picturesque'. Critics grasped at the types identified by the cartoonist Osbert Lancaster, which he dubbed 'By-Pass Variegated', 'Wimbledon Transitional' and 'Stockbroker's Tudor,' saddling the semi-detached suburbs with the first of these (Lancaster, 1938).

**Figure 19.1**
Trade advertisements for semi-detatched houses from the 1920s and 1930s.

**Figure 19.2**
Semi-detached houses with walls of knapped flint, using a treatment common in the regional vernacular tradition. Worthing, West Sussex.

Picturesque or nostalgic in a sense the semis were, and are. To the modernist architects and to designers still, such echoes of history are anathema and by the same token, the occupants are retreating into a cosy, unrealistic world of their fantasies. This may be true in some, even many, cases though it is arguable that the authors, writing in their protected and often economically cushioned ivory towers were in no position to criticize. What the writers did not consider was the massive social revolution which the growth of the suburbs represented: a shift of the population to the south-east of England, the

**Figure 19.3**
Detached houses in Reading with 'Tudor' timber framing details, one having a 'jettied' upper floor. Seldom structural, the framing was usually applied decoratively.

**Figure 19.4**
Variations in the treatment of façades of semi-detached pairs reflect differences in plan, notably entrances at the centre, or at the sides. Headington, Oxford.

resettlement of millions of people in new and alien circumstances, the creation of totally new communities without precedent in their scale, their numbers or their function. In the face of this extraordinary re-organization of the population and of the landscape, there was none of the security which the Hampstead and Kensington critics had enjoyed for generations. Small wonder that the new house-owners sought the comfort of elements that assured them of the essential Englishness of their new dwellings, while they enjoyed the satisfaction of newly-built houses that were sufficiently different from past forms to give them confidence in their venture into the suburban world. Clearly, the whole subject cannot be viewed outside the social context of the times in which they were built. New suburbs grew at phenomenal rates, changing a region completely in the space of 6 months, creating new roads, gardens and parks, new shopping parades and cinemas, and only occasionally retaining the small core of a former village or church to give a sense of historic continuity. Yet the new suburban dwellers did not wish to maintain a sense of the frontier indefinitely; above all they wished to settle, to put down roots, to make their homes in their new, 'olde-worlde,' surroundings (Oliver *et al.*, 1982).

For the intending suburb-dwellers who migrated from all parts of Britain to the cities, but especially to the south-east and London, the experience was unsettling enough; what they required was a feeling of identification with their neighbours in the unfamiliar surroundings, while retaining their own sense of personal identity and self-respect. 'Keeping up with the Joneses was a critical cliché of the aspirations of the suburbs at the time, and the phrase has remained as emblematic of a striving, and basically anti-social competitiveness. Yet the term is not an inaccurate one: the suburban family sought to keep apace with its neighbours but not to exceed it by more than a small and tolerable margin. The accusation of being 'stuck-up', of 'snobbery' was levelled at the household that attempted to 'show up' its neighbours. Social controls were subtle and accepted. Everyone was seeking to better their economic position, and this was understood. But neighbourliness was a highly prized virtue in the suburbs, and overt competitiveness or 'swanking' with ostentatious acquisitiveness was deplored. So the unstated problems of living in the suburb were ones of attainment within the accepted mores, of individualism within the context of uniformity. It was probably subconscious imagery that gave the semi-detached pair of houses their face-like appearance and the pair were locked together like the reciprocating halves of the human brain. Each family within the suburb sought to confirm its selfhood through the home while according to the domestic norms.

Through its builders and merchant suppliers, the suburban house offered many routes to these ends. The first was through the choice of house design: whether, for example, adjacent entrances with central hallways which provided a measure of sound insulation was preferred to access at the wings of the house which emphasized detachment but placed living rooms in proximity. Most builders offered both, and many also had houses with corner doorways or side entrances in their folios. The gables that were so disliked by the

**Figure 19.5**
Swept gable type, inspired by C.F. Voysey's 1905 design for a 'homestead', at Frinton-on-Sea, Essex.

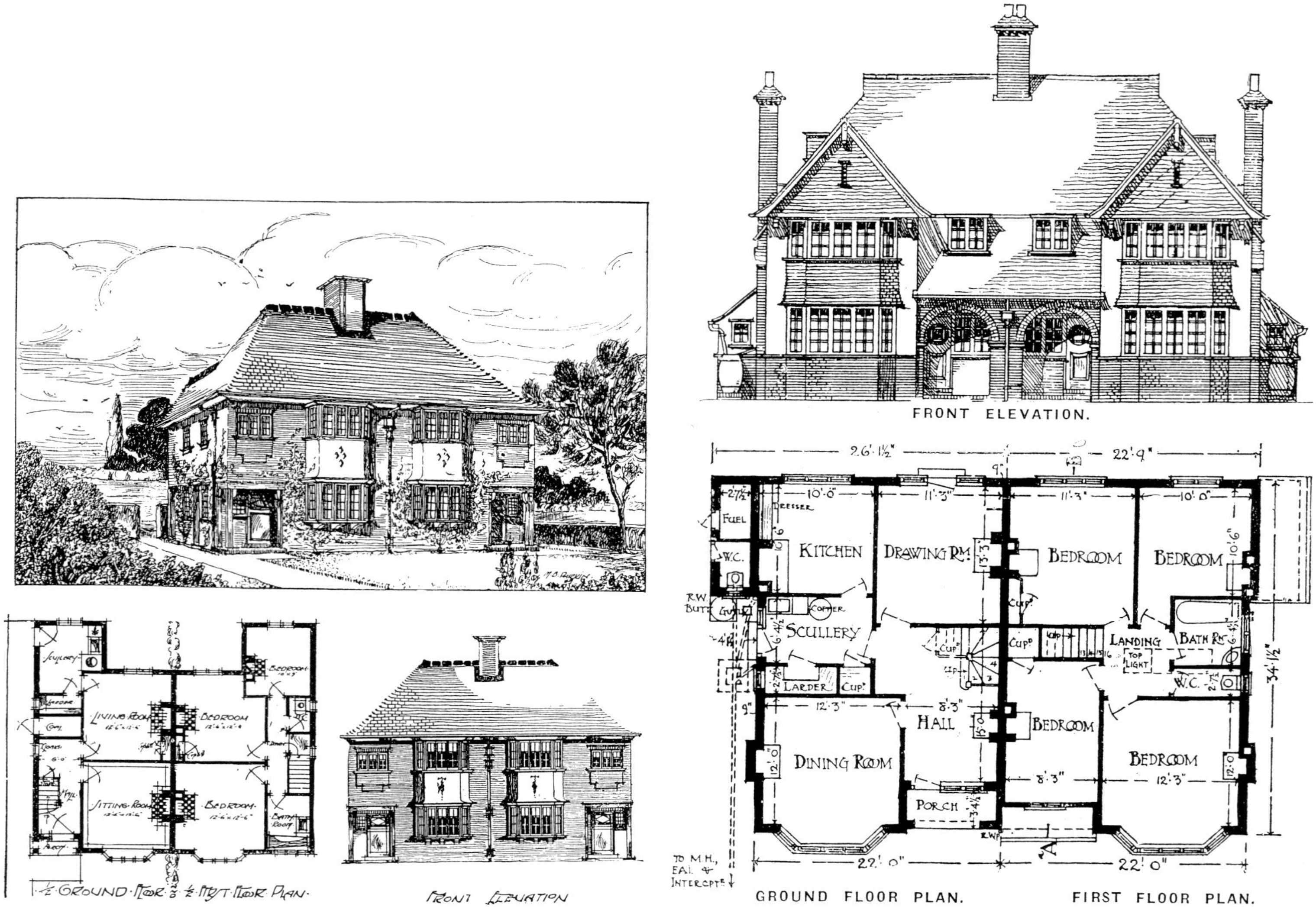


**Figure 19.6**
A pair of villas, designed by Maurice B. Parkin, circa 1912 (left), with an estimated price of £520 for the two, and a pair by J. Gordon Allen of similar date (right) price £800. Such designs were influential on house design in the 1920s and 1930s.

critics came in many forms, the swept gable reaching from roof to ground floor being a popular alternative that had its origins in the Arts and Crafts designs of C.F. Voysey. In the modernist taste of the time this was sufficient to condemn it (Jackson, 1973). Though they were 'handed', one semi-detached house being the mirror reflection of its neighbour, in 3 years (when the cycle of house-painting was normally begun) mouldings were delineated, textures changed or rendered over, and colour schemes were introduced that enabled the householders to exercise their individual taste while retaining the character of the suburban 'Crescent', 'Avenue', 'Close' or 'Gardens'. Frequently, the names of the streets reflected those of the fields, farms and estates on which they were built; others, named by local councils, were given the names of trees: 'Acacia Gardens', 'Elm Grove', or improvingly, the names of poets, 'Dryden Avenue', 'Keats Lane'. But whatever the name of the road, the name of the house was an important aspect of personalization. Former home towns, honeymoon venues, views and aspects, or portmanteau combinations of the owner's own names were common. The frequent 'Chez Nous' and 'Holmeleigh', were enlivened by 'Ardwun', 'Wedydit' or 'Dunroamin' (Miles, 1982). 'Dunroamin' was favoured by the London Scots – people who had migrated from Scotland to south-east England, leaving the country of Dunfermline, Dunelme and Dunedin, where the popular song hero of the day, Will Fyffe, sang of 'roamin' in the gloamin'. To them the punning house name was a statement of satisfaction at having settled and a memory of the land they'd left behind.

Popular songs of the times like *My Blue Heaven, The Folks Who Live On The Hill* or *Me and My Gal* reflected the hopes of the newcomers to the suburbs: 'we'll build a little home for two, or three or four, or more.' Some came with their families, others were first-time buyers hoping to start new families in the suburbs when they could afford to do so. They tilled their front garden soil, planted their flower beds and shrubs and sometimes populated their plots with figurines. Gnomes, engaged in creative activities that reflected their own, were common, but the diminutive phallic figures were also assertive statements of territory. England is a country of gardeners, but the front garden acts as an intermediate zone between the public and the private domains. An arena for displaying accomplishment in shaping and controlling nature, it is also a protective transitional space, guarded even today by symbolic motifs (Oliver, 1982). Within, builders offered a selection of alternative plans, extending from the placement of the main entrance, to the hall, living room, dining room and kitchen on the ground floor. On the upper floor the

**Figure 19.7**
With skilful topiary on display, the hedge of a front garden defines the private domain. Kidlington, Oxford.

three or four bedrooms and bathroom were variously deployed in relation to staircase and landing (open corridor). Internal details and fixtures included fireplaces and surrounds: as many as 70 alternative designs fully tiled, were offered by a single builders' merchant, to be ordered and installed by the builder (Metal Agencies, 1937). Stained glass windows, bathroom suites and kitchen fittings could be selected from the large catalogues of the suppliers. Picture rails and dado rails, shelving recesses and mantelpieces afforded wall surfaces and places for the display of memorabilia and, like the panelled doors and moulded window and door frames, these could be painted, while the walls might be papered or distempered.

Given the many planes of choice available to the intending house purchaser, there was considerable room for personalization. But this was further enlarged by the motifs and details of such elements. Study of the symbolism of the motifs on suburban domestic stained glass windows reveals much of the values and aspirations of the new householders as they made houses into homes. Some of these superficially accorded to conventions of design, but they were made considerably more expressive in suburban contexts: the sunbursts, rosebuds, peacocks, windmills, galleons and bridges of the figurative motifs may be seen to have significant associative meanings. Many convey a sense of future promise or of imminent maturity; others speak of industrious activity, of transformation, of adventure and safe return. Closer examination of the objects and accoutrements of the suburban interior – such as lampshades, fireside 'companions' (tool stands), mantelpiece ornaments or objects on the bedside

**Figure 19.8**
Designs for stained glass in the house include the reassuring sunrise, a peacock about to spread its wings, a wise owl, an adventurous galleon and a bridge to the future, 1937.

table reveal further symbols of lifeways and values, of prosperity, fidelity and fecundity. As the home was moulded out of the house, the significance of individual choice in details increased: nostalgic souvenirs, family photographs and portraits, shells and found objects from holidays spent beachcombing – the intrinsically valueless articles of personal attachment assumed significance with their deep emotional and sentimental meanings or associations. When eventually, a family might move to make a home elsewhere, it was these that went with them. But it was the suburban house which provided the context and the cabinet for these personal curiosities.

At the heart of the attacks on the suburban houses was objection to their 'individualism' which was regarded as anti-social. Suburban details and personalization were condemned: 'individualism run rampant' was a frequent epithet with its implications of an

**Figure 19.9**
A typical council housing estate, with some variation in group and roofscape, but none in windows and details, designed to inhibit 'individualizing'.

uncontrollable epidemic. Modernist architects and the designers of rentable council housing alike, sought to inhibit all individualization. When the contemporary council house estates and the relatively few examples of middle-class housing designed by architects of the period, are compared with the developer-built housing of the suburbs, the repression of personalized detail is evident (Bentley, 1982a). Features and relief that could animate the elevations were deliberately omitted. Plain and unrelieved surfaces were justified on the grounds of harmony, 'clean lines', efficiency or 'decency'. Of course, the dreary anonymity of the council estates cannot be solely attributed to the total inhibition of individual expression without and within the dwelling. But it is clear that the motivation for 'home-making', from which sprang the sense of identification and the establishment of associative roots, was systematically frustrated through the deliberate application of an ideological opposition to individualism. No less overtly stated, their design ethic was also rigorously opposed to any historic or antecedent referents that could give a sense of identification with place and past, which the new residents needed. After the Second World War, the opponents of the suburbs seized their chance to propagate modernist ideals in the form of Corbusier-influenced slab blocks of flats. On the high-rise apartment blocks, all means of identifying the home from the outside were totally and rigorously excluded. Internally, the council houses and the modernist buildings alike eliminated all elements that might provide vehicles for the expression of individualism. In spite of the changing social climate, the suburbs survived and flourished. Far

**Figure 19.10**
High-rise apartments with intimidating upper level access. Killingworth, Yorkshire. Scenes of social disruption and discontent, these have now been demolished.

from being in decline, those built in the 1920s and 1930s with over half a century of occupancy, exposed the lie of forecasts of criminality and misery. On the contrary, it was the bleak council housing estates and high-rise modernist point blocks and slab blocks of flats that became the seats of crime, rather than the suburbs (Coleman, 1985). It would be wrong to imply that the cause of civil unrest was the characterless nature of the buildings; unemployment and the lack of community facilities were largely responsible. Nevertheless, pride of ownership and a sense of belonging that can be confirmed by appearances play their part in maintaining social stability. Again provoking the contempt of the architectural press, the humanizing and transforming of modernist high-rise blocks by reducing their height and enriching their forms and spaces, has proved successful in the small number of such projects so far completed.

While other high-rise and mass housing complexes have been demolished in recognition of their social failure, the suburbs and their semis have continued to prosper. Half a century after the last of the pre-war semis were built they are still highly sought after. In spite of the abuse poured on the suburbs and the contempt in which both the houses and their residents were held by the aesthetic establishment, they have never lost their popularity nor their capacity to provide an agreeable and satisfying environment for half the population of Britain. This depends in large measure on the land available for homes, the configuration of the suburban estates, and their proximity to communications and commercial or public services. Such planning elements are important, and demand serious consideration, though they are beyond the concerns of this paper. Neither the planning of the suburbs nor the semi-detached houses have had much said in their favour (Richards, 1946). In a 280-page book on *The Design of Suburbia* published in 1981, Arthur M. Edwards devoted less than two pages of text to the three million houses built by private enterprise between the world wars. He did not hide his contempt: 'It was the combination of extent, monotony and restlessness which made inter-war speculative suburbia so hideous in its appearance and so alarming in its spread. Every part of its [sic] was restless. The contrasting black and white of its half-timbering, the jagged regularity of its silhouette, the variety of its facing materials, the fragmentation of its front gardens, carriageways and pavements, the shapelessness of its spaces, the patchy colours of its hedges and boundary walls – all contributed to a scene which was both unsettled and invariable. For wherever it might be, speculative suburbia was the same', he wrote, his prejudices over-riding the contradictions in his statement. He concluded that 'among them all it is difficult to find a single decently designed estate' (Edwards, 1981).

By far the majority of the migrants to the cities who settled in the suburbs in the 1920s and 1930s were first-home buyers without roots in their new milieux. In order to 'be at home', they had to create new places with which they could identify themselves; in this, the choices of type, plan, external and internal details assisted them (Bentley, 1982b). Echoes of a collective history were available in a variety of forms, while the personal selection of colours, of fixtures and memorabilia helped them to establish their individual identities while participating in the creation of new communities and their emerging values. The building and the occupation of the semi-detached suburbs took place a lifetime ago. Those who vilified the suburbs at the time were convinced that they would be hot-houses for crime, yet their social achievement has been conspicuous, difficult though it may be for many of its critics to accept, even now. The aspects of the design of the suburban houses which they condemned were, ironically, the very features which ensured their success (Oliver *et al.* 1982).

Today's suburban dwellers are often the children and grandchildren of the original occupants, who have found that the semis of the 1930s are still the desirable homes of the 1990s. Now though, their roots are the suburbs themselves, and the details of the suburban houses have acquired their own historic associations over time. In the 1960s, many were altered, with garage extensions and inner walls removed to create 'through' living rooms or 'open plans'.

**Figure 19.11**
Adaptation of a semi-detached house, inspired perhaps, by a memorable vacation in Mykonos. Headington, Oxford.

Slowly, some of the stained glass windows that were shattered in the Second World War were replaced, often with more abstract designs; to some of the gardens, figures were to return, now grey with the instant patina of an implied history. House walls were sometimes transformed from brick and pebbledash by the application of stone veneer; aluminium window frames are being replaced with mouldings in white plastic: the suitability and taste of such measures may be questionable but the symbols of permanence and pride are clear. The opportunities afforded for the further individualizing of the dwellings, which is taking place in thousands of semis at this very moment, may ensure their appropriateness to express the values of a new century.

The semi-detached houses of the suburbs of Britain do not offer a model for new developments; this chapter is not an argument for replicating them. But I contend that they can teach domestic architects the importance of choice, and the provision of design elements which can facilitate the personalization of the home within community norms.

## References


Bentley, I. (1982a). Individualism or community? Private enterprise housing and the council estate. In: Oliver, P. *et al. Dunroamin*, Chapter 4, London: Barrie & Jenkins.

Bentley, I. (1982b). The owner makes his mark. In: Oliver, P. *et al. Dunroamin*, Chapter 6, London: Barrie & Jenkins.

Betjeman, J. (1937). Slough. In: *Continual Dew.* London: John Murray.
Boumphrey, G. and Cadbury, J. (1935). Suburbs or satellites? *The Listener*, 17 February, p. 147.
Carey, J. (1992). Massacre in metroland. *The Sunday Times Books Supplement*, 5 July, extracted from Carey, *The Intellectual and the Masses*, London: Faber & Faber.
Coleman, A.E. (1985). *Utopia on Trial: Vision and Reality in Planned Housing.* London: Hilary Shipman.
Davis, I. (1982). One of the greatest evils: Dunroamin and the modern movement. In Oliver, P. *et al. Dunroamin*, Chapter 4, London: Barrie & Jenkins.
Edwards, A.E. (1981). *The Design of Suburbia. A Critical Study in Environmental History.* London: Pembridge Press.
Jackson, A.A. (1973). *Semi-Detached London.* London: George Allen & Unwin.
Jordan, R.F. (1959). *The English House*. London: Vista Books, p. 135.
Lancaster, O. (1938, 1958). *Pillar to Post. A Cartoon History of Architecture.* London: John Murray.
Maspero, F. and Frantz, A. (1992). *Beyond the Gates of Paris: A Journey Through the Suburbs.* London: Verso Books. Quotation from undated review in *La Quinzaine Litteraire* cited in Verso catalogue.
Metal Agencies. (1937). *Catalogue No. 66.* Bristol: The Metal Agencies Co. Ltd.
Miles, J. (1982). *The House Names Book: Ackybotha to Zeelust.* London: Unwin.
Oliver, P. (1982). The galleon on the front door: Imagery of the house and garden. In Oliver, P. *et al. Dunroamin.* Chapter 7, London: Barrie & Jenkins.
Oliver, P., Davis, I. and Bentley, I. (1982). *Dunroamin: The Suburban Semi and its Enemies.* London: Barrie & Jenkins (reprinted 1994, London, Pimlico, Random House, UK).
Peattie, L. (1982). Aesthetic politics: Shantytown or new vernacular? *Traditional Dwellings and Settlements Review*, VI 111, p. 24.
Richards, J.M. (1946). *Castles on the Ground.* London: Architectural Press.

## Additional references

Barrett, H. and Phillips, J. (1988). *Suburban Style. The British Home, 1840–1960.* London: Guild Publishing.
Honer, J. (ed.). (1999). Saint, Andrew (introduction). *London Suburbs.* London: Merrell Holberton, with English Heritage.
Ward, N. and Ward, M. (1978). *Home in the Twenties and Thirties.* London: Ian Allan Ltd.

# 20
# Round the houses (1983)

It takes only the most cursory glance at a batch of international architectural magazines to confirm that what is illustrated between their laminated covers bears only an occasional, glancing resemblance to what most of us experience in the built world around us. Wade into the stream of dreams and schemes that has flowed through *Architectural Design* during the early 1980s, for instance. How many of those neatly docketed and documented buildings do you personally know; how many encountered, walked through, experienced, lived in? Of course, there are diligent critics and enthusiastic students who will tot up a score of such works of architecture visited, the icon-images of the colour plates being matched against a highly selective reality. New 'canonical' buildings are being defined to replace the discarded classics of Modernism coolly appraised by Juan Pablo Bonta (Bonta, 1979). That's as it should be, one can argue. After all, publications on art or literature do not have to concern themselves with pavement portraits or wire-rack novels – though some of them do. They need only be concerned with what is judged as innovatory or of worth (aesthetic or financial). To say that architecture is different is to state a truism, but for all that it may be banal to repeat it, the fact remains that buildings serve the needs of their users in ways that are far wider in implication than do paintings or fiction, and architecture relates to the adjacent built environment in juxtapositions that have no parallel in other areas of creative endeavour. Lifted out of the pages of the periodical and into the street, buildings are prone to unexpected transformations, sometimes exciting, often disappointing, frequently demanding a perception of the immediate environment that was missing before. Anyone who has ever innocently sought out Rietveld's Schröder house, that canonical De Stijl building, and discovered that it was stuck like a bookend at one extreme of a suburban terrace and overshadowed by a flyover highway, has experienced a shock. It may be,

**Figure 20.1**
Ludwig van Rietveld's iconic Schröder House, in Utrecht, is rarely depicted in its suburban setting, with three-storeyed apartments adjacent.

in Lautréamont's words, 'beautiful as the chance meeting on a dissecting table of a sewing machine and an umbrella' (Lautréamont, in Rubin, 1968), but if so, it's a beautiful encounter that hasn't hit the pages of most esteemed architectural publications.

However, it's my contention that getting to know the environment 'out there' is of far more importance than the serendipitous shoulder-rubbing of selected architecture and anonymous buildings. I believe that we stand to know more about the nature of architecture and the shaping of a humane environment, if we seek to know more about buildings in all their manifestations, uses and meanings. If the study and understanding that this involves has scarcely begun, and if an overall, comprehensive view even of the 'buildings of England' seems virtually impossible (just think what's left after the ecclesiastical buildings, castles, manor houses and town halls have been deleted from Pevsner's work under that title (Pevsner, 1951)), there's much to be gained by seeking to comprehend at least some of the environment that we share. It's a chip-shop, garden-centre, tractor-store, holiday-chalet, side-street, back-alley, closed-cinema, garden-shed, furniture-warehouse, signal-box, bungalow, cow-byre, double-garage, your-street, my-street, you-name-it, he'll-call-it-something-else mélange we live in; making sense of it isn't easy and most of the time we have no mind to do so. But if, for the present purposes, we restrict our discussion to houses, the diversity of types, forms, let alone details and plans, is extraordinarily rich in any county in Britain. It's our unwillingness to perceive the distinctions, and our inability to

**Figure 20.2**
Allotments, or land rented for small-scale cultivation, often have self-built sheds for tools and temporary shelter. These are on the outskirts of Ljubliana, Slovenia.

identify unfamiliar characteristics that induce us to dismiss much of the housing we see as monotonous, bourgeois, stockbroker belt, blot on the landscape, or whatever other chosen epithet we employ to screen off the challenge it poses to our entrenched habits of architectural thinking.

One broad category which we are more inclined to acknowledge, if not pursue, is that of 'vernacular architecture'. Quite what the term means is almost as much in doubt as is 'neo-vernacular' (which, for some, means 'responding to a local tradition' and for others, as at an architectural education conference in Turkey, means 'illegal settlement' (EAAE, 1982)). Regional, frequently anonymous building using indigenous skills and local materials for the use and accommodation of the common populace, generally comes within the compass of building types acknowledged by those engaged in its study. But there are those that contend that there was no vernacular architecture in Britain after the mid-nineteenth century; others who acknowledge minor industrial or hand-labour buildings within its broad category; still others who would extend the term to embrace speculative builders' suburban estate housing in the 1920s and 1930s. Professor R.W. Brunskill didn't go that far, but his *Illustrated Handbook of Vernacular Architecture* (Brunskill, 1970) did provide a framework for the identification and classification of vernacular traditions in Britain. Its publication in 1970, though he himself saw it as appearing when systematic study had 'just reached its majority', was certainly a significant landmark in the field. A dozen years later the handbook had proved its worth to scores of schools, local history groups, WEA classes and the like throughout the country, as well as having provided a valuable tool for the identification and recording of building types, forms, materials, structural systems, and so on. The Cordingley-Brunskill system for recording buildings offered encoded descriptions and gave examples of their application under the heading 'How to Study Vernacular Architecture'. Unfortunately, the system was a shade too neat, the 'how to study' instructions buttoned up the process. Hundreds of amateur house-hunters have beavered away producing record cards, or similar documentation, and have got very little nearer to understanding the buildings: why they were built, what needs they met, or how they have been transformed through changing demands over time.

This latter aspect is particularly evident. An obsession to trace the 'original' building, to 'date' its construction and to recapture its nature when it was first built has pervaded much of this work. And it is to be seen in the sanitized, disinfected historic houses that have been herded for their own protection into the reservations of 'museums of folk architecture'. Interest in the minutiae of vernacular architecture has also reached obsessive lengths, with detailed analyses of the distribution of different kinds of scarfed joints, and exhaustive inventories of particular architectural features, being common among the members of the Vernacular Architecture Group. Formed in the early 1950s, it has undeniably added to the sum of human knowledge on British traditional building, but the plethora of publications and articles on cruck construction, from F.W.B. Charles' 1967 monograph on *Mediaeval Cruck Building*

**Figure 20.3**
A fourteenth century house with exposed cruck frame. Later alterations are evident in the raised roof line, severed original tie beam and dormer windows. Didbrook, Gloucestershire.

**Figure 20.4**
The Leadenporch House, a former hall house with concealed cruck framing. Estimated date, 1325, and altered in the seventeenth century, Deddington, Banbury region.

*and its Derivatives* (Charles, 1967) to Nat Alcock's *A Catalogue of Cruck Buildings* (Alcock, 1973) and the seemingly unending lists and descriptions of other cruck structures that have been published by the group since, suggests that the cruck has metaphorical as well as literal significance. A number of important books on the subject of English vernacular architecture were published during the 1960s and 1970s including Maurice Barley's *The English Farmhouse and Cottage* (Barley, 1961) which made considerable use of documentary evidence, particularly the '*true and perficte inventories*' of '*all the moveable goods, cattles and chattels*' of a number of seventeenth-century householders, to create a fuller picture of the relationship of dwelling to society. Among the many regional studies R.B. Wood-Jones' *Traditional Domestic Architecture of the Banbury Region* (Wood-Jones, 1963) remains among the most comprehensive, while Eric Mercer's *English Vernacular Houses,* published for the Royal Commission on Historical Monuments, is monumental in more ways than one (Mercer, 1975). To these must be added the, literally, hundreds of articles which have appeared in *Archaeologia Cantiana, Oxoniensia, Mediaeval Archaeology* or the *Transactions, Notes or Newsletters* of numerous county or local historical and archaeological societies. Local publications range from the cyclostyled booklets of the Robertsbridge and District Archaeological Society (Martin, n.d.) to the carefully produced booklets of *Traditional Kent Buildings,* edited by Jane Wade from work done by students of Canterbury School of Architecture (Wade, 1981). These latter publications were among the few that had 'architecture' as their source; for the most part the publications reflect the emphases and the biases of historical and archaeological enquiry. If at first the volume of published material suggests that little remains to be done, in fact this is far from the case. Not only is the recording of traditional building in large areas of Britain still sketchy, but it is also limited in its scope. It would be wrong to suggest that 'the outside view' predominates, but it is arguable how much architectural thinking permeates much of the literature. Of formal or spatial analysis there is very little; cultural relationships are seldom hinted at. There is much to be done in such areas for the better understanding of the tradition.

Yet this is not, in my view, the principal omission from current studies. Most serious is any real consideration of the changes of use and adaptations that have taken place over time and their bearing on changing values. The meaning of vernacular buildings to their present and recent occupiers is scarcely hinted at; when it is, as in the writings of George Ewart Evans (Evans, 1966) it is often buried among the wart-cures and hag-stones. A more searching study, which was nonetheless weak on architecture, was hinted at in W.J. Turner's immediately post-war *Exmoor Village* (Turner, 1947) backed up by researches made by Mass Observation. But the promise of this start was never realized in later works. In spite of the changes in philosophy and anthropology which have occurred since then, and which have been reflected to some degree in architectural writing, there hasn't been much evidence of their influence on thought concerning the vernacular in Britain. There is, for example, no work that brings structuralist thinking to vernacular studies in the way that Henry Glassie combined both structuralism and the analysis of architectural structural innovation in his *Folk Housing in Middle Virginia* (Glassie, 1975). And we surely can take no pride in the fact that one of the very few works that relate the architecture of a folk community in the British Isles to its historic and present culture in the way in which the dwellings are built, used, lived in, comes from the same author: *Passing the Time in Ballymenone: Culture and History of an Ulster Community* (Glassie, 1982).

There's something cosy about vernacular architecture; it's a sheltered retreat for many who fondle the adze-marks, feel the fit of the ashlar or marvel at the assembly of post, wall-plate and tie-beam. Somehow, there's not the craftsmanship any more; all that honest workmanship with simple tools and muscle – it's gone. What is a comfort for some is a turn-off for others – except, that is, when it comes to buying a house in Devon or Wales to visit with the family at weekends, and get away from the practice and the telephone.

Recently sold, because the farmer's family wanted a bungalow just up the road – you know the sort of explanation. But *why* did he prefer the bungalow – if he did, which is a moot point – what values does it represent for him? We make our assumptions as we generally do, and are quite ready to back them by designing in accordance with them. Though frankly, we seldom know. For the truth of the matter is, the major proportion of housing in Britain is vernacular no longer, unless you happen to belong to the category that does extend the term to speculative builders' semis. Half the population of Britain lives in the suburbs of our cities, and a lot more live in housing of a similar kind that clusters round our small towns and villages. This includes not only detached and semi-detached houses, but terraced houses too. And in the outer suburbs, where land was cheaper and there was room to spread a little, bungalows, chalet bungalows and detached houses range in size from three bedrooms to five or six. The latter may be few in number, relatively speaking, but they are at one end of a scale that embraces a wide range of domestic buildings which also includes rows of three or four, maisonettes, flats over shops, and much else.

If the vernacular seems at times to be a comfortable corner of architecture in which to hide, there are not many who have chosen to go out and meet the suburbs. In spite of the fact that the most conspicuous element in the built environment of Britain, must surely be the suburbs around the cities, until extremely recently there has been an almost total disregard of them. Compared with the extent of the phenomenon the extent of the writing on it is still miniscule; nevertheless, within the past few years it has continued to grow. Not all of it, rightly, is concerned with the subject of the suburbs alone, but rather with housing generally, during a period of population growth and considerable social change. John Burnett's *A Social History of Housing* (Burnett, 1978) first appeared in 1978 and on a broad canvas plotted the dramatic developments in domestic accommodation between approximately 1815 and 1970. It is a masterly work within the inevitable limitations, but even here a strange myopia sets in when he discusses the suburbs of the 1920s and 1930s: with literally millions of examples from which to draw for illustrations for his themes he chose to depict them with five watercolours from John Prizeman's *Your Home: The Outside View* (Prizeman, 1975). Later, *The Design of Suburbia: A Critical Study in Environmental History* (Edwards, 1981) by Arthur M. Edwards covered much of the same span of time. By 'critical history' he meant that he was no lover of the suburbs: 'as the narrow house is the cheapest, commonest and ugliest of detached two-storey houses, so the square-plan bungalow is the cheapest, commonest and ugliest of single-storey dwellings'. Edwards cannot be accused of being dispassionate. Others more coolly examined an aspect of the housing issue, like Professor John Nelson Tarn, whose *Five Per Cent Philanthropy* was a scholarly appraisal of the housing of the urban poor over the three-quarters of a century that culminated in the First World War and the commencement of the Old Oak Estate at Acton. Or a particular building type is documented in a specific area, of which Alan A. Jackson's *Semi-Detached London* (Jackson, 1973) is an informative example.

All this activity has not promoted, as far as I know, a society to match the Vernacular Architecture Group, though a Suburban Architecture Group would have plenty of work to do. If there is as yet no inventory of vernacular houses and even a comprehensive typology still remains to be compiled, as far as suburban housing is concerned the work has scarcely begun. To which no doubt, the answer comes readily that there is little variety to document and what there is, would not merit the effort. But only a few hours spent in Hastings, Harrow or Hull reveal that such is not the case. Although the types of semi-detached house are modest in number they still add up to a sizeable range, while the forms encompassed within the bungalows and chalet-bungalows of the inter-war years extend far beyond the 'cheap and common' square plan. The activities of individual builders of the 1930s, the much-maligned speculative builders, about whom so little is known, also provide an area for research that could be done at local level. In fact there are local

**Figure 20.5**
'Station Road', in the outer London suburb of Pinner, with a characteristic 1930s general post office (left) and shops with living accommodation above (see also Figure 20.6).

**Figure 20.6**
Traditional buildings, adapted to contemporary use in the High Street, the village core of the suburb of Pinner. Two supermarkets are concealed behind the High Street.

studies to match in type of approach, if not in abundance, the studies made by local history groups and the like in the vernacular field, such as *Pinner Streets Yesterday and Today* by Elizabeth Cooper (1976), or James Murphy's *The Semi-Detached House: Its Place in Suburban Housing*, from the School of Architecture, University College, Dublin (Murphy, 1977).

Much of the writing on the suburbs (well, there isn't much, but a good proportion of what there is) reflects the archaeological and socio-historical emphases that are to be found in the vernacular field. Very little has been considered in essentially architectural or planning terms, if only because the architects and planners have been the bitterest in their attacks on the homes of half of Britain's population. Their spokesman of another era, the *Architectural Review,* bestowed 'a name in the hope it will stick – SUBTOPIA' (Nairn, 1955). Unhappily the patronizing term and its definition ('Philosophically, the idealization of the Little Man who lives there; from suburb + Utopia') did stick, and the mud-slinging has hardly abated. The times seemed to be a-changing when *Architectural Design* published at the close of 1981 a profile on 'the Anglo-American suburb' (Stern and Massengale, 1981). Hearts sank as we padded round the paths of Park Town, sipped again at Bourneville and bathed in Port Sunlight. The American bit would not be familiar to many, though it was comfortably conventional. Here was the architect congratulating other architects on their tasteful ventures

**Figure 20.7**
Suburban houses in an Ottawa street, with roofs, porches and other details designed to protect against the onslaught of winter. Quebec, Canada.

into the suburbs – which bear only tangentially today on the suburbs of either Britain or the United States. As for their occupants, they as usual, hardly came into the picture – or the pictures. It's all the more surprising because studies of the suburbs have been made in the United States since at least 1925, when Harlan Paul Douglass published *The Suburban Trend* (Douglass, 1925). Thirty years later though, David Riesman was still complaining that 'we know very little about the relatively settled suburbs and . . . almost nothing about the suburbs (old and new) surrounding the smaller cities' (Riesman, 1957). His work, and that of Herbert J. Gans, William H. Whyte, William Dobriner, A.C. Spectorsky, Stanley Buder and many others have largely repaired the omission. They aren't always in favour of the suburbs, but they do base their conclusions on considered research and not cliché responses about 'monotony', 'soul-destroying environments' or 'little men'. Largely, of course, they remain as unread by planners and architects in the United States, as their few counterparts in Britain are similarly ignored. We might have been spared the débacle of high-rise housing, for example, if the warnings in Willmott and Young's *Family and Kinship in East London* had been taken seriously (Young and Willmott, 1957). There are studies of suburban houses and communities of comparatively recent date, but they are far less well known than those undertaken by the Institute of Community Studies and likely to be even less influential, while architects' resistance to, or ignorance of them persists. I have in mind Lynette Carey and Roy Mapes' *The Sociology of Planning* (Carey and Mapes, 1972) for instance. The daunting title is not likely to induce architects to respond to their work on social interactions within eight new housing estates of differing configurations. Or again, there is *Mental Health on a New Housing Estate* by E.H. Hare and G.K. Shaw (Hare and Shaw, 1965) which compares the incidence of neuroses in an old and a new housing estate in Croydon. Of course, these are sociological and psychological works, and they use the tools and the methods of those disciplines. Still, their conclusions should surely have some significance for designers, though they may not be the ones they'd expect.

'If an architect is really concerned with the way in which a realized design is used and enjoyed by the people who will have to experience it as part of their lives, then the architect must become something of a sociologist or must at least employ one', wrote Carey and Mapes. Tables and statistics do not express the values of the householders and their families, it's true. How do you ascertain what those values are, and how they bear upon house and home? *Voices from the Middle Class* by Jane Deverson and Katherine Lindsay (1975), used free association and the tape recorder to try and get an answer in two South London suburbs, but though some of what they documented has design implications, the bulk of the book is concerned with other domestic matters. More original and more thought-provoking was the work of Stephen Willats with his West London Social Resources Project (Willats, 1976). He was the editor of *Control Magazine*, and an artist with a concern for the social roles of art. Willats' Social Resources Project was conducted in Greenford, Osterley, Hanwell and Harrow and it involved the participation of local residents, not only in the recording of their activities, needs and responses to their own environment, but also in qualitative decision-making after the completed record sheets had been publically displayed. Its purpose was to demonstrate the 'externalization of art' but it offers lessons in the externalization of architecture. And by that I mean getting far more feedback from the community for whom architects are theoretically working, and gaining far more of its participation in their design processes. Even so, the significance of the personally-shaped, embellished, planted, wall-hung, done-it-yourself environment of the home, whether it's in the village, the town or the suburbs, has not been examined closely in Britain. Not as closely, at any rate, as when Mihaly Csikszentmihalyi and Eugene Rochberg-Halton sought to uncover the empirical relationships between objects and

**Figure 20.8**
Artificial stone and 'roughcast' applied to adjacent council houses after purchase by their occupiers. Standard council houses are beyond. Old Oak Estate, Acton, London.

their owners, 'people and things' in Rogers Park and Evanston in the northern limits of Chicago (Csikszentmihalyi and Rochberg-Halton, 1981). Their exhaustive study of the home as a symbolic environment was concerned mainly with the values attached to objects gathered, kept, owned, nurtured, displayed, from beds to bric-a-brac; potted plants to pin-up photos. But if the significance of domestic symbols in relation to the self is treated with contempt, as 'good taste' (or whatever guise is worn to distinguish 'our' taste from 'theirs') ensures that it is, there's little likelihood that the message of *The Meaning of Things* is going to get through to the design professions.

Rochberg-Halton and his partner were concentrating on the internal, personally-shaped home and did not extend their work to the houses in which their subjects lived. This Ian Davis, Ian Bentley and myself attempted to do in *Dunroamin: The Suburban Semi and Its Enemies* (Oliver *et al.*, 1982). But our intention was also to reveal how virulent, biased and irrational were the attacks of the modernist architects on the suburban environment of the inter-war years. It was only the identification of a reasonably defined period that made us end with the outbreak of war; there's massive evidence to show that such attitudes not only persisted throughout the 1950s and 1960s, but with few exceptions, are flourishing today. In a way it's hardly surprising. Much post-Modernism was old-style Modernism in a recut suit and the attitudes of formalist designers to the qualities which appeal to those who never hear, let alone learn, the language of their formal games are not noticeably different. One of the fascinating aspects of the breaches in the modernist ranks, brought about by the sharp critiques of Brolin (1976) and others, was how rapidly and securely the ranks closed again. If the old attitudes were shaken it wasn't for long: the condescension to the vernacular and the patronizing of the suburbs persisted, where either are considered at all.

Does it matter? Well, obviously I think it does. I believe we should learn by the successes, even if they were not of our making, and we should acknowledge and learn from the mistakes, especially when they were. It is proper that architectural magazines are largely concerned with the schemes of innovatory designers, but only if it is recognized that the entire spectrum of environmental research and thought does not reside within them. Nor is it encompassed by a few photographs of sturdy examples of functional vernacular barns or the games that architects occasionally play with the textures and motifs that they may extract from the mass of houses on the urban periphery. It's not only the values of architects that matter in the design of houses or community buildings; its the values of those that live in them, work in them and adapt, extend or remodel them when they can. And that goes as much for our understanding of the vernacular traditions as it does for the necessary recognition of all the other kinds of building that are overlooked 'out there'. Rather than select a number of examples to discuss in this chapter, I've chosen to comment on the state of research and writing in vernacular and popular architecture. I've tried to show what kind of emphases there are, to indicate some of the aspects that are little pursued in this country, and to suggest some of the lines along which, in my view, potentially valuable work is being done which can have direct bearing on architectural design for a humane environment. Vernacular architecture in the conventional sense may have come to an end in Britain, though it is still lived in and adapted. But while I write the popular environment is evolving and changing. In the Old Oak Estate at Acton, mentioned above, many of those LCC estate council houses have been sold off and their new owners were intent on expressing their new home ownership by remodelling them. It's not easy of course – as in all council estates where architects were in control, the houses were deliberately designed to suppress any hints of individualism. But it's happening, here and in scores of other estates around the country: new messages are being uttered in the vernacular but, as far as I'm aware, no one is devoting much attention to finding out what they mean.

# References


Alcock, N. (1973). *A Catalogue of Cruck Buildings*. Chichester: Phillimore for VAG.

Barley, M. (1961). *The English Farmhouse and Cottage*. London: Routledge & Kegan Paul.

Bonta, J.P. (1979). *Architecture and Its Interpretation*. London: Lund Humphries.

Brolin, B.C. (1976). *The Failure of Modern Architecture*. London: Studio Vista.

Brunskill, R.W. (1970). *Illustrated Handbook of Vernacular Architecture*. London: Faber & Faber.

Burnett, J. (1978). *A Social History of Housing, 1815–1970*. Newton Abbot: David & Charles.

Carey, L. and Mapes, R. (1972). *The Sociology of Planning: A Study of Social Activity on New Housing Estates*. London: Batsford.

Charles, F.W.B. (1967). *Mediaeval Cruck-Building and its Derivatives*. Society for Mediaeval Archaeology, Monograph No. 2.

Comte de Lautreamont (Isadore Ducasse), see Rubin (1968).

Cooper, E. (1976). *Pinner Streets Yesterday and Today*. Pinner and Hatch End Archaeological Society, Vol. V.

Csikszentmihalyi, M. and Rochberg-Halton, E. (1981). *The Meaning of Things: Domestic Symbols and the Self*. Cambridge University Press.

Deverson, J. and Lindsay, K. (1975). *Voices from the Middle Class: A Study of Families in Two London Suburbs*. London: Hutchinson.

Douglas, H.P. (1925). *The Suburban Trend*. New York: Century Press.

EAAE. (1982). Workshop on vernacular and neo-vernacular architecture, METU, Ankara May 16–22.

Edwards, A.M. (1981). *The Design of Suburbia. A Critical Study in Environmental History*. London: Pembridge Press.

Evans, G.E. (1966). *The Pattern Under the Plough*. London: Faber and Faber.

Glassie, H. (1975). *Folk Housing in Middle Virginia: A Structural Analysis of Historic Artefacts*. Knoxville: University of Tennessee Press.

Glassie, H. (1982). *Passing the Time in Ballymenone: Culture and History of an Ulster Community*. Dublin: O'Brien Press.

Hare, E.H. and Shaw, G.K. (1965). *Mental Health on a New Housing Estate: A Comparative Study of Health in Two Districts of Croydon*, London: Oxford University Press. Maudsley Monograph No. 12.

Jackson, A.A. (1973). *Semi-Detached London*. London: George Allen & Unwin.

Martin, D. (n.d.). *The Robertsbridge Wealdens*. Robertsbridge & District Archaeological Society.

Mercer, E. (1975). *English Vernacular Houses: A Study of Traditional Farmhouses and Cottages*. London: HMSO.

Murphy, J. (1977). *The Semi-Detached House: Its Place in Suburban Housing*. Housing Research Unit, School of Architecture, University College, Dublin.

Nairn, I. (1955). Outrage. *Architectural Review*. Special Number, June.

Oliver, P., Davis, I. and Bentley, I. (1982). *Dunroamin: The Suburban Semi and Its Enemies*. London: Barrie & Jenkins.

Pevsner, N. (1951 *et seq.*). *The Buildings of England.* Series by counties. Harmondsworth: Penguin Books.

Prizeman, J. (1975). *Your Home: The Outside View.* London: Blue Circle Group.

Riesman, D. (1957). The suburban dislocation. In: *Annals of the American Academy of Political and Social Science.* Vol 1. November.

Rubin, W.S. (1968). *Dada, Surrealism and their Heritage.* New York: Museum of Modern Art.

Stern, R.A.M. and Massengale, J.M. (1981). The Anglo-American suburb. *Architectural Design.* Profile 37.

Tarn, J.N. (1973). *Five Per Cent Philanthropy. An Account of Housing in Urban Areas Between 1840 and 1914.* Cambridge University Press.

Turner, W.J. (1947). *Exmoor Village.* London: George C. Harrap.

VAG (1969). *Vernacular Architecture.* York: Vernacular Architecture Group.

Wade, J. (ed.). (1981). *Traditional Kent Buildings*, books 1 & 2, School of Architecture, Canterbury College of Art, Kent County Council.

Willatts, S. (1976). *Art and Social Function: Three Projects.* London: Latimer New Directions.

Wood-Jones, R.B. (1963). *Traditional Domestic Architecture in the Banbury Region.* Manchester University Press.

Young, M. and Willmott, P. (1957). *Family and Kinship in East London.* London: Routledge and Kegan Paul Ltd.

# 21

# Kaluderica: High-grade housing in an illegal settlement (1989)

At the time of writing, it was over 20 years since the publication of Charles Abrams' *Housing in the Modern World* (Abrams, 1966). Since then the literature on 'squatter settlements' has grown at a rate comparable with the expansion of cities in the Third World themselves. John F.C. Turner's writings (Turner, 1976) in the 1970s did much to challenge conventional views of the urban 'slums', and while many detailed reports have been made on *bustees, favelas, gecekondus, bidonvilles* and many other types of illegal settlement, positive approaches to 'sites and services' schemes, settlement upgrading and other improvement measures have developed. A variety of building types, environmental conditions, material resources and skills have been noted in them, but in general, illegal housing is built at minimum cost from found and waste materials. They are, for the most part, makeshift constructions, with one or two rooms, single-storeyed and unserviced. Flattened oil drums, kerosene cans, vehicle tyres, sacking and plastic sheeting are widely used, but the ingenuity and resourcefulness of the builders and their capacity to recycle materials testify to the desire on the part of the squatter to have a stake in the city. Settlement upgrading projects have done much to improve roads, to bring services of water, sewage disposal and electricity to the settlements, though the improved locations have often attracted still more migrants as a result. In some cases, there has been little consultation or participation with the settlers themselves in such projects as, for instance, the Kampung Improvement Projects in Jakarta (Silas, 1984). There is, therefore, a hint of paternalism in the bringing of the services, but this nevertheless, is a vastly more constructive approach than was the wholesale demolition of squatter homes which once constituted official response to the 'problem' (Payne, 1984).

A number of writers, including the critics of John Turner's advocacy (Burgess, 1982), have blamed the development of squatter settlements on the adoption by less developed and less prosperous countries, of the western capitalist system. While the issues are complex there is much to support the argument; however, little is known or written about concerning urban problems in socialist and 'Second World' countries. Analyses of urbanization in the former USSR, in Poland, the Czech Republic, Slovakia or the German Democratic Republic has revealed undoubted problems, but population projections and urban growth has often been accurate and contained (Musil, 1980). Nevertheless, in a centrally planned economy, controls on movement of labour and regional development involved losses in personal freedom which many would find unacceptable (Bourne *et al.*, 1984). Whether the living conditions of those who migrate to Third World cities are any more acceptable is a point that might be argued at length, but in another paper.

Yugoslavia was a non-aligned nation with a communist government of a unique kind. Though centrally administered in the immediate post-war years the country was gradually decentralized after 1956, into regional, city and local communes. The economic reforms of 1965 and the new constitution of 1974 consolidated a principle of 'self-management' in the six autonomous republics of the Federal Socialist Republic of Yugoslavia, namely Croatia, Slovenia, Bosnia-Hercegovina, Montenegro, Macedonia and Serbia, which included the autonomous regions of Vojvodina and Kosovo Metchija. Of these, Serbia was the largest. Its capital, Beograd (Belgrade), was also the capital of the country and with 1.5 million population was by far the largest city. Urban development in Yugoslavia is the decentralized responsibility of the commune (*opcina*) which may average some 50 000 people in a broadly historically defined territory. Regional and urban plans were prepared and had to be approved by the majority of the citizens and by the executive city assembly. Master plans (GUP) had to have this approval before they could be issued with building permits, but public discussion was open and urban proposals were fully displayed (Butina-Watson, 1985). I attended one such presentation in Belgrade and was impressed by the sophistication of the participants in their understanding of the issues involved. Belgrade is, however, a typically Central European city in many ways, but even in a provincial town like Titova Ujice a dramatic urban development was taking place.

Belgrade is notable for its many high-rise building developments of apartment blocks and public facilities. They are firmly Modernist; if a number are dull, many are interesting (Stojanovic and Martinovic, 1978). Public participation in the maintenance of gardens and the employment by the residents of concierges had kept the environmental quality of some areas commendably high. But the sheer numbers of apartment blocks inevitably brought the sense of anonymity and loss of personal identity evident in modern cities everywhere. In spite of this, Belgrade could not keep pace with the demand for housing. In theory, all workers were entitled to accommodation either from local government or from the factory or other enterprise which employed them. Rents were low, the standard of public sector housing accommodation generally good. But, because of the shortage, many migrants to the city lived in substandard housing which, unlike most cities, was not in a particular area but was scattered throughout the urban area. This made it less immediately visible, but living conditions for the unskilled and uneducated can be poor. Many workers lived in a *radnicka koloija*, or workers' colony which ranged in size from units of a few dozen bed places to a few hundred. The *samacki hotel*, or bachelor dormitory, was an alternative kind of accommodation run by some of the larger concerns; it was usually better run and better serviced, but suitable only for young migrants without families (Simic, 1983). In the face of this housing problem, peasants might well have been expected to stay in the rural areas, but as the peasant economy declined, the city beckoned more people to migrate and to share some of

**Figure 21.1**
Zemon, Belgrade. A fringe area of the city where some single-storey vernacular buildings still remain. Serbia, Yugoslavia.

its benefits. At one time it was possible to buy cheap land quite near the centre of Belgrade and to erect a squatter home on it. Having done so, one could apply for a building permit and establish a base. But the opportunities inevitably ran out, and homeless migrants turned instead to the outer fringes of the city, staying with peasant homes in one of the farm villages. Many began to build their own houses on plots sold to them by the peasants, illegally and without a permit – the *divlja gradnja*. Kaluderica is one of the 'wild settlements' that have grown up around Belgrade this way.

In the spring of 1985, an international group of staff and students of the Shelter and Settlements Unit of the Department of Architecture of Oxford Polytechnic made a short study of the town. With members from England, Ireland, Turkey, Australia, Botswana, Malawi and South Africa we were hardly invisible, but the people that we interviewed and whose houses we measured or studied were generally welcoming, and in the often miserable weather the patron of the Sangaj let us use the cafe as a base. We were introduced to Kaluderica by Milan Prodanovic, Professor of Urban Design at the University of Novi Sad and we were helped in many ways by faculty and students of the School of Architecture of the University of Belgrade. We were particularly fortunate in having as one of our number Georgia Grzan-Butina, a Yugoslav citizen and faculty member of the Joint Centre for Urban Design at Oxford Polytechnic. We also had the invaluable help of Ljiljana Peric, who was, as far as I am aware, the only person to have studied any part of Kaluderica before our work (Oliver, 1985). Travel to the southern suburbs of

**Figure 21.2**
The advance of high-rise blocks threatened the suburban and rural periphery. South Belgrade, Serbia.

Belgrade was direct, if hardly comfortable, by the crowded bus, but after a change of coaches the route to Kaluderica was less congested. The high-rise blocks were left behind, to be replaced in our vision by an untidy but always interesting mix of suburban houses, farms and farmworkers' cottages, roadside stalls and shops. Significantly, they were interspersed with builders' yards where stocks of hollow pot bricks, breeze blocks, coarse sand and timber were available for purchase. Most appeared to have one or two handlers of the materials and a proprietor; they were small concerns clearly catering for domestic building rather than for the large-scale construction industry of the city. The last of the buildings passed and for a few hundred metres there was rough pasture on either side of the road as it followed the contours above the Bare River. Then curiously dispersed rows of red brick houses with tiled roofs came into view and the bus swung off the road, past a school and health centre, across the river in the valley and up the other side, coming to a stop at a two-roomed depot with a loggia of stained plaster.

Many of the houses in Kaluderica were of local vernacular type, especially in the centre, for it had developed around the nucleus of a small village about seven miles from the city. Even in the 1950s there were still fewer than 200 households, but a decade later it began to grow considerably. Peasant families sold off pieces of land for housing. The method of farming in many ways was medieval and the old strip pattern of fields still applied. A farmer might sell off a strip which could be divided up for a row of houses – and continue to drive his oxen on the strips on either side. Lanes and footpaths between farmholdings had become routes through the growing town, whose morphology oddly reflected the patterns of centuries-old farming systems. Fortunately, the village of Kaluderica was well served by public transport; a bus arrived at the store – proudly termed a 'supermarket' – every quarter of an hour. The service adequately met the needs of the population which was now in excess of 20 000. But Kaluderica had to rely on other services and facilities that served the village, such as the stream in the valley that roughly divided it, and the cistern beside the only cafe-bar, the *Sangaj*, or 'Shanghai', which belies the exoticism of its name. Consequently, like any other illegal settlement, Kaluderica lacked certain services. There was a village standpipe, but no sewage disposal. Occasional 'palladin bins' for refuse disposal appear and were emptied intermittently. There was electricity and telephone lines available for those who wanted them, but only a small number of the roads were surfaced and ditches provided the only drainage. Many householders dug their own wells, which were often 20–30 metres deep, but pit latrines were used by many residents. Recently, individual septic tanks had been installed by some home builders and these were emptied monthly by the local authority as the existence of Kaluderica was gradually recognized.

In spite of its size, Kaluderica was still, in all other respects, a village. On first sight it appeared to have no other shops, but the single 'main' street had several, all of them in domestic premises – a hairdresser, a dress shop, a baker. Further along there was a carpenter's shop and two separate glass-cutter's shops. I was curious about this and talked with Radisa (his name, he explained, means 'hard worker') about it. I was drawn to his shop by an unlikely companion to a framed picture of Marshal Tito's tomb: a framed reproduction of a painting by the eighteenth century British artist, Romney. It turned out that the picture was awaiting collection by a local man; part of Radisa's business was framing pictures and mirrors, though his principal livelihood came from fitting window glass. The other glass-cutter was his cousin; they had fallen out and were now rivals, though Radisa was confident that there would be enough work for them both as Kaluderica continued to grow. Radisa was a fairly typical Serbian craftsman whose work and experience were unexpectedly wide. He had been a guest worker in Saudi Arabia for some time, a country and climate which he greatly disliked but which had enabled him to earn sufficient money to start a small business. Yugoslav law not only permitted modest private enterprise but, though large-scale capital accumulation was neither permitted nor possible, owners of businesses were allowed to employ up to five workers. There was a strong vein of independence in the Serbian temperament and a large proportion of the population were both employees and self-employed peasant farmers. This perplexing dual status arose from a peculiarity of the Yugoslav system which enabled a man (or woman, though less frequently) to be a factory operative or wage-earner for part of the day, and peasant farmer for the rest. Factories usually ran from six o'clock in the morning until two o'clock in the afternoon, permitting workers to engage themselves in self-employment of some kind for the remainder of the day. Theoretically, at least; although the time spent in commuting meant an early departure in the morning and a late start in the 'second economy' in the afternoon. It was demanding and tiring, but widespread, and meant that Serbian loyalties were often torn; at harvest and other critical times they usually favoured work on the family farm. Some of these farms were large enough to be self-supporting – individuals could own up to 10 hectares (about

25 acres) of arable land and, if they could maintain them, additional woodlands if they so wished (Halpern and Halpern, 1972). This applied even in Kaluderica, although it meant that a peasant might only have a few strips within the village area, the rest of the land being further away.

Radislava Markovic was a fairly typical worker. About 65 years old, he was a partisan during the war, injured and partially deafened in the fighting. He lived at Igmatovica 16, a grey, two-storeyed house of brick, rendered and lightly moulded in the fashion of the changing vernacular at the time of his birth. His parents built it in 1922 and it was the only home he had known. The tiny smallholding had a mere two acres by the house, but he owned a dozen more in the hills. His wife Lubinka, 61, was dressed in the typical contemporary peasant clothes of headscarf, long skirt and fleece-lined sleeveless jacket tied with thongs. She explained 'We have a horse, two cows, four pigs, five piglets and a dog. We keep bees, we grow our own vegetables and corn. We use the corn shucks to feed the cows. And we grow potatoes, beans, onions and salad.' Their house was barely furnished, although the doors had traditional flowered pelmets over them and there were plastic flowers in a vase, beside the photographs of their sons, on a small sideboard. They were justifiably proud of their sons. The eldest, aged 45, was an architect and urban planner at Euprea, 200 km away, married to a doctor. The second was a dentist who had been living in Switzerland since 1970; the third trained as an art student but, with no employment available for his talents, he drove a truck. Three houses in line at

**Figure 21.3**
Peasant farm and smallholding of the Markovic family, in the Kaluderica region beyond the city limits.

the bottom strip, close to the road, had been designed by the architect son and built for all of them, a 'little sum' to the district officer helping them to get permission to build by the main road. Yet, when services came to Kaluderica they were likely to have the farm house demolished and they were fearful for the future, while being happy that their sons would be able to return to the village.

The dilemma of the Markovic's and the marked difference of status of the sons, were not wholly typical. Many families were peasant farmers, with no expectations of being more than that. Others, perhaps the majority, were representative of the dual economy, being both peasants and workers in Belgrade; a smaller group were professionals and entrepreneurs who had built in Kaluderica because they preferred the country to the city, the land was comparatively cheap and it was possible to start building. Zoran, who declined to give his second name, was one; a suave, well-dressed man in his thirties who was, in the local euphemism, 'in trade'. His unspecified trade had enabled him to travel as far as England and he was particularly proud of the English-styled garden with flower beds, flowering cherry, evergreen trees and green lawns, which he had tended in front and behind his house. The house itself was on four floors, the lowest having a garage with a car, the upper ones with balconies and a steep pitched roof with deep eaves of apparent Swiss design. He showed me round the house, to admire the push-button telephone, the comfortable nursery, the light attic utility room, the layers of roof insulation, the dining suite, the fully fitted kitchen, the charming children's play-room. There were radiators for central

**Figure 21.4**
Sophisticated self-build, with concrete main frames made by contractors. The view down the road indicates the extent of the 'wild settlement' of Kaluderica.

heating, a low-level flush suite for the w.c., a bathroom *en suite* with the bedroom. It was hard to imagine that this was an illegally built house, but it was. No water went to the w.c., the radiators were not working, but the telephone, at least, was connected. Zoran was ready for the day when Belgrade recognized Kaluderica, or at least his street, and provided the services, the metalled road and general infrastructure, that would have as a by-product the destruction of the Markovic home.

Several of the houses in his short street were of a similar, but not identical design; they were pleasantly individual, but related well to each other. Some were still in the process of being built, Zoran explained. He and a few friends had seen the plans in a 'pattern book' for second and vacation homes, and had bought a set. They gave this to a builder and devised their own variations. A couple, less well-off than Zoran (with his wife, his two cars and their holidays in Greece), were slowly building their own house. Together, they had each given up a metre of their frontage to ensure that their houses conformed in detail with the 1969 development plan; they were confident that connections would soon be made. There were other sections of Kaluderica where the houses were three or four storeys high, in various stages of completion. Some made extensive use of concrete and some were rendered, but most were built in red brick. Rendering, and coloured plaster with textured surfaces, were usually left to a skilled workman, who might be employed to finish the house some years after it was fully inhabited. The rendering was a sign of completion. It was evident that the influences were varied: several houses had the deep eaves, broad balconies, clerestory windows and roof lights that indicated that the builders had been influenced by German, Swiss and Austrian models. They had probably seen these while employed abroad as 'guest workers'. Others took influences from each other: round arches in one house would invariably mean that houses under construction nearby, would also have round arches. Evidence of the influence of the vernacular tradition was apparent in the techniques of brickwork, the use of standard details such as eaves, gutters and finials, often made of metal sheeting, and the use of side entrances and broad balconies. Space use was frequently traditional, especially among the peasant families, with a bed in the kitchen, separate stores for food, and a 'guest room' with spare bed and a 'feast table' for important functions like weddings and Christmas celebrations, which was otherwise unused.

Looking round Kaluderica, the widespread use of brick and the large number (at least 50) of unfinished buildings, gave a certain strange uniformity to the town. But closer inspection revealed

**Figure 21.5**
An incomplete house, in which the builder used arches for a loggia and verandah.

a wide variety of buildings, either under construction or already structurally complete. They included two-storeyed houses, semi-detached pairs, semi-detached groups of four apartments, small apartment blocks, three- and four-storey houses and many, sited on the slopes, which had cellars and basements approached from the front. The standard of building however, was variable. Some houses were rather poorly constructed with evident errors, especially in the placing of reinforcement rods in concrete. But the high quality of much of the building was what really surprised; a great many houses

**Figure 21.6**
Semi-detached houses, of a pattern book design, with one raised on piles. Built by the respective families, the other house had still to be rendered but was near completion.

were skilfully assembled, with some revealing the hand of the *majstor*, the master mason. Why was the building quality as good as it was, and why, with this in mind, were so many houses unfinished? Initially the settlers in the region came, some two centuries ago, from eastern Serbia; a thin trickle continued to flow in, but at so slow a rate that by 1910 there were scarcely a hundred households in the village and its environs. Even after the Second World War, this number had not doubled. The evidence of growth that we witnessed was therefore quite recent; an outcome of the post-war industrialization of Belgrade and its housing shortage, it began to expand only in the 1960s. Many of the new settlers also came from eastern Serbia, and particularly from the south-east. Some were from Crna Trava, which is noted for its builders, who were attracted by the booming construction industry in Belgrade. High-rise blocks meant that many builders were needed and innumerable craftsmen learned to work with reinforced concrete construction, after they had secured employment. For them, building their own houses presented no problems, and many soon found that the 'second economy' gave them the opportunity of setting up small building enterprises. Self-management was an important aspect of the Yugoslav constitution (Seibel and Damachi, 1982).

Working on high-rise buildings may have led to the association of 'modernization' with high buildings. Tall houses also broke with the tradition, further emphasizing the modern trend, while their internal arrangement could still perpetuate long-standing customs of space use. Families pooled their resources and sought to build a house big enough to accommodate the *zadruga*, the extended clan. Unfortunately, their ambitions were frequently far beyond their means, and many houses were abandoned after one or two storeys were built. Often though, the work was merely halted; 10 or a dozen years spent on building the family house was common. Typically, a house may have a cellar, cut into the hill slope where livestock, especially pigs, are kept, above which was the ground (first) floor proper. Though the rest of the house may be constructed as a skeleton, or with infill of hollow fired clay bricks, the upper storeys could remain unoccupied, but used for storage, washing and airing clothes. Eventually these may be completed and occupied, as and when they were ready. But the house is the future of the family and the focus of its activity; delaying completion might have been a part of the process of holding the family together, with responsibility for working on it being shared by all. As years passed, a family would expand into their available space, putting up dividing walls to provide quite frequently, as many as a dozen rooms. Official reaction to the initial development of Kaluderica was the attempt to demolish these houses built without building permits; as late as 1975 a special order forbidding further illegal building was issued. Neither action was in any way successful. It was politically inexpedient to be seen demolishing houses in large numbers, and in any event, they were rising too fast. Nonetheless, the settlement was not officially recognized and was a long way from attaining legalized status that would bring all the facilities, businesses and services that it needed. Clearly, the school, the health centre with its dental surgery, the chemist's shop and the paediatric consultancy designed to serve the original, and officially recognized village, were wholly inadequate for the reality of the town that it had become. No one was in serious doubt that the town would continue to thrive and grow, and there were new sites being prepared, new foundations being dug, and smoke curling from the brick enclosure that marked the first stage of many a future house, which underlined the optimism of the residents.

Kaluderica was not alone. There were other settlements around Belgrade and in many different parts of Serbia and further afield, in Yugoslavia. The town of Split for example, was reported at the time of writing, to have as many as 12 000 illegally built houses. At least a part of the confusing picture of new building in Yugoslavia was the law which permitted the building of up to two *vikendica* – literally, weekend houses – in the country, in any one of the republics. Capital investment in shareholdings in this socialist state was not possible. Hence, families were motivated to put their savings into building. This growth was evident all over the country in the scattered houses standing in the open countryside. Poor understanding of planning principles often accounted for their location and distribution. Many 'pattern books' such as *Vasa Kuca*, published in Zagreb with some 700 designs for houses, chalets and other domestic buildings, with interiors, details of plumbing and heating systems, and 30 pages of building details, were compiled to meet the potential builders' needs (Izdavaea *et al.*, 1972). That hundreds of illegal buildings cropped up between the weekend houses with their official building permits, is hardly surprising. Obviously, the situation was getting out of control and much of the countryside was being marred by indiscriminate building. But there were, nevertheless, many aspects of note and a number of lessons to be learned. On the other hand, there was surprising evidence of consumerism, of a taste for ostentation, individualism and display which was evident in building details and, in particular, in walls and metal-framed gates. Some of these latter had the quality of a flourishing popular art,

**Figure 21.7**
When their houses were finished and occupied many residents found opportunities for personalizing them with decorations and details such as wrought-iron fencing.

with car hub-caps, reflector lights and other items worked into the iron frames by the local blacksmith. There were garden lights and ornaments which would be proudly displayed in any western suburban garden or yard; there were wrought-iron balconies and faience decorations of a lively design, even if they were far removed from architectural canons of taste. This exuberance and materialism alienated the builders and householders from the more strict adherents to the party line and the socialist ethic, and equally separated them from the architects and planners who rejected their 'bad taste'.

**Figure 21.8**
View of a settlement in Kaluderica, with others beyond. The spatial organization reflects the pattern of land areas and strips sold by peasant farmers to aspiring builders.

Nevertheless, there's no question that Kaluderica demonstrated the determination of many families to build their own homes, and generally to do so with audacity, commitment and often, with great skill, which is remarkable.

To my knowledge there are few parallels with such high-grade housing in an illegal settlement elsewhere. Would legalizing the process of self-build of this kind strengthen or weaken the resolve of the builders? And what place has the architect in it – if any?

## Note

The ravages of the subsequent civil war in Yugoslavia led to the destruction of many houses in spontaneous settlements in Serbia and other republics. Kaluderica was not unaffected by this, but the determination to build their own homes persisted in many regions, and contributed to the post-war recovery.

## References

Abrams, C. (1966). *Housing in the Modern World.* London: Faber and Faber.

Bourne, L.S., Sinclair, R. and Dziewonski, K. (eds). (1984). *Urbanization and Settlement Patterns.* Part B: Settlement systems in centrally planned economies. Oxford University Press, pp. 355–411.

Burgess, R. (1982), Self-help housing advocacy: A critique of the work of John F.C. Turner. In: Ward, P.M. (ed.). *Self-Help Housing: A Critique.* London: Mansell, pp. 56–98.

Butina-Watson. G. (1985). Background to Kaluderica. In: Oliver, P. (ed.). *Kaluderica: Observations on a Wild Settlement.* Oxford Polytechnic, School of Architecture.

Halpern, J.M. and Halpern, B.K. (1972). *A Serbian Village in Historical Perspective.* New York: Holt, Rinehart & Winston, pp. 73–85.

Izdavaca, Z. *et al.* (1972). *Vas Kuca.* Pakrac, X11 Prolet. Zagreb: Brigade 2.

Musil, J. (1980). *Urbanization in Socialist Countries.* New York: M.E. Sharpe.

Oliver, P. (ed.). (1985). *Kaluderica: Observations on a Wild Settlement.* A field report made by staff and students of the Shelter and Settlements Unit and Course Area, School of Architecture, Oxford Polytechnic (later, Oxford Brookes University).

Payne, G.K. (ed.). (1984). *Low-Income Housing in the Developing World.* Chichester: John Wiley.

Seibel, H.D. and Damachi, U.G. (1982). *Self-Management in Yugoslavia and the Developing World.* London: Macmillan Press Ltd.

Silas, J. (1984). The Kampung improvement programme of Indonesia. In: Payne, G.K. (ed.). *Low Income Housing in the Developing World.* Chichester: John Wiley.

Simic, A. (1983). *The Peasant Urbanites: Rural–Urban Mobility in Serbia*. London: Seminar Press, pp. 91–107.
Stojanovic, B. and Martinovic, U. (1978). *Beograd 1945–1975. Urbanizam Arhitektura*. Beograd 7, Niro: Tehnicka knjiga.
Turner, J.F.C. (1976). *Housing by People*. London: Marion Boyars.

# PART VII

# MEETING THE CHALLENGE OF THE TWENTY-FIRST CENTURY

# 22

# Tradition by itself . . . (2000)

'Tradition by itself is not enough', wrote T.S. Eliot in *After Strange Gods*, 'it must be perpetually criticized and brought up to date under the supervision of what I call orthodoxy' (1934). That tradition is not, of itself, enough to sustain culture I would agree, and in the modern world it should be examined and brought up to date where this is desirable and practicable. But 'orthodoxy' was a strange god for an innovator like T.S. Eliot to make obeisance, and a false god where tradition in relation to the built environment is concerned. Whatever Eliot called, or meant by 'orthodoxy', it is understood to mean 'agreement with accepted standards, established doctrines, ideas, etc' (*Webster's Dictionary*) or 'of opinions or doctrines: right, correct, true; in accordance with what is authoritatively established as the true view or right practice' (*Oxford English Dictionary*). It was the established, 'right', 'correct' and 'true' doctrines of the Modern Movement applied to housing after the Second World War, that led to the disastrous high-rise developments plastered without respect to cultural differences, in cities throughout the world. The fiascos of Pruett-Igoe and Killingworth, which were among many high-rise blocks and complexes that were subsequently destroyed, were built as the result of measures hardly less Draconian than Ceaucescu's in Romania, however socially committed and well-intentioned they may have been. Supervised by such orthodoxy, the critique of traditional housing and the substitution of the 'up-to-date', contributed substantially to the problems of urbanization, rather than to their amelioration.

The reification of 'tradition' as an entity, rather than an abstraction of processes was, I believe, what Eliot had in mind when he considered it to be 'not enough'. Tradition as mimesis, perpetuated in the name of historical continuity; tradition which is no more than habit or mere repetition; tradition that is principally a vehicle for sentimental associations; tradition that promotes stereotypical imitation and the 'neo-vernacular': these interpretations or expressions should indeed be perpetually criticized. It is debatable whether they can be brought 'up-to-date', if that means what is currently considered as 'the true view or right practice' in design. If tradition is recognized as the transmission of cultural mores over time, and is understood as giving meaning to the utilization of accumulated experience, then this is another issue. If it is acknowledged as the passing on of technical know-how and is respected as the standards and values of a society embodied in its built structures, whether domestic, functional or symbolic, such tradition is not simply 'by itself', detached, insulated and unrelated to reality. On the contrary, tradition is a complex continuity inherited from the past, lived in the present and sustained in the future. It encompasses the concepts, processes and meanings of those aspects of praxis and materiality whose persistence ensures durability, reliability and identity.

At that initial symposium held when IASTE was founded in 1988, I presented a paper on 'Handed-Down Architecture: Tradition and Transmission' (see Chapter 10) in which I endeavoured to illustrate by examples some of the oral and other means whereby traditional values and technologies are passed between generations. Challenging the familiar concept of traditions being 'handed down', I suggested that 'in one sense it can be argued that there is no such thing as a traditional building, no larger field of traditional architecture. There are only buildings which embody traditions' (Bourdier and Al-Sayyad, 1983). That this conclusion was, in the words of the editors, 'provocatively arrived at' was only partially true, in that I wished to shift the emphasis from the common notion of the building as being 'traditional' to a recognition that it is the human transmission of tradita pertaining to its erection, occupation and meaning, that is of fundamental significance. The definition of spaces, the means and methods of construction, the forms and features of dwellings and the mores of living in families and communities, together constitute the lifeways and habitats of diverse cultures over time. Conceiving 'traditional buildings' as distinct entities, divorces their creation, occupancy and continuity from the socio-cultural and psychological realities. When this is recognized the processes whereby change is effected in vernacular traditions become more apparent, modifications of traditional practices being communicated to successors within a society. As Malinowski demonstrated a lifetime ago, the

**Figure 22.1**
Continuity and maintenance of tradition is evident in the stages of building in a small Bozo fishing settlement on an island in the Bani river, Lake Debo region, Mali.

'dynamics of social change' operate in all societies, though at differing rates (Malinowski, 1945). In vernacular architecture they may be as prolonged as the persistence of the black tent, as profound and permanent as the adoption of the chimney stack, or as immediate as the use of concrete blocks in masonry. Vernacular builders are not resistant to change, but by experiment, trial and evaluation, they embrace new technologies or details when their employment is perceived as beneficial. This is not to argue that mistakes do not occur, or that vernacular builders and the occupants of

**Figure 22.2**
A woman gathers hay from the rack of a *kozalec*, a structural type unique to Slovenia, reinstated after the health of herds declined with introduced mechanical baling.

their constructions are impervious to fashion, or external influence. Superficially, bearing in mind the pressures of commercialization, exploitation and economic repression, it may seem remarkable that vernacular traditions persist at all. Yet, the values by which they flourish or evolve are of the cultures to which they belong; they are not necessarily coincident with those of nations, still less with those of multinational corporations, whose hegemonic domination is inimical to their survival.

Take Peru, for instance, where vernacular traditions are apparent, and where their underlying presence is fundamentally significant. More than half the buildings in the capital city of Lima, whose population is creeping up to ten million, are built by their owners, their families or friends, or to their direction, by jobbing builders. In the rural areas and in the smaller towns, the proportion is far higher, exceeding 80 per cent of the housing stock. While the foundations of major buildings are often of closely fitted dressed stone of Inca origin and construction, the base of most buildings is of rubble stone, the walls being built of adobe blocks, made and moulded on site, and frequently mud plastered. Internal walls and second storeys, where they occur, are generally made of *qincha*, or panels of cane lengths, bound or wired together. Spaces are spanned with logs, poles or thick bamboo, and layers of *qincha*, mud mixed with straw, and packed mud, together make a secure roof. In a seismically active region, heavier materials are eschewed, the tying of beams and cane walls permitting some elasticity of movement without life-threatening collapse. Such building techniques are ubiquitous in rural regions, but mass adobe

**Figure 22.3**
Use of stone, earth, and fired tiles in an outer settlement, Chocechaca, Cuzco.

walling is prevalent in the second city of the country, Cuzco, situated in the mountains above 3300 m (Hartkopf, 1981).

In the raw, yellow-brown hills that form the backdrop to the capital city, Lima, literally millions of people live in the self-built *barriadas*. Many years ago, I was privileged to include the results of the work of William Mangin and John C. Turner on the *barriadas* or 'spontaneous' settlements of Lima, in my edited volume, *Shelter and Society* (Oliver, 1969). Their research and advocacy changed attitudes to the 'illegal' and 'squatter' settlements and promoted a more positive approach to the masses of self-built structures which rose on the hillsides and desertic plains that surround the city. Mangin and Turner (1969) held that the great majority of 'settlers' were from the slums of the inner city, rather than from the rural regions. This may have been the case, but the squatter settlements, later known as the *pueblos jovenes* or 'young towns', continued to grow in number and scale. Within a decade or so, by far the majority of the participants in the 'invasions', as the occupation of barren lands were termed, came from the rural areas lying to the north and east, and from the Andes, as traditional pastoralism and small farming declined. The activities of the *Sendero Luminoso* (Shining Path) guerillas in the 1980s forced thousands more to flee to the city. Many were Quechua, members of a widely distributed native American people. Others were *mestizos*, and some were *criollos* from the Lima hinterland, but the indigenous rural people predominated. Some brought a few materials with them, or carried mats of cane strips which could be used as windbreaks and temporary roofing, but the majority had to build their houses out of the resources available. Of these none was more common, nor more familiar, than earthen adobe block. With skills in building with earth that had been passed through many generations, the families who settled in the new towns had few problems before them in building sound, single-storey structures. As time passed and they found their niches, however small, in the Lima economy, many were able to purchase sufficient timber to construct the roofs and even the balconies with external stairs, to which many aspired. Yards were small, and in time, often built over, but living space was adequate if not ample, for the growing families. Land invasions were not legal and were often contentious, but the city learned to adopt them. With a trade-off of projects, such as the preparing by a community of basket-ball courts for their youth, 'traded' against the provision of surfacing of a road, the local government gave its support to the new citizens. Water availability was limited, but street lighting which gave protection to all at night, was one of the facilities which the city afforded many of the new settlements.

In some instances more substantial provision was made, most conspicuously with the provision of 'sites and services' schemes, in which a plot of land to which title was attached, and electricity, water supply and drainage were installed, for each family unit. As is the case with many such schemes, they were rigidly planned to an inflexible grid. To the inheritors of Inca planning and the 'Laws of the Indies' of their Spanish conquerors, imposition of the squared plans and rectilinear streets was not as repressive as it would have been, for many other cultures with a more organic approach to settlement. Once established, and as a measure of economic independence came, some families built second and even third floors, sometimes with a cantilevered or 'jettied' upper storey, to gain more space and a better view over the landscape. The houses that they built might be to an urban plan, and in some cases were larger than those which they had left; but they represented both their heritage and their aspirations. The *pueblos jovenes* or 'young towns' of Lima owed most of their form, their construction and their image to the vernacular traditions which they had inherited. Lima's young towns are not a model for other cities and other countries; to many settlers in other cultures they would be inimical to their values. The accommodation of three million of Lima's residents has largely depended on their initiative, mutual cooperation, skills and vernacular know-how, and on the seemingly limitless resource of earth for building. When the inhabitants find employment and as their families grow and the employable members increase, they may engage small contractors – usually enterprising inhabitants of the *pueblos jovenes*

**Figure 22.4**
Example of the *pueblos jovenes* (young towns) of Lima, Peru. As their presence is accepted and savings permit, many families extend or add floors to their houses.

themselves – to erect a concrete frame, or even floor slabs, for their buildings. Traditional techniques and building materials may thus be augmented with reinforced concrete where the situation demands and the domestic economy permits, while market stalls and shops, village centres and recreation spaces become part of the building and settlement layouts. For the *pueblos jovenes* to succeed, however, they require support in services, access to transport, schools and other amenities (Lloyd, 1980).

Among the most remarkable of the young towns was Villa El Salvador, created when state-owned land some 20 km to the south of the central city was allocated in 1971 by the then revolutionary government, to several thousand families who had invaded public and private land. Within 2 months some 20 000 families had settled on the designated plots. In 5 years, a quarter of a million people were living in the young town which, with the help of SINAMOS, the National System to Support Social Mobilization, had established its own community administration, CUAVES, or the autonomous urban community of El Salvador. A people's bank had been inaugurated, electricity supplied, schools opened and thousands of temporary dwellings transformed by their owner-builders into adobe and fired brick houses. Regrettably, a planned industrial development programme failed, when a new CUAVES committee lost popular support as it engaged in party politics following the right-wing coup in 1976 (Skinner, 1982). Reorganized in partnership with the municipality in the 1980s, Villa El Salvador witnessed substantial urban improvements including black-top roads and drinking water on tap. Support for self-help housing remained inadequate for the poorest families, and there were many problems relating to changing government policies, inadequate funding and the investment of small industries which employed too few of the settlers. Squatter settlements are a drain on the city's resources and at times, interests may be opposed – such as the obstruction by small traders of the streets used for transportation. These have sometimes resulted in restrictive measures, such as the relocation of market stalls in an underused underground car park (Maskrey and Turner, 1988).

There are many other problems in the urban districts, such as the many city slum *corralones* that still persist, even in the Santa Cruz sector of the affluent Miraflores district of Lima. The residents of the slums are packed within enclosing walls, narrow walkways threading between the self-built, single-cell dwelling units. As many as 30 families may share a couple of rudimentary latrines, with adjacent, a single tap sputtering an intermittent supply of water. Working as drivers, home helps or cleaners for the Miraflores wealthy and the

**Figure 22.5**
*Corralones*, or enclosed and gated slum areas, are where domestic servants and casual labourers live in minimal units. Santa Cruz, Lima, Peru.

even more affluent residents of San Isidro district, they prefer to stay in their enclave in the suburbs, to squatting in the distant mountains. Lima is built on a dry desert where it never rains, the waters of the Rio Rimac scarcely meeting the city's needs. But at least, there is a water supply of sorts for the inhabitants of the city slum quarters. Situated on the outskirts of the city, surrounded on three sides by congested slums and on the fourth by squatter settlements, the University of Lima has been sufficiently mindful of the plight of its neighbours to build a gravity-feed water filtration plant to service them. Although government and muncipality support has been variable in its extent and intensity, it has remained at a level matched by few cities in the world of comparable size and rate of expansion. Aid has come from non-government agencies and foreign aid organizations, many of them voluntary. Several hundred such aid

**Figure 22.6**
The single standpipe tap and lavatory shared by all resident *corralones* families.

organizations operate in Peru, over 150 of them in Lima itself. Their efforts are uncoordinated and special interest groups may overlook factors that lie outside their remit, so that inequalities in assistance are inevitable. Only a small number have directed their attention to building assistance, but with French co-operation agencies and the Government of the Netherlands among its partners, DESCO's Home Densification Program is aimed to effect better use of the land and the training of master builders, as well as continuing to support self-help housing (Sahley and Danziger, 1995). CALIDAD, is a municipal service linked with DESCO, which facilitates professional and technical advice and aid for families, while protecting their independence (CALIDAD, 1999). A number of official publications give advice on construction, for example in adobe to approved standards, for building in seismic zones (SENSICO, 1999).

These examples drawn from the experience of Lima indicate what can be done to assist traditional builders to cope in new settlements, reducing costs by providing their own labour, but aided by measures that give them title to land, and appropriate servicing. Problems there are, in this ever-expanding city, and it is not my intention to minimize or ignore them. But the city of Lima in a developing country has given some indications of the way in which traditional living patterns and building skills, brought with them in this example by migrating Quechua Indians, can be accommodated and supported, rather than replaced or repressed. This discussion does not permit detailed consideration of the 'push' and 'pull' factors that forced them to migrate from the rural regions in the first place. Clearly, the need for the regeneration of the rural areas is of paramount importance in reducing the outflow of people from the provinces; not merely in Peru, but in all developing countries. Urban expansion and settlement is a fact of the contemporary environment and it will increase exponentially. The almost total failure on the part of most nations to face the realities of this population growth and the housing crises it will generate, is culpable in the extreme. Where do we hear of any serious discussion of the means whereby these thousands of millions of people will be responsibly and appropriately accommodated? By any criterion, vernacular architecture constitutes by far the majority of world housing. Never costed or accounted for in the expenditure of human effort that it represents, the building and maintaining of vernacular architecture remains a prime, but grossly unrecognized, constituent of national economies in all continents.

'Tradition by itself is not enough' to solve the impending housing crisis, but neither can it be brought 'up to date' by 'perpetual criticism' and what Eliot termed 'orthodoxy'. Only support through the responsible management of resources, the encouragement of inherited skills and training in new ones, the availability of sites and access to services, and respect for the requirements and values of those who build and occupy the dwellings, can adequate housing be achieved. We need not despair of the end of tradition: on the contrary, we need to acknowledge, celebrate and actively promote it, if unimaginable misery is to be averted. The Lima experience has given some pointers as to the means whereby some of the problems may be met, while indicating many of the issues that have to be confronted. Aided with sensitivity, with the partnership of state and people, and with the autonomy of the new communities assured, traditional vernacular means of building and of organizing space to meet cultural needs, may secure the identity and integrity of future settlements around the globe.

## References


Bourdier, J.-P. and Al-Sayyad, N. (eds). (1983). *Dwellings, Settlements and Tradition*. Lanham, Maryland: University Press of America.

CALIDAD. (1999). *Un Servicio Tecnico Municipal para la Vivienda (STC)*. Lima, Peru: CALIDAD for the Municipality of Lima.

DESCO. (1996). *Enlarging Residences: Densification de la Vivienda en Villa El Salvador-Peru*. Lima: Centro de Estudios y Promocion del Desarollo, Lima, Peru.

Hartkopf, V. (1981). *Tecnicas de Construccion Autoctonas del Peru*. Washington, DC: Agencia Para El Desarollo Internacional.
Lloyd, P. (1980). *The Young Towns of Lima. Aspects of Urbanization in Peru*. Cambridge University Press, 1980.
Malinowski, B. (1945, 1961). *The Dynamics of Culture Change*. New Haven: Yale University Press.
Mangin, W.P. and Turner, J.F.C. (1969). Benavides and the Barriada movement. In: Oliver, P. (ed.). *Shelter and Society*. London: Basrie & Rockliff.
Maskrey, A. and Turner, B. (1988). Villa El Salvador. Low-income Peruvians build a new township. Turner, B. (ed.). *Building Community. A Third World Case Book*. Building Community Books, London: pp. 153–160.
Oliver, P. (1969). (ed.). *Shelter and Society*. London: Barrie & Rockliff, The Cresset Press.
Oliver, P. (1983). Handed-down architecture: Tradition and transmission. In: Bourdier, J.P. and Al-Sayyad, N. (eds). *Dwellings, Settlements and Tradition*. Lanham, Maryland: University Press of America. (Chapter 10 in this collection).
Sahley, C. and Danziger, J. (eds). (c. 1995). *Rising to the Urban Challenge? The Roles, Strategies and Performances of NGOs in Lima, Peru*. Oxford: INTRAC, Occasional Paper, No. 26.
SENSICO. (1999). *Norma Tecnica de Edification NTE E. 080: Adobe*. Lima: Reglamento de Construcciones, SENSICO, December.
Skinner, R. (1982). Self-help, community organization and politics: Villa El Salvador, Lima. In: Ward, P. (ed.). *Self-Help Housing: A Critique*. London: Mansell, pp. 209–29.

# 23

# Ethics and vernacular architecture (2000)

Those who are seriously concerned about the built environment, whether from a purely architectural viewpoint, or with particular concern for its aesthetic, ecological, sustainable or other qualitative considerations, frequently use the perceived merits of vernacular architecture to further their arguments. Examples drawn from the Greek islands, or from the Middle East for instance, may be used to illustrate the beauty and simplicity of form, the structural and economic merits of materials such as earth, or the passive modification of the internal environment by wind-scoops. Sometimes the examples may be practically based, though more often they are employed to demonstrate intuitive responses to mankind's psychological needs for meaningful spaces, harmonious forms and human scale. There is a fair measure of self-gratification in this admiration of the vernacular aesthetic and an inclination to disregard those vernacular traditions that do not satisfy the criteria of the viewer, who is rarely an ordinary member of the culture that produced the buildings. Such criteria are generally ethical, the 'purity of form', the 'truth to materials', the 'economy of means' being ascribed moral value.

Whether we can speak of the 'ethics of vernacular architecture' or even, of the 'ethic' of a specific vernacular culture, is a debatable issue and one which is seldom, if ever, addressed. For the present discussion, vernacular architecture is understood to mean the buildings of the people, built by the people. It does not refer to buildings designed and constructed by professional architects and builders for the people which, in suburban housing for instance, may be considered as 'popular' architecture. In Britain, we are accustomed to regarding vernacular architecture as the past traditions of predominately rural building, including farmhouses, barns

**Figure 23.1**
Fisherman's houses in Looe, Cornwall. Fishing tackle was usually kept in a storage space below the external stairs, where in some cases, a dinghy might be housed.

and granaries, but also village churches and chapels, windmills and watermills and, in specific regions, the workshops of craft industries. Houses, shops and premises of urban workers and artisans may also be included, as well as the boat sheds and other buildings of fishing communities (even if the buildings of fishing villages are conspicuously absent from writing on English vernacular architecture). Specialists in the British traditions generally accept that they ended with the development of the railways and the free movement of building materials, which brought about the demise of regional building. Such a determinist position has led to a concentration on the early history of those traditions and marginal attention to the cultural factors that influenced their foundation, development and continued use. Much of European vernacular study has a similarly retrospective view, but in Eastern Europe vernacular traditions have continued until recently, and in some instances still persist. When the focus of attention is shifted from the history of the buildings to their adaptation to meet changing uses and needs, it becomes apparent that vernacular architecture still constitutes a large proportion of the European, including British, domestic building stock.

Considered on a world scale, the picture is dramatically different. Bearing in mind that in broad statistical terms, all but a very small proportion of the billion people living in the Indian subcontinent dwell in vernacular buildings which they have inherited or have themselves constructed, it is evident that in any discussion of world housing the vernacular has to be seriously reckoned with. When the majority of the 1.2 billion Chinese who are similarly accommodated are added, a third of the world's population are included in the reckoning. If the dwellings, workplaces and places of worship of the peoples of South-East Asia and Indonesia, Central Asia, the Middle East, most of Africa, non-urban Latin America and a not inconsiderable proportion of the North American population are also considered, it becomes apparent that somewhere above 80 per cent of the world's buildings, and possibly even 90 per cent of dwellings, are 'vernacular' in kind (Oliver, 1997). Seen from this perspective, not only does vernacular architecture constitute the majority of all domestic buildings, it is likely to remain so for most, if not all, of the twenty-first century. At the turn of the century the global population reached six billion; predictions based on demographic trends indicate a global population of nine billion people by mid-century. Who is to build the houses that will be needed to accommodate the extra three billion people, let alone replace or maintain the bulk of the existing housing stock? It seems inescapable that the peoples of cultures the world over will be obliged to build their own. Just as the inhabitants of the burgeoning peri-urban squatter settlements are self-built with the detritus and scrap materials of the cities by the occupants themselves with no recognition or aid from national or city funds and resources, so the rapidly expanding millions, urban or rural, will find themselves in the same position.

In those countries whose wealth may grow and which recognize that their continued prosperity, let alone their political futures, will depend on the well-being, health, occupations and accommodation of untold numbers of the general populace, measures may be taken to build 'mass housing' for them. In view of their lack of concern for all but the wealthiest of clients, it seems unlikely that such housing will be initiated by multinationals and large construction companies, unless it can generate considerable profits, or is subsidized by governments or other funding agencies. Whether 'affordable'

**Figure 23.2**
An example of mass, low-cost housing. For economic reasons, such housing is to a standard design and the plan follows the inflexible grids of service systems. Costa Rica.

or 'low-cost' housing (it will not be other than low-cost) is generated by governments, by international charities, or by religious bodies to meet the inevitable demand, it raises important ethical issues. For instance, it can be argued that all people are entitled to fundamental services for their dwellings – water supply, disposal of waste including sewerage, provision of electricity, insulation or defence against extremes of weather as appropriate to the climate, rooms that ensure privacy, labour-saving devices within the kitchen, and so on. A number of these ethically justified entitlements would require technological solutions that may in themselves create problems elsewhere – such as the pollution risks arising from the nuclear generation of electricity, or the consumption of water that flushing systems for the disposal of human wastes can incur. This in turn leads to the problems of waste recycling, or composting, on a massive scale. Land is inevitably consumed with housing, but the theoretical 'saving' of land by the development of high-rise housing has often failed, further divorcing the occupants from the productive use of domestic farm plots. So it can also be argued that an ethically responsible approach to large-scale or 'mass' housing should give careful attention to the consumption of materials and the need to use renewable resources; that 'green' solutions to housing are essential for the survival of life on the planet.

Even if the problems and paradoxes of such ethical concerns for the housing of the world's poor can be resolved, the question arises as to who has the right, let alone the political will or the financial resources, to make and implement the design decisions necessary to meet these demands? Can they be made independently of the people who need to be housed? Can they in fact, be effected without their active participation? Can the vernacular, the architecture of the people and built by the people be ignored, and can such rejection of the values and traditions of cultures, however large or small, be ethically justified? Mass housing, low-cost housing, community architecture, participatory building – however termed, and at whatever scale, the external 'solution of the housing problem' means intervention: intervention by the design decisions of those beyond and outside a culture, intervention through introduced technologies, intervention by builders, contractors, services engineers. Whatever the charitable motivations and ideological justifications – the settlement of space-circulating nomads, the rehousing of the poor believed to be living in inadequate shelters, the upgrading of urban squatter settlements, the relocation of ethnic, religious or other minorities, the provision of emergency shelter and housing for the victims of disasters among them: all such measures intervene (from *inter venire*: to come between). The ethics of intervention and their relevance to vernacular architecture are therefore of paramount importance in the vital issues of the ethics of the built environment in the twenty-first century.

When considering the ethics of intervention in vernacular architecture it is necessary first to question whether there is a fundamental incompatibility in the very concept of 'the greater good'. Is ethics essentially a part of western philosophy and if so, what bearing does it have on the value systems of vernacular culture? For instance, many vernacular traditions have been used to illustrate particular architectural qualities of form, use of resources, and environmental responsiveness, of which the Dogon of Mali are among the most frequently cited. Living on the *talus*, or rock-fall of the Bandiagara escarpment, they are poised between the desert and marginally more fertile lands. Their architecture has been the subject of both anthropological and architectural study, its structural forms and anthropomorphic symbolism being much illustrated. But to speak of 'good design' being superior to 'bad' design in building would have little meaning to a people for whom the balance of the desirable and the undesirable is an essential aspect of life (Griaule and Dieterlen, 1954). Similar concepts of maintaining a balance between stability and adversity are to be found among peoples across the world. Although generalizations about the nature of the world's cultures are fraught with problems and subject to numerous exceptions, it may be argued that for the most part the ethical

**Figure 23.3**
Village of the Dogon who live on the talus slopes of the Bandiagara escarpment. The plans of their compounds are anthropomorphic and symbolic. Mali, West Africa.

issues in vernacular architecture are not abstracted by the cultures that produce it. Rather, they are part of the moral climate of a culture which may relate to ancestry and lineage, social and family structures, dependence on and nurturing of the environment, cultivation and the raising of livestock and other fundamental aspects of community life. In contexts that may vary with climate, topography, altitude, proximity to water, access to materials and many other factors, including those of accumulated knowledge and the transmission of skills, vernacular traditions have evolved and have been perfected to meet socio-cultural needs. They may range from transitory tented camps to compounds, from farm settlements to urban complexes; they may be built of animal products or moulded earth, wrought timber or dressed stone, grasses, palms and a variety of other natural and manufactured materials. Systems for modifying the climate – to protect from the weather, to promote air circulation, to cool or to insulate – will depend on prevailing climatic conditions. But these and innumerable other aspects of vernacular architecture traditions are special to the environmental and social circumstances of every culture, which largely account for their diversity and, in certain respects where conditions are comparable, their similarities.

Generating the commitment and responsibility necessary for the continuity of traditions and for development through them, are the belief systems that unify distinct cultures. Often these may relate to religions, whether pantheist or monotheist wherein the rights of the community and of the individual with respect to building,

**Figure 23.4**
Hindu *lontars*, or manuals made of dried palm leaves on which are written ancient Hindu texts on medicine, architecture and beliefs. Bali, Indonesia.

may be enshrined in sacred law. They may require rituals and customs, from dedication to obtaining materials, from the sequence of construction to 'topping-out', through which the spirits of land and household are respected, worshipped and placated. Or they may guide and prescribe all stages in the layout and raising of buildings, as do the Hindu manuals of building, the *vastu sastras*, the *manasara* or the *lontars* (Chakrabarti *et al.*, 1997). In many societies, to be a member of a household or of an extended family may involve obligations in building, while in others, guild systems may define the specialist roles and skills of craftsmen and builders. Whether obedience or default, observance or omission, are matters of ethics within vernacular cultures may remain an open question in philosophical theory, but there is little doubt that interventionism in their building practices by alien groups, whatever their reasons, raises fundamental ethical issues.

When the complexity of environments, of social life, building needs and processes, obligations and beliefs that give form and meaning to the vernacular architecture of countless cultures, are borne in mind, one might wonder under what conditions, and by whom, can intervention in vernacular architectural traditions be justified? Yet there are many circumstances, from post-war resettlement to housing following natural disasters, when external intervention is necessitated, requested, even demanded. Over the past four decades scores of such occasions have arisen, when long-term housing needs have been anticipated and design solutions implemented after initial periods of temporary or emergency accommodation.

**Figure 23.5**
Resettlement housing, Kete Krachi, Volta River, Ghana.

The methods employed and the acceptability or otherwise of the resultant housing, have afforded lessons in the ethics of intervention which, in many cases, have still to be learned.

In my personal experience, the first of these arose through the building, under President Kwame Nkrumah's direction, of the Akosombo dam across the Volta River at Tema in Ghana, West Africa in 1964. Though the dam was designed to create a great lake system which would provide the resource for the generation of hydro-electric power to advance Ghana's aluminium industry, it was also a threat to the livelihoods, the lands and the housing of many tribes and peoples in the hinterland of eastern Ghana. The greatest concentration of new housing was required in the Kete Krachi region and agriculturalists, sociologists, planners and architects were involved in effecting the transition from traditional villages to planned settlements. 80 000 people were to be displaced and resettled, for whom four types of 'core houses' were designed. With families ranging from five to 25 members, the houses had to have sufficient space for expansion, even though the compound and settlement plans were designed to a regular quadrilateral geometry.

For my part, I had been charged with developing graphic systems which would enable young Asante architects to communicate with Gurunsi (Nabdam) tribes people in the north of Ghana in the event that they too, would have to be relocated, should the Volta waters rise still higher. The compounds of the Nabdam were complexes of

**Figure 23.6**
A Nabdam family compound, northern Ghana.

cylindrical, single-cell units of moulded mud, linked with enclosing walls. Dwelling units were often flat-roofed, with low parapets and notched log ladders; granaries and stores were capped with cones of elephant-grass thatch (Prussin, 1968). The land on which the houses were constructed belonged to the ancestors, to whom libations were offered by an intercessionary priest, the *tendaana*, who determined where new compounds should be built. I was deeply concerned that the compound forms and customs of the northern people would be overlooked in the urgency of resettlement. A subsequent book on the project confirmed my fears: a misleading photograph of 'a northern compound' showed rectilinear buildings with *brise soleils*, which were in fact, of one of the standard house types designed for the new settlements (Chambers, 1970). Four house types were used, all employing lateritic soil-cement blocks, 4 × 2″ timber purlins and aluminium sheet roofs. Generally, one room of 150 square feet was completed, a further roof provided for a 120 square foot room, and an L-plan floor slab permitted the building of a kitchen, stoep and porch. Soon a settlement near Akosombo presented a 'problem of controlling a large number of unauthorized structures', mainly kitchens and 'bathrooms' made of used corrugated iron, bamboo and old packing cases (Danby, in Chambers, 1970). Entitled *The Volta Resettlement Experience*, the book gave accounts of the 'experience' of designers, agronomists and sociologists. Needless to say, it expressed nothing of the experience of those who were resettled. E.A.K. Kalitsi, the Ghanaian in charge of the Volta project, acknowledged that 'it is easier to evacuate people to the settlement towns than to keep them there'. Many of the evacuees soon drifted from the new sites: 'the spectre of the ghost town hangs over every settlement we have built', he wrote (Kalitsi, 1970). I did not remain in Ghana long enough to learn their eventual fate, but the problems of the ethics of intervention arose repeatedly, in diverse cultural contexts across the world. Some were in the name of 'improvement', others as 'advocacy planning' or 'aided self-help' in diverse contexts that generally involved 'emergency' methods.

It was a story that was repeated scores of times in diverse cultural contexts, as I witnessed for myself in Central America, Eastern Europe, Turkey, East Africa, the Indian subcontinent, China and elsewhere. Design decisions were taken on behalf of national and regional authorities in circumstances of resettlement or post-disaster housing, often with little or no regard for indigenous values and patterns of settlement. While the intentions were often with the interests of the subject communities in mind, the planning policies, building forms, spatial allocation and arrangement, and the use of 'modern materials' in construction, were determined by professional planners and architects. In the majority of cases, they had scarcely visited the selected sites, much less discussed the proposed developments with those who were to live in them. In some instances, there appear to have been ulterior motives for this, that bring the ethics of intervention further into question. Such was the case in Borneo, where indigenous peoples such as the Dayaks, Dusun, Kenyah and others, live by traditional systems that they pursued long before Indonesia and Malaysia assumed power over their territories. One of the largest of the Dyak cultures are the Iban, who live in contiguous family units, or *bileks*, beneath common roofs that form 'longhouses'. In effect, the longhouse is a village on piles, within the length of which runs a broad 'street', the *tempuan*, linking the individual family *bileks*. Communal work and social space, sleeping space for guests, and often an outdoor platform, the *tanju*, also run in parallel along the longhouse which, in some cases, may be as much as 200 m in length. Animist in their beliefs, the Iban are swidden farmers, whose movement, settlement, territorial claims and boundaries have brought them into conflict with government regulations and administrations for most of the present century (Freeman, 1970).

Living on land which contained sought-after minerals and gravels, the Iban of northern Sarawak and Brunei were still under pressure when I visited some of their longhouses in the early 1990s. The

**Figure 23.7**
A fine example of an Iban longhouse, virtually a village under one roof, which was threatened with destruction, as excavation for gravel rapidly advanced. Brunei.



longhouses ranged from a traditional structure built more than 60 years previously, to a large painted longhouse, only 3 years old, with vinyl floor covering and strip-lighting in the *tempuan*, and glazed windows to the *bileks* that opened on to it. The residents of both were being induced to move to the outskirts of the city of Brunei. By the customary standards of resettlement housing, the houses on offer were superior in quality, with high concrete piles, tiled and pitched roofs, spacious accommodation and garden plots around each building. A house could be secured with a minimal payment which could be spread over several years. My Iban informants told me that the only other considerations were that the residents would give up swidden farming and move to the city, that they would no longer live in a longhouse, and that they would adopt the Muslim faith. The cost of the new houses was the abandonment of their culture and the loss of their identity. At the time of viewing, all but a couple of the new houses were standing empty. If the price to pay for new housing was unacceptable to Iban in this region, related groups of Iban in other parts of Sarawak and Kalimantan have had their longhouses destroyed. They have been forced to move from their forest homelands, being accused of causing destructive fires by the 'slash-and-burn' methods of swidden farming. Whether or not the conflagrations were deliberately fired to clear the undergrowth during the reckless plundering of the forest hardwoods for short-term profits is a matter of debate, but it is clear that other, ethically questionable, interests than those of the Iban are served by their removal and resettlement. Apart from dubious motivations, ethical problems arise when the housing is constrained by concepts of design that are not compatible with the life-ways, needs and values of the victim culture. Yet rehousing, as in post-disaster and refugee circumstances, is often initiated for altruistic reasons, and the results can be sympathetic.

Traditional building on the Greek island of Santorini in the Cyclades, has long been admired by architects (Philippides, 1983). Subject to piracy and invasion in a long and troubled history, the islanders were prone to many influences. Yet they developed a way of building that was appropriate to the rough and undulating terrain, which was distinctive in its forms and construction. The volcanic explosion of Thira reputedly destroyed the Minoan civilization in Crete, but the crater rim which constitutes Santorini island has supported a small population that has farmed its volcanic soils for many centuries. Typically, the peasant houses were vaulted, though they were often extended with flat-roofed terraces, built of black and red volcanic rock, and later with pumice, bonded with tephra (pozzolana), which 'is rich in silica and poor in lime, so that on mixing with a quantity of lime and water a solid homogeneous mass is produced, absolutely impervious to water'. The vault was 'laid on a framework of branches and weeds, tephra mortar joining long stones carefully placed in horizontal bands from springing to crown' (Radford and Clark, 1974). The single cell was often internally divided into living

**Figure 23.8**
Vernacular houses at Emborion village, Santorini. Several houses are cubic in form, while many with a rectangular plan have vaulted roofs. Cyclades, Greece.

and sleeping areas, while light and access were gained by two windows and a door in the gable end wall, and a skylight in the upper semicircular gable. A plaster of pozzolana and water was laid over the wall surfaces which were often colour-washed with ochre. Underground cisterns for the storage of rainwater were used in all houses. To defend themselves against invaders and pirates the wealthier families in the seventeenth century enclosed themselves in hilltop fortified settlements, or *kastelia*. Pyrgos, in the south centre of Santorini, was typical, the vaulted houses of the peasants being outside the *kasteli* on the lower slopes of the hill. This differentiated village structure continued until the island was hit by disaster.

In 1956, a powerful earthquake on Santorini caused extensive damage, such that only one church or chapel among more than 200 on the island, survived unscathed. In the town of Pyrgos, the *kasteli* was totally destroyed and large areas of the rest of the town were demolished. Even so, partial vaults of severely damaged houses were still in evidence over 40 years later. To avoid further landslides much of the ruinous hilltop had been capped with concrete, when the reconstruction programme of the Greek Ministry of Public Works Housing Department commenced. The architectural team endeavoured to restore houses where possible, but approval for loans against rebuilding meant that many houses were replaced. However, literally hundreds of houses were constructed to accommodate the homeless. Following discussions with local people, the vaulted roof of the vernacular buildings was 'chosen as a form in

**Figure 23.9**
Post-disaster houses, built with a pair of vaults and a courtyard. Some owners made vertical extensions to provide dowry houses for newly married daughters. Santorini.

the new construction since it offered economy in cost, speed of construction and reflective qualities' (Noussia, 1992). Most housing units consisted of parallel vaults, sometimes opening on to a loggia or a yard in which a cistern and wash-house could be built. The side walls of the house had a partially exposed ring beam so that a bearing ledge for subsequent extension was possible, a provision which acknowledged the local ethic that a family head should provide a dowry house or extension for his eldest daughter.

Over 35 years later, in the town of Pyrgos and in similar villages where the earthquake victims had been extensively rehoused, the success of the building policy was evident. Large numbers of short rows of vaulted homes, or free-standing single and double-vault units stood with little or no modification. Local builders had been instructed in the new methods, including reinforced concrete construction, and had been capable of extending other houses, setting further vaults at right angles, and even building above the vaults by spanning them with raised slabs. The over-riding impression was one of a continuing vernacular tradition, which did not hinder those who wished to enlarge their properties, but which established continuity between the past and the future while meeting, with safety and sensitivity, the physical, social and environmental needs of the culture. Regrettably, recent housing developments, hotels and the 'second homes' of Athenian vacationists have not recognized or responded positively to the example set by the reconstruction programme. However, this does not bring into question the achievement of its architects and builders, who did not intervene, but who worked with the community to produce a rare model of rehousing appropriately within a vernacular context.

When these instances of intervention in housing are considered, certain fundamental lessons emerge. The ethics of one-off elite architecture may require that the designer meets the brief to the best of his creative abilities, but the ethics of housing for communities requires more. The architect may design responsibly, but the process fails when he ignores the values, mores, building skills, experience and wisdom of the cultures whose housing needs are to be met. Housing that involves the active participation of the community, which accommodates its values, relates to its vernacular traditions while meeting its aspirations. That which retains or remains substantially as the housing of and by the people, is the housing most likely to succeed. If the housing of the billions in the twenty-first century is not to result in design debacles of unprecedented scale, these and many other lessons in the ethics of building must be learned, understood and effected in practice.

## References


Chambers, R. (ed). (1970). *The Volta Resettlement Experience.* London: Pall Mall Press.

Charkrabarti, V. *et al.* (1997). Vastu sastras, 552–553; and Sulistayawati, A. Lontars (Bali) 560–561. In: Oliver, P. (ed.). *The Encyclopedia of Vernacular Architecture of the World.* Cambridge: Cambridge University Press.

Danby, M. (1970). House design. In: Chambers, *op cit.* 164–178.

Doumanis, O. and Oliver, P. (eds). (1974). *Shelter in Greece.* Athens: Architecture in Greece Press.

Freeman, D. (1970). *Report on the Iban.* London: The Athlone Press.

Griaule, M. and Dieterlen, G. (1954). The Dogon. In: Forde, C.D. (ed.). *African Worlds.* London: Oxford University Press.

Kailitsi, E.A.K. (1970). Present and future problems of administering resettlement towns. In: Chambers *op. cit.* 217–225.

Noussia, A. (1992). Revisiting the tourist landscape: The dynamics of change of the traditional environment in Santorini. In: *Traditional Dwellings and Settlements.* Working Papers, Vol. XXXV, 55–98.

Oliver, P. (ed.). (1997). *The Encyclopedia of Vernacular Architecture of the World*, 3 vols. Cambridge: Cambridge University Press.

Philippides, D. (1983). Santorini. In: Philippides, D. (ed.). *Greek Traditional Architecture*, Vol. 2. Aegean: Cyclades. Athens: Melissa, 147–178.

Prussin, L. (1968). *Architecture in Northern Ghana. A Study in Forms and Functions.* Berkeley: University of California Press.

Radford, A. and Clark, G. (1974). Cyclades; Studies of a building vernacular. In: Doumanis and Oliver, *op. cit.* 64–82.

# 24

# Necessity and sustainability: The impending crisis (2002)

Although the history of vernacular architecture studies remains to be written, the close of the nineteenth century witnessed an increasing awareness in the west of the significance of buildings in the lives of indigenous peoples encountered in newly explored regions. A growing interest in 'folk' traditions also alerted some European investigators to the loss of traditional buildings through military conflicts, industrialization, expansion of the railroads and colonization. Early studies in, for instance, the pueblo architecture of Native American peoples of the south-west United States by Victor Mindeleff (1891) or the pioneering work on the *Houses and House-life of the American Aborigines* by Lewis H. Morgan (1881) are among the first serious examples of documentation. Admiration of the work of medieval craftsmen inspired William Morris and the Arts and Crafts movement – but also had the negative effect of consigning the study of the vernacular to archaeology, history or nostalgic imitation.

While valuable work was done in many countries by explorers, anthropologists, geographers and by no means least, by military surveyors and colonial officials, their work was often achieved in isolation or in the pursuit of another objective. Anthropologists paid a little more attention to buildings in the 1930s, a landmark in vernacular research being the publication of *Conversations with Ogotommeli* by the French anthropologist Marcel Griaule (1949) which revealed the symbolism and values attached to the buildings of the Dogon of Mali. If there was little co-ordination of research activities until after the Second World War, a concerted effort to document the rural architecture of the French provinces was conducted during the Occupation, even though it remained unpublished until

**Figure 24.1**
*Kanaga* symbol on a Dogon granary or shrine. The *kanaga* is the symbol of creation, expressed in binary pairs, parallels and oppositions (see also Figure 23.3). Mali.

the 1980s. This work placed particular emphasis on typology, an approach which was also to dominate American studies of vernacular traditions. In Great Britain, research into Welsh vernacular building by Iorwerth Peate, Sir Cyril Fox and Lord Raglan among others, led to their post-war publication, but it was L.F. Salzman's documentary history of *Building in England down to 1540* that was markedly influential on the archaeological approach of British specialists in the field (Salzman, 1952). Mapping the distribution of cruck frames, dating by means of dendrochronology, the recording of regional techniques in carpentry, or the pursuit of the earliest incidence of certain architectural features, still remain dominant in British vernacular studies.

Research in various parts of the world, such as Japan or Nepal, tended to favour the more monumental architecture, as it did

**Figure 24.2**
Masked dancers in the Dogon *dama* funeral ritual. Several wear the *kanaga* mask. Part of the village lies up the slope to the left. Tireli, Bandiagara escarpment, Mali.

in Europe, but some studies were made, including J.-P. Lebeuf's *Habitation des Fali* (Lebeuf, 1961), revealing to a scattered and specialized readership the richness in form and meaning of some vernacular traditions in the Middle East, South and West Africa, and Asia. Prompted by a number of architects, the exhibition *Architecture Without Architects* organized at the Museum of Modern Art, New York by Bernard Rudofsky, attracted a much wider audience. Mainly pictorial, it tended to fix an aesthetic image of the vernacular which has persisted in a large number of popular books on the subject (Rudofsky, 1964). At the end of the 1960s, the publication of Amos Rapoport's *House Form and Culture* (1969) and the essays based on fieldwork in *Shelter and Society* and subsequent works in the 'Shelter' series, which synthesized architectural documentation and anthropological research into culture and building, indicated an alternative approach (Oliver, 1969). In the ensuing decades, the volume of research increased greatly with important works on the building traditions of Scandinavia, the Netherlands and Belgium, the Balkans and Greece, Mexico, Venezuela, India and South-East Asia joining the considerable number published on the vernacular of Africa, North America and the British Isles. Almost without exception, these studies were made as records, in Morgan's terms, of 'houses' or 'house-life', often with the intention of documenting them in anticipation of their imminent destruction. Frequently they were perceived as traditions that had passed or were in decline, or as appealing testimonies to a way of living that was of another era; there was little consideration of the role they might play in living in the future.

International and cross-cultural studies of the vernacular in architectural education were slow to develop. One of the most accomplished of studies to be made in the early post-war years was by a group of architectural students from L'Ecôle des Beaux-Arts de Paris who spent 6 months (1949–1950) in the Cameroun. Published in 1952, *L'Habitat au Cameroun* was exemplary in the quality of the draughtsmanship, photography, identification of spaces and functions, and record of the building processes (Beguin *et al.*, 1952). In some schools of architecture there had been a slowly growing awareness that vernacular architecture might have lessons for the student. At the New Bauhaus directed by expatriate Laszlo Moholy-Nagy in Chicago in the 1930s, G.F. Keck organized a programme for each new student intake which involved, somewhat paradoxically, 'the design of a primitive house'. By designing log cabins, grass huts and skin tents he believed that they would make the 'resourceful discovery of fundamental principles by the diligent evaluation of technological and biological requirements' (Moholy-Nagy, 1956). It was influential and adopted by a number of schools in the United States and Europe, among them the Architectural Association School of Architecture in London, where I joined the staff in 1961. For many years, Professor Giancarlo Cataldi and faculty at the Universita degli Studi di Firenze, Italy, developed a *Tipologie Primitive* programme with their students (Cataldi *et al.*, 1987), while at the Polytechnique Federale de Lausanne under the direction of Professor Frederic Aubry, students built rigorously dimensioned large-scale models of the vernacular architecture of many cultures (Aubry and Berilacqua, 1980).

While I admired the thoroughness with which these models were constructed, and had no doubts as to their benefit to architectural students in learning some of the fundamentals of their chosen subject, I felt that there was much more that they needed to learn. One problem was that the 'primitive hut' programme in whatever form it took, was confined to the first year of their education, whereas I believed that as they confronted the world as it is, students needed to study vernacular architecture in their final year. It was not a commonly held view, but at the Architectural Association, even in the 'Archigram' decade, it was possible for me to lecture extensively on traditional building in many cultures, and later to introduce the subject in the newly formed graduate school. To my great satisfaction, numerous past students – such as the Development Workshop team – have made important contributions to housing in Africa and other parts of the developing world, often through technology transfer and with deep respect for local vernacular traditions.

**Figure 24.3**
Section of a Matakam compound, drawn by students of l'Ecole Nationale Superieure des Beaux Arts de Paris. Cameroun, 1950.

**Figure 24.4**
Model of a ma'dan, or Marsh Arab, *mudhif* which was a meeting house constructed of reeds in Southern Iraq. First year architectural student project at the Ecôle Polytechnique Federale de Lausanne, Switzerland.

It was the growth in specialist publications on vernacular architecture, but the lack of a more widely accessible book which brought together some of the range and diversity of vernacular traditions, that prompted me to write *Dwellings; The House Across the World* (Oliver, 1984). I make no apology for the autobiographical nature of much of this paper, for a year later, in 1988, I was invited to compile the first world encyclopedia of the subject. With Oxford Brookes University School of Architecture providing us with a base, and with the support of a number of grants, a small but dedicated team set about tracing sources, building the database and finding contributors. Potential authors all over the world were identified, invited and in many cases, visited, so that they could be briefed as to the purposes, content, mapping and referencing of entries. Even so, I had to write 250 entries myself, not on the themes of most interest to me but largely on subjects such as sanitation in vernacular buildings, on which relatively little had been published. A decade in the making, *The Encyclopedia of Vernacular Architecture* was intended above all, to be an educational tool which would ensure that basic information on vernacular architecture extant in the twentieth century would be available. In my view an understanding of the vernacular is essential to the education of architects and the practice of architecture in much of the world. In fact, I believe that it should be part of the education of every politician, social scientist and economist who ventures an opinion or decision concerning the built environment, in any continent.

If design professionals have only a limited understanding of traditional environments, most politicians, businessmen, scientists, journalists and even many educationalists are frequently uninformed about them. As evidence of this, we may consider the extent to which there are references in their pronouncements, their publications, teaching, or the media to issues related to vernacular environments of any period, let alone the immediate future. Except for archaeology or medieval history, passing references to poverty and living in 'mud huts' is about as much as we are likely to hear. This is a situation that must not last, for the implications of this neglect could be devastating, especially in view of the rapid growth in world population. Less familiar to many of us are the projections of global population expansion. There are many factors to be considered when making these projections, such as natural increase, greater longevity and reduced infantile deaths due to improved health programmes, family planning, food production and distribution, climate change, whether cyclic or induced, ethical or religious objections and dictats, civil and international agreements and disputes, and much else. But generally, the demographers are in accord with the estimated growth of the global population by 50 per cent during the next half century.

Where, we may ask, and how, and by whom are these extra three billion people to be housed, notwithstanding the need for adequate housing for those who are alive at present, and who may still be living in extreme impoverishment in the future. Many planners state that already nearly half the world's population is urban. Rather than consider that, by definition, this means that half the world is non-urban and rural, they discuss the effects of continuing urban expansion. It is illuminating to note that the plethora of conferences held in the year 2000 by architects and planners were devoted, almost without exception, to the future of the city (see list of architectural conferences at the end of this chapter). There was a considerable measure of self-interest in this, with speakers repeatedly advocating a return to high-rise building in view of land shortages and communication costs, even though this solution has failed demonstrably in many contexts. Obviously, the problems vary in complexity and scale in different parts of the world, and are made greater still in regions, for example, with high birth-rates, with disadvantaged economies or with susceptibility to natural disasters. In varying degree such measures for conservation, or the lack of them, may be the fate of many of the traditional environments, including their vernacular architecture, of Europe. Yet, in much of the rest of the world, including the Middle East, the Indian peninsula, Central

**Figure 24.5**
With every space utilized, migrants live wherever they can, some building rudimentary shelters on the pavements. Khaligat, Calcutta, India.

and Eastern Asia, South-East Asia and Oceania, West, Central and southern Africa and non-urban Latin America, vernacular traditions have been sustained and, in a great many cultural contexts, are thriving. Building in naturally occurring materials, including earths, stone, timber, bamboo, palm and grasses, is to be found in a remarkable diversity of forms, in accordance with the socio-environmental and symbolic requirements of the cultures that construct them. A variety of technologies is employed, with specialized skills developed in response to environmental conditions and physical properties.

**Figure 24.6**
A man prepares stripped bamboo to tie components of the house that he is building for himself, and his family. Central Java, Indonesia.

In some regions, cultures are under pressure to 'modernize', but the realities of political and economic constraints make this unachievable, except in some cases in electronic hardware. Water supply, sanitation and waste disposal, the consumption of renewable resources and the exhaustion of others, remain as problems which are often scarcely addressed, especially where disparities between the affluent and the impoverished are endemic. Traditional environments are sustained extensively in the non-urban half of the world, but with the global expansion of multinationals they could be threatened with extinction. The concept of 'mass housing', which developed with the patronizing disassociation of architects and planners from the people and their perception of the majority of the populace as an unsophisticated 'mass', persists today. It may be expressed in the revival of arguments in favour of the multistorey point and slab housing blocks of the 1960s, but even more so in advocacy for prefabricated, professedly low-cost developments of standardized components, subordinated to rigid planning. Many projects of this kind were embarked upon in areas left devastated in the wake of the vast destruction of houses and environments, created by the South-East Asian *tsunami* at the close of 2004.

When people are forced by economic or environmental decline to migrate from the rural regions to the cities, they rarely share in the urban prosperity but suffer as the most disadvantaged of the populace. Without their skills and knowledge, developed and passed on by successive generations within the vernacular context, few would be able to build a dwelling or simply survive within the peri-urban squatter settlements which constitute a high proportion of target cities. They continue to expand unremittingly, while the future 'sustainability' of the world's cities is optimistically projected and glamorized in a seemingly endless stream of reports and conferences. Problems of the continually expanding and scarcely sustainable cities, though rarely addressed, are largely the outcome of the neglect or ignorance of the impoverished rural regions of the world (the world's cities even now occupy just 2 per cent of the land). In the lists of keynote papers and the catalogues of contributions to these hothouses of architectural dialogue, one looks in vain for serious consideration of the regeneration of rural regions, of the alleviation of distress in both city and country through decentralized economies, or of supportive infrastructures for the half of the world's population that has no system of sanitation and the billions who have no access to clean water. Even the worldwide dependence on the massive contribution to housing made by vernacular builders is scarcely recognized, let alone the importance of culturally and contextually appropriate architectural and environmental design which respects it.

By the phrase 'sustained traditional environments', I refer not only to the monumental religious and civic architecture inherited from the past but also to the vernacular dwellings, functional and symbolic structures, and other architectural expressions in their environmental contexts, whether natural, adapted or modified, sustained by indigenous cultures the world over. Although it is a much-used term in the discussion of the design of future, notably urban, environments, 'sustainability' is seldom employed with any reference to the inheritance of the vernacular architecture traditions of the past and present. By its very nature, one might even say by its very definition, vernacular architecture is *sustained* architecture, sustained over generations by the persistence of traditions, but subject to appropriate modification as changes in the needs of different societies have arisen. While it may appear to be economically less justified, monolithic resettlement programmes should be replaced, I believe, by numbers of smaller, regionally based schemes centred on existing cultural identities and involving community participation at all levels. It would be fundamental for such schemes to be initiated in the light of the ethical, cultural, economic and practical implications of resettlement, while seeking to determine and promote sustainable local economies. Housing schemes and settlement plans based on European models should be eschewed. Each culture has its specific identity, expressed in innumerable ways, but of which

**Figure 24.7**
A bustee, or settlement built by migrants to the city, which has been 'consolidated' with basic services and extra materials for improving the housing. Changula, Calcutta, India.

dwellings and other buildings, whether social or functional, are of exceptional importance in relating to its values and pursuits. A community should be consolidated rather than relocated, remaining as close as is practicable to its present situation, in order to reduce the trauma of resettlement. To achieve re-establishment, a great many cultures would be able to construct their own houses to meet their needs and in accord with their traditional norms. The cost in terms of organization would be largely offset by the deployment of local skills and building know-how, and immeasurably by the involvement of the people in the resuscitation of their societies.

## The educational challenge

While the economies of many nations and cultures are not in a position to finance extensive housing, they could support the continuity of traditional environments and respond to their trends in development by careful planning and appropriate servicing. The embodied values of existing vernacular traditions should be recognized rather than repressed, with respect for indigenous cultural norms and environmental knowledge. This also applies to the employment of local resources and the recovery of traditional building skills. For such a programme in the sustaining of traditional environments to be successful there would be many unavoidable implications for governments and local administrations. In particular, they would profoundly affect policies of education, both in general terms and in the specialized education and training of architects, planners, engineers and social scientists. In this, professional ethics, inter- and cross-cultural studies, the economic recognition of aided self-help and many other principles and practices all play their part. But, by whom, and in what circumstances, will these challenges of necessity, continuity, cultural values and the sustainability of the vernacular, be met in the new millennium?

How are architects and designers to be prepared for the tasks that face them and, in an era of global opportunities when 'more and more UK architects are heading overseas', how are they likely to cope without such preparation? A feature in the *RIBA Journal* highlighted these problems when a few expatriate architects summarized their experiences: 'Most westerners who spend time in Asia soon realize that the more they learn the less they understand', wrote one. Another observed that 'it was difficult to meet ordinary Russians. Life tended to revolve around a rather closed, ex-pat community'. 'Japanese culture and etiquette is different from ours. My advice is, recognize this but don't worry about it', another recommended. Less insulated was the caution of an architect in Saudi Arabia: 'Take time to first understand the culture here, founded on Islam, before getting to grips with business ethics and requirements.' Only one acknowledged indigenous skills. 'Traditional buildings skills in stone laying, woodworking, wood carving, thatching and plastering are very good in Zimbabwe.... We arranged for bricks to be manufactured on site. Not only were these cheaper... they make use of the largely unemployed local labour force' (Stungo, 2000). Such lessons, largely learned on site and for which there is generally no preparation, are common enough. Frequently, indigenous values are insensitively treated, and in the pursuit of lucrative design projects and contracts, local cultures are simply ignored, and traditional building practices disregarded. While in some instances this may be wilful, the inevitable result of an unwavering commitment to, and belief in, western technology and social systems, in other cases it may be simply due to a lack of knowledge and understanding of the diversity of building traditions and their relationship to the distinctive qualities of the cultures that produce them. *The Encyclopedia of Vernacular Architecture of the World* was compiled in part to provide such information. Concerned as I was that to leave the situation was untenable, I believed it to be important that a resource be developed that would give opportunities for study for those who were concerned about the world's vernacular environments.

Nevertheless, publication was not enough; based on the publications and ephemera that I had gathered over several decades, the International Vernacular Architecture Studies Unit (IVAU) was established at the Department of Architecture, Oxford Brookes University in 1997. Moreover, it was clear that the preparation of architects, and those who were concerned about the global environment issues, but particularly housing in the developing world, offered a major challenge to design education. Concurrently, I sought and obtained university validation for an unprecedented Master's course in International Studies in Vernacular Architecture (ISVA). With the issues summarized above borne in mind, faculty members who have taught on the course over the years endeavoured to confront many of the problems of world housing, and to review the part that vernacular architecture in both country and city will play in meeting them. Certain components were requisite, for participating students. Among these are the philosophy and theory of vernacular architecture; the anthropology of shelter, including houses and house-life seen from a cross-cultural perspective; project-based studies in tradition

**Figure 24.8**
Students on the ISVA course commenced by examining the fundamental factors of environment, economy and security which were met by Bronze Age settlers. Grimspound, Dartmoor (see also Figure 1.3).

and sustainability; vernacular resources and technology in different environmental contexts; field studies and workshops abroad; and experience and skills exchange between participants. Optional studies included the cultural geography and sustainability of vernacular architecture on a worldwide basis; climate and building; natural hazards and traditional building, emphasizing vulnerability and safe practices; policies and practices relating to the conservation of the vernacular; designing in a vernacular context, based on specific projects and international fieldwork; and vernacular architecture in development, which considered the role of building traditions in the twenty-first century (Latter, 2005).

Students from all continents have taken the course, but IVAU does not desire, nor intend, to remain unique; on the contrary, it considers that vernacular architecture studies, and others that engage with the impact of globalization, or the economics of development, should be components in the course in every school of architecture. They should be supported and given full recognition by the Royal Institute of British Architects, and by equivalent bodies in all other countries offering graduate courses in architecture. As the ISVA Position Statement (1997) makes clear: 'We believe it to be essential for the welfare of the environment and of present and future generations that much more should be known about vernacular traditions, so that they may be supported all over the world, and architect-designed buildings can relate to them. Architectural responses to building needs must be developed that respect local traditions, rather than attempt to apply universal design solutions, irrespective of cultural diversity and differing aspirations.'

Vernacular architecture may be regarded by some as a romantic and engaging inheritance from the past, but it has proved to be remarkably enduring all over the globe. Whether the 'technological revolution' of the new century will principally serve the wealthier nations and the multinationals, or will have value and benefit for the impoverished peoples of the developing world, remains to be seen. Whatever the outcome, the implications of future housing and other building demand on land, on the environment, on material resources, water and energy consumption, climatic change from industrial and other emissions, among many other factotrs, will be massive, perhaps incalculable. Their impact on countless cultures, embracing their social and domestic life-ways including, in terms of building, labour and skills, could be profound and probably irreparable. The challenge to architects and to architectural education cannot be disregarded any longer. Vernacular traditions, recognized and encouraged, appropriately supported and serviced, augmented and complemented, may prove to be the only realistic and sustainable solution to the housing and building demands of the future, throughout much of the world.

## References


Aubry, F. and Bevilacqua, M. (1980). Constructions rurales du canton du Vaud. *Architecture et Comportement* No, 1. Saint Saphorin.

Beguin, J.-P. *et al.* (1952). *Habitat au Cameroun.* L'Office de la Recherche Scientifique, Outré-mer Paris.

Cataldi, G. *et al.* (1987). *Typologie primitive.* Florence: Universita degli Studi.

Cuisenier, J. Raulin, H. and Francois, C. (1980). *L'Architecture Rurale Francaise.* Lyon: La Manufacture, (40 vols).

Griaule, M. (1949, 1965). *Conversations with Ogotemmêli. An Introduction to Dogon Religious Ideas.* Oxford University Press.

Latter, R. (2005). Educating architects to be more culturally sensitive. In Asquith, L. and Vellinga, M. (eds). *Vernacular Architecture in the Twenty-first Century. Theory, Education and Practice.* London: Routledge.

Lebeuf, J.P. (1961). *L'Habitation des Falis, Montagnards du Cameroun. Septentrional.* Librairie Hachette.

Mass observation reports and projects 1940s *et seq.*

Mindeleff, V. and Mindeleff, C. (1891). *A Study of Pueblo Architecture: Tusayan and Cibola.* Bureau of American Ethnology, 8th Report. Washington DC: Smithsonian.

Moholy-Nagy, L. (1956). *Vision in Motion.* Chicago: Paul Theobald & Co., p. 98.

Morgan, L.H. (1881, 1965). *Houses and House-Life of the American Aborigines.* North American Ethnology, Vol. 4. Washington, DC. Republished, University of Chicago Press.
Oliver, P. (ed.) (1969). *Shelter & Society.* London: Barrie, Cresset Press.
Oliver, P. (ed.) (1973). *Shelter in Africa.* London: Barrie & Rockliff.
Oliver, P. (ed.) (1975). *Shelter, Sign and Symbol.* London: Barrie & Jenkins.
Oliver, P. (1984). *Dwellings: The House Across the World.* Phaidon, Oxford, revised and enlarged edition (2003) *Dwellings: The Vernacular House World-Wide.* London: Phaidon Press.
Oliver, P. (ed). (1997). *The Encyclopedia of Vernacular Architecture of the World.* Volume One: 'Theories and Principles'; Volume Two: 'Asia and Europe'; Volume Three: 'Americas and Sub-Saharan Africa'; Bibliography, Glossary, International Lexicon, Index of Locations; General Index.
Position Statement *ISVA Course Handbook* (1997), p iii. Course modules in detail, pp. 17–37. International Studies in Vernacular Architecture (ISVA) MA Course, Centre for Vernacular Architecture Studies Unit, School of the Built Environment, Oxford Brookes University.
Rapoport, A. (1969). *House Form and Culture.* Englewood Cliffs, NJ: Prentice-Hall.
Rudofsky, B. (1964). *Architecture Without Architects.* Museum of Modern Art.
Salzman, L.F. (1952). *Building in England Down to 1540.* Oxford University Press.
Stungo, N. (2000). World service. *RIBA Journal* May, pp. 86–88. Contributions by Appli, G. (Singapore); Davies, R. (Russia); Barr, J. (Japan); Young, J. (Saudi Arabia); Vermeulen, B. (Zimbabwe).

## Architectural conferences in year 2000

*Millennium Conference: Cities and Sustainability.* University of Moratuwa, Sri Lanka.
*Sustainable & Humane Cities.* University of San Tomas, Manila, Philippines.
*Sustainable Cities, Sustainable Development.* 17th Inter-Schools Conference.
*City 2K.* RIBA, with University of Cambridge.
*Sustainable Cities for the 21st Century.* Oxford Brookes University.
*Cities for the New Millennium.* Lowry Centre, Manchester.
*Urban Futures.* Johannesburg, South Africa.

# Conferences and publications

## Introduction

The introduction summarizes the contexts in which papers were given, and themes discussed in the seven parts.

**1. Why study vernacular architecture?**
Address to the Ecôle d'Architecture, Universitaire Polytechnique, Lausanne, Switzerland, c. 1980 (unpublished)

**2. The importance of the study of vernacular architecture**
Keynote paper to ICOMOS Seminario Internacional Mexico City, 1993 (unpublished)

**3. Problems of definition and praxis**
Keynote paper to 8th International Conference on Theoretical and Practical Issues of Monumental Conservation, VA Heritage, Tusnad, Rumania. 1999. (Published in *Vernacular Architecture Heritage*, Dorottya Makay (ed.). Transylvania Trust Foundation, 1999, pp. 7–10)

**4. Learning from Asante**
Keynote Paper to Environment and Behaviour Studies Conference, Southeastern University, Nanjing, China, 2000 (unpublished)

**5. Cultural traits and environmental contexts: Cultural specificity and cross-cultural comparability**
Keynote paper to IAPS-CSBE Conference on Culture and Space in the Home Environment, Istanbul, Turkey 1999

**6. Huizhou and Herefordshire: A comparative study**
Keynote Paper to Second International Symposium, IAPS-CSBE Network, Amasya, Turkey 2001: Traditional Environments in a New Millennium (published Istanbul, 2002)

**7. Tout confort: Culture and comfort**
Address to the School of Architecture, Louisiana State University, Baton Rouge, 1986. (Unpublished)

**8. Vernacular know-how**
Keynote paper to International Vernacular Workshop, EAAE, School of Architecture, METU, Ankara, Turkey, 1982. (Published in *Vernacular Architecture. Paradigms of Environmental Response*, Mete Turan (ed.). Avebury, 1990, pp. 146–160)

**9. Earth as a building material today**
Paper presented at St. Catherine's College, Oxford. (Published in *Oxford Art Journal*, Vol 5, (2). 1983, pp. 31–38)

**10. Handed down architecture: Tradition and transmission**
Keynote paper to IASTE Conference Dwelling, Settlements and Tradition, Cross Cultural Perspectives. Berkeley, Ca, 1988. (published J.-P. Bourdier, N. Al-Sayyad (eds), Universities Press of North America, Lanham, 1989, pp. 53–75)

**11. Technology transfer: A vernacular view**
Keynote paper for Vancouver Workshop on East–West Technology Exchange 2002. (Published in *Buildings, Culture and Environment*, Raymond J. Cole and Richard Lorch (eds), Oxford, 2003, pp. 246–268).

**12. The cultural context of shelter provision**
Paper to conference on Disasters and the Small Dwelling, Oxford Polytechnic, 1978. (Published Ian Davis (ed.). Pergamon Press, 1980, pp. 39–42)

**13. Earthen housing and cultures in seismic areas**
Paper to conference on Earth Building in Earthquake Zones. University of New Mexico, 1984. (Published in *Transactions*, Intertect, Santa Fe, 1984)

**14. Factors affecting the acceptability of resettlement housing**
Paper to Conference Built Form and Culture Research. Kansas, 1984. (Published in *Architecture in Culture Change*, David G. Saile (ed.), University of Kansas, 1986, pp. 117–128)

**15. Rebirth of a Rajput village**

Paper to IASTE Conference, First World/Third World. Duality and Coincidence in TD&S 1990. (Published in Traditional Dwellings and Settlements Review No 11, 1992)

**16. Conserving the vernacular in developing countries**

Conference, Oxford Polytechnic, 1979. Published In Festschrift for James Walton (Franco Fescura (ed.). *South Africa Architectural Record* c.1986)

**17. Re-presenting and representing the vernacular: The open-air museum**

Paper to IASTE Conference Manufacturing Heritage and Consuming Tradition, Cairo 1998. (Published in *Consuming Tradition and Manufacturing Heritage*. Nezar Al-Sayyad (ed.). Routledge, 2001, pp. 191–211)

**18. Perfect and plain: Shaker approaches to design**.

Shaker Symposium, University of Exeter, Centre for American and Commonwealth Arts. 1989. (Published in *Locating the Shakers*. Mick Gidley (ed.). University of Exeter, 1990, pp. 63–70)

**19. Individualizing Dunroamin**

Paper to Symposium Dwelling in Scandinavia. Norwegian Institute of Technology, Trondheim, Norway, 1982 (unpublished)

**20. Round the houses**

Paper given at Oxford Brookes University, 1982 (Published in Andreas Papadakis (ed.). *British Architecture*, Academy Editions, Architectural Design, London, 1983, pp. 16–19)

**21. Kaluderica: High-grade housing in an illegal settlement**

Paper to 'Built Form and Culture Research' Conference on Purposes in Understanding Socio-Cultural Aspects of Built Environments. (Published in Conference Proceedings, J. William Carswell and David G. Saile (eds), University of Kansas, 1989, pp. 84–90)

**22. Tradition by itself...**

Paper to IASTE Conference: The End of Tradition? Trani, Italy. 2000 (Published in *the International Association for the Study of Traditional Environments Working Papers*)

**23. Ethics and vernacular architecture**

Keynote Paper to Conference *Ethics and the Built Environment*. University of Central Lancashire, 2000. (Published in *Professional Ethics Series*. Warwick Fox (ed.). Routledge, 2000, pp. 115–126)

**24. Necessity and sustainability: The impending crisis**

Keynote Paper to Conference *Traditional Environments in a New Millennium* 2002. Amasya, Turkey. (Published by IAPS-CSBE Network. Hulya Turgut & Peter Kellett (eds), 2003). With paragraphs from a Paper to the Conference on Teaching in Architecture. Somerville College, Oxford, 2001 (Published in *TIA Papers*, Susan Roaf (ed.) 2001)

# Index

Note: Authors of books or publications whose work is cited or discussed are included in the Index. Other authors are listed in the References. Information which is conveyed by illustrations and captions is included in **bold**